THE SAPPER VCs

The decorations and medals of Major General Sir Howard Elphinstone VC, KCB, CMG.
Shown here are (from left to right): the Victoria Cross; The Most Honourable Order of the Bath (CB),
Military Division; The Most Distinguished Order of St Michael and St George (CMG);
Crimea medal, clasp Sebastopol; 1887 Jubilee medal; Turkish Order of the Medjidjie, 5th Class;
French Légion d'Honneur, Chevalier; Turkish Crimea medal, 1855 (Sotheby's, London).

GERALD NAPIER

THE SAPPER VCs

The Story of Valour in the Royal Engineers and its Associated Corps

London: The Stationery Office

ISBN 0 11 772835 7

Catalogue in Publication Data

A CIP catalogue record for this book is available from the British Library.

A Library of Congress CIP catalogue record has been applied for.

First published 1998.

Note
In some cases it has proved impossible, despite every effort by the author, to contact the copyright holders of certain illustrations and maps. Any such copyright holder wishing to ensure that a correct acknowledgement appears in any future edition of this book, should contact The Stationery Office.

Published by The Stationery Office and available from:

The Publications Centre
(mail, telephone and fax orders only)
PO Box 276, London SW8 5DT
General enquiries 0171 873 0011
Telephone orders 0171 873 9090
Fax orders 0171 873 8200

The Stationery Office Bookshops
59–60 Holborn Viaduct, London EC1A 2FD
temporary until mid 1998
(counter service and fax orders only)
Fax 0171 831 1326
68–69 Bull Street, Birmingham B4 6AD
0121 236 9696 Fax 0121 236 9699
33 Wine Street, Bristol BS1 2BQ
0117 9264306 Fax 0117 9294515
9–21 Princess Street, Manchester M60 8AS
0161 834 7201 Fax 0161 833 0634
16 Arthur Street, Belfast BT1 4GD
01232 238451 Fax 01232 235401
The Stationery Office Oriel Bookshop
The Friary, Cardiff CF1 4AA
01222 395548 Fax 01222 384347
71 Lothian Road, Edinburgh EH3 9AZ
(counter service only)

Customers in Scotland may
mail, telephone or fax their orders to:
Scottish Publications Sales
South Gyle Crescent, Edinburgh EH12 9EB
0131 622 7050 Fax 0131 622 7017

The Stationery Office's Accredited Agents
(see Yellow Pages)

and through good booksellers

J30953 C15 3/98 039462

With gratitude to all members of the Royal Engineers Museum Foundation
who have generously given of their time and treasure
to create a permanent home for the memorabilia of the Corps
and particularly to their chairmen in the years 1991 to 1997:
Colonel Peter Williams, ADC, TD, DL; Colonel Sir Idris Pearce, CBE, TD, DL;
and Mr John Fitzmaurice to whom I owe the idea for this book.

'For titles do not reflect honour on men,
but rather men on their titles'

(Machiavelli, *Dei Discorsi*)

THE SAPPER VCs **C**ONTENTS

List of Maps

'First in, last out' is a common catchphrase to describe the sapper contribution to a battle. It is something of an oversimplification, perhaps, but the stories told in this book go a long way to explaining its origin. The fact is that sappers are soldiers first and foremost and although many of the Victoria Crosses won by them derive from their role as engineers, many more have resulted from the straightforward fighting which is the inevitable consequence of being 'at the sharp end'.

I am delighted to endorse this book, the first ever complete account of the sapper VCs, and welcome the fact that the stories are told as a narrative in the context of the operations in which the incidents arose. In this way, military engineering is seen as an integral part of war rather than a mysterious isolated activity undertaken by a strange body of men often regarded by the rest of the Army as 'mad, married or Methodist'.

The 55 subjects of this book were heroes to a man but many of them, as the author remarks in the final chapter, were ordinary men who rose to the occasion when called upon to do their duty. Reading how they did it provides an insight into the potential of the human spirit for selfless bravery and endurance and I hope will also inspire all those who take up arms as a profession.

General Sir John Stibbon, KCB, OBE
Chief Royal Engineer

A sapper officer was once asked how he had enjoyed being a visitor for some weeks in the officers' mess of a distinguished battalion of the Brigade of Guards. He replied that his hosts had been models of hospitality; the only complaint he had about them was that, never quite sure what subject would interest him most in conversation, they would invariably start talking to him about drains. For some this image of the sapper persists and so it comes as something of a surprise to discover that of the 1354 VCs awarded since the inception of the decoration in 1856 some 50 have gone to sappers of one sort or another. There is no current record of these in a single volume other than the two comprehensive books of reference, *The VC and DSO* by O'Moore Creagh and E.M. Humphris (up to 1920 only) and *The Register of the Victoria Cross* published by This England, both of which necessarily give little more than the bare facts of every VC award. It is to fill that gap that this book has been written, and also to present the story chronologically in the context of the campaigns in which the events occurred and of the evolution of the Corps of Royal Engineers itself.

The immediate problem that presents itself is whom to include. Until 1856 the term 'Royal Engineer' defined a professionally qualified officer in the eponymous corps. Rank and file, including the technicians and artisans without whom the Royal Engineer could not accomplish his responsibilities, were found from a quite separate body, the Royal Sappers and Miners (RS&M), which had been formed only in 1813 but which was absorbed into the Royal Engineers after the Crimean War. Royal Engineers' and RS&M's Crimea VCs are all included in this book. A rather similar difficulty of identity exists over the Indian Army. Until after the 1857 Mutiny,* the individual Presidency armies of the East India Company had their own Bombay, Madras and Bengal Engineers and Sappers and Miners. The officers of these corps underwent exactly the same training as those of the Royal Engineers, except that from 1809 they attended the Company's college at Addiscombe rather than the Royal Military Academy at Woolwich. Both categories went on to the School of Military Engineering at Chatham for their professional military engineer training. Queen's and Company Sappers fought together in the 1857 Uprising winning eight VCs, of which two were by NCOs of the Royal Engineers, who by then were part of the corps. In 1862 the Company's Engineers were amalgamated with the Royal Engineers.

There is then the question whether or not to include VCs won by former sappers serving with other regiments at the time of their award. At first sight they should perhaps not qualify for this book. However, this would mean omitting the

---

*Hereinafter the term '1857 Uprising' or just 'Uprising' has been adopted in this book to refer generally to the overall period of unrest that followed the mutiny of the Bengal Army as opposed to the more frequently used but misleading 'Indian Mutiny' or 'Mutiny'.

three Royal Flying Corps VCs. Who could have been more a sapper than James McCudden, the blood of the corps coursing through his veins from his distinguished quartermaster father and his own days as a bugler? So much did his family regard him as a sapper that they presented his medals and those of his father and two RFC brothers to the Royal Engineers Museum. Again, Major Lanoe Hawker is referred to in the Commemorative Scroll presented to his family after his death in action as 'Royal Engineers and Royal Flying Corps'.

I have therefore followed the principle 'Once a sapper, always a sapper'. This implies no intention to poach credit from other arms, corps and regiments but simply to provide as complete and accurate a record as can be accommodated in a single volume. By the same token, I use the term sappers to refer to all military engineers, whatever their rank, speciality or national allegiance. Readers familiar with the Army will know that 'sapper' is also the rank of the private soldier in the Royal Engineers but that all ranks are proud to be referred to generically as 'sappers'. However, where I use the term 'the corps', this refers solely to the Corps of Royal Engineers.

Gerald Napier
Tavistock, January 1998

Anyone embarking on a project connected with the Victoria Cross soon discovers they are not alone. There is a bewildering number of sources of information and other individuals working on different aspects in this field and I am most grateful to all those who have generously shared the product of their own hard work with me, principally Dennis Pillinger of the Military Historical Society and keeper of the Lummis files held in the National Army Museum; Dave Harvey, indefatigable researcher and stickler for accuracy whose lifetime work on the last resting places of the VCs should be coming to fruition in the near future; Lieutenant-Colonel Paul Oldfield whose detailed work on all the Western Front VCs is bound to become a definitive source when it is complete; Donald C. Jennings of the United States for his help also on last resting places; and John Cunningham of Belleek, County Fermanagh.

My thanks are also due to the authors of various published works for their permission to draw on them, particularly Roger Perkins, Gerald Gliddon, Stephen Snelling and Tommy Riordan. Expert advice in specialist aspects of military history is essential in such a wide-ranging work as this. That from the Victorian Military Society, personified by Chris Kempton and Neil Roberts; from the Crimean War Research Society, by Andrew Sewell and Major Colin Robins; and from the Indian Army Association, by Lieutenant-Colonel Patric Emerson and Colonel Bill Adams, has been invaluable.

The families, descendants and friends of many of the sapper VCs have been a most rewarding source of information and encouragement, generously sharing their family archives with me: Sue Smithson, Marion Shephard, William and Catherine Urquhart, the Colvin family, Mabyn Martin, Richard Martin, Cyril Coffin, Katrina Barling, Colonel John Osborne, Tim Waters, Charles Trollope, Derrick Martin, Reg Durrant, Major Travers Cosgrove, Major-General Logan Scott-Bowden and the late Robin Williams. I also owe much to Derrick Vernon of Wath-upon-Dearne who made contact on my behalf with Mrs Freda Warren, granddaughter of Sapper William Hackett, VC, resulting in much material. Messrs Spinks kindly gave me access to the Dundas papers prior to their sale.

Representatives of regimental museums and associations and similar bodies whose help I most gratefully acknowledge include Hugh Forrester of the Royal Inniskilling Fusiliers, Major Ron Morris of the Middlesex Regiment, Howard Chamberlain on behalf of the Royal New Zealand Engineers Association, Major P.V. Williams of the Military Engineers Museum of Canada, Lieutenant-Colonel I.P.S. Ahuja of the Bombay Engineer Group and Centre, Brigadier Spike Barker-Wyatt of the Royal Bombay Sappers and Miners Officers Association, Lieutenant-Colonel Patrick Love of the Worcestershire Regiment Museum Trust, Major Ted Green of the Staffordshire Regiment and Bill Tyrwhitt-Drake of The Haileybury Society.

From the libraries, museums and other official bodies who have helped beyond the call of duty my gratitude goes to Fiona Watson of the Northern Health Services Archives, Siobhan Convery (Archivist, Aberdeen City Council), Lucy Harland of the Birmingham Museum and Art Gallery, Robert Woosnam-Savage of the Art Gallery and Museum, Glasgow, Diana Condell and Philip Dutton of the Imperial War Museum, and the staff of the reading room at the National Army Museum.

Above all, none of this would have been possible without the help and support of my own corps, the Royal Engineers, from whose archives the bulk of the material for this book has been drawn. Colonel Mike Cooper, Corps and Institution Secretary, and, in the museum, Colonel John Nowers and his team – Dr John Rhodes, Dr James Rattue, Beverley Williams and Andrew Gladwell – have been unfailingly courteous and patient. Captain Bob Arnold, Maggie Magnuson and Vivienne Blaker made the library into a second home for me, produced seemingly endless material and drew my attention to many sources which would otherwise have been missed.

My special thanks are due to Graham Hornby who, having for many years given the Royal Engineers the benefit of his considerable knowledge on medals, has done the same for me, including writing part of the Introduction. He, with Derrick Vernon, has also read all my drafts and offered valuable suggestions for their improvement. I owe much, too, to David Goad whose early encouragement and generous use of his design skills and contacts helped me off first base.

Many others have helped along the way and I apologise to anyone whom I have omitted from these acknowledgements. That said, despite this most valuable expert advice, any errors and omissions in the book are fully my responsibility.

Last but not least, I now understand why authors need to thank their spouse for their support through what is a long process involving frequent periods of detachment from the real world. Such loyalty is, in the words of one of the subjects of this book, a jewel beyond price.

Gerald Napier
Tavistock, January 1998

All illustrations other than those listed below were provided by the Royal Engineers Museum and Library. The sources of the remainder are as follows and permission to reproduce them is gratefully acknowledged:

Roger Perkins (p.ii); William Clowes (p.6); Mrs Marion Shephard (p.17); David Harvey (p.20, top left); Peter Archer Prints (A&J Partnership, Barton-on-Sea, Hants BH25 7AJ) (p.20, bottom); Mrs Sue Smithson (p.56, top); Royal Collection Trust (p.89); Spink & Son Ltd (p.108, top); James Colvin (pp.125, 126); *Illustrated London News* Picture Library (p.135); Imperial War Museum (pp.157, 164, 165, 169, 175, 180, 181, 199, 247, 250, 251, 252, 256, 258, 271, 273, 276); William Kimber (p.168); Herbert Jenkins Ltd (p.185); South Yorkshire Newspapers Ltd (p.191); The Staffordshire Regiment Museum (p.202, top); The Middlesex Regiment Association (p.210); Mrs Katrina Barling (p.212); The Royal Canadian Engineers Museum (p.222); Stuarts Holdings (p.232, top); Hodder & Stoughton (p.234, top; p.236, top); Collins (p.273, bottom); Reg Durrant (p.274, both pictures).

Cover illustration (also on title page, p.iii): *The Defence of Rorke's Drift* (OMV 186) by Lady Elizabeth Thompson Butler (1846–1933). The Royal Collection © Her Majesty Queen Elizabeth II.

LIST OF ABBREVIATIONS

AAG	Assistant Adjutant-General
ADC	Aide-de-camp
AG	Adjutant-General
BEF	British Expeditionary Force
C-in-C	Commander-in-Chief
CB	Companion of the Order of the Bath
CBE	Commander of the Order of the British Empire
CE	Chief Engineer
CGM	Conspicuous Gallantry Medal
CMG	Companion of the Order of St Michael and St George
CO	Commanding Officer
CRE	Commanding Royal Engineer
CSI	Companion of the Star of India
CSM	Company Sergeant-Major
DCM	Distinguished Conduct Medal
DCRE	Deputy Commanding Royal Engineer
DL	Deputy Lieutenant
DSO	Distinguished Service Order
GBE	Knight Grand Cross of the Order of the British Empire
GCB	Knight Grand Cross of the Order of the Bath
GCIE	Knight Grand Commander of the Order of the Indian Empire
GCMG	Knight Grand Cross of the Order of St Michael and St George
GCSI	Knight Grand Commander of the Order of the Star of India
GHQ	General Headquarters
GOC(in-C)	General Officer Commanding (in-Chief)
GSO (1,2)	General Staff Officer (Grade 1, Grade 2)
IDSM	Indian Distinguished Service Medal
ILH	Imperial Light Horse
IMA	Indian Military Academy
KCB	Knight Commander of the Order of the Bath
KCMG	Knight Commander of the Order of St Michael and St George
KCIE	Knight Commander of the Order of the Indian Empire
KCSI	Knight Commander of the Order of the Star of India
KCVO	Knight Commander of the Royal Victorian Order
KT	Knight of the Order of the Thistle
LDV	Local Defence Volunteers
MC	Military Cross
MGO	Master General of the Ordnance
MM	Military Medal
MP	Member of Parliament
NCO	Non-commissioned officer
NNC	Natal Native Contingent
OBE	Officer of the Order of the British Empire
OC	Officer Commanding
OCTU	Officer Cadets Training Unit
OTC	Officer Training Corps
PVSM	Param Vashist Seva Medal
QMS	Quartermaster-Sergeant
RA	Royal Artillery
RAMC	Royal Army Medical Corps
RCE	Royal Canadian Engineers
RE	Royal Engineers
RFC	Royal Flying Corps
RIMC	Royal Indian Medical Corps
RMA	Royal Military Academy
RNVR	Royal Naval Volunteer Reserve
RSM	Regimental Sergeant-Major
TAVR	Territorial and Army Volunteer Reserve
TD	Territorial Decoration
VC	Victoria Cross
WO	Warrant Officer

Sixthly *It is ordained with a view to place all persons on a perfectly equal footing in relation to eligibility for the Decoration that neither rank nor long service nor wounds nor any other circumstance or condition whatsoever save the merit of conspicuous bravery shall be held to establish a sufficient claim to the honour.*[1]

Until the Crimean War, official rewards for gallantry existed only for officers. They were either the Order of the Bath or brevet promotion, the latter often the direct outcome of a mention in a commander's despatches. However, the Bath was limited to senior officers and, being an order, the number who could be accepted into it was finite. In the war against Russia, both in the Baltic and the Crimea, the British position in this matter contrasted unfavourably with their French allies whose Legion of Merit, with its various grades, was also awarded to British soldiers and sailors and much envied. Before that time there had been cases where commanding officers of a regiment or ship, recognising a need, had, as a private venture, struck medals for individuals. However, the first official decorations for bravery by rank and file were the Distinguished Conduct Medal (DCM) for soldiers and its naval equivalent, the Conspicuous Gallantry Medal (CGM), introduced by Royal Warrant in 1854 and 1855, respectively. For some reason these did not meet the need of the time, possibly because they tended to be awarded for distinguished service in the field as opposed to signal acts of valour in the face of the enemy.

The question of a new gallantry award for all ranks was first raised in Parliament in December 1854. From there it took a little time, mainly for officialdom to work out the nature of this new award as distinct from anything previously in use, but the Victoria Cross was eventually instituted by the Royal Warrant dated 29 January 1856. From the time of its conception right up to its birth the new infant had the full encouragement of Queen Victoria and Prince Albert. The Queen is said to have influenced many of the decisions on the design of the simple bronze cross. For example, she felt that the first pattern was too dull and coppery and that true bronze would give a better finish. She also pointed out that the motto 'For Valour' would be better than the proposed 'For the Brave' which would have 'the inference that only those are deemed brave who have got the Cross'.[2]

The Cross

The design of the cross seems to reflect the British penchant for simplicity and understatement. It succeeded, where anything flashier would have failed, in encapsulating the whole concept of modest, selfless bravery regardless of rank or station, an ideal of which the cross is itself symbolic. Its history has

The Victoria Cross
obverse

The Victoria Cross
reverse

triumphantly belied the carping criticism of *The Times* when the Victoria Cross first appeared in public after the original investiture: 'nothing could be more plain and homely, not to say coarse … poor looking and mean in the extreme.'[3]

Made originally from the bronze of captured Russian cannon, the cross is 1.375 inches wide and was first cast in gunmetal and then chased and finished by hand. The overall dark brown effect was obtained by chemical treatment. The cross, described in the warrant as a Maltese cross, might more accurately be referred to in heraldry terms as a *cross patée*, and bears on the obverse the royal crest of Queen Victoria in the centre partly within a scroll bearing the legend 'For Valour'.

Suspension is by means of a straight bronze bar, slotted to take the ribbon, and decorated on the obverse with laurel leaves. The bar is attached to the cross by means of a V-lug and link. The ribbon is now crimson, 1.5 inches wide for all services, although originally Royal Navy recipients wore the Victoria Cross with a blue ribbon. Provision is made in the warrants for bars, similar to the suspension bar but without the V-lug, to be awarded for further acts of gallantry.

Details of the recipient are engraved in capital letters on the reverse of the suspension bar and the date or dates of the action are engraved on the centre of the reverse of the cross.

The Conditions of the Award

The main feature of this unique decoration is the rarity of its award. One of the strongest influences in setting the tone for this was Queen Victoria herself and how this quality has been maintained and strengthened over the years will be illustrated as the story unfolds. The various circumstances of the sapper VCs will also provide examples of how the regulations for the award have evolved since its original inception, correcting some of the anomalies in such matters as posthumous qualification and taking account of the position of the VC in relation to other gallantry awards. Some of the more interesting facts and figures to date are:

- In all, 1354 VCs and three bars have been awarded. They are made up as follows:

1856–1913	522
1914–1919	634
1920–1938	5 (including one to the USA Unknown Warrior)
1939–1945	182
1946–date	11

- Of these, 294 have been awarded posthumously.

- The warrant allows for VC recipients to be selected by ballot among their comrades in cases where units have performed collective acts of 'heroic gallantry' in such a way that no individual can be identified as especially pre-eminent. The number of such awards is determined by the size of the unit.
- Awards do not have to relate to a single incident. There is nothing to prevent several acts performed over a period being cited.

- The award is accompanied by an annuity, originally £10 to other ranks (at that time officers did not receive an annuity) rising to £100 in 1959 to all recipients regardless of rank and, in 1995, to £1000.

- The award has been made to civilians, four such having been made, all during the 1857 Uprising in India.

- Both sexes are eligible although so far no female has received a VC.

- Forfeiture for various crimes and infamous acts was allowed for in the original warrant but no longer is. There were eight such cases in the history of the VC, none of whom were sappers.

- The youngest recipient so far was 15 and the oldest 69 years of age (neither was a sapper).

- There have been three cases of father-and-son VCs and four of brothers, but none of these were sappers.

Sapper Awards

This book tells the story of the 55 sapper VCs. Of these, 31 would have been on the strength of the Royal Engineers at the time of their incidents. Thirteen more belonged to corps such as the Royal Sappers and Miners or the Indian Presidency Engineers which were later absorbed into the Royal Engineers. Five individuals were former and two future Royal Engineers. Last but not least, four were sappers of the engineer corps of the Dominions, fighting alongside the British Army in two world wars.

The events which led to these awards vary from those which only occurred by virtue of the participants being sappers, such as at the Kashmir Gate in 1857 or on the Sambre–Oise canal in 1918, to those in which sappers had to revert to their primary role as soldiers, such as at Wagon Hill in 1900.

The story starts in 1854, by which time sappers could look back with some pride to many incidents of bravery in their history, such as in the trenches at Badajoz or San Sebastian, or before the gates of Ghazni in the First Afghan War. The first war in the Victoria Cross era was, however, scarcely a matter of pride for the Army as a whole although immensely so for the manner in which it was fought.

The Crimean War (1853–1856)

Towards the end of June 1855 Dr Robert Graham received a letter at his home at Eden Brows, Cumberland, from his son:

> It shows that we were blindly confident of success or we should never have fixed upon the Anniversary of Waterloo as the day for the assault ... Of my party of 210 men 90 were sailors who displayed throughout a daring and coolness worthy of the reputation of the British tar. As soon as we had advanced from under cover of our trenches, the Russians opened up a withering fire on us from about 20 guns. The fire they had been chary of before, they lavished on us now and the ground was ploughed and the air torn by the volleys of grape, canister and musketry. They were undoubtedly quite prepared for our attack for directly we came out they manned their parapets in great numbers. The firing from their guns was so rapid and continuous that I could only account for it by supposing the majority of them to be field pieces as I do not think they could load and fire their heavy guns so rapidly. It was very soon evident that our men could not face this iron shower ...[1]

Gerald Graham (1831–1899)

Lieutenant Gerald Graham of the Royal Engineers had just taken part in one of the most severe reverses of British arms in recent history, the first assault on the Redan at the siege of Sebastopol. His letter had much else to say of the disastrous planning and muddled thinking that had been responsible for this humiliation and the needless death of so many good men. It did *not* mention that, even though his own role had been frustrated by the fearsome fire, he then applied his energies to rescuing wounded men and carrying them back to safety through the inferno until the whole operation was called off. His actions, from which he could hardly have expected to emerge unscathed let alone survive, were to win him one of the eight VCs to be awarded to sappers in this war.

To understand how the young Graham and his colleagues had found themselves in this unenviable predicament, we need to take a few steps back in time.

The Start of the War

Russia's mid-19th century imperial ambitions had become obvious enough to cause even the British and the French, traditional enemies from time immemorial, to co-operate to frustrate them. The major concern was the threat of Russia's taking advantage of the debilitated state of the Ottoman Empire to expand south either side of the Black Sea, through Bulgaria and the Caucasus, to obtain its historic goal, a warm-water outlet into the Mediterranean. Czar Nicholas I had fished for the likely British attitude to such a move in his famous reference to Turkey to the British Ambassador: 'We have on our hands a sick man, a very sick man'; and received no encouragement. Quite the reverse, an urgent reconnaissance of the area was undertaken by a team under the Royal Engineer Sir John

Lieutenant-General
Sir John Burgoyne GCB

Map 1

The Sebastopol area of
the Crimea.

Based on a map in *The*
Crimean War by Dennis
Judd (Granada, 1975).

Burgoyne, Inspector-General of Fortifications and, at 72 years of age, universally respected for his military judgement. The French agreed to support the Turks with joint military action and both countries began to send their armies to Gallipoli from where the defence of Constantinople (now Istanbul), seen as the first priority, could be mounted.

Although this war against Russia is almost invariably called the Crimean War, it was in fact much more widespread, with violent actions in the Baltic and eastern Turkey as well as the Crimea, which had not originally been foreseen as an objective. The first shots of the land war were fired in Bulgaria where a Turkish force bolstered by a British brigade drove off the Russian Army on the Danube boundary of the Ottoman Empire. Captain Bent and Lieutenant Burke of the Royal Engineers, together with Lance-Corporal Swann and Private Anderson of the Royal Sappers and Miners who accompanied Burke, all distinguished themselves in these operations. Burke unfortunately became the first British Army fatality when a Turkish force attacked the Russians across the river at Rustchuk.

When he [Burke] first leaped on shore from the boat six soldiers charged him; two he shot with his revolver, one he cut down with his sword, the rest turned and fled. While he was encouraging the Turks, who were in the stream, to row quietly to the land, and forming them in line ... a number of riflemen advanced from behind

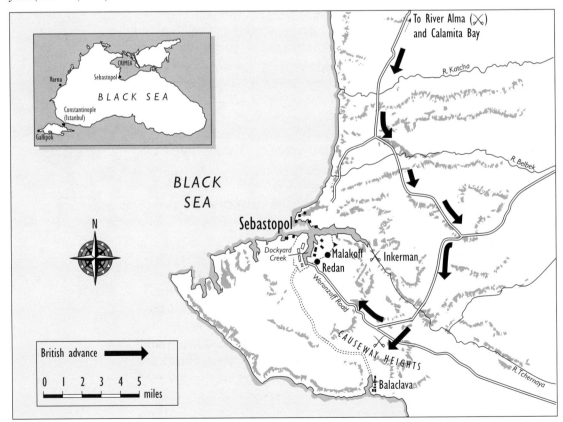

a ditch and took deliberate aim at him. Poor Burke charged them with headlong gallantry. As he got near he was struck by a ball which broke his jaw-bone; but he rushed on, shot three men dead at close quarters with his revolver, and cleft two men through helmet and all into the brain with his sword. He was then surrounded, and while engaged in cutting his way with heroic courage through the ranks of the enemy, a sabre-cut from behind, given by a dragoon as he went by, nearly severed his head from his body, and he fell dead, covered with bayonet wounds, sabre gashes, and marked with lance-thrusts and bullet-holes.[2]

The party withdrew to the home bank. Swann was badly wounded but Anderson, who also fought heroically, was unscathed and returned the next morning to recover his officer's mutilated body. He was decorated by the Turkish Commander-in-Chief in person with the Order of the Medjidjie.

By this time the joint British and French force had concentrated at Varna on the Black Sea coast ready to move against the Russians should affairs on the Danube go against the Allies. Some hint of troubles to come appeared at Varna where the Army's administrative deficiencies began to show themselves and morale deteriorated. The worst torment, however, was an epidemic of cholera which killed over 500 men before the force embarked for the Crimea. The decision to invade the Crimea had arisen from strong pressure for action once it became clear that the threat to the Bulgarian border had ebbed away. In Britain a public mood for retribution against Russia had already been stimulated by the annihilation of a large part of the Turkish navy at Sinope and this mood was 'thundered' in *The Times*, which was to have the same sort of media influence on events in the coming campaign as television does today. What was required was the invasion of the Crimea and the destruction of the naval base at Sebastopol. As Porter in *The History of the Corps of Royal Engineers* puts it, 'that once accomplished, the power of Russia in the Black Sea would be at an end for many a long day.'[3]

At this stage late in the summer of 1854 the idea of overwintering in the Crimea was not a consideration in the British high command. Two clear months of good weather were available and these were considered sufficient for the required expedition. We now know what a fatal, almost criminal, misjudgement this was to prove. Given a well-integrated unified command with common political aims, good leadership from experienced commanders and sound logistic support it all might have been possible. None of these applied. The two armies had to answer to two governments between which historic animosities and mistrust still lay deep. Neither had been tested in battle since Waterloo. The senior commanders were too old and backward-looking in their attitudes and lacked any effective staff system such as Wellington had developed in the Peninsula. The British commander, Lord Raglan, was aged 66. In his youth, as the dashing Lord Fitzroy Somerset, he had been on Wellington's personal staff in the Peninsula and at Waterloo but had never commanded troops at any level. Personally very brave and a quintessential English gentleman, Raglan was too easily swayed by stronger personalities in the interest of seeking compromise. His orders, often given against his own better judgement, were to have a direct effect on the individuals who are the subject of this chapter.

Above all, particularly in the British force, those essentials of any military operation – transport, a supply system for food and ammunition, accommodation and adequate medical back-up – were virtually non-existent. Superhuman efforts by individuals responsible on the ground for delivering these services, and by the soldiers themselves to improvise, simply could not compensate for the lack of straw with which to create the bricks.

The Royal Engineers in the Crimea

The British force was reasonably well represented by Royal Engineers and sappers. It must be remembered that the Corps of Royal Engineers was then still the all-officer organisation that it had always been. In war Royal Engineers were responsible for planning and controlling siegeworks and operations as well as logistic and construction engineering such as bridging, road-making and providing camps. The manpower available for such works might come from the infantry or from civilian tradesmen and labourers, or even sailors. However, since the Peninsular War there was also available a body of trained soldier-engineers, the Royal Sappers and Miners, generally known as sappers. By the 1850s the sapper companies were invariably commanded by Royal Engineers and in the British Army reforms which followed the Crimean War the two bodies became integrated into the Royal Engineers as we know them today.

The other feature of the Royal Engineers at that time was that they and the Royal Artillery were still the responsibility of the Board of Ordnance, a completely separate government organisation from the office of the Commander-in-Chief at the Horse Guards. The Master-General of the Ordnance (MGO), normally a senior Army officer, was directly responsible to the Cabinet for his department. In 1854 the MGO was the future commander in the Crimea, Lord Raglan, who had replaced Wellington on the latter's death in 1852. Raglan had a clear memory from his Peninsular War days of the need for engineers and sappers. No doubt that memory was firmly prodded by his Inspector-General of Fortifications, General Sir John Burgoyne.

So it was that two companies of Royal Sappers and Miners arrived in Turkey in February 1854 and were employed in constructing piers for the landing of stores and preparing buildings as hospitals. They also dug fortifications on the Gallipoli peninsula. Two further companies arrived in time for the move to Varna. When the force eventually embarked for the Crimea it included 23 officers (Royal Engineers) and 323 sappers organised into five companies. More were to follow.

Three Battles

The force (27,000 British, 30,000 French and 7000 Turks) was landed unopposed in Calamita Bay, some 20 miles north of Sebastopol, on 13 September 1854. In the course of the next two months it was to fight three notorious battles which led up to the siege of Sebastopol, during which action the sapper VCs were won. It is worth recounting briefly these three extraordinary battles if only to show how the siege came about.

The first took place on the River Alma on 20 September, a few miles down the armies' route of march towards Sebastopol. The river, dominated by hills some 150 feet in height rising to 400 feet at the flanks, offered the Russians the first natural obstacle and a golden opportunity with which to destroy the invaders. The British bore the brunt of this affair as the Russians had left the sector opposite the French almost unmanned, believing the slopes at that point to be impossible to scale. None but the most senior of the British force had been in battle before and one can only imagine the soldiers' feelings as they moved forward in glorious autumn sunshine, through the vineyards and up on to the downland facing them, waiting for their first taste of action.

There were few orders issued for this frontal assault. Years of peacetime drill and manoeuvres were, however, replayed like clockwork to the astonishment of the onlooking Russians. This, combined with the extraordinary courage and perseverance of the soldiers, seems to have sufficed. Sir John Burgoyne was present throughout:

> The Russians fought gallantly, but could not withstand the steady, persevering gallantry of our troops ... our attack was over a river that, though fordable, could only be crossed in broken order, from natural impediments, above which was a fine range of heights ... that on the right (the key to the whole), with a steep sloping rise as smooth as a glacis; midway up it a trench of some hundreds of yards long for cover, and both sides flanked by artillery. This eminence was boldly assailed and carried, and so close was the contest that it was literally covered with killed and wounded, the most advanced of which, Russians and British, were heaped together.[4]

By 17 October the Allies' guns were bombarding Sebastopol from prepared positions and the armies had established their bases and encampments surrounding the city. Sebastopol lies at the point where the north–south coastline down which the Allied force had been advancing turns west, creating a tongue of land some ten miles wide jutting out into the Black Sea. The British base was the small harbour of Balaclava about eight miles south of the centre of the plateau from which they would need to mount any operations against Sebastopol. The French base was out on the tongue with no harbour but a reasonably well-protected bay through which stores could be landed over the beach. These dispositions, themselves the cause of some controversy, were fundamentally to affect the fortunes of the armies. Further debate surrounded (and still surrounds) the issue of whether a quick assault at this time, when the balance of morale was so much in favour of the Allies, would have sufficed to snatch the prize. There is plenty of hindsight evidence to suggest that, after the Alma, the Russians were badly off balance and ill-prepared to resist an assault. For example, Lieutenant E.R. James, RE, who became a prisoner-of-war in Russian hands, wrote a memoir of his career in which he records conversations with the Russians to that effect.[5] The deployment of the armies on the dominating ground to the south of Sebastopol and the occupation of Balaclava as the British base had been undertaken following a careful appreciation by Sir John Burgoyne. Not to have adopted his advice and thus risk an inexperienced army in a *coup de main* with no base other than the fleet at sea, could have resulted in ignominious and tragic failure. A brief reconnaissance then showed that the defences were too strong to risk an immediate assault. Nevertheless, even now a prolonged siege was not envisaged and by 17 October the bombardment opened from 126 pieces of ordnance: 73 British and 53 French, based on a rudimentary trench line. At first the artillery duel went in favour of the Allies and preparations were made for an assault. Then the Russians intervened.

Their second attempt to remove the invaders from their country was to advance upon the Balaclava base moving in from the east with 3400 cavalry and 22,000 infantry. Their intention was to wheel left to where their objective lay to the south. Between them and their goal was a line of gun positions manned largely by Turks, on what was known as the Causeway Heights, and a single battalion, the 93rd Highlanders (later The Argyll and Sutherland Highlanders), the rest of the infantry being encamped on the high plateau above the Balaclava plain and not yet within reach. However, the British cavalry under the command of Lord Lucan was deployed on the plain and as the Russian cavalry poured over the Causeway Heights the Heavy Brigade, some 300 strong, under General James Scarlett, attacked them with such vigour that they were induced to withdraw, although not before the 93rd Highlanders (to be dubbed 'the thin red line' by William Russell, correspondent of *The Times*) had seen off three squadrons which had detached themselves from the main Russian body.

There then followed the senseless and tragic charge by the Light Brigade under Lord Cardigan along the 'valley of death' which lay parallel with the Causeway Heights to their north.[6] The Light Brigade was effectively destroyed in this action (of 668 who charged, 103 were killed in the action and 196 wounded, many of them mortally);[7] but whether or not out of sheer bewilderment at this eccentric British behaviour, or just poor finishing power, the Russians failed to exploit the advantage they had won and by mid-morning the situation was stabilised with the active help of the French cavalry. Raglan had to settle for a situation in which Balaclava was secure but the Russians held an inconveniently forward line which to some extent circumscribed future British movement.

Attention was then concentrated on the business of the siege which the Allies still hoped to bring to a successful conclusion before the winter. However, just ten days after Balaclava, on 5 November, the third great encounter occurred, with the Russians making a massive effort to dislodge their enemies from the heights above Sebastopol. They sent dense columns of infantry, supported by well-sited artillery, all of which emerged from Sebastopol as well as from the army in the field outside the garrison, to strike at what they rightly perceived to be the weakest part of the British line. These columns took the besieging army completely by surprise early on a foggy morning. Altogether the Russians committed 65,000 infantry with 134 guns to this battle. From the Allied point of view the resulting Battle of Inkerman was a miracle of improvisation and individual enterprise by small groups of men, thrust into the conflict as and when they arrived at the chaotic scene from their divisional locations several miles away.

Inkerman has come to symbolise more than almost any other battle the courage and endurance of the British soldier fighting with scant orders or coherent plans from his leaders. At the end of that long day the Russians left 4400 dead behind out of a total of 12,000 casualties. British casualties were 2573, of whom 635 died in the battle but far more succumbed to their wounds and the dreadful conditions they had to endure on board ship or in hospital at Scutari.

Inkerman effectively put paid to any idea of a quick assault on Sebastopol. Both sides appear to have been so debilitated by their experiences and, in the case of the British, by sickness, as to be incapable of further action. 'The attack and defence both gradually subsided into a sullen tranquillity.'[8] Any lingering hopes of an early assault were buried by the appalling hurricane which struck on 14 November, heralding one of the worst Crimean winters in living memory. The loss of 12 ships in this storm, including the steamship *Prince* with its cargo of warm clothing, is often blamed for the subsequent nightmare conditions suffered by the troops in the winter which effectively destroyed the army, but it is insufficient excuse. Gerald Graham wrote to his sister two months later, on 17 January 1855:

> It is a terribly trying time for the troops. With all your kind sympathy at home you have a very faint idea of what they suffer. To understand that you should see the poor fellows (I mean the private soldier) toiling out to the trenches in the slippery snow, having probably had no breakfast, or see him fagging out to Balaklava for his rations; or wandering about in search of roots to make his fire and lastly to see him lying in his tent amid snow, mud and filth of every description – that article in *The Times* of the 23rd was only too much needed – There is a criminal neglect among the high officials and it will be a heavy day for them when called upon by an indignant nation to account for the noble army which had been entrusted to them.[9]

The Siege

Our concern now, however, is with the siege. Here the Russians made up in energy and skill for all their inexplicable deficiencies in the field. They were inspired by their Chief Engineer, the dynamic 36-year-old Colonel Franz Todleben (a Russian of German descent), who not only made the defences of Sebastopol effective so early in the campaign that it is doubtful if any attempt at a quick assault would have succeeded, but also marshalled a labour force with the necessary resources which, throughout the siege, was able to make overnight repairs to defences which had received terrific battering from the Allied artillery the previous day.

Sebastopol as a whole was in two parts separated by the Dockyard Creek, with the town on the west and the dominating ground containing some suburbs on the east. The west side was the responsibility of the French and no actions of significance were to take place against its fortifications. Their importance lay in the capability of their batteries to give interlocking supporting fire to the main defences protecting the eastern side, particularly from Flagstaff Bastion (Bastion du Mât). Initially the eastern sector was entirely the responsibility of the British. After Inkerman, the brunt of which was borne by the British, the French were persuaded to take over the most easterly section. Thus on the east there were three clearly defined sectors separated as it happened by steep ravines: the British Left and Right Attacks[*] divided by the Woronzoff Ravine; and the French works with the Middle Ravine as their boundary with the British Right Attack.

The Russian works were continuous but their principal features were the Redan and the Malakoff Tower – in front of the British and French sectors respectively. The Redan was a triangular earthwork with 70-yard-long faces, 15 feet in height and with a 20-foot-wide and 14-foot-deep ditch, giving a total height for escalade of some 30 feet. The Malakoff was a semi-circular masonry tower which completely dominated the area. Early in the campaign Sir John Burgoyne had identified it as the key to the whole position and after Inkerman he had recommended attacking it. This could only have been done with the support of the French who, however, demurred.

On the Allied side there was nothing for it but to settle down to the tedious business of digging forward until a point was reached sufficiently close to the enemy works from which an assault could be launched. The main object of this process, a well-established siegecraft drill since the 18th century, was to bring guns

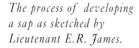

The process of developing a sap as sketched by Lieutenant E.R. James.

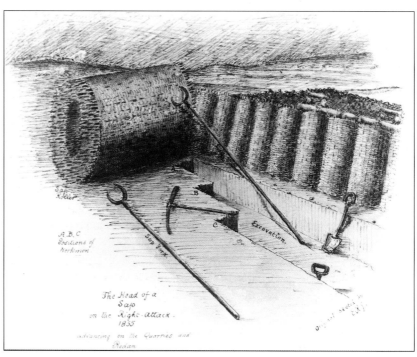

[*]This use of the term 'Attack' to denote a sector of responsibility is unique to the Crimean War and should not be confused with 'attack' meaning assault.

forward into protected batteries from which the enemy's fortifications could be battered until a breach was created. By the time of Sebastopol the range of artillery had improved so as to allow a dispersion of guns from the rear. The requirement therefore was to dig a trench system to accommodate the guns and allow the forward movement of infantry. The parapets of the trenches and batteries would be protected by cylindrical containers of earth and rubble known as gabions and often reinforced by sandbags. The main trenches in the system would be more or less parallel to the enemy's works so as to be protected from his fire along its length. To work forward to the next 'parallel' a short connecting trench known as a sap or sometimes a boyau would be dug. The resulting system would be a complex zigzag, in constant need of repair from the depredations of the enemy's artillery and the occasional sally.

When the time came, infantry would concentrate in the protection of the foremost trenches and mount the assault. In a classical siege the ditches protecting the fortress should be filled by the material knocked down from the walls, but as a safeguard it was normal to carry forward large sacks of wool to enable the assaulting force to jump down safely. These wool sacks would certainly be required in any attack on an earthwork such as the Redan. The walls would then be scaled with the help of ladders.

It was the sappers' task to plan all this work, direct the digging parties, make all the necessary materials available and lead the assaulting force forward to the point of attack. They acquired an expert knowledge of the trenches and of the enemy's works which it was their job to assess, if necessary by reconnaissance. Thus 'Follow the sapper' became the key phrase for the infantry force finding themselves in this system possibly for the first time.

The First VC – Lieutenant Wilbraham Lennox

Naturally the enemy was not going to let all this happen without interference. By the end of November 1854 a good start had been made in the very rocky soil and the Left Attack's Second Parallel was under way when the Russians established some rifle pits 250 yards or so to its front, which menaced both the Left Attack's works and, by enfilade, those in the French sector. It was there that the first VC to be awarded to a Royal Engineer was won by Lieutenant Wilbraham Lennox.

Wilbraham Oates Lennox (1830–1897)

Lennox, the son of Colonel Lord John Lennox, MP and grandson of the 4th Duke of Richmond, was born at Molecomb House on the Goodwood estate. He was privately educated and, after attending the Royal Military Academy at Woolwich, was commissioned into the Royal Engineers in 1848 at the age of 18. He was posted to Ceylon where he spent a few idyllic years in which sport seems to have been his principal occupation (he is reputed to have shot 100 elephants during his tour). He arrived in the Crimea just after the Battle of the Alma and was put in charge of the engineer park* for the Left Attack as soon as the siege

---

*An engineer park was responsible for providing the siege materials.

Map 2

*Development of the
trench system in the
Right and Left Attacks,
Sebastopol.*

began. He was also present throughout the Battle of Inkerman. It was Lennox's
job to deal with the Russian rifle pits which had been established in front of the
Left Attack's Second Parallel. His part in this is recorded in his journal written
two days later:

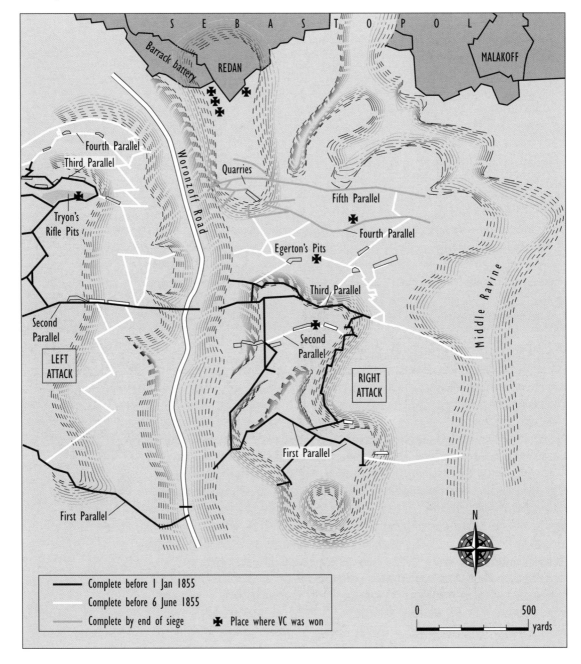

At 4 p.m. 200 of the Rifle Brigade, under Tryon, Bourchier,* and Cunningham, paraded at our park, and were conducted by self and Phillips, R. E., to the advanced trench, where Tryon made his arrangements. He and Bourchier, with 100 men, were to sneak round by the right, and Cunningham, with the rest, were to remain as a reserve and advance when the pits were taken.

Tryon's party got within about 80 yards of the Russians before being twigged, and then went forward with a rush, the Russians bolting away; they rallied about 100 yards off, and then commenced a sharp musketry fire. In the meantime the forts of Sebastopol opened with shot and shell as Phillips and I brought up our working party of 100 men in rear of Cunningham's rifles, out of the left of the advanced trench. We found Bourchier's party (poor Tryon was shot dead while leading) in possession of the pits, and we were only annoyed once more by the Russians advancing; but a few rounds sent them back, and, as the Rifles were short of ammunition, I extended some of my working party, and set the rest to work to make a trench to connect the pits we had taken, and to convert them into English instead of Russian ones … We worked hard all night, and in the morning had the satisfaction of having provided cover for the Rifles to hold the ground during the day and keep the Russians well away from us – altogether a good night's work, and one which pleased, I hear, General Canrobert much.[10]

This 'good night's work' earned VCs for Lennox, Bourchier and another Rifle Brigade officer, Lieutenant William Cuninghame. The rifle pits have been called by the name of the gallant Tryon ever since.

Corporal William Lendrim and Colour Sergeant Henry McDonald

The work continued as far as possible during the appalling winter. On 9 April morale in the trenches was raised by a massive week-long bombardment which the troops hoped was a prelude to the final assault on Sebastopol. However, the Russians started to dig counter-works into the French sector and had also made a lodgement about 250 yards in front of the Third Parallel of the Right Attack, established in two large rifle pits which would have to be occupied before further progress could be made. Colonel Egerton of the 77th Regiment (later 2nd Battalion The Middlesex Regiment) with 600 men achieved this in a night attack, taking with him a working party of 150 men, under Captain Owen and Lieutenant Baynes of the Royal Engineers, who were to turn the pits into a defensive position to be incorporated in the Right Attack's trench system. This was an extremely sharp action in which Egerton and Owen were killed and Baynes wounded. Command of the working party fell to Colour Sergeant Henry McDonald of the Royal Sappers and Miners. Unquestionably his intervention had a significant effect. At one point McDonald had helped carry Baynes back on a stretcher.

Henry McDonald (1823–1893)

In retracing his steps, McDonald was astonished to find the working party running from the lodgment. Asking the reason, he was informed that the Russians, in some strength, had driven up the work and forced them back. At once

---

*The *Royal Engineers Journal*, from which this extract is taken, gives this name as 'Boucher'. However, it must have been Tryon's close friend, Lieutenant Claude Thomas Bourchier, 1st Battalion Rifle Brigade.

McDonald ordered them to stand, and after facing them to the right-about, drew his sword and placed himself at their head. [Private] Ewen was there ready to second his authority with any amount of daring he might find it necessary to command. Seeing the Russians still creeping over the works, the sergeant desired the workmen to kneel, and after firing a volley, to charge. Strictly obeyed were the orders; the charge was gallantly made, and the enemy having vanished before the cool volley and the bayonet point, the pits were reoccupied and the lodgment resumed.[11]

The left of the Second Parallel on the Right Attack, sketched by Lieutenant E.R. James after June 1855. The sketch shows the Sandbag Battery on the left and the eight-gun battery on the right. In front is the Third Parallel with its approach and beyond that, Egerton's Pits (where McDonald's VC was won) and the Quarries. On the high ground beyond is the Redan.

This was not the end of the affair. Lieutenant-Colonel Tylden, commanding the Right Attack engineer work, now arrived and learned about McDonald's fine action from Egerton. Together they set about extending the trench system when, after further exertions, McDonald was badly wounded. 'Colonel Egerton was near at the time and administered his brandy-flask to sustain, in a measure, the drooping head of that brave soldier.'[12] This urgent sapper work paid off when the enemy made a strong sortie to recover the pits but were beaten off. At this point, however, Egerton was killed. Lieutenant James of the Royal Engineers, who arrived just at the time McDonald was wounded, helped carry him to the rear and then remained directing affairs until daylight.

Henry McDonald hailed from Inverness. By family tradition he was originally destined to become a monk but he joined the Royal Sappers and Miners in December 1840 at the age of 17 and served with them in various parts of the world. By the time he reached the Crimea with the 10th Company he was a married man with at least one child, a small daughter called Lydia Emily. He was present at the battles of the Alma and Inkerman before joining the siege. On the occasion of the attacks on Egerton's Pits, as they later became known, it was undoubtedly Egerton's report on McDonald's gallantry which told in the eventual consideration for his VC. He was also awarded an annuity of £20.

However, the honour of being the first other-rank sapper VC falls to another man who was in the rifle pits on that occasion, Corporal William Lendrim. Lendrim (né Lendrum) enlisted into the Royal Sappers and Miners in 1845 at the age of 15 as a bugler. He set sail for the Crimea in 7th Company in his trade of miner, landing at Gallipoli in April 1854 where he took part in the fortification works on the Gallipoli peninsula. He reached the Crimea in November 1854 shortly after the Battle of Inkerman. His mining skills were immediately in great demand in the trenches and he quickly made his mark for his steadiness under fire and initiative. On 14 February Lendrim was supervising a French working party on a battery in the Second Parallel of the Right Attack. The Russian artillery soon found the range of this work, as the newly placed gabions showed up against the snow, and began to knock down the gabions with round shot, causing several casualties among the French. Lendrim took over and went from gap to gap replacing the gabions under a heavy fire. The French officer in charge, who saw the whole affair, reported to Lendrim's officer that his action had saved the battery. The incident subsequently formed part of his VC citation.

*William Lendrim
as a young man*

There were several more occasions when Lendrim distinguished himself. On the night of 11/12 April, he was working in the huge 21-gun battery, manned largely by the Royal Navy, when a Russian shell ignited the sandbags on the magazine roof. Still under fire, he and another sapper, Corporal Wright, climbed on to the roof, removed the sandbags and made good the damage. For this action both sappers received the commendation of the naval commander present, the remarkable Captain William Peel, who was also later to be awarded the VC.

It was just over a week later that the rifle pits incident occurred. While Colour Sergeant McDonald was battling away in Egerton's Pits, Lendrim was in another detachment detailed to destroy what were known as the advanced pits, some 40 yards further forward. Shortly before daylight they charged forward and took the pits with little trouble, dealt with the enemy's defence works and returned. This incident also contributed to Lendrim's VC citation.

The Assault on the Redan, 18 June 1855
<u>Lieutenants Howard Elphinstone and Gerald Graham, Colour Sergeant Peter Leitch and Sapper John Perie</u>

The hard, dangerous but unglamorous work in the trenches ground on with little to relieve monotony apart from the occasional enemy sortie and the seizing of new territory as the trenches crept steadily forward. Before the long-anticipated assault on Sebastopol could be undertaken, both the British and the French on their right had to secure two heavily fortified Russian posts known respectively as the Quarries and the Mamelon. They did so with distinction in a co-ordinated attack on 8 June but only after a long process of painful negotiation between the French commander, Pélissier, and his home government over the newly established tele-

View through an embrasure on the right of the 21-gun battery from an original water-colour by Lieutenant E.R. James. This was where Corporals Lendrim and Wright climbed on to the roof under full enemy fire to extinguish the burning sandbag roof.

graph – an example of the political interference which was to have much influence on the whole campaign. There had been severe casualties, too, in some of these preliminaries. The French had lost over 2000 in a single night attack on 22 May. Total Allied casualties in the Mamelon and the Quarries were over 5000.

Nevertheless, these objectives gave the Allies the springboard for the final onslaught against the Malakoff Tower, the key to Sebastopol, and the Redan. After such successes this last effort was expected by many to be a formality. Captain Gerald Goodlake of the Coldstream Guards, whose performance in an earlier fight at Windmill Ravine on 24 October 1854 had earned him a VC, is quoted: 'You cannot conceive the excitement. We are all the world like tigers. I believe the men would go in without arms.'[13] This mood of optimism was reinforced by a crowd of onlookers including many women and other camp followers who crowded the hills overlooking the doomed city to witness the break-in. How tragically wrong they were to be.

The four men who were to win abiding fame by their exploits in the forthcoming battle were Graham, Perie,* Elphinstone and Leitch. Lieutenant Gerald

---

*The name was spelled Pirie, or sometimes Pirrie, in official records in Scotland later in his life but no record of his birth has been located and the spelling used at his attestation is adopted here.

Graham, then ten days short of his 24th birthday, was immensely tall and strong. His early training, after school at Wimbledon and in Dresden, had followed the normal pattern for a Royal Engineer. He had been among the first to arrive in the Crimea, having been attached to the 11th Company Royal Sappers and Miners in the Dardanelles and at Varna. He was present at the Battle of the Alma and by the time of the battles of Balaclava and Inkerman he was fully engaged in the siege-work. He was a shrewd observer of the scene, and his letters home showed that he understood the strategic setting. Although he was disappointed that the opportunity for an early attempt on Sebastopol had been missed, he was not an impetuous character, being reserved in nature and, in the case of the forthcoming attack, realistic enough about his chances of survival to have written a farewell letter home to his sister.

Closely in support of Graham was Private John Perie of the Royal Sappers and Miners. John Perie was born in Huntly, Aberdeenshire in the 1820s and he enlisted into the Royal Artillery in January 1848, giving his age as 18½. He transferred to the Royal Sappers and Miners in March the same year. In due course he joined 4th Company and, at some point before they were sent to the Crimea, he married Jessie Hay, daughter of a farm labourer and some ten years older than him. They had two daughters born respectively in 1851 and 1853. Perie made a good impression in his new profession being acknowledged as 'an unlettered man but a first-class sapper and leader'.[14] Graham was later quoted as saying: 'Who of the sappers here know anything of the ground?' 'I do, sir,' cried Perie with an impatience that evinced his desire for selection, 'I know every inch of it'; and he was accordingly appointed to head the sailors with the ladders.[15]

John Perie
(1829–1874)

Lieutenant Howard Elphinstone was 18 months older than Graham although nearly three years senior in the corps. He was a determined man of many talents. He had been born in Riga on the Baltic coast where ironically his father was in service in the Russian navy. Educated both in Britain and at the University of Bonn, he had travelled extensively in continental Europe and spoke several languages. He was also an accomplished artist and since his commission he had been employed by the Ordnance Survey. In the summer of 1854 he was ordered to the Crimea. He reached Balaclava in September and was immediately engaged in the work in the trenches. Here he was not inclined to settle for a quiet life and had performed with distinction in the attack on the Quarries. Sir William Gordon, the senior Royal Engineer under Sir John Burgoyne, is quoted in Elphinstone's biography as being

> keenly appreciative of this 'young subaltern, who was full of quiet humour, very observant and quick at detecting humbug or affectation.' 'He was singularly cool in danger,' wrote a fellow officer, 'as I well remember walking in an advanced trench on the Right attack with him when we had to pass a gap where there was no cover at all, thereby affording the enemy a sport like rabbit shooting – with us for rabbits. When it came to Elphinstone's turn, he merely made a quiet remark after getting across, "that was a good shot considering I was running", the shot having just grazed his coat.'[16]

*Peter Leitch
(1820–1892)*

Last but not least there was Colour Sergeant Peter Leitch who had served as a corporal in 2nd Company Royal Sappers and Miners earlier in the war in the Baltic. This was the first campaign of the war in 1854. A fleet under Admiral Sir Charles Napier had been dispatched with the aim of imposing a blockade on the Russian fleet, to prevent it from emerging from the Gulf of Finland; and to examine the prospects of attacking the Russian bases at Kronstadt, Sveaborg (off modern Helsinki) or Bomarsund. Leitch's work as a carpenter, building the platforms and protective works for the guns during that campaign, had been outstanding and he reached the Crimea with his company just before Christmas 1854 with a high reputation. Since then his experience and talents had been put to good use in the trenches.

As already noted the key to an Allied victory was to be the Malakoff Tower, the French objective; the British attack on the Redan was to be in support, and unlikely to be achieved until the Malakoff was secured. Raglan realised this but felt obliged to display strong support for the French. Due partly to a change in plan by the French of which they failed to notify Raglan, the co-ordination of the attacks was disastrous. Although there had been a tremendous bombardment during 17 June, Raglan had accepted a French decision that, for the sake of surprise, none should precede their attack on 18 June. As a result the Russians were ready. The genius with which Todleben had managed overnight repairs to the defences throughout the siege was again displayed. Although the French made some progress the British had to go forward 450 yards under a hail of grape and canister, leap into the ditch, clear the abbatis (obstacles of branches), erect such ladders as had survived the advance and enter the Redan in the face of massive and determined opposition.

Private John Perie leading a party of sailors in the 18 June 1855 attack on the Redan.

By kind permission of the artist
Peter Archer

Three columns were to make the assault on the Redan itself (there was also a second offensive by the British Left Attack). Each column comprised some 1500 men of whom 100 were the leading skirmishers from the Rifle Brigade followed by the sapper parties, the latter divided into about 30 for the clearance of obstacles and 200 carrying ladders and wool sacks; and finally the storming party, 400 strong with reserves of 800. The sapper parties comprised the Royal Engineers, members of the Royal Sappers and Miners and various Royal Navy and infantry of the line. Number 1 column was commanded by Brigadier General Sir John Campbell. Their sapper party under Major Bent included Lieutenant Graham and Sapper Perie. Number 2 column's sappers of which Colour Sergeant Leitch was a member were led by Lieutenant-Colonel Tylden. Lieutenant Elphinstone was one of two assistant engineers attached to the Commanding Royal Engineer, Major-General Harry Jones.

Number 1 column attacked on the left (the right flank of the Redan). As they emerged from the cover of the Fifth Parallel and looked across to the looming earthworks a quarter of a mile ahead the enemy artillery opened up such a terrible fire that Raglan claimed later, 'I never before witnessed such a continued and heavy fire of grape combined with musketry from the enemy's works which appeared fully manned',[17] although he must have realised that his acquiescence to the French plan was the direct cause. The result was described in Graham's letter:

> Before five minutes were over we had lost many men, without making much advance. My Brother officer preceding me [Lieutenant Murray] had his arm shot off and died shortly afterwards. Brigadier General Sir J. Campbell had been killed at the outset, having with extraordinary valour, gone out in front of the skirmishers. Colonel Tylden of the Royal Engineers … was struck down by a grapeshot whilst I was at his side. The men were drawn back under cover of our advanced trench and though some abortive attempts were made to advance on the Salient, the attack may be said to have been repelled as soon as Colonel Tylden fell.[18]

In fact, according to Graham's biographer,[19] Graham had been in process of obtaining the Colonel's permission to redirect the assault at the moment when Tylden was struck. After carrying him to the rear, Graham moved forward again but was eventually pinned down, along with his gallant sailors, 'exposed to this tremendous fire' whilst waiting in vain for another storming party to come forward. It was only then that he withdrew his men.

Number 2 column attacking on the right (left face of the Redan) under the inspiring leadership of Colonel Lacy Yea fared slightly better as some of the Russians' murderous fire was engaged with the French attack further to the British right. A few of the storming party made it to the parapet but, with so many of the officers and senior ranks having become casualties, nothing would induce the raw soldiers now forming the bulk of the force to emerge from the scraps of cover they had found. It was here that Colour Sergeant Leitch made his great attempt to stabilise the situation by dragging material off the defence works to create a position in the ditch around which the men could rally.

*Artist's impression of
the Redan, Sebastopol.*

It was in the aftermath of this carnage that both Graham and Elphinstone, who must have come forward from his place at the side of the Commanding Royal Engineer, carried out the rescue missions that were to win them their VCs. It is probable that Graham had done enough already but it seems that he was indefatigable in pulling wounded men back to safety. Elphinstone's citation credits him with saving 20 wounded men.

It is worth mentioning one other Royal Engineer who was present on this occasion, Lieutenant Charles Gordon. Gordon, who was eventually to achieve even greater lasting fame than any of the VC winners in this story, was with the reserve in the same column as Graham and fretting at not being involved with the action. He demanded to be allowed forward after Graham had returned from his exploits but Graham told him that it was too late. Nevertheless, Gordon, Graham and Elphinstone all remained close friends for the rest of their lives and were to influence each others' careers.

Although the French had made some progress against the Malakoff at huge cost, the British repulse at the Redan deterred the two commanders from any further action and the whole operation was called off.

British morale suffered badly after this disaster in which so many of their finest leaders had been so needlessly sacrificed. Lord Raglan was in particular despair and shortly afterwards contracted cholera and died. His place was taken by General James Simpson who lacked even Raglan's modest abilities to take decisions.

Nevertheless the Allies stuck to their task. Nor was all sweetness and light in the Russian camp. In the first place, Todleben, so much the inspiration for their performance in the siege, had been badly wounded and was now out of action. Also, in May, a highly successful expedition had taken place against Kertch and Yenikale, the Russian bases guarding the Sea of Azov to the north-east of the Crimean peninsula. Russia's ability to reinforce and resupply the Crimea was now at the mercy of the Royal Navy. Furthermore, despite their high morale after their victory, Russian casualties on 18 June had been severe, over 5000, and in mid-August they were to lose a further 8000 in a failed attempt by their field army, still encamped to the east, to dislodge the Allied force by means of an attack across the River Tchernaya. Lastly, the British received several new siege companies of artillery to boost their already considerable firepower. Attrition would now surely win the day but not before yet another severe reverse to British arms and the winning of the last sapper VC of the war.

Corporal John Ross

Corporal John Ross was born in Inch near Stranraer, and enlisted into the Royal Sappers and Miners at the age of 21 at Glasgow. He was a mason by trade. By the time he arrived in the Crimea he had some 13 years' service, six of them spent in Gibraltar. He was obviously a steady soldier but had one lapse in his career when a day's absence had earned him a regimental court martial and a month's imprisonment. However, he was promoted second corporal in October 1854 and corporal on the fateful 18 June 1855.

Ross clearly performed with distinction throughout the siege. Conolly called him 'untiring, patient, intrepid'. However, the first incident quoted in his VC citation was on 21 July 1855, in the aftermath of the Redan setback, when Ross was allocated 200 men (line infantrymen plus two of his own sappers) to push a trench connection forward from the Fourth Parallel of the Right Attack to join up with some Russian rifle pits. This work was conducted under intense fire albeit at night. He duly marked out the task which, because it was solid rock, had to be constructed from a line of gabions filled by soil brought forward from the rear. The way in which he positioned his men and organised the work so inspired his men that enough was achieved to enable further parties to carry on the work by day, protected by what had been put up overnight. A month later Ross undertook a similar task with 25 men forward of the Fifth Parallel described in his eventual citation (see Annex A) with pleasant understatement 'whilst annoyed by the presence of light balls'. With this sort of work the trenches crept ever nearer to the Redan.

The Russians, for their part, had realised from their defeat on the Tchernaya that the Allies would prevail in the end and, to facilitate their evacuation, had started building a bridge of boats across the Dockyard Creek to connect the eastern and western parts of Sebastopol. The bombardments that were now being wrought on the Russians were causing frightful casualties and it was plain from the traffic that began to use the bridge that the game was nearly up. All that the Allies needed to do was to keep up the pressure and bide their time. French politics could not, however, allow such a supine end after so much pain and loss of life. One last great assault was agreed upon. This was to take place on 8 September after a three-day bombardment. The French, who now had three times the number of troops as the British, took charge of the planning. The objectives were to be much the same as for the 18 June attack albeit with a much stronger effort against the western sector, particularly against the Bastion du Mât, by the French.

At noon on 8 September the French took the Malakoff in a fierce fight which caught the Russians by surprise. It held against determined counter-attacks. For the British there was one last, tragic humiliation in store. This time a more concentrated attack on the Redan was made across a shorter distance. Nevertheless the same withering fire of grape and canister took its bloody toll. This time the parapet was reached but once again there were simply insufficient resources of determination and courage amongst the inexperienced soldiers to win the day in the face of a plan that the young Garnet Wolseley, then a subaltern in the 90th Regiment (eventually the Cameronians) acting as a field engineer, a task for which he had volunteered,* later condemned as 'faulty in every detail as it was puerile in conception'.[20] Lieutenant George Ranken, one of the two Royal Engineers involved in the assault, wrote his own account later.

> I heard directly after I had regained our trenches that three officers of the 41st after vainly striving to induce the men to advance rushed forward together and were all three shot down like one man by the cross fire of the Russians behind their parados. This was the turning point according to this account of the men's indecision – they wavered and fled.[21]

Ranken went on to describe the apocalyptic scene as the mass of men gave way and hurtled down the collapsing face of the Redan, a tangle of broken bodies, collapsed ladders, weapons and missiles hurled by their jeering enemies, only to have to run the gauntlet of the fire-swept 250 yards that lay between themselves and the sanctuary of the trenches.

The overall casualties were worse even than on 18 June. Indeed, in two hours on the Redan, more men were lost than in the eight hours of fighting at the Alma. Howard Elphinstone was nearly one of them. He was badly wounded in this final

---

*It was common practice for a number of non-sappers to be employed in this role in siege warfare. The arduous, round-the-clock duty called for many more officers than the Royal Engineers could provide. This experience of the future field marshal gave him an understanding of sappers and formed friendships which were to bear fruit in later life.

John Ross; an artist's impression of his investigation of the evacuated Redan.

assault and in fact given up for dead. He owed his life to his soldier servant who noticed his unconscious body among a heap awaiting burial, having recognised his boots. However, the last ultimate irony still remained to be revealed by none other than Corporal John Ross. That night, anxious to investigate the whereabouts of two of his missing soldiers, Ross worked his way forward through the trench system and out into the ditch where a wounded sapper had been reported under the abbatis. Explosions were occurring from within the fortifications but, having found his man and given him succour, Ross went carefully on to investigate. Conolly's somewhat lurid account may need a pinch or two of salt:

> [he] clambered up the escarp made during the storming, and entered the jaws of a broken embrasure on the right of the salient of the Redan. The gun was there but no artillerymen … All was silent, and with a burglar's creep, soft and wary but determined, he gained the neck of the aperture. At either side he looked, but nothing started up to show that the batteries were occupied. He looked ahead with straining eyes and onwards; still, nothing could he see but huge broken works, and streams of light shooting from burning buildings. All indeed was quiet save the crackling timbers in the distance, the booming of mines and the falling of houses. The Redan, that furnace of the siege, was indeed deserted and desolate![22]

This was the third incident that contributed to Corporal John Ross's VC citation.

Aftermath

The siege of Sebastopol was over. Though a victory for the Allies, throughout it the Russians had displayed leadership, ingenuity, courage and honour which had to be admired. From the British point of view the hard-earned victories in battle before the siege and the extraordinary fortitude of the soldiers stood in stark contrast to the inept leadership and administration. The war continued through another winter with the armies confronting, but not moving against, each other in the field. The sappers busied themselves with the massive task of demolishing the Russians' defensive installations in Sebastopol and improving the living conditions for the Army. Across the Black Sea another epic siege had been in progress at Kars with the protagonists' roles reversed. In November it too ended in victory for the besiegers after an extraordinary gallant defence by the Turkish garrison led by a British general. Peace was finally signed in March 1856 and the armies went home.

It was not until February 1856 that the announcement of the inauguration of the Victoria Cross was made and that its award was to be retrospective to the autumn of 1854 to include the Crimean War. Lists of names were called for straight away although it was not until December of that year that the board of officers, under the chairmanship of General Simpson, began its sessions to decide on the recipients.

The process cannot have been easy. Looking back over the campaign there must have been countless occasions when individual men undertook actions which they never expected to survive. It seems clear from the citations that a single act of valour was often not enough to qualify for this inaugural list and men were selected for consistently outstanding performances. Many of these first submissions were 'multiple incident' citations, raising the question of whether bars should be awarded. This matter was soon settled as the warrant stipulated that a bar could only be awarded for a further act of bravery *after* receipt of the cross.[23] Altogether 111 Victoria Crosses were awarded, of which eight went to the Royal Engineers and the Royal Sappers and Miners. Bearing in mind that these were all won in the siege this achievement speaks highly of the regard in which the sappers were held in the Army for the unglamorous but dangerous work in the trenches and its associated actions. Several sappers were also honoured with French decorations. The *Medaille Militaire* (French military war medal – 'for valour and discipline') went to nine of the Royal Sappers and Miners including Ross, Lendrim and Perie, and Colour Sergeants McDonald and Leitch both became knights of the Imperial Order of the Légion d'Honneur.[*]

The first investiture, at which 62 crosses were presented by Queen Victoria, took place at a magnificent parade of some 4000 troops in brilliant sunshine in Hyde Park on 26 June 1857, before an audience estimated at over 100,000. Lieutenant Graham, Corporals Lendrim and Ross and Sapper Perie took their

---

[*]This is not quite so grand as it sounds, 'knight' being the lowest grade of this order below 'officer'.

turn to march up to Her Majesty from the file in front of the parade to the magnificent charger on which she was mounted. For Graham this was yet another test of his fortitude as he explained in a letter to his father: 'She pinned on the medal with her own hand to our coats. She stuck the pin fairly into me, so keenly I realized my momentary interview with Royalty.'

Of those four first recipients, the subsequent careers of Perie and Ross were not particularly distinguished. In Perie's case it is sad that as early as 1898 the *Sapper* carried correspondence from other soldiers wishing to trace information of this brave man. All we know is that he served in China with the 8th Company for 2½ years taking part in the capture of Hankow and the attack on the forts of Peiho. The *Sapper* correspondent wrote:

> As soon as we embarked at Southampton I was put under the care of old Jock. He used to do all my washing and mending, and in return he drew my allowance at the grog tub.
>
> I was invalided home in 1860, and Perie followed soon after, time expired, first term. He took his discharge, and ... I was sent to Canada ... [where] ... one of the company drew my attention to a paragraph in a Scotch paper, and to my surprise I saw it referred to Perie. He was either in an infirmary or a poor house ... and he was in a very poor state of health. It was a minister of religion who had put this paragraph in the paper so, taking it for genuine, we got up a subscription and sent it to him.[24]

Jock Perie's fondness for the grog was to be his undoing. As early as January 1856 he had been awarded 28 days' imprisonment with hard labour by a court martial at Sebastopol for 'habitual drunkenness'. He and the Army parted company with, it can be assumed, few regrets on either side, on the termination of his engagement in 1860. It seems he settled with his family in Aberdeen and they ran a small newsagent's and confectionery shop at 69 East North Street. Perie's gallant service was, however, recognised in 1868 by the award of a special pension of sixpence a day 'in consideration of wounds and disability'.[25] Only six years later he was dead. The cause on his death certificate was 'Diarrhoea and Liver disease – 16 days. General debility 14 years.' The end of this sad decline was an unmarked grave in St Peter's cemetery where he was buried on 19 September 1864. Jessie outlived her husband by another 20 years and is commemorated on her son-in-law's headstone in the same cemetery.

Ross completed his time in the Royal Engineers, receiving his discharge, in the rank of sergeant, in April 1867. His intended place of residence then is recorded as Pentonville Prison and so it is possible he had found employment there. Certainly he died in London, at Corbett Road, in 1879 at the age of 57.

Lendrim, on the other hand, rose to become a highly respected figure in the Army. Incidentally, by the time of the investiture he had already been presented to Queen Victoria on a visit she had made to Aldershot in 1856 specifically to meet selected men from the Crimea. However, in 1857, shortly after his marriage to the 19-year-old Louisa Hobbey, he was posted to the 23rd Company destined for China, but diverted to India to fight in the Uprising. He was at the relief

William Lendrim
(1830–1891)

of Lucknow and on 11 March 1858 he was wounded whilst overcoming a rebel assailant whom he disarmed. Later he became a sergeant major of field works at the Royal Military and Staff Colleges at Sandhurst. He died there aged 61 leaving a wife and 12 children. The magnificence of his funeral bears testimony to the respect with which he was held:

> At 11.10 am the procession formed up, six horses drew a gun carriage bearing the coffin, 'William James Lendrum V.C.' was inscribed on the coffin plate … Lendrum's tunic, belt and sword were laid on the top of the coffin escorted by a firing party of twenty-one sappers with arms reversed. Regimental Sergeant Major Hapgood RE led eight Warrant Officers as bearers of a Union Jack used as a pall, four sons represented the family, the Royal Engineers (Aldershot) and Royal Military College Bands provided the music and many distinguished officers who had fought around the world as glimpses of their medals under their cloaks testified (two who were present were in the famous 'Death Charge' (Balaclava), one of whom sounded the 'charge') took their places in the solemn cortege, which was increased by the unmounted Riding Troop and a detachment of the Infantry. General Clive the Governor of the Royal Military College received the procession at the church and the service was read by the Chaplain of the Forces the Rev F Murphy …[26]

Of the Crimean War VCs, it was Graham who had the most distinguished career as a soldier. The personal charisma noted by the Crimean War chronicler Kinglake, 'The vast stature of the young Engineer who directed their energies made him strangely conspicuous in the field, and it was on Gerald Graham and the sailors that the praise of observers converged',[27] continued throughout his life. He was badly wounded in the trenches only a few weeks after the 18 June attack on the Redan but returned to take part in the demolitions in Sebastopol. After the Crimea he went to China via India, taking command of the 23rd Company from Lennox (see below) for the duration of the 1859–60 war. He again displayed extraordinary courage and leadership in the fighting to capture the Taku forts and returned home a brevet lieutenant-colonel. In 1862 he married Jane Blacker, the widow of a Norfolk parson.

By 1881 Graham was a major-general and was selected (influenced by Sir Garnet Wolseley, with whom he served in the Crimea) to command the 2nd Brigade of the 1st Division in Egypt in the 1882 war to put down the revolt under Arabi Pasha. He was in the field immediately after landing on 20 August and less than a month later he led his brigade in the battle of Tel el Kebir, rushing the enemy's works in the face of heavy fire after a night march. Graham's natural modesty was commented on by a sapper colleague who had visited him during the march before the battle, 'thinking solely of the work he had to do, he had made no arrangements for his own comfort … I found that he had absolutely nothing to eat in his tent, but had just gone out and sat down among the men, to their great delight, and shared with them their bit of biscuit and bully beef.'[28]

Graham's next assignments now had much to do with the tribulations in the Sudan of his old friend General Charles Gordon whom he had accompanied for part of Gordon's last journey to Khartoum. In March 1884 Graham was in the eastern Sudan in command of an army to secure the area from the ravages of the rebel leader Osman Digna whom he defeated at the decisive battle of Tamai. The following year saw him commanding another force in the area when, in the domestic furore after the fall of Khartoum and Gordon's death, it was decided to operate against the Mahdi from the Red Sea coast. Good progress was made but the political scene at home changed and the force pulled out. Graham returned to England and all the honours that were his due. He retired from the Army in 1890 and died in 1899.

At the time of the first investiture, the crosses for two of the Royal Engineers' recipients, Lieutenant Lennox and Colour Sergeant Leitch, were sent overseas for presentation in their new stations, Hong Kong and South Africa respectively. However, although Lennox was the senior subaltern in the 23rd Company, the same unit as Corporal Lendrim, he must have already embarked on an earlier ship. He was later diverted to India when his ship reached Singapore. He took part in the same operations as Lendrim and gained command of the company when his commanding officer was killed at Lucknow. Although he handed over command to Graham, his VC must have followed him round the world and back again as there is evidence he was presented with it on his return to England.

At the end of this very active campaign, Lennox was promoted brevet lieutenant-colonel and awarded the CB. From 1859 he served in a number of different posts in England until 1870 when, as brevet colonel, he was sent as military attaché to the German army during the Franco-Prussian War. In 1876 he was involved with the Turks in the Balkan wars, and in 1878 he actually joined the Turkish army and took part in a series of battles before returning to Britain in 1878. After three years as Commanding Royal Engineer at the Curragh, promotion then caught up with him and he, like Graham, was put in command of a brigade in Egypt on the outbreak of the rebellion in 1882. His brigade, at Alexandria, had the hectic task of running the garrison and coping with the reinforcements and the base administration for the army in the field. He also became responsible for handling the logistics including the movement of men, boats and stores for the ill-starred Nile campaign launched too late to rescue Gordon from Khartoum. These tasks suited Lennox's by now renowned reputation for meticulous attention to detail. After Alexandria Lennox went to Ceylon in command of the troops there and his last job in the Army was as Director-General of Military Education in the rank of full general. In 1861 Lennox had married Mary Harriett Harrison and they had one son, but Mary died in 1863 and four years later Lennox married again, Susan Hay Sinclair, by whom he had a further three sons. He died in 1897 just two years after retirement.

Colour Sergeant Leitch, the other overseas recipient of the Victoria Cross, was still serving with the 2nd Company which had gone to South Africa from the Crimea in 1858. He received his VC in November of that year from the hand of the Governor of Cape Colony, Lieutenant-General Sir James Jackson. The company returned to England in 1867 and thereafter Leitch received due promotion becoming a sergeant major in 1870 at the age of 50 when based at Gravesend. He retired two years later and although there is no record of his having taken up any permanent employment, he may have worked as a temporary foreman at Dover docks in the 1870s. His son, William, was born around 1849.

Two more sapper VCs remained to be presented, to Lieutenant Howard Elphinstone and Colour Sergeant Henry McDonald. Their names were among a batch of nine submitted to the Queen by the Commander-in-Chief on 14 May 1858. This raised the question as to how far in retrospect names could be submitted as claims continued to be pressed on the War Office. Following a strong hint from the Secretary of State, only two more were put forward.[29] The ceremony took place during a visit to Southsea by Queen Victoria in August. *The Times* reported this as a colourful and fashionable event, commenting on the bravery of the recipients and remarking, '… at the same time it must be remembered that this coveted reward must never become too cheap. None but those who have actively been campaigning can understand the tense feeling with which this decoration is regarded in the army, and what perils officers and men will encounter in their efforts to gain it.'

Little is known about McDonald's life and career after the Crimea except that he rose steadily through the ranks, was commissioned in March 1862 and in 1867 became the garrison quartermaster in Gibraltar. He was compulsorily retired from that post in 1876 due to ill-health. McDonald's commissioning was the subject of one of the earlier questions that arose from the Royal Warrant that instituted the VC. At that time the pension was only granted to non-commissioned ranks. However, a new ruling was made by the Secretary of State in April 1890 to allow for it to carry over into commissioned rank. McDonald was a beneficiary of this although only for three years as he died in Glasgow in 1893, three months before his 70th birthday. The *Glasgow Herald* reported his death as having followed 12 years of suffering despite which 'his bright and genial manner never forsook him'.

As for Howard Elphinstone, as Her Majesty pinned his cross to his breast, his links with the royal family were already being forged, as he was shortly afterwards appointed tutor to the Queen's youngest son, Prince Arthur (Duke of Connaught). Elphinstone took up his duties in January 1859, initially for a year, but eventually he became so indispensable to the Queen that he was never fully released from her service even when occupying career appointments, exacting enough in themselves.

Elphinstone seemed to possess exactly the right temperament for his unusual appointment, being quietly discreet but sufficiently mentally robust to withstand the relentless flow of concerned enquiry from the Queen as to the progress of her son. His artistic talents and eye provided an important cultural dimension in the young prince's upbringing. His experience of the wider world from his origins, his travels and his professional life must have provided Prince Arthur with an invaluable grounding for the public affairs with which he would inevitably become involved.

Howard Elphinstone (without hat), seated in a group with Prince Arthur of Connaught, newly commissioned into the Royal Engineers.

Somehow Elphinstone managed to fill a variety of military appointments, mostly in Aldershot where he eventually became Commanding Royal Engineer. But he was always at the beck and call of the Queen who seemed to find reassurance from his advice on a wide range of topics, particularly after the death of the Prince Consort. A proposed posting as Commanding Royal Engineer, Mauritius, in 1881, caused a crisis of loyalties which was fortunately solved by his lifelong friend Charles Gordon volunteering to take his place.

Even Elphinstone's private life was constrained by his commitments to the Queen but he eventually married at the age of 47, and had two daughters, one of whom became Elphinstone's biographer.

In 1887 Elphinstone, now a KCB and CMG, was promoted to major-general and was selected to command Western District based at Plymouth. Early in 1890 he set off with his family for a long-sought-after holiday in Tenerife but shortly after they set sail he lost his footing on deck during a heavy swell and fell overboard to his death.

The Queen's personal feelings on learning of this tragedy were obvious even from the normally formal wording of the Court Circular of 14 March 1890 in which she describes her 'profound grief at the terrible news of the untimely death of Sir Howard Elphinstone. Sir Howard enjoyed Her Majesty's entire confidence, esteem and friendship for 31 years ... The Queen and still more the Duke of Connaught have lost a dear and most devoted friend to whom the latter could always turn for wise advice and counsel ...'[30]

It was a dreadful end for one who had survived the shot and shell of the Crimean trenches with such distinction. He and his fellow heroes might have gained a little satisfaction that, whatever the political results of the final peace agreement over the Crimea, some long-overdue reforms began in the British Army. For the Royal Engineers the most obvious were that from 1855 the Board of Ordnance ceased to exist (it effectively died with Lord Raglan) and in 1856 the Royal Sappers and Miners became Royal Engineers, the unified corps now answering, like the rest of the Army, to the Commander-in-Chief. By the early 1860s the head of the Royal Engineers became responsible to the Commander-in-Chief for all works including barracks and hospitals. Thus the separation of responsibility which had been the cause of so much grief in the Crimea was abolished.

The war had also seen the start of so many of the Royal Engineers' wider responsibilities from which the Royal Engineers earned their reputation for versatility. They had, of course, been responsible for the erection of prefabricated hutting in the Crimea. As early as January 1855 this had been the first task of the young Charles Gordon on his arrival at Balaclava. By the second winter such hutting accommodated the whole army in reasonable comfort. Telegraph had been successfully introduced and communications in the Army remained a Royal Engineers' responsibility until the formation of the Royal Corps of Signals in 1920. A railway had been built from Balaclava to the heights above Sebastopol to ease the transportation of supplies along the notoriously boggy route on which the

Army had depended in the worst part of the winter of 1854–55. It had been the work of civilian contractors but henceforth such projects were to become the responsibility of the transportation branch of the Royal Engineers.

However, although the Crimean War did indeed have far-reaching consequences for the Army, many of the soldiers who had taken part in it scarcely had time to lick their wounds before their services were, once again, urgently in demand. This time it was the greatest crisis so far to confront British imperial policy.

India – the 1857 Uprising

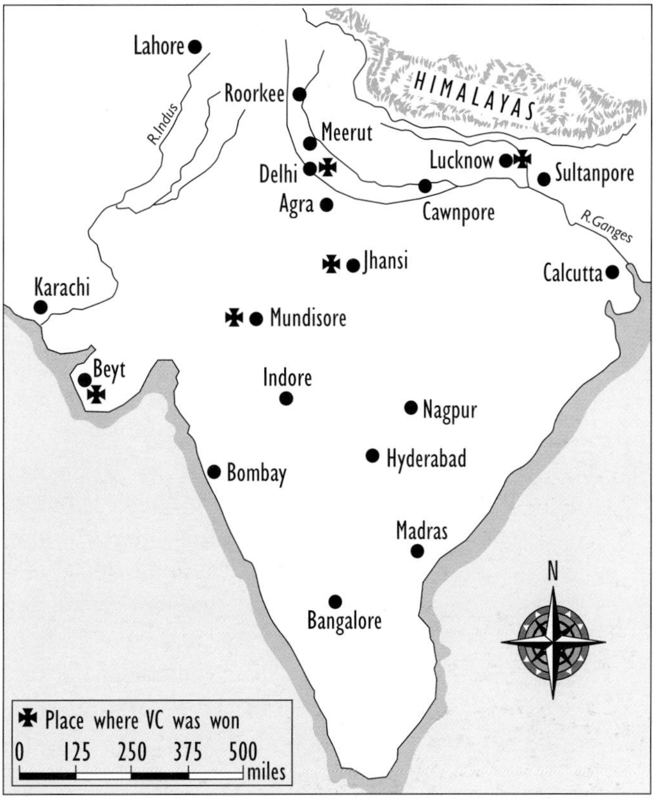

On the morning of Saturday, 16 May 1857, Captain Edward Fraser of the Bengal Engineers was shot in the back and killed by an Afghan sapper under his command at Meerut, a station of the Bengal Army some 40 miles north-east of Delhi. Fraser had arrived the previous day with six companies of the Bengal Sappers and Miners from their own station at Roorkee. He had travelled (by barge on the Ganges canal) in response to an order received from the commander of the Meerut station, to help in the tense situation following the rebellion which had occurred there the previous Sunday. In the fierce reprisals which had ensued, those sepoys who had not either been killed or escaped to join the other mutineers, many of them by then en route to Delhi, had been disarmed and all ammunition safely stored. The sappers, however, still held their ammunition and many soldiers took Fraser's order for it to be secured

Map 3

India, showing where the sapper VCs were won.

elsewhere both as a breach of faith in their loyalty and a threat to their own safety. Fraser's fatal dilemma, balancing the need to show trust against the terrible consequences of that trust being misplaced, was soon to be replicated in scores of situations throughout the Bengal Army.

Edward Fraser was the first engineer officer to fall in the 1857 Uprising. In the subsequent two years of fighting, characterised by acts of great barbarity and extreme heroism on both sides, a total of 182 VCs were to be won, eight of them by sappers. Their stories are best introduced with a short explanation of the circumstances that led to these events.

At the time of the Uprising, India was still governed by the East India Company although, since the end of the 18th century, the home government had exercised control over the Board of Directors through a minister of the Crown known as the President of the Board of Control. The country was divided into the three presidencies of Bengal, Bombay and Madras from which the three separate armies with their own corps of engineers took their name. Exactly how these corps evolved, along with the units of Sappers and Miners and Pioneers, is too long a story for this brief summary. It is enough to record that by the 1820s all were well established and had already earned their laurels in many campaigns.

Competition for service with the Company's armies had always been intense. India offered a young man excitement, sport, professional experience and responsibility far beyond any obtainable or affordable at home. While fame and fortune beckoned, the risks were considerable. Survival rates from the perils of disease, exhaustion, banditry or shipwreck, let alone actual warfare, were low. Captain James Rennell, one of the early pioneers of the Indian Survey, was once nearly killed by a group of hostile fakirs:

> One Stroke of a Sabre had cut my shoulder bone thro', and laid me open for nearly a foot down the back, wounding several ribs, besides a Stab in the same arm, and a large cut in the hand, which has deprived me of the use of my forefinger … I must not forget to tell you that about a month ago a large Leopard jumped at me, and I was fortunate enough to kill him by thrusting my Bayonet down his Throat. Five of my men were wounded by him, four of them very dangerously. You see I am a lucky Fellow at all Times.[1]

Since 1809, to obtain a commission in the Artillery (gunners) or Engineers (sappers), a young man had first to attend a course at the Company's cadet school at Addiscombe, near Croydon, an education roughly equivalent to that at the Royal Military Academy at Woolwich. Those destined to become sappers then went on to attend a course at the Royal Engineer Establishment at Chatham, along with their contemporaries in the Royal Engineers. There they learnt their military duties, the sciences of fortification and siegecraft and other field engineering skills such as bridging and pontooning, the use of explosives and survey. From 1826 a course in practical architecture was added to the syllabus.

The product of all this training was a valuable asset in a country thirsty for professional skills. The newly fledged officer would normally join one of the units of the Bengal, Bombay or Madras Sappers and Miners to be swept up into military duty and later, particularly in times of peace, to be detached for civil works either as an individual or with his unit. He learned quickly, necessity being the mother of many inventions. Versatility was the sappers' stock in trade. Many became distinguished engineers in such fields as architecture, road and railway engineering, irrigation and survey. Few of those who left their mark so enduringly on the face of India in the form of some exceptional feat of engineering had not also had a record of long, hazardous, sometimes violent campaigning behind them.

For example, one celebrated sapper surveyor, Lieutenant J.T. Walker of the Bombay Engineers who took an active part in the operations which are the subject of this chapter, eventually became one of the most distinguished Surveyors General of India.

Another case in point was General Sir Arthur Cotton. He had been commissioned into the Madras Engineers in 1820 and served with great gallantry in the First Burma War in 1824. Later he became one of India's greatest irrigation engineers, still venerated today for the prosperity his work, against many odds, brought to the regions where he worked.

One last example will serve to illustrate the nature of the soldier-engineer. In 1819 Lieutenant William Forbes of the Bengal Engineers started work building the Calcutta Silver Mint with the complex machinery whose manufacture he had supervised in England. Halfway through the project he was recalled to his unit to take part in the siege of Bhurtpore, the Jat Sikh stronghold which 20 years earlier had successfully resisted attack by the Company's armies at the end of the Second Maratha War. This heavily fortified town was invested by a 10,000-strong army under Lord Combermere (a kinsman, incidentally, of Arthur Cotton). The siege-craft tested the sappers' skills and courage and several were killed and wounded before success was finally achieved. Forbes survived, however, and not only completed the Silver Mint but went on to build St Paul's Cathedral in Calcutta amongst many other fine buildings.

Origins of the Uprising

The origins of the events which led up to the death of Edward Fraser at the hands of one of his own men, and were to engross the entire Bengal Army, are hard to define and still the subject of much debate. It seems that whereas in the early days of the Company British and Indians had enjoyed a considerable degree of mutual respect and friendship, as the 19th century developed, European society took on a more exclusive character. More and more laws were passed which appeared to threaten the fundamentals of Indian life. Deep suspicion grew amongst Indians as to the future of their land ownership, the status of their traditional rulers and above all their freedom to observe their traditional religion.

These strains were also reflected within the Army where the normal loyalties between officer and soldier had themselves been eroded by a whole variety of factors, including the attraction – for regimental officers – of the more glamorous (and better paid) career of the political officer. The roots of mutiny when it came, however, derived from and were sustained by society at large and did not lie simply within the Army itself. The well-known *casus belli*, which can not be investigated in detail here, was the refusal of the sepoys to use new ammunition which they believed to have been prepared with tallow containing the fat of cows or pigs. To have been contaminated by either of these would have been deeply offensive to Hindu and Muslim troops.[2] Whether or not such substance was contained in the new rounds, the sepoys certainly believed it to be so and refused to use them. On Sunday 29 March 1857 the dissent had reached such a pitch that a sepoy named Mangal Pande, of the 34th Native Infantry stationed at Barrackpore near Calcutta, attempted to raise rebellion, resisted arrest by firing at his European officers and eventually shot himself, though not fatally. Pande was hanged for his crime – mutineers were thereafter generically referred to as 'pandies'. Soon further disturbances brought stern and humiliating retribution upon 85 troopers of the 3rd Cavalry at Meerut where the storm finally broke on 9 May.

Early Events

A series of terrible events now followed in which men, women and children of the European communities, in the region extending from the Punjab through the United Provinces and eventually south into central India, became the victims of unco-ordinated attacks by groups of disaffected sepoys and their supporters. Many of these Europeans were cruelly and irrationally slaughtered. Others found sanctuary in more fortunate regions after hazardous journeys in which they endured awful privations. But many were caught up in the sieges that soon closed around the garrisons in Agra, Cawnpore and Lucknow. The Army was now faced with a multiple problem. There was the immediate need to secure the safety of the European civilian population, including their own womenfolk and children. At the same time the regiments had to be disarmed or their loyalty established, a process often beyond the comprehension of British officers whose almost mystical relationship to their soldiers had never before been threatened. Finally, the means had to be found of defeating the rebellion and restoring authority. Only in the Punjab was the leadership up to coping with these events and this resulted in a degree of stability, albeit on a knife-edge, and the ability eventually to spare some troops, both British and loyal Indian, for the conflict further south. Fortunately mutiny was almost entirely confined to the Bengal Army and even there some troops remained loyal, including five Indian officers and 124 other ranks of the Bengal Sappers and Miners to which were attached 45 British non-commissioned officers and privates. However, the situation called for extremely firm action and reinforcements from the Queen's Army came from England including the first Royal Engineer units to serve in India.

Cawnpore soon fell to the rebels. The torments endured by General Wheeler's small garrison in his entrenchment, the latter's subsequent betrayal and the massacre of the imprisoned women and children on 15 July, when news arrived of an approaching relief force, became the symbol of suffering and cruelty which drove the British to a pitiless revenge matching the deeds of the rebels in its inhumanity. The rebel leader responsible, Nana Sahib, personified that symbol. Cawnpore, however, has little relevance to this account. Nor does Agra – it is enough to record that, while it remained an important focus of operations, its eventual relief followed the success of actions elsewhere.

Lucknow, however, is significant both for its strategic importance and because the gallant stand of the garrison there and the drama of its eventual relief have become an epic in themselves. Moreover, it was also the scene of the first involvement of one of the subjects of this book, Lieutenant J.J. McLeod Innes of the Bengal Engineers, although he was still to experience many more adventures before the action which won him his VC. We will return to Lucknow later. By the

time that city was invested effectively on 1 July, events had reached their most serious state some 250 miles to the north-west in the ancient Mogul capital of Delhi.

The Siege of Delhi

It was to Delhi that the mutineers first went after the Meerut insurrection in May. The Emperor Bahadur Shah, the somewhat forlorn descendant of the great Moguls – though now bereft of all power – then resided at Delhi and he also offered some hope of a political focus for the rebel cause. The ejection of the British by mid-May had been achieved with horrific blood-letting and the military position of the rebel forces grew in strength. The recovery of Delhi and its elimination as a centre of rebel power now became the overriding priority for the British forces and such an army as could be spared began to gather on the Ridge, the feature that commanded the north-eastern approaches to the city. In command was General Sir Henry Barnard who had taken over when the Commander-in Chief, General Sir George Anson, had died of cholera. They had had to fight for possession of the Ridge and were seldom free from the danger of attack.

> With 21 heavy guns and mortars, 12 Coehorns [light mortars], 22 field guns, very little ammunition and less than 4,000 men, General Barnard sat down in the terrific heat of June to besiege 9,000 trained soldiers and as many more irregulars, supplied with twice as many guns and unlimited ammunition, in a fortified city which he could not encircle.[3]

An artist's panoramic view of Delhi in 1857, of unreliable accuracy. The right-hand corner of the walls on the river bank is the Water Bastion, beyond which can be seen the Kashmir Bastion with the Kashmir Gate where there is a kink in the line of the wall. The Residency lay in the corner of the walls on the river bank and the magazine where Thackeray won his VC was to its left.

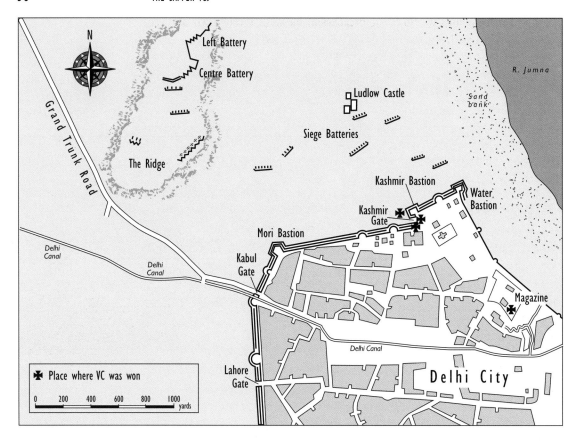

Map 4

Delhi at the time of the siege.

Indeed the force on the Ridge often appeared more besieged than besieging, so frequent were the enemy's attacks and so debilitating their circumstances as cholera and other sickness began to strike in the heat. The sappers were under-manned and hampered by the inactivity and self-indulgent habits of their commander, Major John Laughton, until he was sacked for incompetence. The young engineer officers left to cope, led by Captain Alexander Taylor, rose to the occasion and were soon trying to persuade Barnard that breaching the city walls offered a practical chance for an assault. This nearly occurred but Barnard was induced to postpone the plan and await reinforcements. A new chief engineer arrived in July, Lieutenant-Colonel Richard Baird Smith. The combination of his experience and powers of persuasion, and Taylor's inspiring energies and personal courage, resulted in a bold plan which now had to be sold to the new commander, Brigadier Archdale Wilson, General Barnard having also died of cholera. Any qualms Wilson might have had were dispelled by the presence of the charismatic Brigadier John Nicholson recently arrived from successful operations in the Punjab. His inspirational leadership, together with reinforcements and a siege-train of guns, did much to inject some confidence into the force and the potential of the plan.

The essence of this was to create breaches in the walls through which three columns could assault the city on the left, closest to the river; a fourth column would provide flank protection and eventually force an entry on the right. Two of the breaches would be achieved by artillery bombardment on the Water and Kashmir bastions. The setting up of the batteries within the range of the enemy guns and their manning until the breaches were complete called for extraordinarily careful planning, exertion and courage of a special order. However that story belongs elsewhere. We are concerned here with the third breach, which was to be achieved by blowing in the Kashmir Gate[4] using a charge of gunpowder emplaced and fired by a *coup-de-main* party.

Lieutenant Duncan Charles Home

The officer entrusted with this task was the 29-year-old Lieutenant Duncan Home.* Born in India, the son of Major-General Richard Home of the Bengal Army, at the age of eight he was sent to school in England, at Langley House near Colnbrook. He seems to have been a model pupil, if the memoir[5] published after his death is to be believed, full of life and spirits but diligent in his studies and an inspiration to others. He also attended Elizabeth College in Guernsey before going on to the training at Addiscombe and Chatham described earlier in this chapter. He joined the Bengal Engineers on his arrival in India in 1848 while the Second Sikh War was still in progress and was sent to Mooltan, recently captured after a five-month siege, where he rapidly learned the military aspects of his trade. He took part in the Battle of Gujerat, the final event of that war, in which he served with 3rd Company Bengal Sappers and Miners.

*Duncan Home
(1828–1857)*

He remained with his unit immediately after the war for work on the construction of roads and canals near the Afghan border. Quite soon, however, he became attached (much to his credit) to the Department of Public Works at Aligarh to supervise a section of the Ganges canal, then under construction. After three years on this task he was sent to Malikpore to work on the Bari Doab canal where he remained for a further five years. Again he received much credit both as an engineer and as an upright character who conducted public worship in his own home in the absence of a church and chaplain. 'The gentleness, yet firmness of his manners, and his conciliatory behaviour, won the admiration of the natives; and one of his younger brothers, who succeeded him in his appointment, found that he had inherited the fair fame which Duncan Home had established; ...'[6]

Duncan Home had therefore been away from his unit and normal soldiering for eight years when the call came to join the force at Delhi. Before setting off he had to raise five companies of men to participate in the siegeworks there. This he did by recruiting the most trustworthy and experienced of the Muzbee Sikhs who had formed his workforce in the Punjab. He sent three companies off in advance

---

*Duncan apparently came from that branch of the family which pronounced their name to rhyme with 'dome' rather than with 'plume' as used by Lord Home of the Hirsel with which family Duncan's is related.

and arrived with the remaining two on 20 August after forced marches of 30 miles a day in extremes of heat and rain. The Muzbee Sikhs soon became known as the 'Punjab Sappers', and in fact formed the basis of the Corps of Sikh Pioneers – later to become one of the Indian Army's most distinguished units.

Duncan Home was immediately absorbed into the strenuous and dangerous work on the new batteries. His fellow Bengal engineer, Lieutenant Arthur Moffat Lang, managed to keep a diary throughout the Uprising.[7] His vivid entry for 11 September reads:

> At 1 pm, I went with twelve Sappers and sixty pioneers to No 2 Right to make the traverse and epaulments longer. The enfilade fire from the right-rear was dreadful; the gun-wheels, carriages, trails, platform ribands and traverses were struck again and again. Six Sappers and I on the parapet got lots of grape plugged at us; all missed, but men in the batteries were hit.

Duncan Home and Lang then took part in the final hazardous reconnaissance of the breaches to assess their adequacy for the infantry assault.

Lieutenant Philip Salkeld

Philip Salkeld (1830–1857)

This representation is taken from the Bengal Engineers memorial to those who died in the Uprising.

Appointed as second-in-command to Duncan Home was Lieutenant Philip Salkeld. Two years younger than Duncan, he was the son of a country parson, the Reverend Robert Salkeld, the incumbent of the parish of Fontmell Magna near Shaftesbury in Dorset. Philip's maternal grandfather had been a soldier and, perhaps with this influence, he attended Dr Bridgman's School at Woolwich and later obtained a place at Addiscombe, moving on to Chatham in 1848. He reached India and the Bengal Engineers in June 1850 and after some language studies was employed on canal and road projects. In 1853 he was given responsibility for a stretch of the Grand Trunk Road until moving to Delhi in 1856 as an executive engineer with the Department of Public Works.

In the harrowing events that followed the arrival in Delhi of the mutineers from Meerut, Philip Salkeld was to display qualities of calm courage and cheerful fortitude which he would need when he eventually returned to join the force at Delhi. He narrowly escaped death in the early rioting; he was trapped with a number of Europeans near the Kashmir Gate. As many of their party were being cut down or shot, he led a group to the top of the bastion and helped form an escape 'rope' from swordbelts. Many more were now killed and injured, either falling from the walls or by rebel muskets but Philip managed to escape with a party of four officers, two ladies and three girls, the youngest aged nine.

The party then endured a series of terrifying ordeals as they made their way north towards Meerut which they believed offered the best chance of sanctuary. They had to wade the River Jumna and the Ganges canal, march through hot dry country, hiding up where they could. They were robbed, though not otherwise harmed by a gang of criminals. Eventually they were helped by some friendly Indians, and fed and sheltered by an elderly German Jew who had settled with his Indian wife in a village some 15 miles from Delhi. A message they wrote in French (the code commonly used in case of interception by rebels) finally found its way to an officer in the 3rd Cavalry who mounted a rescue operation and the party reached Meerut by bullock cart.

Philip Salkeld made a quick recovery and then took part in the operations of the Delhi Field Force which fought its way back to the city in June under General Barnard, distinguishing himself during the advance. He was then immediately involved in the construction of the batteries required for countering the fierce fire directed on the Ridge from the city's ramparts, one of which became known as Salkeld's Battery. He took part in the demolition work required to secure the positions on the Ridge, destroying the bridge carrying the Grand Trunk Road over the Najaafgarh Jhil Drain on 21 June. He then remained part of the sapper team which so indefatigably worked to prepare for the forthcoming assault, until finally being detailed to join Duncan Home in his great enterprise.

John Smith

John Smith was a 45-year-old experienced senior non-commissioned officer when he was detailed to join Duncan Home's party on 14 September 1857. By then he had many years' operational service to his credit. He was born the son of a Derbyshire cordwainer in 1814. The family then fell on hard times and his mother died young. Although he completed an apprenticeship with his uncle, the young John was persuaded by a recruiting sergeant for the East India Company to sign up for service in India. In 1841 he joined 5th Company Bengal Sappers and Miners and with them took part in the latter stages of the First Afghan War, fighting in a number of actions in the country around the Khyber Pass and taking part in the reoccupation of Kabul.

John Smith saw further service in the Sutlej campaign of 1845-6 and later served in 3rd Company at the Battle of Gujerat where he must have met and worked with Duncan Home. By this time he had married the widow of a trooper of the 12th Dragoons and after Goojerat he was able to share a few years' family life with her in Lahore. After some ups and downs in his career John Smith found himself at Roorkee, the Sappers and Miners' depot, and accompanied Captain Fraser's party to Meerut when the trouble brewed up there. On 27 May, along with Lieutenant Philip Salkeld, he joined the column which left Meerut under the then Colonel Archdale Wilson to join up with the Delhi Field Force, experiencing with them the same battles en route to the Ridge and the hazards and trials of the siege.

The Assault

As well as Home, Salkeld and Smith, one other member of the Kashmir Gate party was to earn the coveted VC at the Gate. This was Bugler Robert Hawthorne, a 37-year-old Irishman of the 52nd Regiment of Foot (later the Oxfordshire Light Infantry). He was the only non-sapper and not strictly a subject for this book; the lack of biographical detail of this brave man is in no way intended to detract from the courage he displayed throughout the operation. Overall the party consisted of the two officers, three British non-commissioned officers, 14 Bengal sappers, ten Punjab sappers and Bugler Hawthorne. The other British non-commissioned officers were Sergeant Andrew Blair Carmichael and Corporal Frank Burgess (aka Joshua Burgess Grierson). Unfortunately, the accounts of the affair do not all agree as to the names of the Bengal sappers, although as late as 1932 the then Commandant of the Bengal Sappers and Miners produced a list.[8] No record exists of the names of the Punjab sappers.

An impression of the action at the Kashmir Gate by the artist Eyre Crome who was Edward Thackeray's brother-in-law. Lieutenant Philip Salkeld is applying the match to the charge. Lieutenant Duncan Home and Bugler Hawthorne are in the ditch.

After a week's bombardment the breaches were deemed practicable and the columns were detailed off for the assault which was to take place at first light on 14 September. The first column led by Brigadier John Nicholson, who was in overall command of the assaulting force, would storm the Kashmir Bastion. A second column would similarly go for the Water Bastion on the left. The column appointed for the Kashmir Gate was to be led by Colonel George Campbell of the 52nd Regiment. The starting point was to be Ludlow Castle, one of the fine residences that lay between the Ridge and the walls, now ruined by the battles that had raged about it. Ironically, it was the former home of Duncan Home's uncle Simon Fraser, the Resident Commissioner at Delhi who had been killed in the earlier fighting in the city.

Campbell's column had to be clear of Ludlow Castle before Duncan's explosion party set off on their perilous mission, in order to ensure they were ready to charge the gate as soon as a breach had been achieved. By the time the column was clear, dawn had broken and Duncan's party had to run the gauntlet of the enemy fire in daylight. He had formed them into two groups. An emplacement party led by himself and carrying the 25-lb bags of gunpowder reached the gate unharmed but Sergeant Carmichael was killed while laying his bag. Then, in the words of Duncan's report later:

> Lieutenant Salkeld, carrying the slow match to light the charge, now came up with the remainder of the party, and with a view to enable him to shield himself from the fire from the wicket which was very severe and (the advanced party having deposited the powder bags) I slipped down into the ditch. Lieutenant Salkeld being wounded in the leg from the wicket, handed over the match to Corporal Burgess who was mortally wounded while completing the operation ... The charge having exploded blew in the right ... leaf of the gate, on which I caused the regimental call of the 52nd Regiment to be sounded as the signal for the advance of the storming party ...[9]

An extract from Sergeant Smith's more informal and dramatic report is as follows:

> I placed my bags and then Carmichael's bags, arranged the fuse and reported 'All ready' to Lieutenant Salkeld who held the slow match. In stooping down to light the match Lieutenant Salkeld was shot through the thigh and, in falling, held out the 'slow' and told me to fire the charge. Burgess was next to him and took it. He turned round and said, 'It won't go off, sir; it has gone out, sir,' not knowing that the officer had fallen into the ditch. I gave him a box of lucifers, and as he took them he let them fall into my hand – being shot through the body – and fell over after Lieutenant Salkeld into the ditch. I was left alone. Keeping close to the charge I struck a light when the port-fire in the fuse went off in my hand, the light not having gone out as we had thought. I took up my gun and jumped into the ditch, but before I had reached the ground the charge went off. As soon as the dust cleared I saw Lieutenant Salkeld and Burgess covered with dust. Lieutenant Salkeld's arms were broken. Lieutenant Home got out of the ditch leaving me in charge of the wounded and went to the front after the Rifles had gone in.[10]

The Kashmir Gate photographed a few months after the battle. The bridge has been repaired but otherwise the gate is much as it was at the time of the assault, with the right-hand portico filled in with brickwork.

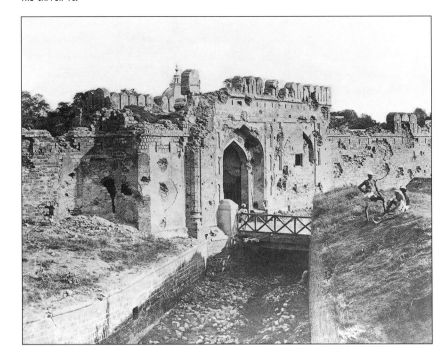

Sandes describes this act as 'the bravest deed ever performed in India by Engineers or Sappers and Miners'.[11] Home, Salkeld, Smith and Hawthorne were all awarded the VC. There seems little doubt that in the spirit of the day Carmichael and Burgess would also have been so honoured, but the rules did not permit this as the VC warrant then made no provision for posthumous awards. In fact there was also considerable debate as to the eligibility of the two officers as both were dead before confirmation of the grant could be made by Queen Victoria. The whole question of posthumous award was thus initiated, not to be resolved for nearly 50 years. The official view was that the VC was akin to an order (analogous to the Bath) and therefore 'for the living'. However, the warrant specifically allowed for on-the-spot awards to be made by the General Officer commanding, and it was under those terms that Wilson had conferred the VC on both Home and Salkeld. It was therefore agreed that 'in cases in which the Cross has been provisionally conferred at the time, but the officer or soldier has died prior to the confirmation of the grant by HM, the Cross has, by HM's command, been forwarded to the legal representative, or nearest relative, with the expression of satisfaction which it would have afforded HM to confirm the grant, had such Officer or Soldier survived.'[12] Thus a precedent was set.

A further precedent was involved as, until the Delhi VCs, eligibility was limited to 'Her Majesty's Naval and Military forces' of which Home, Salkeld and Smith were not members. A further warrant was signed in October 1857 to allow for British officers and soldiers of the East India Company to be included. A further point of discussion was how native soldiers involved in VC incidents were to be rewarded. Indian officers and soldiers, but not British, were already entitled to the much coveted Indian Order of Merit. This was awarded for gallantry and had a number of grades each qualifying for a substantial increase in pay. For this reason none of those in Duncan Home's party had, in fact, been put forward for the VC. The matter did arise in another case, however, but a Cabinet ruling decided against thus extending eligibility to native officers and men. This ruling remained in force until it was reversed by the warrant signed on 21 October 1911.

Philip Salkeld survived only a few weeks. He had been hit twice by musket balls at short range. He was taken back to the field hospital, where one arm was amputated, but there was little hope for his survival despite an attempt by General Wilson to cheer him up by the presentation of a length of crimson ribbon which was pinned on to his bedshirt by one of Wilson's aides. He managed to comment that 'it will be gratifying to send it home'. He died on 10 October 1857.

Miraculously, Home emerged unscathed from the fighting at Delhi in which he took a further active part, including another gate-blowing task, this time of the palace; but he was destined not even to survive Philip Salkeld. He took part in the action at Bolandshahr, some 50 miles to the south-east of Delhi, on 28 September, against some 2000 rebels with 14 guns, which he described in a letter as a 'tolerably sharp action' – something of an understatement as no less than six VCs were awarded for this battle although none to sappers. Home was given the task of blowing up the nearby abandoned fort of Malagarh and after several days' successful work was killed by a premature explosion. Lieutenant Arthur Lang recorded this tragedy in his diary for 2 October:

> The last mine to be blown in was the counterscarp, by which we should make a broad smooth road into the place. Stevenson and I rushed up on the ruins of the bastion and saw Home run laughing up to the mine: he put his hand out and to our horror instantaneously the mine sprung; down we rushed, put every man to work and scrape and dig. … of poor Home for a minute or two we saw no traces. I looked round a little distance and about twenty yards off in the hollow of a well I recognised his body, all mangled and covered with dust: poor fellow, his legs were broken in two places, his arms broken and one nearly torn off; his death must have been instantaneous.
>
> It was like a horrid dream from which I longed to wake. I could not realise that merry Home, so full of happiness just before, was now dead. … He had escaped the dangers of the blowing in of the Kashmere Gate, to meet his end before a deserted fort.[13]

The Delhi Magazine Enclosure
Second Lieutenant Edward Thackeray

To record another act of great gallantry performed by a sapper, it is necessary to return to Delhi. Second Lieutenant Edward Thackeray, a first cousin of the novelist William Makepeace Thackeray, had arrived in India only a few weeks before the Uprising. He had been commissioned into the Bengal Engineers after following the same courses of training as Duncan Home and Philip Salkeld. He was also a member of the Delhi Field Force and during the assault had been

Edward Thackeray
(1836–1927)

allocated to the reserve column under Brigadier General Longfield. He took part in the subsequent fighting and it was on 16 September that he performed an act of

> 'cool intrepidity and characteristic daring' ... With Major Renny of the Artillery and a few men he repulsed a determined attack on the Delhi expense magazine which the British had reoccupied. The enemy gained the top of the high boundary wall, firing onto the defenders and setting fire to some of the thatched sheds which leant against the wall. The fire spread rapidly to the magazine buildings, and while Renny climbed on to a blazing roof and threw shells with lighted fuses among the mutineers, Thackeray followed him and had bags of water handed up to him with which he extinguished the fire before the powder could explode beneath them. All this time he was under musketry fire at close quarters and pelted with bricks and stones.[14]

Thackeray's own account varies from this:

> in the afternoon they returned and attacked the magazine and set the roof on fire. We had to get up on the roof with leather bags of water and put it out while they threw large stones at us. ... I think that day I had the narrowest escape of any. After putting out part of the fire, I was just jumping down when three of them put their heads over the wall and took three deliberate shots at me, all of which missed. They could not have been above ten yards off. I fired my revolver at one, but don't remember whether I hit him or not. A Lieutenant of Artillery [Renny] then got on top of the Artillery Magazine with 10-inch shells in his hand. He lighted the fuse and dropped them on their heads. ...
> Thank God it is all over. I am sick of bloodshed and seeing men killed.[15]

Both Renny and Thackeray received the Victoria Cross for this action. However it was to be five years before Thackeray received his. A whole year elapsed before the sappers became aware that a recommendation for Renny's VC had been submitted. Thackeray's commanding officer then appreciated the significance of his feat, which had previously been somewhat overlooked in the circumstances in which so many brave deeds had been performed. Thackeray had also been the only engineer officer present and afterwards had made light of his own part in the affair. The case started on its way in November 1859, signed by Thackeray's then commanding officer, Major F.R. Maunsell, to the former Chief Engineer, Delhi, Colonel Richard Baird Smith, now Mint Master in Calcutta. By then a witness's statement had been obtained from Lieutenant Vicar of the 61st Regiment, now serving in Mauritius. ('I am quite sure you were one of those engaged ... if you remember, when I was handing up the shells to Major Renny, I begged you to come down when the attack of the rebels slackened, as your close proximity to the lighted shells rendered your position one of extreme danger.')[16]

Colonel Baird Smith's submission to the Adjutant General added his 'cordial admiration of the cool, and I may add from my previous experience, the characteristic daring with which Lieutenant Thackeray took his place on the burning roof of a shed filled with live shells and other combustible matter, and there remained under a heavy fire of musketry from the enemy until he had entirely extinguished the flames ...'[17] When this was rejected as being too long after the event, Baird Smith returned to the charge, asserting that the case had been raised without delay as soon as Thackeray had become aware of Renny's recommendation and pointing out, *inter alia*, that no prize money had yet been paid for the campaigns of 1857–8 and, if it was not too late for that, surely it was also not too late for an authenticated claim for an honour won in battle. Moreover, Baird Smith observed that the British Government had only relatively recently approved cases for honours earned in the Peninsula and that 'only a few days ago I had to deliver a decoration of this class, which bore on its face that it was granted for services rendered between 1799 and 1826.'[18] Baird Smith's persistence won the day, and Thackeray's name went forward, together with several others, to the India Office 'for the honourable distinction of the Victoria Cross'. A further 18 months elapsed before final approval and the Duke of Cambridge, Commander-in-Chief at the War Office, was able to give his decision to Thackeray at a personal interview when he was on sick leave in London in 1862.*

Lucknow

Although the fall of Delhi ensured the defeat of the Uprising the fighting was still actively being pursued at Lucknow. The story of the historic siege of that city, which started on 1 July, is only relevant to this book because of the involvement of Lieutenant J.J. McLeod Innes of the Bengal Engineers and must be read in full elsewhere, although the events at Lucknow, more than anywhere else, encapsulate so much of the spirit of the time. In the demeanour of the Commissioner, Sir Henry Lawrence, in command of the garrison until his death in early July, it reflects the calm but firm resolution of the best of the Indian Civil Service. In the experiences of the civilian families whose women and children endured unimaginable hardships and terror, it reflects the dignified and selfless courage of so many innocent people caught up in those bewildering events. On the military side the operations during the siege of Lucknow and its subsequent relief reflect the impact of bold action, exemplary courage and ingenuity in unanticipated circumstances.

There were five engineers in the garrison of whom only three, including Innes, survived. Innes had written home: 'it was a matter of interest to me for family reasons to have to do with Lucknow, the chief attraction being that my grandfather [Lieutenant-General Duncan Macleod, d. 1856], the head of my own corps, had been for many years the Engineer Officer at Lucknow, had built most of the important palaces there and had designed and collected there the framework of the Iron Bridge which spans the Goomjee [sic].'[19] They were continually on the go, one of the main problems being the determination of the enemy in

---

*More straightforward cases could also take some time to work their way through the system. As Annex A shows, the period between the event and the announcement in the *London Gazette* could be considerable; e.g., Prendergast, 2 years; Goodfellow 3$\frac{1}{2}$ years.

tunnelling under the protective works of the Residency area, the main point of defence, in an effort to break in. These attempts had to be defeated by counter-mining, a task which enormously stretched the slender resources of the garrison. Innes was engaged in this work and also distinguished himself in the defence of a post known as Innes' Post which had borne the brunt of one of the enemy's more determined attacks on 20 June. Innes later wrote an account, a copy of which is in the Royal Engineers Museum, which gives a vivid picture of life (and death) during the siege.

The garrison was reinforced, although not relieved, by the force under General Henry Havelock that broke through after fierce enemy resistance on 25 September – a few days before Duncan Home was to meet his death at Malagarh. Relief came nearly two months later when General Sir Colin Campbell, the Napoleonic and Crimean War veteran not long arrived in India as Commander-in-Chief, forced his way into the city and the garrison with all the families withdrew. However, yet more weeks were to elapse before Lucknow was finally recaptured and it was in those operations that Lieutenant Innes performed the action which won him the VC.

Lieutenant J.J. McLeod Innes

Lieutenant James John McLeod Innes was the son of a surgeon in the Bengal Army and, after Addiscombe and Chatham, arrived in India in 1850. Before the

A group of officers of the Bengal Engineers taken c. 1865. James McLeod Innes is the first on the left seated.

Uprising he had been employed with the Public Works Department on the Bari Doab canal in the Punjab but, on the annexation of the province of Oudh, had been transferred there as assistant chief engineer. After the operations at Lucknow already described, Innes was attached to the force under General Franks that was to approach Lucknow from the south-east. By this time Sir Colin Campbell had advanced on Lucknow from the south-west, had inflicted a severe defeat on the rebels in December and joined up with Sir James Outram's division to the south of the city giving him a total force of some 19,000 men with 120 guns.

Franks's force made successful progress winning several battles on the way. One of these took place at Sultanpore, about 80 miles from Lucknow, on 23 February. General Franks later reported:

I have already mentioned [Innes's] distinguished conduct in the attack on Dhowrara [he had been severely wounded whilst endeavouring to burst open the door of a house, within which some mutineers had barricaded themselves]. It is now his due to relate that at the action at Sultanpore, far in advance of the leading skirmishers, he was the first to secure a gun which the enemy was abandoning. Retiring from this, they rallied round another gun further back, from which the shot would in another instant have played through our advancing columns, when Lieut Innes rode up, unsupported, shot the gunner about to apply the match, and remained at his post, the mark for a hundred matchlockmen sheltered in some adjoining huts, and kept the artillerymen at bay until assistance reached him. For this act of gallantry, surpassed by none within my experience, it is my intention to recommend him for the honourable distinction of the VC.[20]

Innes's own version is recorded in a letter he wrote to his wife the following day, which starts 'We had a capital fight yesterday my darling – one that may really be called a battle, while all hitherto I would designate only as affairs ...' and later tells an appropriately breathless story of the two hours in which nine guns were taken and the enemy put to flight from a strong position.[21] In rather more fulsome language at the presentation parade in Calcutta in July 1859 (Innes was then garrison engineer at Fort William), the Governor-General, Lord Canning, extolled Innes's virtues 'by this noble act of well-timed daring you turned aside sweeping death from the advancing ranks of your comrades' and goes on to make the point that the 'Engineers of Her Majesty's Indian forces – men, all of them of proved ability and highly cultivated intellect, have been called upon to achieve great tasks for the protection and advancement of India ... when summoned to meet an enemy in the field, can carry their lives in their hands as lightly as any men ...'[22]

Franks went on to join up with Campbell and Outram at Lucknow on 4 March, making a total force of 31,000 with 164 guns. Innes again distinguished himself in the fierce fighting when, with Lieutenant William Greathed, he was involved in the capture of the Kaisar Bagh on 14 March. On the same day Lieutenant Wynne and Sergeant Paul of the 4th Company Royal Engineers gained recommendations for the VC for removing a barricade under direct fire at the Iron Bridge, a critical point on the rebels' flank which was being attacked by Outram's force.[23] By 21 March 1858, after nearly three weeks' fighting, they had finally recaptured the city.

Campaigns in Central India

While these dramatic events were in progress in Oudh some bitter struggles were taking place further south. The Uprising had had little effect on the Bombay Army and none at all on the Madras Army. However, there was trouble in the provinces of Malwa and Bundelkhand, centred on Indore about 400 miles to the south of Delhi, and swift action had to be taken to forestall a general uprising among the Marathas in the region, particularly as the Nana Sahib, the villain of

Cawnpore, came from that area. Fortunately the political officer in Indore was Colonel H.M. Durand, the Bengal engineer who nearly 20 years earlier in the First Afghan War (before the institution of the VC) had performed a feat at the Kabul Gate, Ghazni almost identical to that of Duncan Home at the Kashmir Gate in Delhi. Durand, who had had to evacuate Indore at the beginning of July, saw the urgency of the situation and led a column which had already been despatched from Poona to deal with the trouble under the overall command of Brigadier-General C.S. Stuart's Malwa Force. In five weeks they advanced through Aurangabad, Asigarh and Mhow to Mundisore fighting numerous engagements on the way and finally disarming the disaffected troops in the area.

If Durand's political insight and purposefulness had been the major factor in the success of this column, it was Second Lieutenant Harry Prendergast of the Madras Engineers who was to win his spurs in this arduous campaign. Harry Prendergast, the son of a member of the Madras Civil Service, had been educated at Brighton College and Addiscombe where he made a name for himself as a sportsman. He was commissioned into the Madras Engineers in 1854 and arrived in India two years later. He was initially posted to undertake irrigation work on the Godavery, but in 1856 a war against Persia arose as a result of the breaking of a treaty obligation by the Shah not to attack Herat in Afghanistan. Harry Prendergast joined B Company of the Madras Sappers and Miners for the resultant expedition and saw action in the south of the country around the Shatt el Arab.

At the end of the Persian War, B Company returned to India landing at Bombay in time to join up and march with Stuart's force from Poona. Together they covered colossal distances subduing various incipient revolts and included in their achievements the successful siege and capture of the fortress at Dhar. They then moved northwards and met a rebel force at Mundisore 90 miles north of Indore. Prendergast was sent forward with a Captain Mayne and 300 cavalry. On 21 November the party was attacked by the enemy who were then checked by a charge of the cavalry. Prendergast, while gallantly charging with the cavalry, saved the life of Lieutenant Dew of the 14th Dragoons by attempting to cut down one of the foreign mercenaries then fighting for the mutineers,[*] who was covering Dew with his musket. Whilst so doing, Prendergast was shot in the chest just to the left of the heart. Fortunately a Major Orr dealt with the rebel and Prendergast went on, after what seems a miraculous recovery, to perform further deeds of valour which are also mentioned in his VC citation.

These occurred during the subsequent campaign in central India under the leadership of Major-General Sir Hugh Rose who had only recently arrived in India for the first time and was now faced with campaigning in extreme conditions

Harry Prendergast
(1834–1913)

---

[*]The citation for Prendergast's VC describes this man as a 'Velaitee'. This word, in various spellings, is related to the modern Urdu word 'wilayat' meaning overseas or, more specifically, UK or European. In the mid-19th century, however, it simply meant 'outside India' and a 'velaitee' was a foreign soldier or mercenary, in this case almost certainly Afghan.

of heat. Rose's force, initially comprising just the 2nd Brigade under Brigadier-General Charles Steuart, but due to be joined later by Brigadier-General C.S. Stuart's 1st Brigade from Indore and a division under Major-General Whitlock, performed prodigies in these extreme conditions. In a period of five months they cleared the area of a determined, warlike and well-organised enemy force. The idea behind the operations was that by driving north-east, Rose's force would distract the attention of the rebels in Gwalior from threatening the operations of Sir Colin Campbell against Lucknow.

Prendergast was then offered the post of Engineer at Mhow by Sir Henry Durand but decided that a quiet life was not to his taste and remained with his company, who now joined Sir Hugh Rose's force on their march with 2nd Brigade. They reached a place called Ratgurh on 25 January and there Prendergast accomplished another act of gallantry (just two months after his life-threatening wound at Mundisore). For some weeks the pattern of life for the sappers was one of forced marches and the demolition of enemy fortresses interspersed by short sharp actions. For example, after destroying the fort at Ratgurh, the force marched some 28 miles to relieve Saugor. From there Prendergast took half his company to another fort 14 miles distant, prepared the mines for its demolition by sunset and returned the same night.

However, over 100 miles to the north lay the fortified city of Jhansi, centre of the rebellion in this area and power base for the Rani of Jhansi, whose furious reaction to the annexation of her state by the British had been one of the features of the rebellion. The Rani had become a charismatic and effective military leader of her people. Her city was a crucial objective for Rose's force. He marched north to invest it, arriving on 21 March 1858. It was a tough assignment in a strong position 'with a perimeter of about four and a half miles and ... surrounded by a wall from 18 to 30 feet in height with numerous bastions in which guns were mounted'.[24] The garrison was estimated at 12,000 with 30–40 guns.

As Rose's force was in process of investing the city he had to take swift action against a relieving force of 20,000 under the rebel leader Tantia Topi. They met at the River Betwa and Rose won a decisive victory. It was at this battle that Harry Prendergast performed the third feat of gallantry that is mentioned in his VC citation. Taking a leading part in yet another charge, he was severely wounded by several sabre cuts on his left arm, his left thumb being all but severed. At last Prendergast was out of action. He was evacuated to Calcutta and then to England for two years' leave where he received his decoration from the Queen.*

---

*Once asked his feelings on being wounded he replied, 'Oh they vary. I had a bullet wound close to my heart, and in consequence could do no active work for a month or so. We were in the field and I had to be carried about. Then, in the following year, in addition to receiving a wound in the finger and having my thumb all but severed in a cavalry charge, my left arm was nearly cut off. The bullet wound ... was a nice clean wound, and the velocity was so great that it did me very little harm. The sword wounds, on the other hand, carried bits of cloth and flannel right through and I found them extremely painful.' (*Chums*, Lummis files, National Army Museum)

Michael Sleavon
(1827–1902)

The Siege of Jhansi
Corporal Michael Sleavon

Immediately after his success on the River Betwa, Rose ordered the storming of Jhansi to take place at dawn on 3 April. By this time his force had been joined by Brigadier-General C.S. Stuart's 1st Brigade from Indore to which had been attached 21 Field Company Royal Engineers. A breach in the walls had been achieved in one place and this was to be attacked by one column from 1st Brigade who formed the left attack. However, three more columns including two from 2nd Brigade on the right were to escalade. The breach was taken fairly easily but the escalading parties had considerable difficulty against a determined defence and suffered severe casualties.

It was during the subsequent street fighting which lasted for three days that Corporal Sleavon won his VC. Michael Sleavon was born in Fermanagh in 1827. Like so many Irishmen he almost certainly enlisted to escape the terrible privations of the Great Hunger. By the time he reached India he had nine years' service, five of them with the company in Bermuda, and had been promoted corporal the previous year. His background, character and the incident which earned him his VC were fully reported in the *Fermanagh Times* of 28 August 1902,[25] from which the following extracts are taken, after his death and funeral.

> The funeral of Michael Sleavin [sic] … was attended by several of the local gentry and a large proportion of the respectable inhabitants of Kesh and the surrounding neighbourhood who, by their presence, testified their respect and esteem for the deserved hero. Sleavin though one of the bravest soldiers the British Army has produced for a century, was a man of the most unassuming character, never parading his deeds of fame in India or elsewhere, living very quietly on a farm on

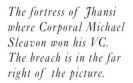

The fortress of Jhansi where Corporal Michael Sleavon won his VC. The breach is in the far right of the picture.

the Archdale property and whenever alluding to the part he took in the taking of Jhansi, for which he received the Victoria Cross, always ended by saying that '... in doing a soldier's part, he only did his duty to his Sovereign and Country.'

Sleavin was enlisted for the Royal Artillery in Lowthestown (Irvinestown) so far back as 1847. Being a mason by trade (it is said of him that at the age of 20 he had already built several houses in Kesh for the late Mr William Archdale) he was soon transferred to the Royal Engineers.

The report continues by quoting from Sleavon's 'commanding officer', Captain John Baillie.

Capt John Baillie, Executive Engineer Jhansi. To Lieutenant J.B. Edwards, RE,* commanding 21st Field Company Royal Engineers Gwalior. Dated Jhansi 26th October 1858.

Sir – I reply to your semi-official letter of the 4th inst requesting me to state the circumstances of an act of gallantry performed by Corporal Sleavin 21st Company Royal Engineers, at the capture of Jhansi. I have the honour to forward the following detailed statement for your information.

On the failure of the attempt to escalade on the left attack to which I was attached as assistant field engineer, I proceeded round to the breach and joined the column of the right attack under Brigadier Stewart [sic] which had forced its way to within a short distance of the Palace. In reaching this position the column suffered very severely from the flank fire of the Fort at a point where it had to cross a small open space at the junction of several streets, upon which the enemy's matchlock men concentrated their fire. Dr Stacks HM 86th Regiment was killed there as I reached it, and several other officers and a number of the men had been wounded. It occurred to me that by running a rough parapet across the opening, a direct communication with the breach and the safe removal of the wounded would be secured and the line of buildings thus connected would form an advanced parallel of great importance in the event of the enemy (as was to be expected) holding out on the front.

Edwards then ordered Corporal Sleavon with some of his men to construct this, using such materials as could be found from the surrounding houses. Immediately they were fired upon. 'Scarcely a plank was laid without being struck and frequently perforated by bullets ...' and so close were the enemy that it became almost impossible to raise the parapet.

Corporal Sleavin, however, who was at the head of the sap [sic – not a dug trench in the usual sense of the word] and consequently much exposed, maintained his position under this heavy fire with a cool and steady determination worthy of the highest praise and he continued his work until the capture of the Palace had placed the greatest portion of the town in our possession and opened up a safe line of communication with the camp by the Poncha and other gateways. ... Capt Coley, Major of Brigade 1st Brigade CIFF and Lieut Gossett CE who personally assisted in the construction of the parapet will, no doubt, add their testimony in support

*Later Lieutenant-General Sir James Edwards, CB, KCMG.

of this statement and I shall be most gratified if with their aid, it may be the means of obtaining for this brave man the due recognition and reward of an act of gallantry unsurpassed, if not equalled throughout the campaign.

The same account also reports that Sleavon led a party 'in the face of death' to rescue the body of the surgeon, Dr Stacks, to save it from mutilation by the enemy. Captain H.E. Jerome and Private J. Byrne of the 86th Regiment, and Bombardier J. Brennan, RA, also received the Victoria Cross for their part in this fierce fighting.

The campaign in central India continued on into 1859, a story which belongs elsewhere, by which time Sir Robert Napier of the Bengal Engineers, after a highly successful period in command of 2nd Brigade, had taken over the chief command from Sir Hugh Rose when he was appointed Commander-in-Chief of the Bombay Army. The Rani of Jhansi was killed in this later fighting and Tantia Topi was finally caught up with and hanged. However, there remains one more event to record.

*Charles Goodfellow
(1836–1915)*

Lieutenant Charles Augustus Goodfellow

The Uprising was effectively over by the end of 1859, but as late as September, Lieutenant Charles Augustus Goodfellow of the Bombay Engineers received orders to take 4th Company of the Bombay Sappers and Miners to join a force operating in Kathiawar north of Bombay. Goodfellow was the son and grandson of Bombay Engineers both of whom became generals after very distinguished service. He was born at Poona in 1836 and in due course followed the Addiscombe and Chatham path before arriving in India in 1857. Like Harry Prendergast he was a proficient sportsman and a particularly good boxer.

Charles Goodfellow had served with Sir Hugh Rose's force in central India. He took part in the sieges at Ratgurh and Jhansi. At the storming of Jhansi, he was one of only two out of the eight officers with the Sappers and Miners who did not suffer death or severe wounding.

The expedition to Kathiawar receives little attention in histories of the Uprising and the fact that the Mutiny medal was not awarded for it rather suggests it was a separate affair. Nevertheless it was quite a sharp action which arose from the rebellion in April 1859 of the Waghers, a fanatical Hindu people descended from the west coast pirates who were based on the island of Beyt in the Gulf of Cutch. Their fort was not captured on that occasion but the insurgents were brought to terms by a force consisting of a detachment of Her Majesty's 4th Foot and a company of Bombay Infantry. In the autumn there was a more serious rebellion. An expeditionary force was mounted and set sail from Bombay on 29 September in 11 of Her Majesty's ships. It comprised Her Majesty's 28th Foot, 6th Bombay Infantry, 200 marines, possibly 17th Bombay Infantry, a Royal Artillery detachment and a party of Bombay Sappers and Miners (under Goodfellow). The force was under the overall command of Lieutenant-Colonel Donovan of Her Majesty's 33rd Regiment. The troops were landed on 6 October and the fort stormed. According to a contemporary account attempts to escalade failed 'owing to the very heavy fire poured upon the assailants from the curtains, which had been extensively loopholed'.[26] Twenty-four officers and men were killed and 47 wounded. It was during this assault that Charles Goodfellow rescued a wounded soldier from under the intense enemy fire, a most gallant act, although unfortunately the man was dead. The troops were then withdrawn and the bombardment resumed. The Waghers evacuated the fort soon after dark. It was occupied the next day and then levelled by the sappers. When Goodfellow died at the age of 78, his obituarist maintained that the VC had been awarded for 'uniform gallant behaviour through the war'. It was the last award of the Uprising.

Later Careers

At the end of the Uprising John Smith was the only survivor of the Kashmir Gate VCs and he too was to be denied old bones. His immediate employment after Delhi is not clear but subsequently he was attached to the flying column under Brigadier-General George Barker engaged on punitive expeditions over a period of 18 months. After the Uprising he was employed, as so many experienced senior NCOs were, as barrack master in various locations. He received his commission as Ensign in 1860 and settled down to an agreeable family life with his wife and four daughters. Sadly, he contracted dysentery in 1864 while on leave at Jullundur and died on 26 June, aged 50. He was buried there in the Artillery Cemetery with full military honours.

Edward Thackeray, however, was the longest survivor of the Uprising VCs. He continued to be engaged on operations for the remainder of the Uprising, first with the Rohilcund Field Force with whom in April 1858 at the capture of Fort Rooyah he had his horse shot from under him. Later he also joined Barker's force in Oudh. For 20 years thereafter he led a quiet life in the Public and Military Works building barracks in Oudh, acting as personal assistant to the Chief Engineer in the same province and then becoming Executive Engineer in Upper Assam.

In 1879 Thackeray was appointed Commandant of the Bengal Sappers and Miners and he took them to the Second Afghan War. He was Commanding Royal Engineer and advanced with the Khyber Column under General Charles Gough. When Gough moved forward to Kabul Thackeray was left in command of the post at Jagdalak Kotal and was severely wounded while defending it against a number of strong enemy attacks (see also Chapter Five). On returning to India he resumed command of the Bengal Sappers and Miners at Roorkee; then after a long period of service with the Intelligence Branch at Army Headquarters he retired as a full colonel in 1888. After retirement Thackeray was appointed KCB for important work in connection with the Order of St John of Jerusalem. In 1898 he went to Bordighera in Italy where he spent the rest of his life. During the First World War he worked for the British Military Hospital in Bordighera and received the two war medals. Thus he had the rare distinction of wearing medals for the Uprising and the First World War. He died at Bordighera on 3 September 1927.

Edward Thackeray was twice married; in 1862 to Amy Crowe, sister of the artist of the Kashmir Gate sketch but who died in 1865; and, in 1869 to Elizabeth Pleydell. There were two daughters from the first marriage and four sons from the second.

Fortune seems to have favoured J.J. McLeod Innes, at least as far as rank is concerned. His heroism in the Uprising happened at a good time in his career for, as well as receiving the VC, he was granted the rank of brevet major. From then on promotion was almost a foregone conclusion. However, Innes was clearly a most able man even though he had no further war experience. Like Thackeray he spent much time with the Public Works Department, in his case in the Central Provinces and in the Punjab. Later he was employed on the commission investigating the failure of the Bank of Bombay. In 1870, after starting the upper section of the Indus Valley Railway, he became Accountant General of the Public Works Department and held this important post for ten years. In 1881 Innes was appointed Inspector-General of Military Works retiring in 1886 as a lieutenant-general. In retirement General Innes took to writing and published several works on India. He suffered severe illness towards the end of his life and died in Cambridge on 13 December 1907.

James McLeod Innes in old age. The admiring young girl is Innes's grand-daughter.

Harry Prendergast was the sort of soldier who was almost inevitably going to win a VC at some time, provided he survived. We have seen how that came about. Dashing and determined, his experiences in central India were nevertheless insufficient for his ardent spirit. Whenever a war occurred somewhere in the world Harry Prendergast felt he must be involved. His biography by Colonel H.M. Vibart, RE is subtitled 'The Happy Warrior'. He volunteered for the Second China War, but was turned down; he travelled to Vienna in a vain attempt to join the Austrians against Italy and France in 1859; he tried, unsuccessfully, to participate in the Ambela campaign in 1863. However, he finally succeeded in joining Sir Robert Napier's Abyssinia Expedition in 1867 commanding three companies of Madras Sappers and Miners. He was present at the storming of Magdala and was mentioned in despatches.

Field Marshal Lord Napier of Magdala

Now a brevet lieutenant-colonel, Harry Prendergast was appointed Commandant of the Madras Sappers and held the post for 12 years. He made a brief excursion to the Mediterranean in 1878 as Commanding Royal Engineer, deploying Indian troops for the first time in Europe. Prendergast returned to India later that year, and filled a number of senior posts, before being put in charge of the Burma Expeditionary Force in the Third Burma War. This was perhaps the climax of his career. The war required rapid movement of a 9000-strong force in a country beset by physical difficulties and ruled by a king (Thibaw) who harboured a passionate hatred of the British. By careful preparation Prendergast achieved a brilliant success in five weeks, forcing Thibaw to surrender and removing him and his family to exile in India. Thus Burma was added to the Queen Empress's dominions in 1886. Prendergast's accomplishment has many parallels with the Abyssinian Expedition and earned him the KCB. In the odd way that promotion worked in those days, Prendergast had to give up his post in Burma on becoming a lieutenant-general and return to India but, because he was still only 51, it was difficult to find him a job. He became a full general at 52, and retired from the Army five years later. He was promoted to GCB in 1902, 16 years after his Burma success, and died in 1913 aged 78.

The contrast between the personality and character of Prendergast and that of Corporal Michael Sleavon, serves well to illustrate the non-discriminatory nature of the VC. In accordance with Queen Victoria's personal wishes, valour was the only criterion. Neither rank nor station in life entered into it. Sleavon was promoted sergeant in May 1858. His unit went to Mauritius about that time and there are hints that the boredom of a peacetime station may have got the better of him. There is a note in the files of the Royal Engineers Museum: 'Regimental Board held on 5 April 1861 at Fort George, Mauritius, enquired into the loss of the Victoria Cross of Sergeant Michael Sleavin [sic] on or about 2 Feb 1861. Probably lost on his return at night from Port Louis. It was recommended that he be permitted to purchase another one.'[27] Whether or not there was some disciplinary incident connected with this is not recorded but Michael Sleavon's career came unstuck in 1862 when he was court-martialled for some offence, also unrecorded, and served the rest of his time as a sapper, obtaining his discharge on 25 April 1871 at the age of 44, after 24 years' service. His discharge papers state with commendable but tantalising lack of detail that 'His name appears in the regimental defaulters book and he has been tried once by Court Martial/the same offences.'[28] Nevertheless with a VC and five good conduct stripes to his name his conduct was graded 'Very Good'. Whether or not he was able to follow his recorded plan to reside at Canterbury is not known; at some point he returned to his native Ireland and died there in August 1902.

As we have seen, about the time Michael Sleavon was winning his VC, Charles Goodfellow was engaged in the desperate fight on the walls; however, it is unlikely they ever met. After the Beyt fort affair Goodfellow's career followed the quieter paths of works in the Bombay area until the Abyssinian Expedition of 1867. There he obviously made an impression with his Commander-in-Chief, General Sir Robert Napier, as he was awarded his brevet majority. Thereafter a successful series of civil engineering posts followed and he became Chief Engineer First Class of the Southern Division in 1888, eventually becoming a lieutenant-general in 1892. A fine sportsman, Charles Goodfellow spent much of his spare time in India shooting big game – he once shot a rogue elephant after tracking it for two days – and fishing. However, he was a modest man who shunned publicity. A devout Catholic, he helped with numerous charities until his death in Leamington Spa in 1915.

Charles Goodfellow

Aftermath

After the 1857 Uprising the East India Company's rule came to an end as the government of India passed to the Crown. In due course the presidency armies developed into the Indian Army which served with such distinction in the two world wars. These wars will be the subject of later chapters of this book. Essential to those achievements was the unique relationship of mutual trust and respect between Indians and British which was patiently built up from the bloody turmoil of the Uprising. How this came about to the point when in 1947 Britain was able to hand over a professional army steeped in traditions which are still followed with pride in the new India, Pakistan and Bangladesh is another story. It was not to be a smooth path. The securing and consolidation of Britain's Indian dominion was to cost more blood and lead to six more Victoria Crosses for the Royal Engineers before the end of the 19th century.

Bhutan (1864–1866)

To have been beaten by the men we have been despising is too much, and I feel thoroughly sick. One of the first maxims of war is 'Never despise your enemy'. Would we have thought of it.[1]

So wrote the commander of the Eurasian Artillery in the Duar Field Force in a letter to his father after they had been humiliatingly ejected from Bhutan in January 1865. Up to then everything had gone so well in what to the outside world must have seemed a minor border skirmish when compared with the challenging struggle of the 1857 Uprising, still fresh in people's memories, to say nothing of the cataclysmic events then taking place in America.

The trouble which broke out in 1864 in the remote north-eastern state of Bhutan was also an early test for the newly forged Indian Army restructured as it had been in the aftermath of the Uprising, and for British resolution in securing the Empire for which the Crown now had full responsibility. It was not until 1 April 1862 that the formal reorganisation of the engineer corps had taken place by the amalgamation of the Bengal, Bombay and Madras Engineers with the Royal

Map 5

Bhutan, approximate boundaries 1865.

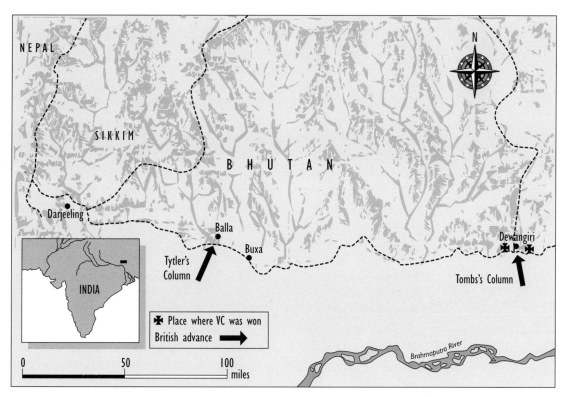

Engineers. There had been little change in the strengths of the Sappers and Miners, however, and when the trouble blew up in Bhutan the sappers were well represented in the punitive force.

The origins of the Bhutan War typify the way in which the fringes of the Empire would creep outwards like a spreading ink-blot almost more by accident than design. A common three-stage pattern would be:

- Stage One: disagreement about a boundary arising from territorial claims from the neighbouring state, probably involving historic 'rights' fought for over generations.

- Stage Two: a treaty drawn up by the British authorities aimed at achieving some sort of permanent peace, almost invariably on terms unfavourable to the troublesome neighbours which would then be either declined, or reluctantly accepted and almost immediately broken.

- Stage Three: a punitive expedition to restore British dignity and establish some form of presence across the border leading eventually to virtual or actual annexation.

In the case of Bhutan, the disputed territory lay along the line of the Bengal 'Dooars', the strip of foothill country now important for growing tea, that divides the high plateau of Bhutan from the lower-lying area of Assam to the north of the Brahmaputra. A diplomatic mission in the autumn of 1864 under a Mr Eden had not only been rebuffed but its members held in captivity until being obliged to sign, under duress, an agreement relinquishing British control of Assamese territory. An ultimatum demanding an apology for the insult and the restitution of property taken in the border raids was ignored. An expedition, known as the Duar Field Force, was duly mounted under Brigadier General W.E. Mulcaster to occupy the significant fortresses along a 180-mile line some 20–30 miles inside the Bhutanese border. It was entirely successful, achieving its aim in six weeks with negligible casualties.

However, the Bhutanese (known as Bhooteas in many contemporary accounts) were playing a crafty game. Mulcaster's force was just about to break up to hand control over to the Bengal police when, on 25 January 1865, they were surprised in a series of attacks which eventually forced a complete withdrawal. In fact, at Dewangiri, the most significant of the posts which had been occupied, lying on a dominating ridge at an important junction of the main routes in the area, some 40 miles inside Bhutan at the eastern end of the disputed area, a note from the Bhutanese leader had been delivered to the force giving one week's warning of an attack unless they withdrew. However, as the note was written in Tibetan, no one could read it and it was set aside. A particularly embarrassing and serious incident then occurred there. The Bhutanese had managed to creep into the camp unnoticed and create considerable havoc. The garrison responded with energy as soon as daylight enabled them to identify their enemy and, in an attack in which the sappers took a prominent role, drove the latter off, unfortunately losing two officers and four men in the process including Lieutenant J.H. Urquhart, RE. However, the enemy then cut off the water supply which made their position untenable. They held out for a few days but on the night of 4/5 February they withdrew in considerable disorder and the other posts to their west had to follow suit.

Mulcaster was sacked and replaced by Brigadier-General Henry Tombs, VC, CB. A gunner, Tombs had made a considerable reputation as a young officer in Gwalior and in the Sutlej campaign of 1845–6. He had performed a very brave act in the Uprising during the siege of Delhi when he went to the aid of another gunner officer who was in the process of being overwhelmed by a patrol of mutineer cavalry. Between them they saw off the patrol and both were awarded the VC.

Tombs's plan was to advance in two main columns, the westernmost, with which this account is not concerned, being under the command of Brigadier-General Tytler. Tombs himself took the right-hand column which, with the reinforcements that had now been sent, amounted effectively to four battalions of native infantry, the headquarters and right wing of the 55th Foot, two batteries of artillery and No. 7 Company Bengal Sappers and Miners. Among the Royal Engineer officers with this column were Captain W.S. Trevor and Lieutenant J. Dundas.

Captain William Trevor

William Spottiswoode Trevor had joined the Bengal Engineers after an unusually adventurous childhood. His father was Captain R.S. Trevor of the Bengal Cavalry who had taken part in the disastrous First Afghan War. In this, the British had invaded Afghanistan in response to what they saw as an unacceptably close relationship between that country and Russia, of which more in later chapters, and occupied Kabul in August 1839 placing their preferred candidate, Shah Shuja, on the throne. By the end of 1841 the occupying force had been greatly reduced and dangerously dispersed despite a serious insurrection that was gaining strength in support of the deposed ruler, Dost Mohammed. The British political head of mission in Kabul, Sir William Macnaghten, had completely misjudged the situation and believed he could successfully negotiate a solution. He accepted an invitation from Dost Mohammed's son, Mohammed Akbar Khan, who was in command of the rebel force, to attend a meeting to consider terms. He went to the meeting accompanied only by three of his political officers, including Captain Trevor. It was a trap. Macnaghten was taken away and murdered. The three political officers were escorted from the scene but Trevor, through some accident, fell from his horse and was hacked to pieces leaving his wife and sons, William aged ten and Arthur, an infant in arms, to face the terrible consequences that now unfolded.

For most of the British community, this was quite simply annihilation in the ghastly retreat that then was forced upon them, through the Afghan mountain passes back to India. Although promised safe passage, in fact they were harried every inch of the way. Despite the epic last stand of the survivors of the 44th

William Trevor
(1831–1907)

Regiment at Gandamak, and the incredible adventures of Dr Brydon, in popular belief the only survivor from the whole of the force which marched, 16,000 souls who had left Kabul eventually perished either from the extreme cold or at the hands of the Afghan tribesmen.

However, some of the families, including the Trevors, had better fortune having been taken captive by Akbar Khan.

> The events of this captivity made a deep impression on Trevor and he carried through life the recollection of the scenes he had witnessed at that time. He had been taught to read and write Hindustani and Persian and he used to relate how Akbar Khan endeavoured without success to avail himself of this knowledge to discover what was being talked about by the prisoners, and to induce him to translate letters received from India. A favourite amusement of Akbar's was to get up fights between Trevor and the Afghan boys, offering as prizes legs of mutton.[2]

The Trevor family survived their captivity* and returned to Britain where Trevor attended Edinburgh Academy 'as befitted the grandson of William Spottiswoode, Laird of Glenfernet in Perthshire, whose name he bore. He and his two brothers then followed their late father into the army of the Honourable East India Company, William being commissioned into the Bengal Engineers on 11 December 1849.'[3] Trevor also attended Addiscombe, and was selected for special duty under the Commissioners of the Great Exhibition of 1851 before going to India in 1852.

Almost immediately Trevor was attached to the expedition to Rangoon under General Godwin to punish the Burmese for their unacceptable treatment of some British nationals. This developed into the Second Burma War† in which Trevor displayed great gallantry and initiative, particularly on two separate occasions. In the first, on 12 August 1852, he led a storming party up one of the ladders in the attack on a fortification called the White House Picket stockade; and in the second, under Sir John Cheape, he led the break-in to the stronghold at Donabew, shooting down the occupants with his pistol.[4] For these services Trevor received the thanks of the Government.

After Burma, Trevor was engaged in a variety of works appointments. In 1857 he was sent to Darjeeling on a barrack construction project, where he married Miss Eliza Ann Fisher. They had two daughters before Eliza died in 1863. Trevor then spent three years superintending the construction of the Ganges-Darjeeling road before becoming Controller of Public Works Accounts in Bengal and responsible for the reform of a system of which he had been a vociferous critic.

Thus, by the time Trevor was appointed to the Duar Field Force in 1864, he was by no means a stranger to the area in which he was to operate, and a soldier of proven experience and courage.

---

*There were eight children in all; the youngest, Jessie Macnaghten, was born in captivity and died five months later at Ferozepote.

†It was on this campaign that the two guns and magnificent bronze bell were taken, which at the time of writing this book adorned the square in Brompton Barracks, Chatham.

Lieutenant James Dundas

James Dundas, by contrast, was new to the game of soldiering. He was Trevor's junior by 11 years. He was the son of George Dundas, one of the judges of the Court of Session in Scotland, and Elizabeth Mackenzie of Peeblesshire. Educated at Edinburgh Academy, Trinity College, Glenalmond and Addiscombe, he was commissioned in 1860 and, after his Chatham course, went to India in 1862. Very shortly afterwards he was attached to the Public Works Department in Bengal and became an Executive Engineer. Bhutan was therefore his first experience of operations.

The Action at Dewangiri

Tombs's column's objective was Dewangiri, a settlement which occupied a commanding position on the easternmost route into Bhutan. His problem was how to approach the enemy position without suffering severe casualties on one or other of the steeply rising tracks surrounded by thick jungle. He solved it by a ruse. He sent a strong party along a route to the west of the position. This attracted a large proportion of the enemy who entrenched the route and constructed palisades. This left Tombs's chosen route from the south open and unprotected so that by 2 April his force was able to concentrate at a point half a mile from the ridge without a single casualty. At this, many of the Bhutanese fled but a number (150–200)

James Dundas (1842–1879)

Copy of the sketch map drawn by Lieutenant Kellow Pye that accompanied Tombs's report. On the original the single lines are in red, the double (artillery) in blue.

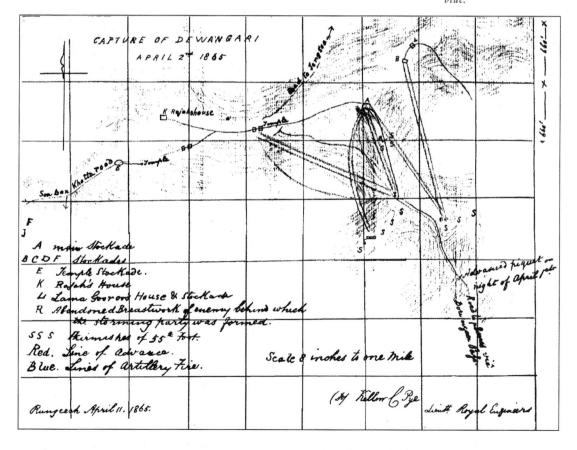

barricaded themselves into a blockhouse to which the only apparent access was through a 2-foot space between the top of the 14-foot high walls and the roof.

This blockhouse (marked 'A' on Kellow Pye's map) with its commanding position became the main target. Tombs decided on a frontal assault up the steep zigzag approach the next day by the 12th Native Infantry and the Sikhs of the 29th Punjabis. A secondary assault on a smaller blockhouse to the left by a company of the 55th Regiment and a detachment of native police was timed to match the main assault. These attacks would be preceded by a bombardment from two howitzers and two mortars.

On the left, the Bhutanese moved out to meet the 55th but were so severely mauled by the musketry of the redcoats that they fled in disarray. In this way the flanking movement got ahead of the main attack which had become bogged down because of the ineffectual gunnery and was now somewhat exposed. Tombs needed swift action to prevent any danger of the Bhutanese from returning and reinforcing the position so imperilling his flanking force and jeopardising the whole operation.

Trevor (who incidentally was suffering from a severe fever) had been watching developments from a vantage point just behind the guns where he had been supervising the sapper work. As he expressed it later:

> warned by an arrow through my trousers and one or two shaves from some half cut blocks of stone, not to loiter unnecessarily near, I turned to join the general who however was quite close by, trying to get the men to close and make another effort for the capture of the place. I heard him call out several times for officers to lead and at last make a general and it struck me reproachful appeal to those within hearing, in the terms – Will no officers here set an example to the men and show them the way in – more to the same effect … [5]

He charged forward, followed by Dundas and a third volunteer, Tombs's Brigade Major, Major Sankey. Tombs could not spare Sankey as he was required urgently for his staff duties and, with a touch of farce, Tombs had to pull Sankey down with his own hands. Trevor and Dundas succeeded in scaling the walls and squeezed through the gap. 'How [they] escaped death was a marvel; perhaps the restricted space at the point of entry had something to do with their success, the defenders being unable to use their swords effectively …'[6] Perhaps also Trevor's marksmanship with his revolver was another factor. At any rate, both were wounded but they were able to hold the occupants at bay until the storming force followed them in.

Terrible revenge was then wrought: 'Some few may have escaped, but the rest were shot down where they stood, and lay in heaps. If Englishmen had not been present, even the 45 prisoners whom we took would not have escaped with wounds, but would have been numbered with their dead comrades, for neither Sikh or Pathan has the vaguest idea of mercy to an enemy.'[7] This, and the further slaughter that followed as the Bhutanese fled, caused much controversy later. Trevor complains in the course of later correspondence that there were 'many false statements which have appeared in print among others a book called *A Story of the Bhutan War* in which the writer says that the Sikhs massacred their prisoners in cold blood after they had ceased to resist …' and that he had wanted to write to the Commander-in-Chief to ask the writer 'who is an officer in the Army but was not in any column to retract the falsehood …'[8] Tombs also strenuously denied these rumours but the accusation contributed to his feeling that his force's achievement in defeating an enemy more numerous and strongly positioned had been denigrated and this also was a factor in the argument which followed over the rewards.

At the centre of this was the fact that, in his admiration for the action that Trevor and Dundas had performed at such a crucial stage of the battle, Tombs had publicly declared that he would recommend them for the VC. The Commander-in-Chief, Sir William Mansfield, however, rejected the recommendation. Trevor himself had not been thinking in those terms at the time:

> I never even remembered there was such an institution until my friends began congratulating me after the action on the intention expressed by the General of recommending Dundas and myself for it. Since then, encouraged by what I heard of the general belief that I had earned the distinction and unconscious of any thing in my conduct which was likely to lead to its being refused I have rather cherished the hope of having it conferred on me.[9]

Sir William Mansfield apparently wanted to discourage any precedent for unorthodox intervention in infantry battles by those whose business lay elsewhere.

> in his opinion Dundas and I as Engineer officers had acted officiously and altogether out of order in entering at all into the struggle … In fact he considered we had been guilty of an irregularity which if repeated might prove seriously detrimental to the discipline of the army and which he was determined not to encourage. He added that the other branches might be excited to jealousy if Engineers who had their own field for distinction and many opportunities were allowed to intrude on the special functions of other arms.[10]

As Trevor saw it, implicit in this was the suggestion that he had acted dishonourably by seeking merit at someone else's expense and this was the main motivation for his taking the unusual step of asking for the case to be reopened. 'As my choice lies between submitting to an implied censure … and being importunate, I adopt the latter alternative.'[11] Tombs, whose success at Dewangiri owed so much to the bravery and swift action of the two sappers, also had strong motives for supporting the case. He had felt ever since that his campaign had been 'pooh-poohed' on the grounds that 'because the Bhooteas are a wild half-civilised race there could have been no fighting worthy of the name and no act of gallantry performed against them.'[12]

Trevor had some experience of bureaucracy having some years earlier put forward criticisms of the system of accounting in the Public Works Department with such skill that he had eventually been appointed to the post of Controller of Accounts only the year before the Bhutan War. Now back in England he made his

A group of Bengal Engineers photographed in 1864, just before the Bhutan War. The figure seated centrally is Colonel Henry Durand, the political officer, former Bengal Engineer, who acted with distinction during the Uprising. William Trevor consulted Durand over making his case for the grant of the VC which had been promised him in the field. Trevor is on Durand's right (seated second left) and James Dundas is sitting on the ground.

appeal through his brother, Captain S.T. Trevor, garrison engineer at Fort William, who submitted to the Commander-in-Chief a letter which had been written in England. Sir William Mansfield did 'not consider it expedient to reopen the case'[13] but, perhaps hoping to keep Trevor quiet, recommended brevet promotion. Undeterred Trevor decided, after consulting Tombs, to go over Sir William Mansfield's head and make his case to the Adjutant-General for presentation to the Governor-General's Council. Before so doing he privately took advice from Sir Henry Durand, the distinguished and influential ex-Bengal Engineer whom we have already met during the Uprising as a political officer in Indore, and who was now the military member of the Governor-General's Council, and received sufficient encouragement from Durand to proceed.

The Council considered that Tombs was the best judge of the affair and forwarded the case to the Commander-in-Chief at the Horse Guards, albeit with Sir William's continuing disapproval. The Commander-in-Chief duly put it forward to the Queen and success finally came with the publication of the awards for Trevor and Dundas in the *London Gazette* of 31 December 1867, nearly three years after the event. The crosses were presented by Major-General Fordyce at a parade of the entire Fort William Brigade on 23 March 1868. It had cost a great deal of patient effort and doubtless a fair amount of champagne for the brigade officers who, in spite of the heat at 6.30 am, had to turn out in long blue frock coats, pouches and 'cock it up hats'. Maybe it cost Trevor even more. He never received any further reward for his services. This has been contrasted with the public recognition of his brothers, Sir Arthur (KCSI) and John (CSI) although 'whether Trevor's own tenacious pursuit of the VC was held against him by those in authority in India remains an open question'.[14]

In all this James Dundas seems to have been a passive junior partner. Like Trevor, he must have felt let down that Tombs's public declaration had not borne fruit but doubtless, as a young man with his career in front of him, was able to shrug off any disappointment as one of the exigencies of army life. One can only imagine his delight when Trevor won his case, since it would, of course, have been impossible to exclude him. His own courage was again proven, however, in 1878 when, at great risk to his own life, he saved an Indian from death in a burning house in Simla bazaar. After his death, Dundas's obituarist in the *Royal Engineers Journal*, remarked of this incident, '[his] … intimate friends will not be surprised to learn that till mentioned to them a short time ago, the members of his family were entirely ignorant of this exploit, for poor Dundas' bravery was only equalled by his modesty.'[15] By that time he had served for many years in the Public Works Department to which he had returned after Bhutan. He had been back to Britain twice on leave, once following the Bhutan War and again, in 1877, having succeeded by the death of his uncle the Right Honourable David Dundas, to the estate of Ochtertyre in Stirlingshire.

He was not, however, to enjoy this new status for long. In 1879, having only just been specially selected to the Secretariat of the Government of India in the Public Works Department, he opted for a spell of more active work joining Roberts's force in the Second Afghan War. During the time Roberts was securing his position at Sherpur outside Kabul (see Chapter Five) James Dundas and a brother officer Lieutenant Charles Nugent were killed on 23 December 1879 by a premature explosion whilst helping with the destruction of a line of forts held by the enemy; an improvised fuse in place of the unserviceable one provided had brought him the same fate as Duncan Home, VC. The tragedy deeply affected the small team of sapper officers at Sherpur. Dundas had earned a reputation for hard work. A junior officer, Lieutenant John Burn-Murdoch, who incidentally produced some fine water-colours of campaign scenes including one of the Sherpur military cemetery reproduced in this book, called him 'a most anxious fellow [presumably in the old sense of the word "full of desire and endeavour"] … frightfully hardworking … he does not give us subs enough to do of the work … always gets up at most unearthly hours though not a coolie shows his face until some hours later.'[16] The letters of condolence[17] to the family throw more light on his character. From Colonel Stansfeld:

> He was naturally shy and reserved with strangers, but there was a peculiar charm about his manner and conversation that soon attracted men to him. His utter absence of 'self', his modesty, his consideration for others, and his honest upright sterling character, endeared him to all of us who had the privilege of calling him friend.

Sir Alexander Taylor,* for whom Dundas had worked for some years, wrote of him:

> In him the Corps has lost one of its 'very best'. A man of high abilities, well cultivated – a modest, high-minded English gentleman, brave, gentle and courteous, I do not know that he ever gave offence to anyone; far less do I believe that he ever had an enemy. To me he was an invaluable professional assistant, and I owe much to his varied and accurate engineering knowledge, to his trustworthy character and universal popularity.[18]

It is curious that almost the same phrase 'he never made an enemy' was used of William Trevor, in the memoir of him in the *Royal Engineers Journal*, although it was to be a long time before these words had to be written. He spent some time in

---

*This was the same Alexander Taylor who, as a captain under Richard Baird Smith, had earned so much admiration at the siege of Delhi in 1857.

England after the Bhutan War recovering his health. His injuries on top of the fever he had been suffering continued to plague him. 'I am sorry to say that in addition to diarrhoea and its concomitants I have ever since writing to you, undergone all the tortures of martyrdom from a kind of feverish neuralgia which has taken possession of me. That cut on the forehead is the focus and centre of my torments and from it radiate the most exquisite pains you can conceive, all over my head face and neck until at times when the paroxysms are at their height I attain a mental state little distinguishable from insanity.'[19]

Nevertheless William Trevor's career continued to progress. From 1867 to 1870 he was a superintending engineer and served for a time as consulting engineer to the Bengal Irrigation Department. In 1872 after two years' home leave, in which he arranged to visit the Franco-Prussian War as an observer on the German side, he became superintending engineer in charge of 'First Circle' military works. In 1874 he was appointed Special Chief Engineer for Famine Relief Works North of Ganges. He returned to Burma, the scene of his triumphs as a young officer, in February 1876, as Chief Engineer, remaining there until 1880 when he succeeded his elder brother, John, as Director General Railways in India. He took up his final appointment, as Secretary to the Government of India in the Public Works Department, in Calcutta and Simla in 1882 and retired as a major-general in 1887.

His wife having died after only five years of marriage one wonders how his daughters fared with their father involved in such an active career. While one apparently never married, the other very properly married a sapper officer, M.C. Brackenbury, who retired as a full colonel in 1899. By then Trevor himself was living in retirement in Queen's Mansions, Victoria Street, London. He died there in 1907.

Aftermath

In Bhutan the war was concluded to British satisfaction although it was March 1866, a year after Dewangiri, before the Bhutanese laid down their arms. They had been a tough enemy in the short campaign but the climate had been tougher and sickness took a severe toll. The sappers (at one time there were no fewer than five companies in the country) had been employed 'for weeks at a time in hacking a way through dense jungle for the advance of the troops, but the companies were so weak that they could not perform the task properly and consequently there were many delays and heavy losses in transport animals.'[20]

Bhutan is but a single example of the many punitive expeditions undertaken to the fringes of Britain's Indian Empire. In *The Military Engineer in India*, Lieutenant-Colonel E.W.C. Sandes lists over 20 in north-east India (excluding Burma) in the latter half of the 19th century. In this book we shall be including two out of the very many more in the north-west of the sub-continent. But first we move to a very different scene, Britain's commitments in Africa.

Ashanti and Zulu (1873 and 1879)

I go back to Africa to try to make an open path for commerce and Christianity. Do carry out the work which I have begun! I leave it with you! (David Livingstone, 1857).[1]

Livingstone's open path for commerce and Christianity is as good a summary as any for the rationale behind the soldiering that took place in Africa in the 19th century. It was all very different from India. There the British had a firmly rooted position, to some minds for all time. Despite the horrors of the Uprising, India was undeniably civilised in terms of its culture, commerce and scientific advancement. Religion, however misled in Victorian eyes, was at the centre of its life. In contrast, black Africa in the common British view

> possessed no worth-while values of its own. Its people, mostly pagan and almost all illiterate, seemed not far removed from the beasts in the Darwinian scale. Its customs sounded childish, meaningless or repulsive. Its languages were so useless or obscure that until the end of the eighteenth century no European bothered to learn any of them. Its art, expressed in the ambiguities of Obo legend, or the stylized grotesqueries of Ife art, appeared downright debased. The imperialists were at once horrified and fascinated by the cruelty of Africa, the sensuality, the shamelessness. It was, they thought, a continent congenitally inferior, a slate upon which the Empire might scrawl what it pleased, compassionate text or raw obscenity.[2]

The other great difference from India was that there was no equivalent of the Indian Army. Later in the century and into the next, native armies, police forces and militia were formed in individual countries, and indeed played a major role in two world wars. Some enter into the stories we are concerned with in this book. But there was never the same almost mystical affinity between native soldier and expatriate officer that developed into a comradeship of mutual professional respect transcending any superficial servant–master relationship. By and large, in Africa, the job of pacification or punitive action had to be done by the Queen's men sent out on tailor-made expeditions rather than by any locally stationed forces.

This chapter is concerned with two such campaigns where sapper VCs were won: in Ashanti, part of which made up the Gold Coast, now Ghana; and in Zululand, neighbour to British-ruled Natal. Both have their roots in what has come to be known as the 'scramble for Africa', the intensively competitive race to establish colonial possessions involving all the major European powers. These campaigns can not therefore be seen in isolation, and brief reference is made here, and in the later chapters on Africa, to the more significant of the major interventions in other parts of the continent, particularly those in which sappers played an important part, even though no sapper VCs resulted.

By the 1860s military technology had begun to have considerable importance and the sapper was in his element more than ever before. In this respect the 1867 expedition to Abyssinia had set something of a trend. It had been essentially a rescue mission to extract a group of Europeans, including the British consul, from the clutches of the Emperor Theodore who had imprisoned them in the belief that he had been slighted by Britain, having received no replies to a letter he had addressed to Queen Victoria proposing that he should send an envoy to Britain. The British responsibility for the rescue was met by sending a vast expedition under the sapper, Sir Robert Napier, who had greatly distinguished himself in India in the Sikh wars and the Uprising. It was indeed a sapper's war requiring enormous logistic engineering involving the building of a port, 12 miles of railway, roads and a telegraph system. Survey was essential to the operation and the expedition was the first in history to be accompanied by official military photographers. The army of 5000 British and Indian troops successfully marched 400 miles to the emperor's hideout in the mountains at Magdala, stormed the fortress (where Theodore had committed suicide) and returned with the hostages safe and sound. Britain resisted the temptation to acquire the territory and Napier's army withdrew, leaving the country to the preserve of the local warlords until the Italians arrived 28 years later to stake their claim.

The Ashanti Wars

The same sort of scale of approach was really called for in the Ashanti War of 1873. In many ways the difficulties were even greater. The objective was Kumasi, capital of the ruler of the best organised and most warlike of the tribes, in the area known as the Gold Coast. The distance to be marched was less than that to Magdala, only some 160 miles, but the route had to be hacked out through dense forest, the only labour being from the unreliable coast-based Fanti tribe whose motivation was negligible and who lived in mortal fear of the Ashanti. All this had to be achieved in what corps history (published in 1889 before the cause of malaria was fully understood) describes as a pestilential climate 'the moist and steaming atmosphere of the days and the equally moist but chilly temperature of the nights soon striking down the hardiest with fever ...'[3]

Instead of grasping the nettle in the style of the Magdala expedition, the British Government tried to deal with Ashanti on the cheap. They sent their best general, Sir Garnet Wolseley, with his staff and expected them to raise a force themselves from the tribes of the Protectorate who it was thought would be so burning with revenge for the injuries inflicted on them by the Ashanti that they would flock to the colours.

Wolseley was just the man for this task. He was already renowned for his efficiency and attention to detail ('all Sir Garnet') although regarded with suspicion as an upstart by much of the Army, often an indication of true professional merit. He had shown himself to be brave almost to the point of recklessness in battle – we have already met him as a colleague of sappers in the thick of battle: in Burma with William Trevor and in the Crimea with Gerald Graham and Charles Gordon. Wolseley had also been prominent in the relief of Lucknow after which he was convinced that the only reason he was not awarded a VC was because he beat the soldiers of the 93rd Highlanders (his general, Sir Colin Campbell's, own regiment), to a particularly gallant piece of glory. Wolseley's reputation for resourceful planning and command of an expedition had recently been made on the Red River in Canada in which his force had covered 1200 miles in the forests and rivers of Canada in pursuit of a rebel half-caste Indian, without the loss of a single man.

The origins of Wolseley's task in Africa lay in the long history of resentment the Ashanti nation had shown to the presence of Europeans on the coast trading in the two commodities which the area had in abundance: gold and slaves. The Portuguese, with their base at Elmina (El Mina – the mine), had been followed by the British, French, Dutch and Danes. These trading stations had lived in reasonable harmony with the local tribes who profited mutually from their activities but the Ashanti occupied the area further inland from the coastal plain, in the belt of rainforest that lay between it and the Volta river, and were the source of much of the wealth sought by the Europeans. In 1824 a series of quarrels had come to a head with a war in which the British Governor, Sir Charles Macarthy, had been killed (some say committed suicide) after a feebly mounted British-led expedition had been outmanoeuvred and outfought by the Ashantis whose military competence and motivation had been disastrously misappreciated. At one point Macarthy, a sort of musical comedy colonial governor, had employed a military band to play *God Save the King* extremely loudly into the bush wherein the Ashanti army was concealed, in the belief that this was all that was required for them to realise that their true loyalty lay with the British.[4]

Decades of uncomfortable coexistence then followed as the British tried to meet their obligations to their Protectorate on the coast, at the same time as satisfying a pledge to the Ashantis to extradite fugitives from their cruel and vengeful regime back to certain torture and death. For, although there was much discussion in Britain about the extent to which interference in Ashanti affairs was justified, there was no doubt in any minds that the Ashanti practice of human sacrifice on a huge scale, largely to satisfy superstitious beliefs, was unacceptable either in human or Christian religious terms.

Nevertheless, by this time they were thoroughly well-organised militarily. Their strength and unity as a nation dated back to the 18th century when the king of Kumasi claimed the title 'Asantahene' (king of the Ashanti kings), his power resting symbolically in the Golden Stool which was said to have floated down on to his lap from heaven and to contain the spirit of the people. It is important to appreciate that the tribal stool in Ashanti was much more than a throne for the chief. It was emblematic of the tribal spirit and its purpose was not to be sat upon but to be revered for the power it contained. Thus the people of Ashanti allied themselves together under the central power in Kumasi where the king, who was always expected to have proved himself in war, presided over a retinue of courtiers who had military functions and went to war with him.

> Powerful and handsome, the Ashanti warrior was characterised by good discipline and a disdainful view of personal risk. Deviationists on either score risked a swift stroke of the axe. Little was left to chance. Each army group took its own supplies of ordnance and food to war and provided its own medical orderlies, the Esumankwafo, a combatant class who gave aid to the wounded and helped remove their dead from the field. Immense trouble was taken to conceal losses, and Ashanti bodies were seldom found by their enemies, even on the rare occasions of a heavy defeat.[5]

Every male Ashanti was expected to take his place in the army. Tactics were devised, said to be based on a study of ants on the march, by which scouts were deployed ahead of the rest of the army. This consisted of an advance guard, the main army itself and wings of a fixed number of independent fighting groups.

By the middle of the 19th century the Ashanti had gained ascendancy over the tribes of the coastal plain and invaded into the open country to the north. They had also established trading rights with the European stations on the coast without having to depend on intermediaries. Their ambition was to establish their own coastal trading bases. When the Dutch withdrew from their fort at Elmina and sold it to the British, they crossed the River Prah, generally accepted as their southern boundary with the Protectorate, and advanced on Elmina and Cape Coast castle with some 25,000 warriors armed with both traditional weapons and muskets in a vast array of military might – drums beating and all the leaders adorned with ceremonial dress and gold ornaments, marching forward under huge intricately decorated umbrellas, their symbol of office. It was this action that decided the British to try and settle the Ashanti question once and for all.

Wolseley and his staff (including the CRE, Major Robert Home) arrived in September, shortly followed by four more RE officers. A further four officers and 28 Field Company followed in December. Undeterred by the wishy-washy political directives he had received, Wolseley quickly defined his objectives in categoric terms: to free the Protectorate of its Ashanti invaders and then strike a decisive blow at Ashanti power by advancing into their territory and destroying Kumasi. Quite soon it was clear that any hopes of raising sufficient local forces to penetrate Ashanti successfully were unrealistic and three British battalions arrived on 1 January 1874, the 23rd (Royal Welch) Fusiliers, the 42nd Highlanders (The Black Watch) and the 2nd Battalion the Rifle Brigade together with two battalions of the West India Regiment. There was also a naval 'brigade' of 250 sailors from the Cape Coast Squadron. These, added to some 1200 locally raised tribesmen and the sappers and gunners, now made up a respectable force to which had to be added 8500 porters and labourers. Even before the force was assembled, the Ashanti had withdrawn within their own borders, largely because of sickness, and the in-country British forces had pressed forward and carried out effective reconnaissance, not without a few brushes with the enemy. It was soon clear that special

The first steam traction engine to be taken on active service, Ashanti campaign.

tactics would have to be devised to deal with an enemy capable of concealing himself in thick bush, in a familiar environment, with no prospect of deployment into any form of open battle for which the British battalions were trained.

For the challenges that lay ahead the sapper contribution to the force of eight officers and a field company was modest. They had some interesting special responsibilities. The first was to introduce steam traction to active service for the first time. Unfortunately this was not the hoped-for success. The 'steam sappers' had already been in full service in the Royal Engineers for some five years and it seemed that they might provide the answer to some of the hideous logistic problems that would face Wolseley. In the event, Steam Sapper No. 4, which had been brought out in pieces and reassembled, had trouble with leaking boiler tubes and spent an ignominious but useful war providing power for a saw mill. More successful and crucial to the campaign was the electric telegraph, its first use in war by the British Army. Quite apart from the huge task of moving coils of copper wire and insulators up the route, the labour required in training and setting this up was considerable. The work was hazardous too as thunderstorms frequently induced strong currents in the wires. The telegraph link eventually reached some two-thirds of the total distance to Kumasi.

As will be seen all the sappers performed with distinction in this campaign, but outstanding for his achievements, which on one particular day were to earn him the VC, was Lieutenant Mark Sever Bell.

Lieutenant Mark Bell

Mark Bell was the son of Hutchinson Bell originally of Leconfield, Yorkshire. He was born in Sydney, New South Wales in May 1843 and commissioned into the Royal Engineers in June 1862. At the end of his Chatham course he set off for India and joined the Bengal Engineers where he was appointed Superintendent of

*Mark Bell
(1843-1906)*

the Park and Field Train. In the Bhutan War (see Chapter Three) he was Assistant Field Engineer in the column which marched on Dewangiri and in which Trevor and Dundas were to make their names. In 1868, in the same capacity, Bell took part in an expedition against the tribesmen of the Black Mountain region in the North-West Frontier. No fewer than 12,500 men were deployed in what Sandes called 'a spectacular parade of military strength'. To reach their deployment area the two companies of Bengal Sappers and Miners had undertaken a forced march of 600 miles from Roorkee to Abbottabad which they achieved in 29 days. Later, Bell was highly critical of the inadequate equipment of the field companies and the lack of numbers for the tasks they were called upon to perform. He seems to have been a forthright character and doubtless gained no friends for these strictures.

At the end of this campaign Bell was appointed to the Public Works Department at Amritsar, becoming Executive Engineer at Rupar in 1871. The next year he returned to England and was selected for service in Wolseley's force.

Wolseley on the March

Faced with over 100 miles of thick forest with little more than a single-file track on the route to the objective, there was nothing for it but to hack a road through

Map 6
Ashanti, showing Wolseley's route in 1873.

From *The Drums of Kumasi* by Alan Lloyd (courtesy of Irene Josephy)

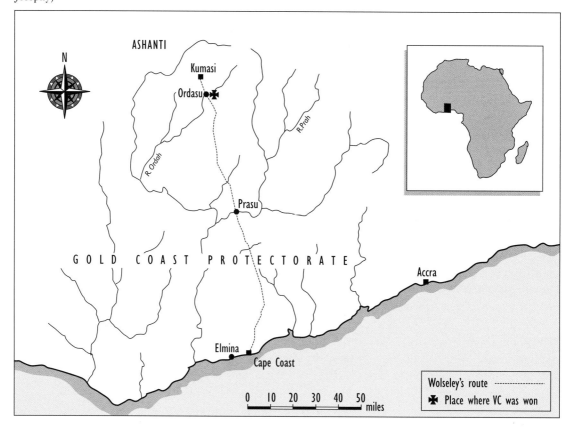

for the entire distance, capable of taking troops with their weapons and supplies, with stations one day's march apart where huts could be erected and rough fortifications constructed with the ground cleared for some distance around them. Eight such stations were built; the largest at Mansue had a central fort with four huts for stores and a guardroom, 11 huts outside the fort for accommodation for the troops, and a further four hospital huts. The principal material for this work was bamboo of which there was an inexhaustible supply.

The obstacles along the route were appalling with numerous streams and rivers to be crossed, and so requiring bridges. These were normally quite simply

The Blanshard infantry pontoon as taken to Ashanti, though in insufficient quantity. The engineer version was much larger and had rounded ends.

made of felled trees capped with a rough timber roadway but, where greater spans were required, they were of more elaborate construction. The widest river was the Prah, for which a 190-foot span was required. This had been anticipated and a certain amount of material was available including some Blanshard pontoons (tinned sheet-metal cylinders pointed at either end to which a bridge superstructure could be attached) and prefabricated trussed girders put together in Chatham before the expedition set sail. Although these were useful, it was soon realised that for the expected traffic something more substantial would be required for which local materials had to be used. Timber was plentiful but winning it from the forest had difficulties unfamiliar to the British sapper: 'Every tree that was cut down was so intertwined with creepers that when cut it would not fall, but remained in its place supported by others until sometimes four or five trees had to be brought down. The mass of branches and foliage knotted together with creepers was very great, and as the trees fell the huge ants nests were broken, and the ants running all over the place actually drove men from their work.'[6]

Almost more difficult than the bridging was the problem of crossing swamps. The only solution was to cut deep trenches either side of the roadway and lay

A prefabricated bridge for the Ashanti war under trial at Chatham.

brushwood fascines and small trees in between, covering the lot with clay.

The fatigue that must have resulted from this arduous work took its toll and with fever rife as well many men had to be evacuated as the work progressed. Nevertheless a routine was acquired and Major Home's report contains a pleasantly vivid account of this:

> A little before daybreak fires were lighted and each European had a dose of quinine, a mug of cocoa and a piece of biscuit. The natives were called at daybreak, and were usually ready about half an hour after; each sapper collected his party, and saw that they were supplied with tools. ... The labourers were extended along the road by an officer, who pointed out what was to be done, the cutlass men cut down the bush, the hand-axe men grubbed up the stubbs [sic] which were so sharp as to cut a boot, the axe men cut down any tree or cut through any that were across the road. Each sapper carried his rifle and 70 rounds of ammunition and kept his own party at work, the officer moving amongst them, and directing from time to time what was to be done. At 10 o'clock word was passed along the line to come in, the whole party returned, rations were issued, and breakfasts, tea, rice and preserved meat, ready by 11 o'clock. At 1 p.m. the men turned out again and worked until it was dark – when they returned to camp, dinner was ready in about half an hour. Large fires were made in front of the *tentes d'abri*, one to every three tents, and a huge fire in the middle of the camp, the men to make these fires and gather the wood having been specially told off. After dinner the rum was served out, and the men smoked, sang glees and turned in about half-past eight.[7]

Fatigue and the physical difficulties were by no means the whole of the problem: disease began to take a severe toll on Wolseley's men. Within a couple of weeks there was a steady flow of hammocks carrying the sick back to base and unit strengths were down ten per cent. Major Home claimed that the sappers fared better due to the precautions in making raised beds for the men to sleep on, in lighting fires, and always carrying filters for the use of the men; these precautions, and the very liberal rations, kept the men in health. Whenever an opportunity offered, the men were made to wash in a stream, and each man was seen daily by a medical officer.[8] It would have suited Wolseley to have achieved a peaceful settlement without having to fight and, in a series of communications with the Asantahene, Kofi Karikari, he offered terms: the release of captives (some men from the coastal Fante tribe and also some missionaries had been held for some time, another bone of contention); the payment of an indemnity of 50,000 ounces of gold; and the conclusion of a new treaty to be signed in Kumasi. There was never any likelihood of acceptance of this ultimatum and the advance continued. That it was not a disaster was largely thanks to Wolseley's minute attention to detail in every aspect of the campaign, from the soldiers' dress and equipment and the tactics they were to adopt, to the means of overcoming the logistic obstacles.

The first serious fighting began at the end of January, about 20 miles south of Kumasi. By then Wolseley had devised a deployment suitable for the conditions:

> in what I may describe as a large open square formation, each side having its own selected commander. The position to be occupied by each battalion was carefully

explained to each commanding officer. The front line was to be between six and seven hundred yards in width, its centre being marked by Rait's guns [two seven-pounders under Captain Rait, RA] on or near the Kumasi road. The rockets were to be at the front angles of the parallelogram. The troops on the side faces were to cut paths as they pushed forward through the underscrub each at a distance of about three hundred yards from the road. My force was too small to enable me to prevent the enemy getting all around us, and he had also the great advantage of being able to move easily through the dense forest where we could only move by cutting paths, a slow, difficult and dangerous operation.[9]

It was in these circumstances that the sappers became involved directly in the fighting, in one instance beating off a party of Ashanti who had infiltrated behind the main advancing force. The sappers, however, would normally be leading, supervising the cutting of the paths and often without infantry cover because of the density of the bush. By 2 February it was a race against time. Wolseley's force was dwindling fast from casualties and sickness and the approaching rainy season would render the return journey down boggy tracks and over swollen rivers extremely hazardous but he was strongly checked at Ordasu just six tantalising miles from the capital. After an overnight bridging operation on 3/4 February, Lieutenant Bell accompanied the advanced guard into the village. Bell had already been noted for his energy if one newspaper report is to be believed:

> If the road was impassable, [Lieutenant Bell and his unarmed native Fantees] was at hand with a party which found a way with more apparent ease than you can find your train in Bradshaw's Railway Guide. Was there a village to be taken? There was Lieutenant Bell knocking at the doors with a flock of dusty pioneers at his heels, like the sheep behind an Eastern shepherd. Was there a bonfire to be made of a collection of huts? There was the Lieutenant with his men lighting fuses with all the accuracy of a Benefit Night at the Crystal Palace … By his example he made his natives work unarmed under fire in the face of his enemy – a thing no European soldier has ever yet been asked to do.[10]

Bridge pier for the River Ordah, Ashanti campaign.

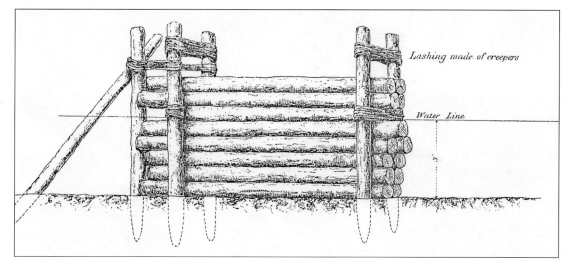

Lashing made of creepers

Water Line

And so it was in Ordasu where his task was conducted under heavy fire. He succeeded in inspiring his own men and his African labourers to such effect and with such gallantry that he was recommended for the VC, which in due course was confirmed, one of only four earned on the campaign.

Wolseley then despatched a flying column of the 42nd to force their way through in a mad dash for the capital, disregarding flank attacks and travelling light. The risk paid off and, after bursting through a series of ambushes, they made it by 5.30 pm and Wolseley joined them by nightfall. The city was deserted but bloodsoaked and stinking of death from the human sacrifices that had continued until the Ashanti had fled. After securing his position and exploring the sinister mysteries of the royal palace, Wolseley gave orders for the collection by the prize agents of as much treasure as could be found and the preparations to be made for the destruction of the city the next day. This was the sappers' last task before the withdrawal, and they worked all night to prepare the palace for demolition and the rest of the city to be burnt.

The army then returned back the way it had come but in appalling conditions as the rain had turned the route into a morass and swept away many of the bridges. During the return journey a treaty was made with Kofi Karikari which required the Asantahene not to take up arms again against Britain, 'to use his best endeavours to check the practice of human sacrifice'[11] and to pay an indemnity of 50,000 ounces of gold. The latter was not forthcoming and Wolseley's army was in no

The Prah bridge.

state to enforce it. Nevertheless, the whole affair was adjudged a brilliant success. It is doubtful if anyone other than Wolseley could have brought it off and he was lavishly rewarded as were many of his triumphant force.

It was not long before the Ashanti began to reassert their authority and to create difficulties for the British. In 1895 a further expedition was mounted in an attempt to force Kofi Karikari's successor, Prempeh I, to accept British protection. After a series of (for him) humiliating episodes he finally did, being in no position to engage the British in a war. In a clumsy follow-up Prempeh was taken captive and exiled to the Seychelles along with several members of the royal family and some other chiefs. In the course of this heavy-handed action the British did their best to exorcise the spirit of Ashanti by desecrating some of the sacred places which had become associated in their minds with the worst excesses of fetishism. One prize eluded them – the Golden Stool. They became obsessed with the idea that possession of this would finally resolve the struggle for supremacy over the Ashanti.

In yet another expedition to Kumasi in 1900 in pursuit of this aim, the colonial government was humiliated when Sir Frederic Hodgson, his wife and small military retinue were besieged in Kumasi fort after a particularly arrogant attempt to demand the Golden Stool. Ashanti pride had prevented any response other than force for this final insult and the governor's party had to endure the most appalling privations both during the siege and the escape which they made – and survived – four months later. Retribution inevitably followed and after a series of fierce encounters the British achieved their final victory over the Ashanti at the battle of Aboasu in September. In 1920 the Golden Stool was found and returned by the colonial government to Kumasi, albeit having lost most of its gold adornment before reaching official hands. In 1924 Prempeh returned from exile and was reinstated as a chief two years later. He died in 1931.

There is a rather happier epilogue to this story. In 1919, a sapper, Frederick Guggisberg, was appointed Governor of the Gold Coast. Guggisberg knew the country well from his time as a surveyor there in 1905 and, indeed the whole region, as he had also been Director of Surveys in Nigeria. After a distinguished war in which he had risen to the rank of brigadier-general he now went to the Gold Coast at what was to be the height of its prosperity as its main cash crop, cocoa, flourished in an expanding world market. On the strength of this and his own administrative abilities and vision Guggisberg was able both to develop the infrastructure of the country and to introduce a far-sighted education system, both of which created the foundation which led eventually to the Gold Coast becoming the first of Britain's former colonies to achieve independence, in 1957.

Mark Bell's Subsequent Career

In 1880, Bell joined the Indian Army Intelligence Branch at Simla in the rank of captain, leaving it eight years later as a brevet lieutenant-colonel. In between he carried out a number of expeditions, 'extended reconnaissances' which in the opinion of the Quartermaster-General's office 'have added largely to geographical knowledge, and the information secured for Government during the adventurous journeys which he has undertaken is especially valuable; while numerous reports and compilations, which are on record in the office, bear testimony to the industry and care with which the observations of an experienced traveller and reconnoitrer may be compiled.'[12] These ventures included northern China in 1882, south-western Persia in 1884, Mesopotamia and Armenia in 1885/6 and, most famously, in western China and Kashgaria in 1887. It was on the 1887 expedition that Francis Younghusband, a junior member of Bell's staff, had asked to join him and had been invited to take an alternative route back to India. Complying with Bell's instruction to explore the route over the 19,000-foot Mustagh Pass on the edge of the mountain K2 called for superhuman effort from Younghusband but established his reputation as an explorer.

Mark Bell's endeavours earned him the first MacGregor Memorial Medal which was founded in 1888 in memory of Major-General Sir Charles MacGregor, first head of the Intelligence Branch, 'for the best military reconnaissances or journeys of exploration of the year'. In 1889 he was appointed Commanding Royal Engineer at Shorncliffe and the following year he was transferred to Dublin in the same appointment where he remained until 1894. After some months on half-pay Bell took up his last appointment, again as Commanding Royal Engineer, this time in Western District at Plymouth.

Mark Bell went on to half-pay in 1898 on the grounds of ill-health; he died eight years later. He married twice: in 1875, Angelina Helen Dickinson who died in 1879; and, in 1890, Nora Margaret Roger. There were two sons by his second marriage, Anthony and Robert, both of whom served in France in the First World War, Robert being killed in action on the Somme.

To return, however, to 1874. If there was any disquiet felt in Britain at the failure of Wolseley's peace treaty with the Ashanti to stick in the longer term, the matter paled into insignificance in comparison with the events that were to unfold within five years in southern Africa – when another black African nation with a military tradition even more highly developed than the Ashanti was to subject Britain to one of its most shattering defeats.

The Zulu War

> My children, the English have declared war against me, for why I cannot tell, and they have already crossed the Umzinyati (Buffalo) and fired on Sihayo's people, killing a lot of them. You are now to go and meet them and see what they are going to do. If they are still determined upon advancing into my country, attack them and show the English dogs how Zulu warriors can fight.[13]

This is how the Zulu king, Cetshwayo, is reported by one of his warriors to have given his orders before the battle of Isandlwana. The warrior in question was Mehlokazulu, the son of Chief Sihayo. With two of his brothers and an uncle he had been at the centre of an incident which sparked off the Zulu War when they

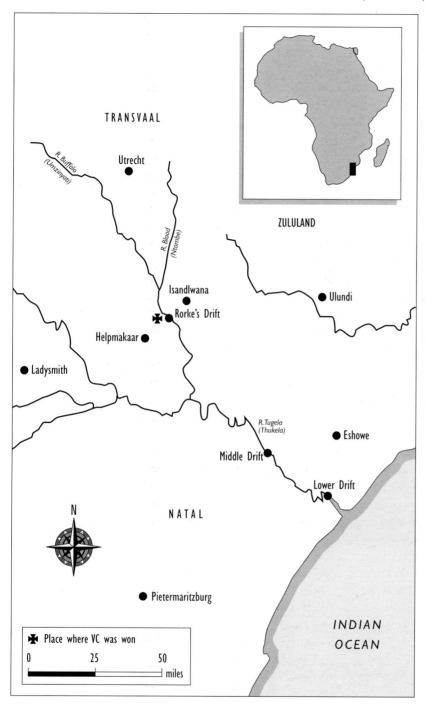

Map 7
The Natal–Zululand–Transvaal border, 1879. Based upon the map of
Zululand in The Road to Isandhlwana *by R.W.F. Droogleever (Greenhill*
Books, 1992).

had led a foray across the border into Natal to bring back two of his father's wives accused of adultery and witchcraft. Both women, now pregnant, were summarily put to death. Six months later Mehlokazulu, as one of the commanders of the iNgobamakosi regiment, participated in the destruction of the 1700-strong British force encamped at Isandlwana in the most humiliating and disastrous start to any of Britain's colonial wars.

The episode of Sihayo's wives had played straight into the hands of Britain's High Commissioner for Southern Africa, Sir Bartle Frere, who was determined to provoke war with the Zulus whom he believed were responsible for the considerable unrest amongst the Blacks throughout southern Africa. The evidence for this was entirely circumstantial but the fact was that the Zulu nation was by far the most organised of the southern Africa ethnic groupings and had developed a powerful and highly disciplined army which had grown ever stronger since the days of its foundation by Cetshwayo's grandfather, the great Shaka. There were some parallels here with the situation in Ashanti and particularly in the, to British eyes, wanton cruelty and savagery of the manner in which law and order was enforced in Zulu society, although in this case human sacrifice on religious grounds was not part of the culture.

The political background was also far more complex than had been the case in the Gold Coast and can only be briefly summarised here. Throughout southern Africa there had been a triangular confrontation between the Boers (the original white settlers of Dutch stock, mostly farmers), the British (who had inherited the Cape from the Napoleonic Wars) and the Blacks who had effectively become the continental race in place of the aboriginal Bushmen and Hottentots. By the 1870s the Boers had extricated themselves from British rule by trekking to the Transvaal, the vast stretch of country lying between the Vaal and Limpopo Rivers. This had become effectively vacant as a result of a major ethnic shake-out among the Blacks, many of whom migrated north as a direct by-product of the uncompromising nation-building by Shaka and his successor, Dingaan. The British had enforced a form of racial settlement among the black tribal groupings in their area of influence in a series of Cape Frontier Wars, the ninth of which had come to an end in 1877.* However, these moves had led to some even greater tensions.

Within Zululand itself, Cetshwayo had become king in 1873 after a bloody power struggle. The British in Natal then attempted to treat Cetshwayo's kingdom as if it were a vassal state owing some allegiance to their own authority. They were concerned to ensure that developments in the relationship between the Zulus and the Boers in the Transvaal did not result in Boer influence in Zululand and access to the sea. The Boer–Zulu relationship centred on a strip of territory between the Transvaal and Zululand where the boundary was in dispute. An

---

*These wars were known in history books until recent times as the 'Kaffir Wars'. However, the term 'kaffir' has become discredited. It derives from an Arabic word meaning 'infidel' and was commonly used by Muslims of any stranger. In modern times it became a term of abuse applied by white South Africans to Blacks.

earlier deal between Cetshwayo's father and predecessor, Mpande, had allowed the Boers grazing rights. Boer and Zulu had established a reasonable coexistence, but who had jurisdiction was unclear. Cetshwayo now needed this territory both to accommodate his growing nation and to give himself control over disaffected factions who had settled there.

The Transvaal Boers for their part had fomented trouble in their efforts to develop a railway link with the coast at Delagoa Bay and, in the wake of a military failure and the financial crisis that these efforts had generated, the British annexed the Transvaal in 1877 in an act of political sleight of hand. It was all part of a master plan by the Colonial Office in London, under the direction of Lord Carnarvon, to build a confederation of states in southern Africa under British control. Two essential ingredients in this were the settlement of the boundary dispute between the Transvaal and Zululand and the bringing of the Zulus under British control, if not actual annexation of their country.

It was for the execution of this policy that Sir Bartle Frere had been sent to Cape Town in 1877 and that in 1878 the local military commander, Major-General Frederic Thesiger, had undertaken the task of assessing the prospects for an invasion of Zululand. Frere was convinced of the necessity of this move although the idea was strongly opposed by the Lieutenant-Governor of Natal, Sir Henry Bulwer. It was also contrary to the policy of the Colonial Office who merely conceded that such action might be required in the future. Also, unfortunately for Frere, a boundary commission early in 1878 had found in favour of the Zulu claim to the disputed territory. Nevertheless, he pressed on with his preparations and persuaded the home government to send some reinforcements for Thesiger (who became Lord Chelmsford in October on the death of his father), though fewer than he needed. Two battalions of infantry and two field companies of Royal Engineers arrived at the end of 1878 to add to the five battalions and two artillery batteries he could immediately call upon. The force was boosted to some 17,000 by the addition of locally raised units based on some that had already been in existence and others that were now to be specially raised as the Natal Native Contingent (NNC) comprising three regiments with seven battalions between them. Frere was convinced that the imperial troops, reorganised as they now were under the Cardwell reforms and armed with modern weapons,* would have little difficulty in bringing the Zulu army to battle and defeating it in a quick campaign, notwithstanding that Cetshwayo now had some 40,000 highly disciplined and well-organised soldiers thirsting for action having had little opportunity to exploit their prowess. But the odds were not all on the British side – to manoeuvre the Zulu army into position to make best use of the modern weaponry required invasion into unfamiliar territory, excellent intelligence as to the enemy's move-

*The Gatling machine-gun made its first appearance in British army warfare in this campaign although curiously manned by the Royal Navy in the naval 'brigade' which made up part of the force. The other significant weapon was the Martini-Henry rifle, firing a .45in calibre round effective to 900 yards at a rate of 55 rounds per three minutes.

ments and the solution of some intractable logistic problems. For example, by the start of the war 'Chelmsford had amassed 977 wagons, 56 carts, 10,023 oxen, 803 horses and 398 mules'. The crippling effect that this had on the economy of Natal can be imagined.[14]

The episode of Sihayo's wives with which this section opened was only one of a series of events towards the end of 1878 which, although in different circumstances might have been shrugged off, now silenced some of Frere's critics and began to give him the excuse to go to war. We need not concern ourselves with the other events.* It is enough to record that, by December, Frere judged the time ripe to deliver an ultimatum to Cetshwayo and on the 11th of that month the conditions were read out to Cetshwayo's representatives at a gathering at Lower Drift, the main crossing point of the Lower Tugela River. The terms required the Zulus to make restitution for the obvious infringements of the Natal border that had been made but, far more seriously, effectively demanded the dissolution of the military-based social structure of the Zulu nation. If these terms were not met in 30 days the British would consider themselves in a state of war with the Zulus. In all this Frere was acting on his own initiative, deliberately timing events to prevent contrary instructions reaching him from London.

Cetshwayo was now in an impossible position. Acceptance of the conditions was out of the question. Equally he must have realised that war spelled the doom of the Zulu nation in the form in which he had inherited it. Cetshwayo was actually prepared to satisfy a number of the points in the ultimatum but he could give no answer on the key question of dismantling the military structure – so war it was. This is how on 22 January 1879 Mehlokazulu, to whom the quotation at the head of this section is attributed, came to be lying with his regiment and 20,000 other warriors of the main 'impi' of Cetshwayo's army, in a deep fold in the ground 5000 yards to the east of the prominent rocky outcrop known as Isandlwana, ten miles inside the border from the crossing point at Rorke's Drift. Isandlwana was Chelmsford's first main encampment, a temporary base set up while he moved forward with half his force further to the south-east along the Ulundi road. Chelmsford had decided to accompany the central of three main columns into which he had split his army and which were now advancing across the border as part of an overall strategy to locate the Zulus and then concentrate for battle in the Ulundi area. The Left Flank Column under Colonel Evelyn Wood, VC started from the Utrecht area crossing the River Ntombe at Bemba's Kop. The Right Flank Column under Colonel Charles Pearson crossed the Lower Tugela at Lower Drift, where the ultimatum had been delivered.

As Chelmsford moved forward he was totally unaware of the massed force concealed a few miles to his left and, planning to bring up his main force shortly,

---

*The most thorough and stimulating of the many accounts of the historical background to the Zulu War remains Donald Morris's seminal work *The Washing of the Spears*, first published in 1966. In recent years Ian Knight's marvellously researched and well-illustrated books, particularly *Brave Men's Blood* (covering the whole war) and *Nothing Remains but to Fight – The Defence of Rorke's Drift 1879* supplement and update Morris's work. This short account owes much to these works.

he had left them at Isandlwana with no particular instructions other than 'to defend the camp'.

Mehlokazulu was well aware of the situation and in the process of reporting to his commander must have seen, off to his right, the umCijo regiment leaping into action as they were discovered at about midday by Lieutenant Raw of the Natal Native Contingent. Before long the entire impi had sprung forward on their way to the stunning and historic victory that was to destroy the reputations of both Frere and Chelmsford.

The story of Isandlwana – of Chelmsford's gradual realisation of the disaster that had befallen him; of the heroic performance of so many of the doomed force and the adventures of the very few who escaped; of the return of Chelmsford's force to pass an uneasy night on that grisly scene of death and mutilation and their eventual withdrawal, much chastened, back across the Buffalo River – belongs elsewhere. However, before we follow the Zulus on to Rorke's Drift, one aspect of the battle has particular interest for sappers.

The first serious engagement that occurred in the battle was between the left 'horn'* of the impi and a force of three companies of the Natal Native Horse, a rocket battery and three companies of the 1st Battalion NNC all under the command of Lieutenant-Colonel Anthony Durnford, Royal Engineers. Durnford was a forthright but complex character, something of an adventurer and a gambler who had left an estranged wife behind in England and become a well-known personality in Natal. Although on the side of those who opposed the war, he was desperate to prove himself in battle having participated in an ill-starred military expedition in 1873 in which he had been wounded. Chelmsford had originally allocated Durnford to cross the Tugela with his own force at Middle Drift, over 100 miles to the south-east but, after some near-insubordinate objections from Durnford, had ordered him up to join his own column.

Durnford reached Isandlwana with his force at about 10.30 am and conferred with Lieutenant-Colonel Pulleine, in command of the camp. Durnford was, in fact, senior to Pulleine and it has often been asserted since that he might have taken over command at that point and, indeed, was thereafter technically responsible for all that occurred. He had no instructions from Chelmsford to this effect, however. His first act was to despatch the reconnaissance parties to try and observe the enemy movements, then apparently of a fairly minor nature and it was his men, under Lieutenants Raw and Roberts, who first stumbled on the impi. Durnford now realised that a movement from the Zulus was developing which might threaten Chelmsford's force out along the Ulundi track, and he therefore deployed forward with his force to cut them off. When the full strength of the enemy materialised he and his men fought an epic withdrawal battle back to the camp but were finally engulfed, fighting with great gallantry along with the rest.

*The standard Zulu formation in battle was pictured as a charging buffalo, two horns which encircled the enemy, the chest which provided the central thrust and the loins, a reserve close behind for deployment as necessary.

The extent, if any, of Durnford's culpability for Isandlwana is a matter for personal judgement. Some believe he was simply a scapegoat for Chelmsford's guilt; others that he behaved honourably by leaving Pulleine in his own command and taking his force away in an independent capacity. Opinions can be coloured by Durnford's romantic association with the daughter of Bishop Colenso and his own equivocal past.[15]

While Mehlokazulu was thus heavily engaged with his regiment on the left, the uNdi Corps in the right horn of the impi had taken little part in the actual fighting. Led by Cetshwayo's brother, Dabulamanzi, they charged round to the north of the great outcrop and then sweeping down to the west of the position, cut off the British line of retreat. For reasons which are not clear they decided to cross the Mzinyathi into Natal, an action which had been expressly forbidden by Cetshwayo, and to head for the Central Column's depot at Rorke's Drift.

> Life at Rorke's Drift had been quiet since Chelmsford had crossed the border eleven days before. The post itself consisted of two low, thatched bungalows facing the river, beneath the shadow of a hill known to the Zulus as Shiyane, 'the eyebrow', and to the missionaries as Oskarberg. ... The current occupant, the Swedish missionary Otto Witt, used one building as his house and the other as a church. ... The army had turned Witt's chapel into a store, where Commissariat staff – Assistant Commissary Walter Dunn, Acting Assistant Commissary James Dalton, and storekeeper Louis Byrne – supervised the mountain of mealie sacks and biscuit boxes which were due to be shipped forward to the column. Witt's house had been turned into a makeshift hospital where Surgeon Reynolds and three men of the Army Hospital Corps tended thirty-five sick including a couple of wounded ... [from an earlier action]. The post was guarded by Lieutenant Gonville Bromhead and the 80 men of 'B' Company, 2/24th.* Down by the river a subaltern of the Royal Engineers, Lieutenant John Chard, was working to keep the ponts in repair ...[16]

*John Chard
(1847–1897)*

Lieutenant John Chard

John Rouse Merriott Chard had only just arrived in Natal with 5 Field Company, Royal Engineers, when he was sent forward to deal with the river crossing at Rorke's Drift. He was then a 32-year-old subaltern with over 12 years' service including time overseas in Bermuda and Malta. He was born the second son of Mr William Wheaton Chard of Pathe House, Othery, Somerset and Jane Brimacombe of Stoke Climsland, Cornwall and educated at Plymouth Grammar School and the Royal Military Academy. He had two brothers and four sisters. His elder brother, Colonel William Wheaton Chard, served with the 7th (Royal Fusiliers) Regiment. His younger brother, the Reverend Charles Edward Chard, was rector of the parish of St John the Baptist, Hatch Beauchamp, Somerset.[17]

---

*The lineal descendants of the 24th Foot are The Royal Regiment of Wales (24th/41st Foot). In 1879 they were, by county affiliation, the 2nd Warwickshires, becoming the South Wales Borderers in 1881. It was unusual for both battalions of the same regiment to be found in the same theatre of operations. It was the 1st Battalion that suffered so disastrously at Isandlwana, the bulk of the 2nd Battalion having advanced with Chelmsford.

Before he went with his company to Natal, Chard's experience had been entirely on construction projects including fortifications in Bermuda and Malta. After the battle at Rorke's Drift Chard wrote an immediate report to his company commander, Major Walter Parke Jones. Later, when he had returned to England, he wrote a more elaborate account at the personal request of Queen Victoria and what follows is based on that version.[18]

Chard arrived at Rorke's Drift on the morning of 19 January. Chelmsford's force was encamped across the river and he saw it move off the next day.

> There were two large ponts at the river, one of which only was in working order, and my sappers were at this time working at the other, which was then nearly finished, to get it also in working order. Late in the evening of the 21st January I received an order from the 3rd Column to say that the *men* of the R.E., who had lately arrived, were to proceed to the camp at Isandhlwana at once – I had received no orders concerning myself.

This was a fatal order for Corporal Gamble and Sappers Cuthbert, MacLaren and Wheatley, all of whom were killed along with Lieutenant MacDowel who had joined No. 3 Column earlier and supervised some essential roadwork early in the advance. Not sure of his own orders (and possibly hoping for the chance of some action, although he does not admit to this), Chard rode out to Isandlwana himself but discovered that he was indeed to remain at Rorke's Drift.

> A N.C.O. of the 24th Regiment lent me a field glass, which was a very good one, and I also looked with my own, and could see the enemy moving on the distant hills, and apparently in great force. Large numbers of them moving to my left, until the lion hill of Isandhlwana, on my left as I looked at them, hid them from my view. The idea struck me that they might be moving in the direction between the camp and Rorke's Drift and prevent my getting back, and also that they might be going to make a dash at the ponts.

This early observation of some of the Zulu force had also been made from the camp. However, no one suspected at that stage that the sighting was anything more than might be expected nor had they any foreboding of the onslaught to come. On his way back, Chard met Durnford still heading for Isandlwana and told him of the enemy movements he had seen. Durnford's men did not spot the main Zulu impi until much later and were still unaware of any serious danger. Even if Chard did foresee some danger at this point, he still did not know the weight of responsibility that was shortly to be placed on him, because the senior officer at Rorke's Drift was the supply officer, Major Spalding, in command of this sector of the lines of communication. But when he arrived …

> Major Spalding told me that he was going over to Helpmakaar [to expedite the despatch of a company of the 1/24th expected as reinforcements]. Just as I was about to ride away he said to me 'Which one of you is senior, you or Bromhead?' I said 'I don't know' – he went back into his tent, looked at an Army List, and coming back, said – 'I see you are senior, so you will be in charge, although, of course, nothing will happen, and I shall be back this evening early.'

*Prince Dabulmanzi
KaMpande, commander
of the uNdi Corps and
Chard's opponent at
Rorke's Drift.*

Prince Dabulmanzi KaMpande, commander of the uNdi Corps and Chard's opponent at Rorke's Drift.

Spalding left and, very shortly afterwards, fugitives arrived from Isandlwana with the story of the disaster, which at first Chard found some difficulty in believing. Their precarious position was then confirmed by a pencil message from the 3rd Column warning them of the enemy's advance in their direction.

> I held a consultation with Lieut. Bromhead, and with Mr. Dalton, whose energy, intelligence and gallantry were of the greatest service to us, and whom, as I said in my report at the time, and I am sure Bromhead would unite in saying again now, I cannot sufficiently thank for his services.

Amongst other things, Dalton had pointed out that any attempt at withdrawal towards Helpmakaar would be suicide and they all realised that there was nothing for it but to fight it out. Bromhead and Dalton had already started fortifying the little garrison by loopholing the buildings and joining them with two walls of mealie bags strengthened by two wagons 'on the ground'. This work went on apace while Witt, the missionary, and the Reverend George Smith, Vicar of Estcourt, Natal who was acting as an army chaplain, walked up the Oskarberg to spot the enemy. Having identified the impi crossing the river and preparing to attack they hastened back. There was still time to get away but Smith elected to stay while Witt escaped with his family. When, at about 4.20 pm, firing was heard from behind the Oskarberg, two other defections occurred: 100 of Durnford's men who had escaped from the holocaust of Isandlwana and had been guarding the crossing point; and 300 individual natives of the NNC under an officer, Major Stephenson, who had been attached for general duties but who were not organised as a unit. The garrison was now reduced to 140 of whom 30 were hospital patients and only the 81 of B Company were a formed body of trained soldiers.

1 Oscarberg.   4 Camp of B C° 24ᵗʰ
2 Rocks and Caves occupied by Zulus.   9 Cook House. 10 20 Ovens.
3 Cattle Kraal.   5 Well built Kraal.   8 Comm' Store. 11 2 Wagons. 13 Hospital. 14 Wall 5ft.
                     7 2 Heaps of Mealies in Sacks
                6 Mealie sack Wall.   12 Wall of Biscuit Boxes.   15 Garden.

Chard's sketch of
Rorke's Drift which
accompanied his report
to Queen Victoria.

We seemed very few, now all these people had gone and I saw that our line of defence was too extended, and at once commenced a retrenchment of biscuit boxes, so as to get a place we could fall back upon if we could not hold the whole. ... We had not completed a wall two boxes high when, at about 4.30pm, Hitch cried out that the enemy was in sight, and he saw them, apparently 500 or 600 in number, come around the hill to our south (the Oscarberg) and advance at a run against our south wall.

Private Hitch was to become one of the heroes of the defence. One of the first to be wounded – and badly, by a bullet which smashed his shoulder – he still managed to help throughout the battle. This first rush against the southern wall was only just held off, largely by some excellent shooting. It quickly flowed on round to the left and the attacks on the hospital began. Soon:

The main body of the enemy were close behind the first force which appeared, and had lined the ledge of rocks and caves in the Oscarberg overlooking us, and about three or four hundred yards to our south, from where they kept up a constant fire. Advancing somewhat more to the left than the first attack, they occupied the garden, hollow road, and bush in great force.

There was plenty of cover for the enemy, there having been no time in which to clear fields of fire. This made it possible for the Zulus to keep closing up to the wall where a desperate struggle took place throughout the battle. The Zulus were unable to leap on to the wall and as they struggled to get a hold they were shot at point blank range and bayonetted, their bodies piling up as they fell. An even hotter fight was developing in the hospital.

> The garrison of the Hospital defended it with the greatest gallantry, room by room, bringing out all the sick that could be moved, and breaking through some of the partitions while the Zulus were in the building with them. Privates Williams, Hook, R. Jones and W. Jones being the last to leave and holding the doorway with the bayonet, their ammunition being expended.

This building, formerly Otto Witt's home, had few internal doors and so as the Zulus struggled to break in from the outside and set fire to the thatch, the occupants were trapped until they could break through the internal walls and make their escape to the main force on the mealie-bag wall or, as it turned out the biscuit-box barricade. The heroism of the men who succeeded in holding off their enemy in ferocious hand-to-hand fighting and, despite wounds and the sickness of the patients, in rescuing all but a few has become an epic.

The Zulu attacks on Rorke's Drift.

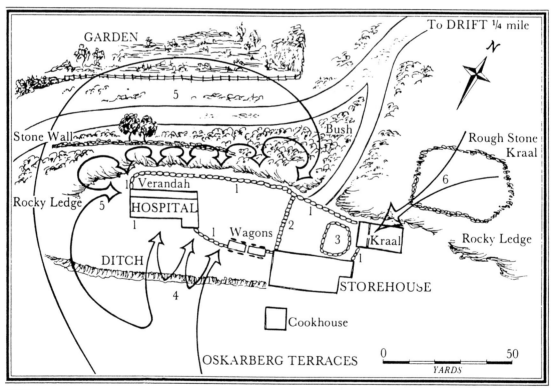

KEY

1. Initial perimeter formed by mealie bag ramparts, two wagons and walls of hospital, storehouse and kraal.
2. Transverse wall of biscuit boxes.
3. Mealie bag redoubt.

4. First Zulu attack.
5. Main Zulu attack.
6. Last Zulu attack.

As darkness came on we were completely surrounded. The Zulus wrecking the camp of the Company 24th and my wagon which had been left outside, in spite of the efforts of my batman, Driver Robson (the only man of the Royal Engineers with us), who had directed his particular attention to keeping the Zulus off this wagon in which were, as he described it, 'Our things'.

And so the fight raged on. The perimeter was now reduced to the storehouse end of the compound and the defence enhanced by the building of a mealie-bag redoubt should the storehouse have to be abandoned. An independent view of Chard's own performance appears later in the diary of Surgeon Reynolds where he records that at 7.00 pm he was beginning to consider the situation desperate: 'Lieutenant Chard here again shone in resource. Anticipating the problem of the Zulus making one more united dash for the fort, and possibly an entrance, he constructed an immense stack of mealies standing in the middle of our enclosure, and originally cone-fashioned, into a comparatively safe place for a last retreat.'[19]

After the first onslaught, the most formidable of the enemy's attacks was just before we retired behind our line of biscuit boxes, and for a short time after it, when they had gained great confidence by their success on the Hospital. Although they… kept up a heavy fire from all sides until about 12 o'clock, they did not actually charge up in a body to get over our wall after about 9 or 10 o'clock.

A few shots went on through the night as the garrison anxiously awaited dawn and the possibility of renewed attacks. But by daybreak the Zulus had gone and the men made cautious excursions into the carnage around them to collect the arms and ammunition of the enemy dead, and continued to strengthen the defences.

a large body of the enemy … appeared on the hills to the south-west. I thought at the time that they were going to attack us, but from what I now know from Zulus, and also of the number we put hors de combat, I do not think so. I think they came up on the high ground to observe Lord Chelmsford's advance; from there they could see the Column long before it came in sight of us.

Thus arrived rescue and glory. The gallant band had held off 4000 Zulus – numerically one-quarter the size of the force that had wreaked such havoc at Isandlwana. They lost 15 killed in the fight, two more died later from their wounds; eight had been severely wounded, including Dalton. Over 370 Zulu dead were counted after the battle but many more were found later in the surrounding countryside. Eleven VCs were awarded for this affair including those to Chard and Bromhead, whose names had been added to the list by Chelmsford himself without consultation with either's superior officer.

Isandlwana and Rorke's Drift symbolise tragedy and triumph so vividly in the popular imagination that the rest of the Zulu War is often regarded as an anticlimax. In fact it contained as much drama, heroism and knife-edge decision in the six months that were to follow before Chelmsford finally achieved his aim of concentrating and decisively defeating the Zulu army at Ulundi on 4 July, a victory he contrived before the newly appointed overall commander, Lord Wolseley (the

The remains of the commissariat storehouse at Rorke's Drift. The loopholed stone wall was erected after the battle in case of further attacks.

former Sir Garnet), could snatch the glory from him. Chelmsford regarded Wolseley's appointment as tantamount to censure and resigned after Ulundi. Although he was promoted and received many honours, he never again held command. For the sappers, the remainder of the war offered the normal challenges presented by operations in a hostile and undeveloped country. For example, the fortifications built at Eshowe for Pearson's Right Flank Column under the supervision of Captain Warren Wynne, RE[*] guaranteed the security of that force after it had become besieged. Similarly, Major Charles Moysey[†] carried out the construction of Fort Khambula, which was critical to its defence in the decisive battle there on 29 March between Colonel Wood's Left Flank Column and an impi of some 20,000 Zulus, many of them veterans of Isandlwana.

As to Chard himself, he fell ill shortly after Rorke's Drift recovering in time to rejoin 5 Field Company and take part in the battle of Ulundi. Something of the envy which his exploit generated can be detected in a letter written by his company commander, Captain Walter Parke Jones, to a friend in England.

> Owing to the deaths at Isandhlwana Bromhead the second in command at Rorke's Drift got his company by promotion & he gets a brevet, this makes my Chard, who was in command, quite sure of a brevet, when he gets his company a year hence. Chard is in great luck, he left us at Durban, came up here quickly & comfortably without all the bother of men sick, wagons sticking &c. He leaves Isandhlwana

[*]Wynne died of disease shortly afterwards.
[†]Later Major-General C.J. Moysey, CMG.

camp an hour before the disaster, being ordered to look after the ponts over the Tugela [sic] at Rorke's Drift. He there becomes a hero, gets a fever & goes away on sick leave to a comfortable and hospitable house near Ladysmith 60 miles off & vegetates there ever since. Not one iota of the work or drudgery does he get.[20]

Chard was ordered home later in the year and, on 2 August, Jones commented in the same vein:

Chard got his orders to leave the 5 Compy for good & departed yesterday. He is a most amiable fellow & a loss to the mess, but as a company officer he is so hopelessly slow and slack. ... [He] makes me angry, with such a start as he got, he stuck to the company doing nothing. In his place I should have gone up and asked Lord C. for an appointment, he must have got it & if not, he could have gone home soon after Rorke's Drift, at the height of his popularity & done splendidly at home. – I advised him, but he placidly smokes his pipe & does nothing. Few men get such opportunities.[21]

Colonel Evelyn Wood had similar disparaging remarks to make about Chard ('ugly ... a dull, heavy man who seemed scarcely ever able to do his regular work')[22] whose demeanour did not impress Lord Wolseley when he presented him with his VC on 15 July 1879 at St Paul's Mission Station.

Nevertheless Chard was the centre of attraction when he reached home and spent several months being fêted, dined and congratulated, and being received by Queen Victoria at Balmoral. Where he could he took his batman, Driver Robson, with him. Normality resumed in January 1880 when he took up a posting in Devonport. However, his subsequent career fitted Walter Parke Jones's predictions, being steady but unremarkable. He served in Cyprus and Singapore as well as England before his last posting as Commanding Royal Engineer, Scotland, and retired in 1897. He had not long to live. He had already contracted cancer of the mouth and after two operations he went to live with his younger brother at Hatch Beauchamp where he died after two weeks of terrible suffering on 1 November 1897. Chard never married although his name has been romantically associated with various ladies including one of Queen Victoria's ladies-in-waiting whom he met at Balmoral.

Epilogue

The Zulu War continues to fascinate people today, thanks in no small measure to Donald Morris's gripping *The Washing of the Spears* and the film *Zulu*, starring Stanley Baker as Chard and Michael Caine as Bromhead. A museum now exists on the site of the mission station at Rorke's Drift and a school has been built nearby. In the summer of 1996 a party of Royal Engineers and cadets from Southampton and Portsmouth Officer Training Corps returned to the site to help build a new community centre, the first British unit to return there since 1879.

This late 20th century interest in the Zulu War contrasts with attitudes in the late 19th century which had seen many tough military campaigns. After

Chard's death it took some time to raise the necessary funds for a suitable memorial in Rochester Cathedral where there were already windows commemorating Durnford and Thomas Rice Henn who had been killed in Afghanistan in 1880 (see Chapter Five). However, Colonel Vetch, writing in the *Royal Engineers Journal* in support of the appeal for the memorial, produced as fitting a summary as any of John Chard's contribution to history with the prescient comment that 'Few military incidents in history had a greater effect at the time, or will, for all time, remain a more memorable instance of gallantry and tenacity … and the fact that a young subaltern of engineers, of no very conspicuous ability, rose to the occasion, and was the hero of the gallant defence of the post … is one that has made the Corps proud of Chard, who had done it honour …'[23]

There is no such thing as a great power. What is spreading out before us is a great weakness. The system in extending its communications always decreases its efficiency; and there never was an empire on this earth that did not go further and fare worse.[1]

G.K. Chesterton, author of this observation, was born just four years before the Second Afghan War which was effectively a showdown between the overstretched Russian and British empires seeking to secure their position in what was then, as now, the homeland of a fiercely independent-minded people with little taste for nationhood beyond their own tribal groupings, let alone submission to any outside power. With all the ingredients of triumph and disaster, military ineptitude and exemplary courage, political miscalculation and strategic vision it is surprising that this war seems to attract less interest nowadays than the events in Zululand told in the last chapter. For the sappers the war entailed overcoming the problems presented by some of the most daunting terrain and climate in which the British and Indian armies had to fight. It also required them to support the army in the field under the constant pressure of a hostile and resentful population intent on making life as difficult as possible, and along vast and vulnerable lines of communication from its sources of supply. The story includes two acts of heroism which earned VCs, the tragic death of one of the earlier VC winners, a last courageous stand by a half company of the Bombay Sappers and Miners at the battle of Maiwand, as disastrous an event as Isandlwana only 18 months earlier, and an outstanding performance by one of the sapper VCs during the subsequent terrible retreat.

The First Afghan War

There are so many parallels and links between the First and Second Afghan Wars, and their roots are so similar, that a short recapitulation of the events of the earlier affair is appropriate. We have already seen in Chapter Three how the young William Trevor, with his mother and brother, survived captivity in the hands of Mohammed Akbar Khan, son of Dost Mohammed who had been deposed in 1839, through British machinations, by Shah Shuja the former king. The latter, as a grandson of Ahmad Shah, the ruler of effectively the first independent state of Afghanistan, had arguably more right than Dost Mohammed to the throne in Kabul. But his kingdom was much reduced from Ahmad Shah's original realm which, as well as Kabul, Kandahar and Herat (the three main areas of the country that lay between the Hindu Kush and Persia that we associate with Afghanistan today) had stretched out to include Peshawar, most of the Punjab and Kashmir, and much of Sind and Baluchistan to the south-east as well as Afghan Turkestan to the north. During the 1820s and 1830s the Punjab had fallen to the Sikhs, under

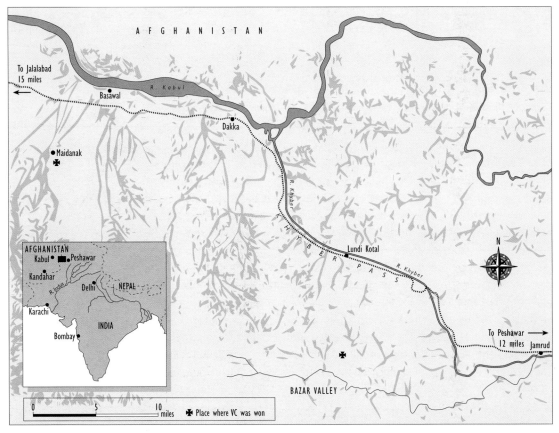

Map 8

The area of the Khyber Pass where Hart and Leach won the Afghan War sapper VCs.

their powerful and charismatic leader Ranjit Singh, in an intricate series of crafty diplomatic and military coups and, by the early 1830s, Shah Shuja was in exile in the Punjab. Shah Shuja's half-brother (but no friend) still retained power in Herat, while Kandahar was in control of Dost Mohammed's brothers. The Afghans had also lost Sind, Baluchistan and Afghan Turkestan to their own rulers.

Shah Shuja's position in power originated with the obsession Britain had developed about the threat to India from the ever-expanding Russian Empire. On the one hand the Russians appeared to be bidding for the control of the central Asian markets of Bokhara, Tashkent, Samarkand and Khiva. The British/Indian government invested enormous effort into discovering the nature of these moves (thus providing opportunities to the adventurous and romantically inclined explorers and spies, both covert and overt, in what became known as the 'great game', inspiration for so much literature from Kipling and lesser mortals to the present day). On the other hand, more immediate and threatening were the Russians' efforts in the late 1830s to back Persian ambitions to regain control of Herat, key to the security of their own north-eastern border region. While all this argued for some sort of forward policy establishing British influence across the Hindu Kush, the Oxus and the Pamirs, the first priority for the British had to be the security of their north and western border along the Indus. Ranjit Singh who was in alliance with Shah Shuja was therefore a friend; and by definition, Dost Mohammed who, incidentally, inflicted a military defeat on the Sikhs at Jamrud in the Khyber Pass in 1837, was an enemy, however much some sort of accommodation with Kabul might be desirable.

The neat solution to the British problem was to put Shah Shuja back on the throne in Kabul and, convincing themselves that such a move would receive popular support, that is what they set out to do by marching him into the country with the 23,000-strong Army of the Indus in the spring of 1839. The combined force deployed was some 39,000 – Shah Shuja, 6000 marching and 4000 at Peshawar; plus 6000 Sikhs.[2] Despite being armed with a firm treaty commitment to Ranjit Singh which would guarantee the security of their base, the Governor-General, Lord Auckland, in deference to Ranjit's feelings, insisted on using the Bolan Pass, the southernmost of the two main routes into Afghanistan, against military advice which favoured the Khyber route. As a result he nearly lost his army even before they entered the country – from starvation, due to inadequate provision of transport (mostly camels) for the daunting 350-mile journey, much of it through waterless desert. The Bengal Sappers and Miners made an early and vital contribution at the start of the march by building a crossing of the 500-yard-wide Indus in three weeks. Materials had either to be brought downriver from Ferozepore 200 miles away or scrounged locally. Cables were made from grass, nails manufactured on site and anchors constructed from timber frames loaded with stone.

Only one major battle took place in the advance to Kabul; that was at the massive fortress of Ghazni, the storming of which required the blowing in of the Kabul Gate. The honour for this was shared between the Bengal and Bombay Sappers and the event was attended by all the drama and determined heroism under fire of the blowing of the Kashmir Gate in Delhi (see Chapter Two). Had the Victoria Cross been in existence at that time undoubtedly Lieutenant Henry Durand,* the main officer participant, would have qualified along with several of the infantry assault party.

But there was little glory in the rest of this war. As we have seen from Chapter Three, Lord Auckland's delusions were proved false and misjudgement was compounded by military incompetence which eventually led to the humiliating defeat of the British force and the terrible massacre of the army and its followers in their doomed efforts to escape through the icy passes back to India. The punitive expedition which returned in 1842 did nothing more than exact revenge. Shah Shuja was murdered by his own people and Dost Mohammed returned to power. The British defeat had two consequences. '[It] destroyed for ever the myth of British invincibility which had grown up since Plassey. This was to have repercussions throughout Asia as well as in India itself where it was to be a significant factor in

---

*Eventually Major-General Sir Henry Durand, KCSI, who died in 1871 after a distinguished career in the political service. See Chapter Two for his contribution to the Malwa campaign during the Uprising and Chapter Three for his involvement in Trevor's Bhutan War VC.

the outbreak of the Mutiny sixteen years later. The war also created an immense bitterness and distrust of the British among the Afghans. Afghanistan became effectively a closed country to the British for more than 30 years. There was no longer any reason why the Afghans should prefer the British to the Russians – indeed rather the opposite.'³

Between the Wars

In the 30 years that now passed before the events that led directly to the Second Afghan War much important water flowed under the bridge. Dost Mohammed remained in power until his death in 1863. His efforts to regain his old empire were generally successful over the long period of his reign but he backed the wrong side in the Sikh Wars with the result that Peshawar, the prize the Sikhs had promised him for his help, was permanently removed from his grasp with the final victory of the British at Gujerat and their annexation of the Punjab in 1849. This event, following shortly after the equally controversial acquisition of Sind, had now brought British India up to the Afghan boundary albeit with a buffer zone, the territory of the border tribes.

The strained Anglo-Afghan relations eased somewhat when Russian attempts to embarrass the British during the Crimean War, by once again causing the Persians to threaten Afghanistan, persuaded the British to a treaty of friendship with Dost Mohammed. This repaid Britain handsomely both at the time and immediately after the end of the war for, when the mutiny broke out in the Bengal Army in 1857, Dost Mohammed made no attempt to stir up trouble. After his death, however, the unity which he had succeeded in bringing to Afghanistan fell apart in the power struggle to establish his successor. The winner after five years of bitter contest between three of his sons was the youngest of them, Sher Ali, the eldest son of his second wife.

The Crimean War had done little to check the advance of the Russian frontier in Asia, however. By the end of the 1860s, Tashkent and Samarkand had fallen, and Bokhara was firmly under control. In 1873 Khiva was occupied. This was no more welcome to Sher Ali than to the British but various attempts to establish firm arrangements for mutual protection fell down as a result of the British Government's policy, generally supported in India, not to become so rattled by the Russian threat as to slip too deeply into involvement in Afghan affairs. This deliberately passive approach (known as 'masterly inactivity', a term which now carries suggestions of idleness but was then a positive technique) was overtaken by the policy of the 'Forward School' when the Disraeli administration took over in 1874.

There was really no reason to fall out with Sher Ali who would have appreciated British support, but the shoals on which any hopes of a working relationship foundered was his reluctance to accept any form of British diplomatic mission in Afghanistan, seen in London as essential to their ability to counter the Russian threat. It was accepted that a mission in Kabul itself might be undesirable to the Afghans, and too dangerous, but one in Kandahar or Herat would serve. The government in India disagreed and the Viceroy, Lord Northbrook, resigned and was replaced by Lord Lytton, a career diplomat with no experience of India but with views which seemed to accord with Disraeli and also with Lord Salisbury, who at the time had the India Office but was shortly to become foreign secretary. Lytton began at once to try and persuade Sher Ali to accept a mission and the diplomatic temperature increased, reaching boiling point when the Russians, frustrated by events in Europe in which determined British opposition had prevented their acquisition of Bulgaria from the Turks, responded by arriving in Kabul with their own diplomatic mission. However unwelcome this might have been to Sher Ali, it was enough excuse for Lytton to set up his own mission under General Sir Neville Chamberlain which was duly despatched into the Khyber Pass en route to Kabul. Chamberlain was accompanied by a political officer, the Commissioner of Peshawar, Major Pierre Louis Napoleon Cavagnari,* who would handle any opposition to their advance. This occurred immediately they reached the gateway fortress of Ali Masjid where they were met by the Afghan governor and firmly informed that any attempt at further progress would be resisted by force.

The home government was dismayed by Lytton's rash actions which cut across the delicate arrangements that had been made with Russia, but had to accept the situation that he had created. Various courses of action short of war were considered but, in the end, an ultimatum was sent to Sher Ali demanding an apology and that he should accept a permanent British mission or he would be treated as a declared enemy. Sher Ali could no more accept these terms than Cetshwayo could accept those presented to him on another continent just six weeks later.

The Invasion

This time three routes were used for the invasion. The Peshawar Field Force of two divisions led by Lieutenant-General Sir Samuel Browne, VC fired the first shots of the war on 21 November 1878 in taking Ali Masjid fort after a stiff fight. Further south, Major-General Frederick Roberts, VC led his Kurram Valley Field Force (ten infantry battalions, one and a half regiments of cavalry and 18 guns) into the valley of that name on the same day, his first fight occurring at Peiwar Kotal on 2 December. This was a major battle for a strongly held ridge, the principal barrier on the route into Afghanistan, and it was won by imaginative and determined tactics in very difficult country. The southernmost route was generally that used in 1839, through the Bolan Pass to secure Quetta and thence to Kandahar. Troops had been despatched in September to this area because of its vulnerability to possible occupation by the Afghan army, from where the Afghans could embarrass the British by a counter-move into Baluchistan. Nevertheless, because of the immense distances to be covered, Quetta was not occupied until 9 November and the main body of this southern column under the overall com-

---

*Although brought up in England, he was the son of an Italian nobleman and an Irish mother.

mander, Lieutenant-General Sir Donald Stewart, started to arrive a month later, two divisions strong. A further month was required before they could set off to Kandahar which they reached with little opposition to their progress on 8 January.

Initially 16 field companies of Sappers and Miners were deployed with the force, nine from the Bengal, three from the Madras and four from the Bombay corps.

> Although there was nothing very spectacular in the work of the Engineers and Sappers, the very existence of every column often depended on it. The Sappers made the roads which brought reinforcements, food and ammunition. Roadmaking and bridge-building may be prosaic tasks, but when carried out in precipitous chasms, scoured by roaring torrents and under the eye of a vigilant foe, they are not so easy as they might first appear. …
>
> Although there was no engineering exploit so striking as the blowing in of the Kabul Gate at Ghazni in 1839, the Engineers and Sappers did excellent and useful work. They bridged the Kabul river many times, constructed dozens of fortified posts, built huts, laid telegraph lines and carried out the hundred-and-one jobs which help an army to advance and fight. Their surveyors covered huge tracts of unknown country, triangulating and mapping as they went and always liable to attack. And far behind the fighting men, the railway engineers toiled night and day to bring their lines through desert and gorge to the advanced bases.[4]

Although there had been many improvements in communications since 1839 – for example, earlier than 1875 trains could run from Calcutta through Delhi and Lahore to the Indus at Multan, and from Karachi to Sukkur on the east bank of the Indus – beyond the railheads the journey to Quetta was still by foot and hoof. In fact the impetus for the improvement of the railways in north-western India came from the experiences of the Second Afghan War: as early as 1882 a railway was in action from Sukkur to Sibi and by 1883 the through journey to both Sibi and Peshawar was possible. Maintenance of the army in the Khyber and Kurram valleys was therefore constrained by the condition of the roads; during the winter of 1878/9, when snow and freezing temperatures added to the difficulties, it was this that determined the extent of the advance. The losses in draught animals were colossal. In Stewart's force, for example, 'The mortality among the camels was at least 40 per cent per month, and, to keep 12,000 camels at work, 1,500 fresh camels *per week* were required.'[5]

The physical difficulties of the country were, however, only part of the story. They were further compounded by the perpetual threat of attack from the local tribesmen through whose traditional lands the routes lay. These tribes, whom the British fought for decades in their attempts to maintain peace in north-west India, were ethnic Afghans or Pathans who owed allegiance more to their own tribes than to Kabul. Although feeling free to negotiate with the British over transit rights, their basic attitude was hostile and supply columns were considered fair game for plunder. Thus a vast proportion of the manpower committed to the war was absorbed in policing the routes. In the Khyber, for example, an entire division was allocated for lines-of-communication work from the start. The only active response that could be made to this menace was the mounting of punitive expeditions into the tribal areas either side of the routes, destroying any opposition that presented itself and burning down the offending villages. It was in one of these that Reginald Hart won his VC.

Lieutenant Reginald Clare Hart

Reginald Hart was the son of Lieutenant-General H.G. Hart and went to school at Marlborough and Cheltenham before passing into Woolwich. He was commissioned in January 1869 in his 21st year and had already demonstrated his personal courage when he rescued a drowning Frenchman in Boulogne harbour, injuring himself in the process on some underwater obstruction after diving off the pier. For this he received the Royal Humane Society's silver medal. He went to India as a young officer and spent some years as an instructor in the Bengal Army before being sent off to the war in Afghanistan after a spell of leave at home. Major-General Sir Louis Jackson, then a subaltern on his first appointment, accompanied Hart, also a subaltern but now with ten years' service, on their journey to the war, both burning with impatience to get involved.

*Reginald Hart
(1848–1931)*

> Hart, of whom I was to see a great deal in the next few months and who became a great friend, was a man of uncommon type whose very quiet, courteous manner and gentle voice masked a regular fire-eater, a Bayard in his thirst for adventure. He was the best of comrades, kindly and cheerful, but had one peculiarity; he was entirely without a sense of humour. It was not safe for a stranger to chaff with him, however good-humouredly, for he might think he was being insulted and want to call the man out. This actually happened once when I was with him, and it took me two hours to calm him down.[6]

After various adventures they reached Jamrud, the most easterly of the Khyber forts, built by Ranjit Singh.

Fort Jamrud at the entrance to the Khyber Pass. The image was used on the reverse of the British Army's 1908–35 Indian General Service medal.

There we had some luck, because a so-called punitive expedition was about to visit the Bazar valley and Hart, having a friend on the staff, managed to get us attached to the 24th N.I. who were going. The Bazar runs into the Khyber from the south-west and was the home territory of the Zakka Khel Afridis.[7]

The expedition to deal with 'these turbulent folk' also included a company of Bengal Sappers to help them over the roads and deal with such tasks as blowing up towers that were stone-built, some 40 feet high and accessible only by a rope ladder leading to a door and a platform occupied by the defenders.

We trekked off up the valley, at first a narrow gorge with a stream which we had to ford every 100 yards as the path went from side to side, but which soon opened out. There were, as well as I remember, some of the 60th Rifles, Gurkhas and 24th N.I. … after three or four days we reached the main Bazar valley and camped, sending out parties on the following days to blow up towers. We were joined in Bazar by the 45th Sikhs and some other troops from Dakka.

The Pathans were now gathering very thickly round us in all the hills, and sniping at night made some casualties. The 24th went out one morning to climb a ridge behind the camp. When we reached the top we could see far over the country, but, of course, the snipers had all gone home to breakfast and so did we. The Gurkhas begged to be allowed to go out at night with only their *kukris* and stalk the snipers, which seemed an excellent idea, but the General refused. He was an old man with Crimean memories, and I suppose he thought it unorthodox. Also there was a nervous horror at headquarters of having to report casualties.

One morning [31 January 1879] Chapman's company of the 24th went back to meet a convoy that was coming across the hills from Lundi Kotal, and escort it in, so Hart and I went with it. We marched a few miles and met the convoy just where they had come out of the hills into the Bazar valley, which here was more of a wide *nullah*. About three-quarters of a mile from this point on our homeward route was a small hillock in the middle of the *nullah*. Here I halted with Hart and Chapman and waited for the convoy to pass. The tribesmen, who had been very keen to loot the convoy, were out in strength in the hills on either side. Just as the last of the convoy passed us, there was a commotion at the point of junction. A post had just come in from Lundi Kotal, carried by 'Catch 'em alive oh's', [*]escort-ed by two *sowars*.[†] As they came into the valley, they were fired on, both *sowars* were wounded; one came galloping towards us, the other went down with his horse in a bed of rushes, in the middle of the *nullah*. The tribesmen came running down from either side to finish them off. I saw Hart talking hurriedly in Hindustani to Chapman and a native officer, then he turned and ran down the hill. I wondered what he had gone for, and presently saw him running down the valley, and Chapman followed more slowly, collecting his men. It was too late to join Hart, and knowing no Hindustani I was rather in the dark as to what was going on, but with field-glasses I could see some Pathans running towards the fallen man. I gathered half a dozen men and fired some long-range volleys at them, and then went down the other side of the *nullah*, to protect that flank. Hart reached

---

[*]Tribal levies paid for by the Indian Government for local defence.
[†]Indian Army cavalrymen.

the man, and then some Gurkha skirmishers came down from the flanks and joined him. They were under fire from a low cliff close by, so they picked up the man and carried him to shelter under the cliff, Hart stopping to save the saddle. It was extraordinary that he was not hit, at such short range. …

　　Then Chapman came up with some more men, and they brought the *sowar* in, but he died on the way. Thus Hart got his V.C.[8]

The convoys for the maintenance of the army in the field were not the only targets for the anger of the hill tribesmen. Survey parties were particularly hated. Apparently there was an Afghan saying: 'First comes one Englishman to shoot birds or beasts, then come two Englishmen to make a map, and then comes an army to take the country. It is better therefore to kill the first Englishman.'[9] Survey of the routes and the country on either side was essential to the operations

> and was carried out in every area, though it progressed more rapidly in the south than in the north as the Engineers and Surveyors with the Kandahar Force were less subject to interruption than their comrades in the Khaibar and the Kurram, and their number was greater. The Peshawar Valley contingent fixed many points on the mountain ranges and began an accurate survey of the route from Peshawar to Jalalabad. Captain R.G. Woodthorpe of the Royal Engineers with Roberts in the Kurram valley, mapped a great part of the valley and accompanied the general in January, 1879, on a small expedition of about 2,000 men in a mixed force of infantry, cavalry and two batteries of artillery, against the Mangals in Khost. The Kandahar Force surveyors fixed a number of peaks and did some elaborate triangulation work. As a rule they could work freely under a proper escort, and in this they were more fortunate than the Khaibar surveyors, who on several occasions had to fight for their lives.[10]

One such was Captain Edward Leach and the action in which he became involved brought him his VC.

Captain Edward Pemberton Leach

Edward Leach was the second son of Lieutenant-Colonel Sir George Leach, KCB, who was himself a sapper officer for 23 years before joining the Civil Service for a distinguished second career, eventually as Secretary to the Board of Agriculture; his mother was the former Emily Leigh Pemberton of Sittingbourne. Edward was born in Londonderry, presumably his father's station at the time, and educated at Highgate School. After his courses at Woolwich and Chatham he was commissioned in April 1866 and left for India two years later. He served with the Bengal Engineers at Rawalpindi but quite soon joined the Public Works Department until being appointed to the Indian Survey in October 1871. It was in this capacity that he joined the 1871 Lushai expedition although in that he accompanied one of the companies of his own corps, the Bengal Sappers and Miners. This rather minor campaign was but slight preparation for the dramatic events in which he was to become involved in Afghanistan although the experience of working in a remote mountainous region must have been useful and earned him

Edward Leach
(1847–1913)

the thanks of the Secretary of State for India and also of the Government of India, together with the Frontier Medal and Clasp. In fact he was much closer to death in an incident on his next posting when he was surveying in central India under Thomas Holdich.* Leach, an indefatigable sportsman but a novice to tiger shooting, shot two during a hunt organised by Holdich. The first was a clean kill but the second went to ground in a bush where Leach discovered it by crawling in on his stomach. 'Just one extension of his great paw and he could have smashed Leach's head in like a nutshell.' There was nothing for it but to inch his rifle forward to the tiger's head and fire and he then 'literally blew his brains out whilst they were still staring into each other's eyes'.[11]

When he arrived in Afghanistan in 1878, as a member of the Khyber Survey Party, he had only just returned from leave in England and started a new job as private secretary to Sir James Caird, Famine Commissioner.

By March 1879 General Sir Sam Browne's column in the Khyber had reached Jalalabad but behind him lay his lines of communication, still under harassment by the tribes bordering the route. The Afridis, whom we have already met in Reginald Hart's affair, and further west the Khugianis and the Shinwaris. An expedition was mounted against the latter in their area round Maidanak, about 14 miles to the south of the route between Jalalabad and Basawal. Leach was undertaking some survey of the area with the protection of an escort from the Guides Cavalry under Lieutenant Walter Hamilton and the 45th Sikhs and Lieutenant Barclay when they were attacked and decided to withdraw. '… for 2 miles everything went well, but when they got close to the plain the tribesmen closed round and a rush was made by a party of them. This Leach was able to check – emptying his revolver in their faces; but then Barclay was wounded, mortally as it turned out, and the enemy, seeing this, again closed up and prepared for another rush.'[12] Taking up the story in Leach's own account:

> There was nothing for it now but the bayonet, and calling to the men nearest I went back to meet them, and held a little knoll which we had just left, hoping to give the men who were carrying Barclay time to push on. Three only closed with us, one was immediately bayonetted by a Sepoy, the other made a rush at me but missed and I floored him with the butt end of the rifle, and the third was either shot or bolted, the remainder, about 50 strong, kept up a shower of stones from 15 to 20 yards off, crouching behind the rocks and assisted by the men with guns from the ridges, who, I am thankful to say, made precious bad shooting though only from 60 to 80 yards from us.
>
> For three or four minutes I simply stood there dodging the stones with an empty rifle in my hand, – of course you will say where was your revolver, but to re-load is a matter of a minute or so, and with these scoundrels so close up I had to keep my eyes open. However, one of the Sepoys realised the situation and

---

*Holdich became one of the leading surveyors in the Second Afghan War, operating largely in the southern sector. He made his name later participating in boundary commissions around the borders of Afghanistan in the 1880s and 1890s, retiring as Colonel Sir Thomas Holdich, KCMG, KCIE, CB in 1900.

brought me a handful of cartridges, I now had my turn and polished off three one after the other, the Sepoys behind me backed me up, and in two or three minutes the whole of this motley crew took to their heels and left us to get down in safety …[13]

Thus in the first few months, sappers had won two of the 15 VCs that were to be awarded in the entire war.

It should be recorded that admiration for Leach's VC award was not universal. After his death a fellow sapper officer who had been in Afghanistan and who claimed to have talked to Barclay before he died, wrote a venomous letter[14] to the Editor of the *Royal Engineers Journal* in which Leach's obituary had been published, maintaining that Leach had been responsible for Barclay's death by working too close to the enemy and that he 'in a civilian capacity [as a surveyor] had not taken over command of the escort whose achievement in saving the party should have been credited to the native NCO.' The author of the letter also took a swipe at Hart maintaining that 'We RE in India were indignant at the occasions and manner in which these VCs were won. But I do admit that Leach thoroughly deserved a VC for Maiwand and that Hart would qualify properly for a VC if he had his chance.' It seems fairly clear that Leach's courage and determination to complete his task were of an outstanding order. Had the party returned unscathed he would have earned nothing but praise. As it was the tragedy of Barclay's death in support of a technical task rather than in some glorious fight must have affected his regiment deeply and no doubt gave rise to such criticism. The idea that Leach was present 'in a civilian capacity' is an absurdity, as is the suggestion, made later in the letter, that the awards were somehow fixed (by two very junior officers!) on a visit to Simla after the campaign. This accusation, never published, simply reflects the sort of envious carping that has accompanied awards of the VC from the earliest times to the present day – viz, H. Jones at Goose Green.

By this time, however, Sher Ali was dead. He had fled to Afghan Turkestan in December. Unable to persuade the Russians to intervene militarily on his behalf, and having had to accept the release of his troublesome son Yakub Khan from imprisonment to take over as regent in his absence, he had resigned himself to his badly declining health and simply allowed himself to die. Negotiations were started with Yakub Khan, now the Amir, and by the Treaty of Gandamak signed on 26 May Yakub Khan agreed an amnesty for all those who had helped the British and accepted a British agent at Kabul, British control of foreign policy and the presence of British officers on his frontiers when necessary. For their part the British would withdraw from their present positions as soon as practicable but retain control over the Khyber Pass and certain areas around Quetta and the Bolan. They would also guarantee military and financial support to Afghanistan against outside aggression, build a telegraph line from Kabul to Kurram and promote trade. The army, still in considerable difficulty along their brittle lines of communication and suffering from disease including the dreaded cholera, breathed a sigh of relief and began to return home to the honours and acclaim

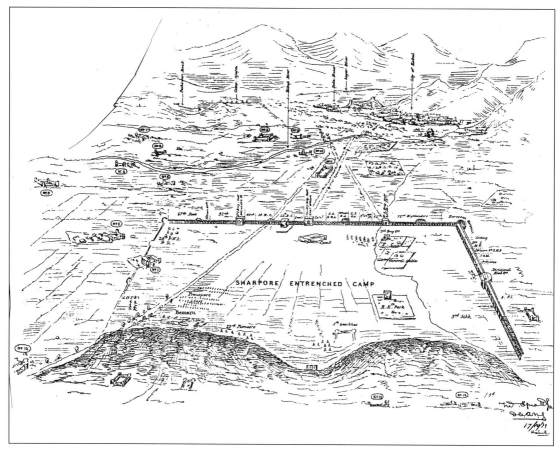

*Sketch of the Sherpur
cantonment during
Roberts's occupation in
1880, looking south.*

that awaited them. Cavagnari moved into Kabul as the newly appointed British
agent or 'Envoy Extraordinary and Minister Plenipotentiary at the court of the
Amir'.

While it might have seemed that all aims had been achieved, without the
general support of the Afghan people these arrangements had no substance and
were doomed. They fell apart with violence and bloodshed three months later
when an angry mob of soldiers from Herat who had marched to Kabul to demand
their back pay from Yakub Khan, stormed the British Residency on 3 September,
the symbol of the cause of their plight, when it was clear that their demands could
not be met. Hopelessly outnumbered in the unfortified Residency, Cavagnari and
his guard of 75 soldiers from the elite Corps of Guides under Lieutenant Walter
Hamilton, incidentally the officer who had escorted Leach's survey party and who
himself had recently won a VC in the Khyber, fought to the death.[*]

---

[*]Even after the deaths of their officers, the Indian soldiers under Jemadar Jewand Singh fought on,
  the Jemadar being the last to die after one final charge.

All arrangements for withdrawal were now put in reverse. Roberts rushed back to the Kurram from Simla where he had returned for a conference. Before long it became clear that Kabul had to be occupied, retribution taken and British influence established unequivocally; and it was Roberts and his column as the only force that was in a position to move quickly on the capital that must do it. In the next three months, while the Kandahar force built up its position under Sir Donald Stewart, and the Khyber column re-established itself under a new commander, Major-General R.O. Bright, Roberts moved on Kabul and undertook the operations to secure the city and subdue the Afghans. In Kabul itself he imposed

The Madras Sappers and Miners guarding their sector of Sherpur cantonment.

One of the fortified villages outside the walls of Sherpur which had to be demolished for security. It was in such a village that Captain James Dundas, VC lost his life in a premature explosion.

A sketch by Lieutenant John Burn-Murdoch of the burial ground at Sherpur where Lieutenants Dundas and Nugent were interred.

order through a number of draconian measures that included the execution of a number of the ring-leaders of any organised resistance to the British moves.

In the field he deployed to deal with the growing threat from enemies who were menacing him from three different directions. After a number of close shaves and the depletion of his own force through disease and casualties, he decided to concentrate on the Sherpur cantonment, the large fortified area to the north of Kabul in the general area where in 1841 the army had so disastrously wasted away from cold, hunger and inactivity brought on by indecisive leadership and from which they set out on their last fateful journey. Now, despite the wintry weather,

One of the bridges over the River Kabul, built by the Madras Sappers and Miners.

it was different. The fortifications had been developed during Dost Mohammed's time and Roberts now ensured that it was well stocked with food, fuel, blankets and ammunition. Under his decisive command he had an army that was experienced, tough and confident. His Commanding Royal Engineer, Lieutenant-Colonel Æneas Perkins, had been at work improving the protection and now all hands were deployed to make the place secure.

Before dawn on 23 December 1879 a massed attack was launched on the cantonment. It had been anticipated and Roberts was ready. For seven hours the Afghans threw wave after wave against the defences, fighting with immense bravery to force some sort of gap, but against the superior weaponry of the defenders (star shells were used for illumination during the early attacks) the defences held. As soon as the attacks slackened Roberts sent his cavalry out in a decisive counter-attack. The outlying area was secured by the destruction of the villages and forts which still held a number of the enemy. In this operation Captain James Dundas, VC and a colleague, Lieutenant Nugent of the Royal Engineers, 'had constructed three mines, and, all being ready, went back to light the fuses. The Sappers were drawn up outside under their European non-commissioned officers and noticed that two of the mines exploded instantly. Their officers were within the walls, and when the dust and smoke cleared away they were still missing. Search was made, and the bodies of Captain Dundas and Lieutenant Nugent were found lying under the debris. Both were dead.'[15] An improvised fuse, made up because of a shortage of serviceable manufactured fuse, was blamed for this tragedy.

It was probably no coincidence that on the same day some 30 miles to the east in the Khyber line, Major Edward Thackeray, VC, whom we first met at the siege of Delhi so brilliantly helping to extinguish the magazine fire, was further proving his worth at the small post of Jagdalak Kotal, high up on the pass some 20 miles to the west of Gandamak. This was one of those vital posts from which operations could be mounted to protect the convoys and which provided the communications links, normally by heliograph, on which much depended. Thackeray's force comprised two companies of Bengal Sappers and some men from the Punjab Native Infantry, 294 ranks all told. There had already been a number of skirmishes connected with the escorting of convoys into and from the fort. Now, on 23 December, the enemy appeared in force along the crest to the north-east and throughout the day closed in to a few hundred yards while within the fort Thackeray supervised the retaliatory fire until he himself was badly wounded in the elbow. The attack was finally beaten off at 10.00 pm.

Yakub Khan had abdicated in October having lost all credibility with his people, and Roberts was now master of Kabul in both a military and political sense. The whole country seethed with anti-British feeling and a long-term political solution was a matter of urgency. In the ensuing six months a number of initiatives, both political and military, were taken, the details of which need not concern us here, until the scene changes to Kandahar for the final and most dramatic episode of the whole war from July to September 1880. By that time the decision to leave Afghanistan had been made and, on 22 July, the new Amir, Yakub Khan's first cousin Abdur Rahman, had been installed in Kabul, a candidate just acceptable to the British in his determination to pursue an independent neutral line, also acceptable to the Afghans.

Sir Donald Stewart was now in Kabul as overall commander, having marched there from Kandahar in April, achieving a fine victory on the way at Ahmad Khel. Military responsibility for the Kandahar region now lay with the Bombay Army in the person of Lieutenant-General J.M. Primrose. The pro-British Wali (ruler) of Kandahar, installed in May, was the Sirdar Sher Ali, a great-nephew of Dost Mohammed and cousin of the Amir Sher Ali, victim of the original British ulti-matum. Sirdar Sher Ali 'has never really been accepted by the Kandaharis. He has been, from the first, looked upon, not as a Governor of Kandahar in his own right, but as a servant of the "Feringhi", and, as such has irretrievably damaged his rep-utation with his own countrymen.'[16]

After the defeats sustained by the Afghans from both Roberts and Stewart, the real cloud on the horizon lay over Herat, where Ayub Khan, Amir Sher Ali's sec-ond son, had established a firm anti-British power base and built up a fine army. He marched this out in early July to threaten Kandahar. Wali Sher Ali led out his own quite inadequate force in response and Primrose sent a brigade under Brigadier-General Burrows in support. Major Edward Leach, VC was on his staff. At Maiwand, on 27 July 1880, Burrows's brigade was destroyed in a disaster as devastating as Isandlwana the previous year. Over 1000 fighting men were killed and the remnants of the army then had to endure the appalling ordeal of escaping back to Kandahar along 45 miles of rough country in searing heat and in desper-ate need of water for horses and men. Subsequent accounts of the battle and the terrible retreat owe much to the reports of Edward Leach whose performance during the battle, the retreat and later operations to save Kandahar earned him the highest praise and a brevet lieutenant-colonelcy.

The Bombay Sappers and Miners under Lieutenant T.R. Henn also earned undying fame at Maiwand, their action illustrating one of the paradoxes of bravery awards such as the VC when extreme heroism goes unrewarded through lack of a witness. The story could only be pieced together later based on an Afghan report quoted in General Primrose's despatch of 1 October and on the deductions made from the positions of the graves seen on a later visit to the battlefield. 'They [a mixed party of the 66th Regiment, the Bombay Grenadiers and the Bombay Sappers and Miners] were surrounded by the whole Afghan army, and fought until only eleven men were left, inflicting enormous loss on the enemy. These eleven charged out of the garden and died with their faces to the foe, fighting to the death. …Thus standing in the open, back to back, firing steadi-ly and truly, every shot telling, surrounded by thousands, these eleven officers and men died, and it was not until the last man had been shot down that the Ghazis dared advance upon them.' According to corps history, Lieutenant Henn in this last stand died 'voluntarily to cover the retreat of the broken column.'[17]

British plans for a clean withdrawal from Afghanistan and the installation of a regime acceptable to both sides were now in jeopardy. The defeat of Ayub Khan became top priority. Stewart, commanding the army in Kabul, was determined to continue his withdrawal back to India. He therefore despatched Roberts on the famous 300-mile three-week march from Kabul to Kandahar. This, with the subsequent operations he undertook to relieve the siege city and wreak revenge on Ayub Khan and the manner in which all this was accomplished, became the crowning glory for Roberts, cementing his military reputation and making him a national hero. In truth, the march was no more of an achievement than Stewart's in the reverse direction earlier in the year. Nevertheless, coming after the disaster of Maiwand, the swiftness with which Roberts then struck to turn a depressing situation into a triumph, generated a national sigh of relief and so the march entered into folklore rather as Rorke's Drift had following Isandlwana. The march was rewarded by the issue to those who took part of the Kabul to Kandahar Star.

Nearly eight months were now to elapse before Kandahar could be evacuated. Further military action was required to stabilise the situation and the political quandary was only solved by persuading the weak Wali Sher Ali to abdicate and offering rule of the province to Abdur Rahman. This achieved, final withdrawal took place in April 1881, thus bringing the war to an end. Ayub Khan's aspirations for power were ended when Abdur Rahman defeated him in battle in September 1881, although he continued to stir up trouble from his exile in Persia until accepting asylum and a British pension in India. It had cost the British and their Indian Army some 10,000 dead from casualties in battle and later from wounds and disease.[18]

Subsequent Careers

If the Second Afghan War made Roberts's career,[*] it did no harm to those of Hart and Leach either. In 1881 Hart joined Major-General Gerald Graham, VC as his ADC, in Wolseley's force in Egypt, and was present at the battles of Kassassin and Tel el Kebir. In 1884 he was back in India where he yet again performed a rescue, earning a clasp to his Royal Humane Society silver medal, this time for saving the life of an Indian gunner in the Roorkee Canal.

In 1897, after many years as an instructor, Hart was appointed to command 1st Brigade in the force under Sir William Lockhart carrying out punitive operations in the 1897 Uprising (see Chapter Six). After an exceedingly arduous six months this ended with operations in the Bazar valley region; thus Hart returned to the area where he had performed the exploit which had made his name nearly 20 years earlier.

[*]He went on to command the Madras Army, was appointed C-in-C India in 1885, became a field marshal in 1895, took overall command in South Africa (Second Boer War) in 1899 with Kitchener as his Chief of Staff and was Commander-in-Chief British Army 1901–4. He was a contemporary and lifelong rival of Wolseley whom he replaced as Commander-in-Chief.

When the South African War broke out in 1899, Hart, who was now over 50, felt frustrated at not being given some part to play in it, and in 1902 he went home to take up command of the Thames District. It was an appropriate enough task for a man of such experience but, as *The Times* put it in his obituary: 'Hart's future was no longer so promising. He had grown older, and long service in India had given him a one-sided experience of war. None of the more recent campaigns in Egypt nor South Africa had known him. Yet his military record fully merited recognition, and in November, 1907, he received command of the troops in Cape Colony.'[19] He was promoted out of the post in 1908 but returned as Commander-in-Chief South Africa in 1911, succeeding Lord Methuen.

There was more to follow. Hart became a full general in 1914 and, now far too old for active service, he became Lieutenant-Governor and Commander-in-Chief of the Forces in Guernsey and Alderney, retiring in June 1918. He died in 1931. In 1881 Hart had married Charlotte Augusta Synnot, daughter of Mr Mark Synnot of Ballymoyer in County Armagh. They had three sons and a daughter.

For his part, Leach had remained in Kandahar until the end of the British occupation in May 1881 and took over the Poona Survey Party. He was made brevet lieutenant-colonel for his performance at Maiwand (one of only two rewards given for that action). He had also been three times mentioned in despatches and received the thanks of the Government of India for his survey work. He then came down from all this glory with a bump, taking command of 24 Field Company in 1885 as part of Sir Gerald Graham's force in eastern Sudan. 24 Field Company were swept up into the Battle of Tofrek during the march across the desert, narrowly avoiding disaster only by great heroism. Leach's reward for his contribution was the CB for gallantry, by then a somewhat unusual use of this honour, and command of a brigade at Korosko on the Nile. Later he was to spend six years in Plymouth in charge of the Sound defences, followed by three years in Canada as Commanding Royal Engineer.

Leach was appointed as GOC Belfast in 1899, where he founded Ballykinler training camp, and as GOC Scotland five years later. He finally retired in 1912 as a full general, KCB and KCVO. In 1882 he had married the eldest daughter of Sir Thomas Bazley Bt of Hatherop Castle, Gloucestershire and they had one son and two daughters. Leach died suddenly in his 67th year at Cadenabbia on Lake Como in Italy.

The North-West Frontier (1891–1898)

How this was done will long be remembered as one of the most gallant things recorded in Indian warfare.[1]

This was the opinion of E.F. Knight, Special Correspondent of *The Times*, writing of Captain Fenton Aylmer's feat in breaking into the fort at Nilt at the end of 1891. It was the quintessential North-West Frontier heroic exploit, albeit in a region so remote that it only just qualifies for this title.

Britain's long love–hate relationship with the North-West Frontier began with the annexation of the Punjab in 1849 by the then Governor-General, Lord Dalhousie. We have seen in the previous chapter how this event occurred in the aftermath of the First Afghan War which led inexorably to the Second. We have also seen how operations in the Second Afghan War were characterised by continued harassment of the supply lines by the Pathan inhabitants of the mountainous area around the Khyber Pass, how this absorbed so much of the military effort and how it gave rise to the two sapper VCs of that war.

The North-West Frontier area stretched from Baluchistan in the south, not part of this particular story, up through the homeland of the Afridis and Shinwaris, northwards through Mohmand country and a further hundred miles towards Chitral, from there sweeping in a broad north-easterly curve where the Hindu Kush gives way to the Pamirs, and into Kashmir to the point where, as the title of Knight's book put it, three empires met, those of

Map 9
The North-West Frontier area of India.

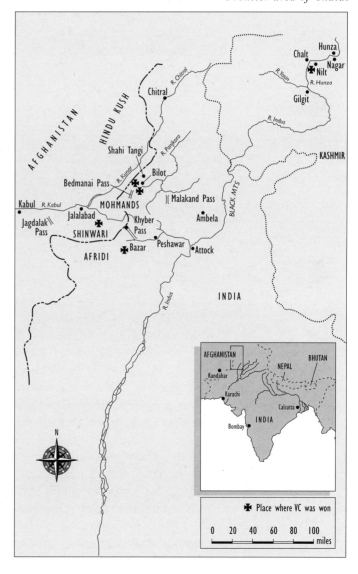

A typical Frontier tower demolition.

Russia, China and Britain.* Within this arc lie the headwaters of the Indus, which rise in this vast mountainous region and flow out through country broken by thousands of rivers and valleys, many of whose names have now become a permanent part of British–Indian history – Swat, Panjkora, Chitral, Gilgit and Hunza to name but a few.

Even before the Second Afghan War the Indian Army was well experienced in fighting the Pathan inhabitants of this region. Sandes lists over 20 such campaigns since 1849.[2] He also criticises these ventures for their failure to take sufficient sappers with them (in many cases none at all), in view of the particular nature of the terrain and the daunting obstacles which had to be crossed, and of the tasks such as the destruction of towers and often whole villages which proceeded more efficiently when undertaken by specialists. The towers, of stone and timber, about 15 feet square and 30 feet high with loopholed walls, built into the villages as protection, were normally destroyed by a mined charge of 15 lb of dynamite. On the two Miranzai expeditions of 1891, 70 such towers were brought down.

The Ambela Campaign of 1863 illustrates Sandes's point about the use of sappers. On a much larger scale than most it involved a force of 5000 under Brigadier-General Sir Neville Chamberlain advancing north from Attock to deal with a group of troublesome Hindu Fanatics near Ambela. There were two companies of sappers with the force, under Lieutenant-Colonel Alexander Taylor, whom we have already met at the siege of Delhi. What was expected to be a routine punitive operation became a near disaster when the Bunerwals, through whose district the force had obtained agreement to march, turned against them and attacked in great strength. The battalions had to build hasty defences but the sappers had been almost fully deployed on work to improve the dreadful route

---

*This point and the whole of the area discussed in this chapter lies within modern Pakistan. However, the term India will be used, referring to the country as it was before Partition.

into the area and could spare little effort for what became a critical situation. The force hung on until reinforcements arrived and the original aim was eventually achieved only after severe fighting, in which 900 casualties were sustained and the Bunerwals had been forced to submit. Even this successful outcome owed much to another sapper. The Indian Government had planned to withdraw on receiving the news of the original set-back but the Viceroy intervened and authorised the necessary reinforcements. As it happened the Viceroy at the time was Lieutenant-General Sir William Denison, a Royal Engineer, now following a career in colonial administration, who as Governor of Madras acted as Viceroy for six weeks after the death of Lord Elgin and before Sir John Lawrence assumed charge.

Although this was a particularly serious affair, many of the expeditions before 1890 were less elaborate and more straightforward, but through them all was built up the understanding of the ways of the Pathans and the skills with which to fight them. Sandes describes the Pathans as:

> fierce, treacherous and unruly: their hands against every man, and every man's hand against them. The bitter struggle for existence in an inhospitable land had produced men who were, and still are, unique, and whose reckless and cruel character is shown by some of their proverbs. 'Keep a cousin poor, but use him.' 'When he is little play with him. When he is grown up he is a cousin; fight him.' 'Speak good words to an enemy very softly; gradually destroy him root and branch.' Yet the Pathan has his good points. At times he is as brave as a lion, and he is bound by his religion to shelter and protect an enemy who comes as a suppliant, and to show hospitality to all who may demand it. He leads a wild, free and active life in his mountain fastnesses. He is a bigoted Muhammedan, proud, strong and defiant, and he values the life of a man no more than that of a jackal. All insults must be avenged in blood. At one moment he may seem a saint: at the next he is a devil.[3]

Of course, behind all the warfare on the frontier lay the anxiety about the expansion of Russia's empire. In the late 1880s, the danger point lay in what Peter Hopkirk has called the crucial gap of 50 miles between Afghanistan's north-eastern border and the south-western extremity of Chinese Central Asia, through which the Russians could obtain access southwards into India.[4] In the course of some adventurous 'great game' activity, it had been established, largely in 1889 by Francis Younghusband who had been sent to confront him, that Safdar Ali, the Thum (ruler) of Hunza, the state which lay at the point where the three empires met, was secretly making overtures to the Russians. By 1890 the Russians had claimed to have annexed the region of the Pamirs and, although after strong British protests in St Petersburg they backed down on this claim, the Delhi government decided to take action to secure certain areas. They installed a political officer, Colonel Algernon Durand,* and a small force of Gurkhas at Gilgit, close

---

*Algernon Durand was the son of Sir Henry Durand who, as a young officer, had led the demolition party at the gates of Ghazni in the First Afghan War (see Chapter Five). His brother was Sir Mortimer Durand, Foreign Secretary to the Indian Government, who gave his name to the line demarcating the boundary between Afghanistan and India.

to Kashmir's most northerly border, at the point at which the Hunza and Gilgit rivers join before flowing into the Indus. Even further north on the Hunza river was the Kashmiri fortress of Chalt. Safdar Ali, believing himself by now safely under Russian protection, made plans to seize Chalt, having enlisted the support of the ruler of Nagar. Learning of this, Durand strengthened the small garrison at Chalt; meanwhile, the Indian Government had become sufficiently alarmed at the Russian threat and influence in Hunza to take steps to occupy the territory and install a friendly regime.

In fact the states of Hunza and Nagar were already technically obedient to the Maharaja of Kashmir to whom they paid a nominal tribute. However, for some years Safdar Ali had pursued his own business interests by plundering caravans on the trade route from Leh to Yarkand by using a secret pass. Finding this pass and ending the attacks on the caravans had been one of Younghusband's missions. Hunza's rulers delighted in expressing their own independence in colourful language. When Durand's small force advanced into the area from Gilgit, setting up his base at Chalt, the Thum of Hunza wrote asking why the British had 'strayed into his country like camels without nose-rings … We will cut off your head Colonel Durand and then report you to the Indian government … The fortress of Chalt is more precious to us than the strings of our wives' pyjamas.'[5]

This force consisted of fewer than 1200 men of whom a half were Kashmiri State troops. The only regulars were 200 men of the 5th Gurkha Rifles, a party of Punjab Infantry with a Gatling gun, 80 men from a mountain battery with two 7-pounder guns, and 12 men of the 4th Company Bengal Sappers and Miners under Captain F.J. Aylmer, RE.

Captain Fenton John Aylmer

Fenton Aylmer had been commissioned into the Royal Engineers in 1880. He was the third son of Captain F.J. Aylmer of the 97th Regiment and had been Senior Under-Officer at the Royal Military Academy from which he passed out second in his batch. After a few months with the Submarine Miners at Devonport, he went to India in 1883 and was with the Bengal Sappers and Miners from then until 1897. In 1886 he went to Burma where a British force under General Sir Harry Prendergast, VC (see Chapter Two) was establishing the authority of the British Empire and was given command of 4th Company Bombay Sappers and Miners. He returned to India in 1888 and three years later, by then a captain, went with his company on the 1891 Black Mountain expedition.

Fenton Aylmer (seated on right) during the 1891 Black Mountain expedition, a few months before setting off to Hunza.

There their task was largely the mundane but arduous one of roadmaking. But when that was ended there was to be little rest for Aylmer as the trouble was already brewing in Hunza-Nagar and by December he was on his way up the gorge of the River Hunza.

In the process of reaching that point Aylmer had had to overcome several obstacles to enable Durand's force to move forward and to be supplied. He had built a 500-foot flying bridge* en route, a clear span bridge at Gilgit, improvements to the track on the approaches to Chalt which ascended 'by nerve-racking zigzags to great heights in certain places, the path being sometimes carried on thin poles jutting out from the face of the cliff',[6] and another bridge across the Hunza above Chalt.

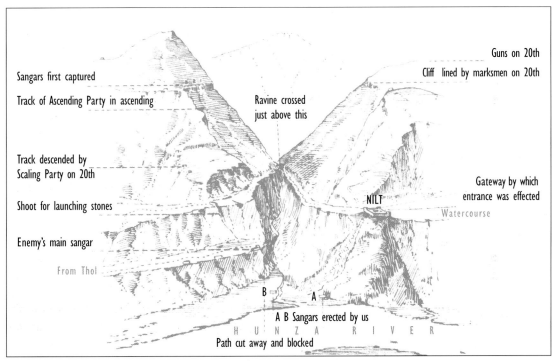

Sangars first captured

Track of Ascending Party in ascending

Track descended by
Scaling Party on 20th

Shoot for launching stones

Enemy's main sangar

From Thol

Ravine crossed
just above this

Guns on 20th

Cliff lined by marksmen on 20th

NILT

Gateway by which
entrance was effected

Watercourse

B   A

A B Sangars erected by us
H U N Z A   R I V E R
Path cut away and blocked

Nilt ravine as sketched for the official report.

A day's march out of Chalt brought the force to the first military obstacle on their route to Hunza. Eight hundred feet above the river was the apparently impregnable Nilt fort which Sandes describes as lying

> on a narrow strip of ground … between the cliff and the mountain behind it, and in the angle formed by the junction of the Nilt torrent from the Rakaposhi Glacier with the Hunza river … The fort was accessible only on the side facing the moun-

*A flying bridge was a standard method of crossing a wide and fast-flowing river and still much used in underdeveloped areas. It consists of a ferry or raft, fixed by a traveller to a cable across the river and caused to cross from bank to bank by adjusting its attitude to the force of the current.

tain, and it could not be seen until the attackers were close to it. Its walls, of large stones cemented with mud and strengthened by longitudinal timbers, were at least 14 feet high and about eight feet thick. Towers at the angles, and in the faces, afforded flanking fire. The main gateway … was flanked by a loopholed bastion at a few yards' distance, and was screened by a walled courtyard swept by the fire from the bastion. Outside the courtyard wall abattis had been formed … The interior of the fort was screened from the mountain above by a high parados wall.[7]

The immediate capture of the fort was essential. The force had found no water during the march, nor was there any in the locality, so a siege from a secure encampment was not possible. It was a question of capturing the fort by storm or retiring. After some preliminary skirmishing, in which the only heavy weapons, the Gatling gun which kept jamming and two 7-pounders which had to be used from less than their normal minimum range, were employed as best they might, the order for the assault was given. Continuing the report quoted at the start of this chapter, E.F. Knight, who observed the whole episode by looking down on the scene from a position further up the mountain, relates:

Captain Aylmer, as our engineer, was now instructed to blow up the main gate of the fort, so as to admit the storming-party … First our guns opened a very heavy fire on the fort, under cover of which 100 of the 5th Gurkhas, led by Lieutenants Boisragon and Badcock, made a rush at the outer wall, and began to cut their way through the abattis with their kukris, the garrison the while firing steadily into them. A small opening having thus been made, the three officers, closely followed by about half a dozen men, pushed their way through it. They then made for the wooden gate of the outer wall, which they soon hacked to pieces. They now found

Sketch plan of Nilt Fort.

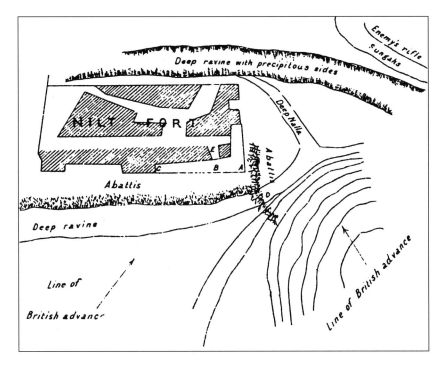

themselves in front of the main wall, and while his companions fired into the loop-holes – the officers using their revolvers – Captain Aylmer, accompanied by his Pathan orderly, rushed forward to the foot of the main gate, which was strongly built, and had been barricaded with stones in anticipation of our coming. The enemy now concentrated their fire on this gallant little band, and it is marvellous that any of them escaped death. Captain Aylmer placed his slabs of guncotton at the foot of the gate, packed them with stones, and ignited the fuse, all the while being exposed to the fire from the towers which flanked the gate, as well as some loopholes in the gate itself. He was shot in the leg from so short a distance that his clothes and flesh were burnt by the gunpowder. He and his orderly then followed the wall of the fort to a safe distance, and stood there awaiting the explosion. But there came no explosion, for the fuse was a faulty one, so Captain Aylmer had once more to face an almost certain death. He returned to the gate, readjusted the fuse, cut it with his knife, lit a match after two or three attempts, and re-ignited the fuse. While doing this he received another wound, his hand being terribly crushed by a stone that was thrown from the battlements.

This time a terrific explosion followed, and at once, before even the dust had cleared or the stones had ceased dropping from the crumbling wall, the three British officers, with six men at their back, clambered through the breach and were within Nilt fort. Enveloped in dense smoke and dust, their comrades, who had been cutting their way through the abattis, could not find the breach; indeed they did not realise that one had been effected and that their officers were within the gate; so for many minutes that little handful of gallant Englishmen and Gurkhas was engaged in a hand-to-hand fight with the garrison in the narrow alley leading from the gate … Soon two were killed and most of them were wounded.[8]

In his own account, Aylmer was accompanied by two of his sappers, Abdulla Khan and Hazara Singh, whose own gallantry and skill clearly contributed to the success of the operation.

While the Gurkhas fired at the loopholes of the flanking bastion, Hazara Singh, who providentially had a guncotton load, assisted me to lay a charge at the foot of the gate. … The enemy began to heave big stones over the top of the wall onto our heads. It was evident that we must get under cover, and the only cover was inside the gate. Four or five tribesmen, with levelled guns, were posted at the end of a covered passage which led from the gate into the interior and it was certain death for the first two or three who might try to lead our little party inside. One Gurkha, exposing himself, was immediately shot dead; but, by putting my revolver round the corner of the gateway and emptying it twice in the direction of the defenders, I succeeded in killing or wounding several, and, seeing the way clear, we rushed inside. We remained for a long time in the covered passage defending ourselves as best we could. … Having been wounded several times, I have not a very clear recollection of what happened but Abdulla pulled me out of the gate to the cut from the water channel. …[9]

Both sappers received the Indian Order of Merit and became Indian officers in due course.

While this was in progress Boisragon went out again to find his Gurkhas and lead them in. The delay had been due to Durand himself being severely

*All that remained of
Nilt in 1927.*

wounded but the day was eventually won. VCs went to both Aylmer and
Boisragon for their part in this affair. Badcock received the DSO. This lesser
award for an equally brave man was queried by the Duke of Cambridge but the
Indian authorities had felt that Badcock had merely led troops to the support of
the others. Some discussion was then provoked as to whether acts performed as
part of normal duty should be considered eligible for the VC as, by that time, a
new warrant was being interpreted to allow for this. This remained a somewhat
ambiguous matter until the 1921 warrant specified 'extreme devotion to duty in
the face of the enemy'.[10]

The Hunza-Nagar campaign was successfully concluded 18 days later,
although not before yet another feat of extraordinary gallantry had been performed in overcoming the next defended position. There the enemy had built a
series of sangars* manned by several thousand men on a 1500-foot cliff which
dominated the route forward. A Kashmiri sepoy succeeded in scaling the cliff at
enormous peril to his own life and, on the strength of this, Lieutenant John
Manners Smith, himself an experienced mountaineer and an infantryman on
secondment from the Political Department, led a small assault party in a nail-
biting climb in which, had they been discovered prematurely, they would have
been swept off the cliff-face to their doom by a hail of rocks. Outflanked in this
dramatic way the enemy gave up after some ferocious fighting in the sangars.
Manners Smith was also awarded a VC for this remarkable feat.

Later Career

After he had recovered from his wounds at Nilt, Fenton Aylmer continued with
his bridging work in the area and developed a design for a suspension bridge with

*Stone-walled emplacements used in country where digging in rocky ground is impossible.

cables formed from bundles of telegraph wire. Starting with a 200-foot span at Gilgit, he built many more until he was posted to the Black Mountain region on another frontier operation, the Isazai Expedition in October 1892.

In 1895 Aylmer once again proved his outstanding courage performing a rescue during the Chitral relief expedition. At that time Chitral Fort was besieged by hostile tribesmen, and its heroic defence by 400 men under Surgeon Major Robertson was to capture the public imagination almost as much as Rorke's Drift had 15 years earlier. Aylmer was with the main relief force which had to fight its way northwards from Nowshera through the Malakand Pass and up the Panjkora valley. When two soldiers were swept away on an overturned raft at a river crossing, 'Major Aylmer immediately slipped down a slack wire that was across the river and just managed to grab the soldier [the other was drowned] as he shot past. The raft was immediately dashed to pieces on the rocks below. With great difficulty they were both hauled on shore and it was then found that the Major was badly cut and bruised by the wire.'[11]

Suspension bridge over the River Panjkora, 98-foot span, built by Major Fenton Aylmer, VC.

From 1897 Aylmer held a number of staff appointments before returning to the North-West Frontier in command of the Bannu brigade. In command he displayed the same degree of imagination as had inspired his engineering innovations, becoming well known for imbuing peace-time exercises with schemes and ideas which made them enjoyable and worthwhile occasions for the participants. In 1907 he was transferred to Quetta, and in 1912 he became Adjutant-General in India. His rapid promotion and senior appointments were no small feat in circumstances in which there were strong prejudices against the employment of sappers in anything other than what was considered their only legitimate sphere, that of bricks and mortar.

It was therefore bitterly disappointing that when his final test came in 1915, as commander of the operations in Mesopotamia for the relief of Kut-el-Amara, he had to take responsibility for its failure. Poignancy was added by the fact that the 6th Indian Division, which Aylmer was attempting to rescue, was commanded by Major-General Charles Townshend who had not only been a colleague in the Hunza-Nagar expedition but had also been one of the leaders of the gallant defence of the besieged fort at Chitral in 1895. The 6th Indian Division had been forced back into Kut in December 1915 during operations against the Turks. The besieged garrison suffered terrible hardships and Aylmer felt enormous pressure to relieve them, even though his resources were inadequate. After two attempts, one in January and the other in March 1916, he had to accept failure. The garrison finally surrendered on 29 April after a siege of 147 days. Aylmer then went on to command the Mhow Divisional Area until his retirement at the end of the war.

Despite this final disappointment, Aylmer remained well regarded for his achievements and his natural powers of leadership. He was made KCB in 1916 and became a Colonel Commandant in 1922. He succeeded to the baronetcy (13th baronet of Donadea, Co. Kildare) on the death of his elder brother in 1928. He had retired from the Army at the end of the war and went to live at Wimbledon. Soon afterwards he was crippled by an accident but he remained mentally active, lecturing and writing until his death in 1935.

Malakand

Whereas Hunza-Nagar was a small war sparked off by events on a vast global stage with two great powers trying to outmanoeuvre each other, what happened throughout the North-West Frontier in 1897 was very much a home-bred rebellion but on such a scale that some 60,000 troops had to take the field before it was brought under control. It created a level of concern about British ability to contain native subversion that had not been experienced since the Uprising of 1857.

It was essentially a 'jihad', a holy war, by what in the late 20th century would be called Muslim fundamentalists. The mullahs had, in fact, been encouraged by external events, particularly the recent military success of the Muslim Turks against the Greeks. They also believed that Afghan support would be forthcoming, on the grounds that the Amir (still Abdur Rahman) was concerned about British intentions to annex areas on his border. The mullahs therefore spread sedition from north to south, fired by religious fervour, and ferocious outbreaks began to occur almost simultaneously.

These started in June with an attack on a political agent in the Tochi valley, west of Bannu, which lies some 120 miles south-west of Peshawar. The trouble spread – and British military posts 50 miles north-east of Peshawar, at Chakdarra in the Swat country, were fiercely assaulted. In August Peshawar was threatened from the north-west by Mohmands from their tribal area north of the Kabul river. It was then the turn of the Afridis and the Orakzais to the south of the river.

It took two brigades and five months finally to subdue the rising in the Tochi valley. The expedition that dealt with it was typical of many such relatively minor operations that characterised this war. There were, however, two on a much larger scale. The Tirah campaign from October through to April 1898, in which Brigadier-General Reginald Hart, VC commanded a brigade, has already been mentioned in Chapter Five. This resulted from the rebellion of the Afridis, the most numerous and widespread of the frontier tribes and the ones who had caused so much trouble in the Second Afghan War. They took the forts at Ali Masjid and Lundi Kotal and for two months the Khyber Pass was closed. The response – punitive action by 35,000 men in two divisions under Lieutenant-General Sir William Lockhart – required every valley in the Afridi Tirah, and the Bara and Bazar valleys where Hart had won his VC, to be visited and the villages laid waste. Losses in the extremely difficult country and awful weather conditions were as high as 1100.

However, we are mainly concerned with the other major operation, the Malakand Expedition centred on the Swat valley. This, although it took fewer troops, involved fighting every bit as bitter as was to be experienced in the Tirah campaign.

> The Swat valley was a special centre of religious fanaticism, and this lent an added fire to the assaults of the tribesmen which only the highest discipline and training could resist. 'At Malakand and Chakdarra,' to quote Nevill, 'and in a minor degree at Nawagai, the same reckless impulse is to be seen which hurled the Mahdists against the British squares at Abu Klea, El Teb and Omdurman, for the sake of a martyr's crown.' Religious madness is usually fleeting: it goes out when the bullet and the sword go in. But on the Malakand and at Chakdarra it gripped the enemy for eight days. It sustained them in those elaborate night attacks which were a new feature in their tactics, and it supported them against an artillery bombardment heavier than any which they had yet encountered.[12]

As the fighting developed in July, a complete division was formed on 1 August under the command of Major-General Sir Bindon Blood. Blood was an outstanding sapper officer who joined the Bengal Sappers some ten years after commissioning and had first seen active service on the Frontier in 1868. He had also taken part in the Zulu War, where he was able to see in action the pontoon he had designed some years earlier while an instructor at Chatham. He also served in the Second Afghan War and two years later was on active service again, this time in Egypt in Wolseley's 1882 campaign.

Blood's leadership and professional qualities were widely recognised and, after taking part as Chief Staff Officer in Sir Robert Low's Chitral Relief Force, in which we have already seen Major Fenton Aylmer, VC engaged, he was chosen to command in Malakand.

As a result of that earlier experience, Sir Bindon Blood (as he then became) was well acquainted both with the country in which his division was to operate and the ways of the tribesmen in the area. His plan was first to deal with the Swatis by advancing north up the Swat valley and then to turn west into the Bajaur region, the home of the Mamund clan of the Mohmand tribe. The first phase was successfully accomplished by the middle of August but not before a considerable battle at Landakai in which Bindon Blood made something of a reputation for himself by concentrating his artillery for his main attack, a precedent for frontier operations.

Blood now moved two of his brigades westwards into the Bajaur area; the 3rd Brigade, with whom he kept his own headquarters, established itself in a defensive position at Nawagai and the 2nd Brigade under Brigadier-General P.D. Jeffreys moved to Inayat Kila in the Mamund valley for the operations in which Lieutenants Thomas Watson and James Colvin were to win their VCs.

Lieutenant Thomas Colclough Watson

*Thomas Watson
(1867–1917)*

Thomas Watson was born in Velsen in Holland in 1867, the son of Thomas Watson of Dovercourt, Essex, and Eliza Holmes (née Reed). He went to school at Louth in Lincolnshire and abroad. At 30 years of age he was a senior lieutenant at the start of this campaign; he had been commissioned into the Royal Engineers in 1888. Four years later he had married Edythe, the daughter of Major-General J.W. Welchman of the Indian Army, and they had one son. His wife had been awarded the Royal Red Cross for her work during the Black Mountain expedition of 1888 and, after the award of Watson's VC, the only other couple to have this joint distinction were the Commander-in-Chief and his wife, Lord and Lady Roberts.

Lieutenant James Morris Colquhoun Colvin

*James Colvin, just
before setting off to
India in 1894*

James Colvin was the son of Mr James C. Colvin, a Bengal civil servant who had earned the Mutiny Medal for gallant service as a volunteer in the 1857 Uprising. James senior had taken part in the defence of Arrah House, an event described in some sources as 'one of the pluckiest things in the Mutiny', and in several expeditions in the district generally in command of Rattray's Sikh Police Battalion. James junior was born at Bijnore where his father was Magistrate and Collector and where his mother died two weeks after his birth. Young James went to school at Charterhouse where he had a brilliant career winning so many prizes that in later life they filled a 6-foot bookcase in his home. He was also outstandingly successful at the RMA Woolwich, passing out top of his batch in July 1889 after having been Senior Under Officer and winning the Sword of Honour and Pollock Medal. He served three years with the Bridging Battalion at Aldershot before going to India in 1894, eventually to join the Bengal Sappers and Miners at Rawalpindi after spending some frustrating months in a works appointment while waiting for a vacancy with the regiment. However, there he had been in good hands as for much of that time he was working for Colonel Bindon Blood who was a distant kinsman and they struck up a good relationship. He was with the 4th Company of the Bengal Sappers during the Chitral Relief Expedition under Major Fenton Aylmer, VC and was involved with many of the daunting bridging operations which were required on that campaign. After a brief return to Roorkee he was back in Chitral and bridge building again, for example a 290-foot

The bridge at Drosht Fort constructed by James Colvin in 1897.

suspension bridge at Drosht in February 1897 followed by a 42-foot cantilever bridge in the same area.

He was one month into some much looked forward to leave in England when the trouble broke out on the Frontier and he was recalled for duty with the Malakand Field Force. He was back in the Swat valley by 29 August.

The Mamund Valley

Jeffreys' brigade had experienced no opposition moving into the Mamund valley. However the local tribesmen were known to be hostile, unlike those at Nawagai where Sir Bindon Blood's headquarters was with the 3rd Brigade. Jeffreys had been ordered to carry out punitive operations throughout the valley by destroying any villages which might become the source of trouble before the force's main task was undertaken, an attack against the Bedmanai Pass further south, in preparation for the advance north from Peshawar of another brigade.

Jeffreys' brigade moved out on 16 September in three columns. One of these, on the right, met such stiff opposition that they were unable to reach their objective and had to return to the base camp before dark. However, the main events of the day were focused on the villages of Badelai and Shahi Tangi at the head of the valley to the north-west. After a promising start the central column, charged with this task, came up against such severe opposition that it had to be reinforced by the third column on its left. This joint force was then driven back off the high ground which it had been laboriously climbing and took up a position in a *nullah*; where they fixed bayonets and faced the enemy. Winston Churchill, accompanying the force as an observer, described the scene in his characteristic style.

> The Sikhs, who now numbered perhaps sixty, were hard pressed, and fired without effect. Then some one – who it was is uncertain – ordered the bugler to sound the 'charge'. The shrill notes rang out not once but a dozen times. Every one

began to shout. The officers waved their swords frantically. Then the Sikhs commenced to move forward towards the enemy, cheering. It was a supreme moment. The tribesmen turned, and began to retreat. Instantly the soldiers opened a steady fire, shooting down their late persecutors with a savage energy.[13]

At this stage, as well as the 35th Sikhs (six companies), there were six companies of the Buffs (Royal East Kent Regiment), five companies of the Guides Infantry, four guns of a mountain battery and the 4th Company Bengal Sappers and Miners concentrated in the area. Jeffreys was determined to achieve his aim and ordered a second attack. After a further hard slog Shahi Tangi was reached and destroyed. But by now it was mid-afternoon and it would be a race against time to withdraw to base before dark. There then followed a confused and desperate fight as the forward troops were extricated from the dangerously exposed position they were now in and the general retirement took place. The enemy, sensing an opportunity, now broke out of the north-western end of the valley 'which had been swarming with them all day' and advanced 'in a great half-moon nearly three miles long and firing continually'.[14] Casualties occurred. A thunderstorm broke, its black cloud blotting out the fading light and its flashes of lightning illuminating targets for the enemy. Contact was lost between units as, by now totally exhausted and having had no food since dawn, individual groups staggered back into camp to spend the night bedded down where they could in the mud, the tents having been struck and the perimeter reduced to facilitate protection. The wounded, who had had to endure torments as they were carried back, now had to wait until daylight and the abatement of the storm before they could be given any attention but the most basic.

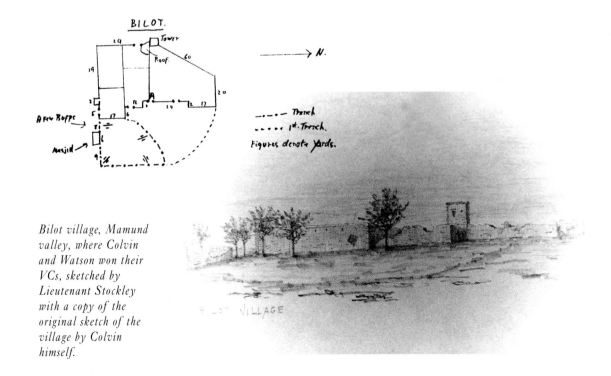

Bilot village, Mamund valley, where Colvin and Watson won their VCs, sketched by Lieutenant Stockley with a copy of the original sketch of the village by Colvin himself.

Worse still, part of the force had not made it back at all. The brigade commander, the gunners and their guns, a party of 12 of the Buffs and 45 sappers including Watson and Colvin had come together at the village of Bilot and decided to take shelter there. Unfortunately, the Mamunds had beaten them to it and a bitter struggle now ensued. The area round the houses was full of burning 'bhoosa', a kind of chopped straw, so that attempts to break in were prevented and the beleaguered party were illuminated as targets for the enemy fire at 30 yards range, from loopholes on two sides of their position. Watson and Colvin led a party of sappers and the 12 Buffs in repeated attempts to break in and drive the enemy out with the bayonet. 'Watson returned, hit in the thigh. He insisted on going out again, telling me to report to the General that we had only a few rounds left. While I was looking for the General, Watson reappeared, swaying about. He had been hit again, in the hand and arm, and was in great pain.'[15] Colvin then led two sorties climbing on to the roofs and firing down on the enemy to try and eject them from their firing positions, and when he brought his men back to the gun position, he learned that Jeffreys himself and another officer had been wounded and that only he and Lieutenant Wynter, RA remained to conduct the defence.

At 9.00 pm there was a pause in the firing while the downpour threatened to wet the enemy's powder but it started again at 10.00 pm. They hung on desperately gaining what protection they could from saddles removed from the mules and continuing to suffer casualties, including Wynter who was shot through both legs, until a relief force arrived at midnight. Churchill said of Watson:

> The attention of the reader is directed to the bravery of this officer. After a long day of marching, and fighting, in the dark, without food and with small numbers, the man who will go on, unshaken and unflinching, after he has received a severe and painful wound, has in respect of personal courage, few equals in the world. It is perhaps as high a form of valour to endure, as to dare. The combination of both is sublime.[16]

Colvin's own account in a letter to his father two days after the event has an immediacy which he obviously later regretted ('I fancy I must have written some rot in my last letter to you, as I was a bit excited.') as he wrote a more sober version on the 22 September enclosing a draft of his official report. The first of these letters ran:

> Next day we all started out i.e. day before yesterday, & were told to burn & destroy & play the dickens all round with the whole Bde. having only 8 coys. in camp. I went with 20 men & dynamite with the 35th Sikhs & Buffs 6 coys. of each & 2 guns & we got into some of the enemy. I was halted to blow up 2 towers & then went on & by gum found the 35th retiring & had to too. I had 2 men wounded. We got the men to stop at last & the Buffs & 2 guns came up & we counterattacked. Meanwhile my mules had gone goodness knows where, also my pony, (the 35th lost their adjutant whose body the brutes got hold of & mutilated fearfully, it was recovered afterwards: another officer was also wounded in the head.) so I went in search of him & found a doctor who asked me to escort his hospital as he was left alone which I did & found my pony there; & got 1/2 coy of 35th Sikhs too. Afterwards as the village was well burnt we retired all round to go to camp.

Meanwhile 2 companies of Sikhs had got lost on the top of a high ridge & the Guides who had come up had some coys sent to help 'em & we continued the retirement Buffs covering. Then Watson R.E. came up to me with 2 more sections of sappers & said we were ordered to escort the 4 guns which had collected there (2 had gone with the Guides Infy.). Just at this point a Gunner officer was killed. Then we went back a bit & it was getting late. Then the General, who is an almighty thunderous fool, by name Jeffries or something like it ordered the 4 guns & ourselves after several contradictory orders to hold a position outside a village, which was on fire & which 3 Coys. of 35th were to occupy but never arrived. It was then dark & we had no tools sent back, but we set to work with bayonets & hands to make a shelter & while we were doing it they began plugging at us around the village. Watson took half a dozen of the Buffs to turn them out & got badly hit 2 Buffs too. So I took 10 of my men & went into the village & climbed on to the roof & plugged the brutes inside over the wall near a tower with my revolver. When I thought it was all right I opened my revolver to refill it & it stuck & the brutes <u>inside</u> the village began plugging & I had to get down on the roof & refill, emptied it, but it was too hot & we went back. I did the same thing again but the men wouldn't come & I emptied my 6 rounds & had to come back. Then we lay in our shelter (which was nothing) round the guns & were plugged at till 11pm when we heard volleys & thought our help was coming. It didn't, & I had given up all hope & was feeling for my sword, when to my horror I found it had tumbled out of the scabbard somehow, so as to be ready in case they came near, but they wouldn't. They only sniped & hove stones. The general & the A.A.G. were knocked out of time with stones & I got knocked over too but I had my helmet on.[17]

All this was from someone who had written home earlier, probably after his first action: 'You can tell Bob [his young half-brother, later to be killed at Neuve Chapelle] I don't like fighting: I funk it,' and 'I think I was in a mortal funk when the bullets came.'[18]

As well as Watson and Colvin, Corporal James Smith received the Victoria Cross, and two members of the 4th Company, Bengal Sappers and Miners were awarded the Indian Order of Merit. For Colvin, the first intimation of his award came at the end of the year as he wrote to his stepmother:

This goes no further [that he might be getting a company], nor does the following bit of intelligence please – of course let Father know – Blood recommended Watson & myself for the V.C. for that 'night out' that we spent at Bilot village. It is most awful rot as far as I am concerned as I achieved nothing. However I don't see how I can get it as nobody saw me do this nothing & that is a sine qua non that there should be eyewitnesses among your superior officers. I may perhaps get a D.S.O.[19]

The operations of the Malakand Field Force did not come to an end until October by which time Sir Bindon Blood had fought a decisive defensive battle at Nawagai in September and Jeffreys' brigade had been in action again in the Mamund valley, capturing two more villages. Overall, it was April the following year before the frontier was quiet again and it then enjoyed a period of relative peace for a further ten years.

Subsequent Careers

Watson was incapacitated for some months and received his VC from Queen Victoria while on home leave in June 1898. In February 1915, he went to Mesopotamia and was appointed Commanding Royal Engineer of 12th Indian Division which was forming up as part of the build-up in that country to oppose the Turkish occupation. While there he contracted an illness as a result of which he had to retire from the Army. He lived in London and died in June 1917.

James Colvin was not much luckier than Thomas Watson as he also contracted an illness in 1915 which, although it was not the cause of his death, seriously inhibited his later career. However, by then he had notched up some considerable successes. He completed the Malakand campaign and the further operations in the Bunerwal country, also under Sir Bindon Blood, and was twice mentioned in despatches. He then went on leave and, while it was agreed that he should receive his VC from the Queen at this time, the cross itself had already been despatched to India. As he would be returning before it could be recovered, a second cross was engraved for the investiture; so, for a few months there were two crosses in circulation with his name on them. According to family tradition, in this way he fulfilled a childhood wish made at Merlin's Well, a wishing well near his mother's home at Bryn Myrddin, when he dropped in a bent pin and wished that he would get a VC, and then further wished that he would get two.

James Colvin
(1870–1945)

On his return to India, Colvin was given command of the 4th Company – an appropriate appointment in view of his gallant performance with them. In 1901 he went to South Africa, for two months as ADC to Sir Bindon Blood. Then in October he became staff officer to one of the columns engaged in the frustrating and arduous business of tracking down the Boer guerrillas, operating in the eastern Transvaal in the area centred on Carolina. His somewhat sketchy diary of those times has survived and records a tough life of marching at short notice on information of Boer activity, quick actions with casualties on both sides and never much progress seen. Nevertheless he was mentioned in despatches and promoted to brevet major in 1902.

He returned to India and for three years he was staff captain of mobilisation at Simla. During that time he met and married (in 1904) Katharine Way, daughter of Colonel J.A. Way, CB. The circumstances of his betrothal tell something of life in India at that time. On 2 September 1903 he wrote to his father:

> The gaieties of Simla still go on & this month is a very bad one – about 10 dances, which is a bit too much, everyone having gone dancing mad. There was a very nice one last night in the covered tennis court here …
>
> You seem very anxious I should get married! I may as well tell you that as far as I know there is not a girl up here – & there are crowds – who has a sixpence to her name! However you may be quite sure that when & if I do get spliced 'she' will not have a stiver[?], as you have always exhorted & expected me to 'look out' for someone with it – & they don't seem to have come my way.[20]

Two days later he wrote again:

In the year of grace 1887 you told me at Greenwich at luncheon that I must marry money. Afterwards in the billiard room we were by ourselves & you said that what you had stated at luncheon was all very well, but that a good woman was a jewel beyond price. I have not forgotten this & have found one – absolutely penniless I believe. What is worse she says she is going to marry me, which is I am afraid foolish of her but very charming. I hope that we have your approval?[21]

After his appointment in Simla, Colvin returned to England for the Camberley Staff College course but was back again on the frontier in 1911, this time at Quetta, as GSO2 24th Indian Division. Although he did well there, earning a recommendation for accelerated promotion, it was then that he contracted the illness which brought his career to an end. In fact he was able to soldier on throughout the war years but never managed to pass fit for active service. His final job was in command of the Bombay Sappers and Miners at Kirkee. It was no sinecure in view of the wartime expansion but he carried on although suffering bouts of illness, retiring eventually in 1921. He went to live at Stanway near Colchester.

His retirement was filled with a variety of voluntary activities in local affairs and in the Second World War, now in his seventies, he even managed to run a successful National Savings Group.

Epilogue

Although there had been a respite from fighting on the North-West Frontier after the 1897 rebellion, inevitably it blew up again and the area continued to be a headache for the Indian Government between the wars (the Third Afghan War occurred in 1921). At the same time it provided a unique field for operational engineering experience, from which those who were lucky enough to be connected with the Indian Army in the inter-war years gained enormous advantages in preparation for the challenges of the Second World War.

However, we must return to 1899 and another field of often bitter experience through which many of those who had fought on the frontier had now to go in South Africa.

The Great Boer War (1899–1902)

For a small isolated post and an active enemy there are no flanks, no rear, or, to put it otherwise, it is front all round. (*Lesson II from* The Defence of Duffer's Drift)[1]

In June 1897, exactly the same month as British rule was being challenged in the high passes of the North-West Frontier leading to the events described in the previous chapter, back in Britain Queen Victoria was celebrating her Diamond Jubilee. The lavish spectacle that this became was far more than a demonstration of loyalty from her British subjects.

> Through the grey and venerable streets of the capital – 'the greatest city since the ruin of Thebes' – there had passed in parade a spectacle of Empire. There were Rajput princes and Dyak headhunters, there were strapping troopers from Australia. Cypriots wore fezzes, Chinese wore conical straw hats. English gentlemen rode by, with virile moustaches and steel-blue eyes, and Indian lancers jangled past in resplendent crimson jerkins.
>
> Here was Lord Roberts of Kandahar, on the grey Arab that had taken him from Kabul to Kandahar in his epic march of 1880. Here was Lord Wolseley of Cairo and Wolseley, hero of Red River, Ashanti and Tel-el-Kebir.[2]

While at the time the Jubilee may have seemed an endorsement of Empire, a glorious apotheosis, in retrospect it was more like a zenith, a high point from which the path lay steadily downwards. No crack in the imperial edifice was more significant than the Great Boer War of 1899 to 1902. When this war broke out volunteers flocked to enlist, not just from Britain, but from the Empire as well, particularly from Australia and Canada. The early reverses suffered by the British Army only served to heighten the sense of threat to an association truly believed by its members to be the hope of the world, and to stiffen their resolve to avenge those reverses.

In fact there had been an earlier reverse, the avenging of which was to become a common rallying cry for the hard-pressed British soldiery in 1899. Nineteen years earlier the Boers had inflicted an ignominious defeat on the British Army at Majuba Hill, on the border between the Transvaal and Natal. This had brought to an end the First Boer War and with it the short-lived British rule in the Transvaal which, as we have seen in Chapter Four, had been annexed in the cause of a southern African confederation, one of the goals of the Zulu War. For Britain, Majuba was a defeat which carried significance out of all proportion to its relatively small numerical scale – the force comprised only 400 men, although losses (dead and injured) were as high as 280 – because, as James Morris points out 'It was the only

Map 10
South Africa c.1900.

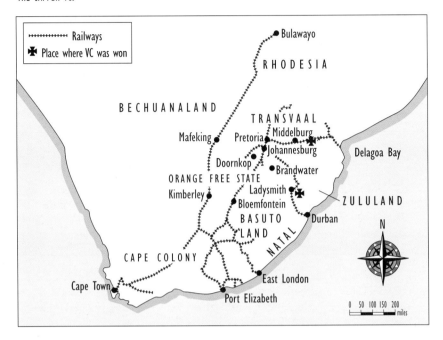

occasion in the history of Victoria's Empire when the British negotiated a peace settlement from the losers' side of the table.'³

There is one other military episode which has so far escaped the telling in this story, solely because it resulted in no sapper VCs, but which does much to explain the mood of imperial triumphalism that prevailed in 1899; and it so happened that the key players were perhaps the two most celebrated sappers in the history of the Corps, Charles Gordon and Herbert Kitchener. Gordon, whom we first met champing impatiently at the bit in the Crimean War, had achieved international acclaim for his conduct in command of a Chinese mercenary army which had helped to defeat the Tai Ping rebellion in the 1860s. Twenty years later, after an unorthodox career, he became the victim of the Mahdist forces in the Sudan after the protracted siege of Khartoum. The fate of this deeply religious and heroic figure, after the narrow failure of Lord Wolseley's elaborate and costly rescue expedition, had greatly moved every loyal Briton from the Queen down. The restoration of British authority (through their Egyptian vassals) and the avenging of Gordon became an aspiration deeply embedded in the national psyche. This was achieved on 2 September 1899 at the Battle of Omdurman by the combined British and Egyptian forces under the leadership of General Sir Herbert Kitchener. It is no wonder that the spirit of revenge invoked at Omdurman should be translated to South Africa as a spirit of revenge for Majuba, both to be symbolic of British power.

But first there had to be a war. This came about because of the total revolution in southern African affairs following the discovery of gold on the Witwatersrand (the Rand) near Johannesburg in 1887. The Transvaal was no longer to be a simple haven for the rugged and religious farming folk as had been the dream of their Voortrekker forefathers. Through gold it became a magnet for adventurers, fortune seekers and international riff-raff with whom the Afrikaner government, determined to maintain the character of their hard-won nationalism, found it hard to cope. These uitlanders, as they were called, who were beginning to outnumber the Boers, had no political status or rights. This became an issue which Cecil Rhodes, the British-born imperialist and now Prime Minister of Cape Colony – who had already made his fortune from the earlier discovery of diamonds at Kimberley, in the Orange Free State – felt he could exploit.

He believed it would be possible to prompt an uprising by the uitlanders and to this end, in 1896, an intimate colleague of his, Dr Leander Starr Jameson, undertook the ludicrously misconceived adventure of leading a motley military force from Pitsani on the Bechuanaland border to Johannesburg. Ill-timed and ill-planned, the incident ended in farce as Jameson and his men were quietly taken into custody by the Boer authorities after a fruitless gun battle and no response whatsoever from the uitlanders. Rhodes had approved the plot, although he had tried to delay its execution, and the episode led to his downfall.

It must also be remembered that, in the British mind at least, Westminster still held a vague suzerainty over the Transvaal. The status of the British colonies of Natal and Cape Colony, and the Orange Free State (which enjoyed internal self-rule) was reasonably clear, but the Pretoria Convention (1881) and London Convention (1884) which followed the Boer victory of the First Boer War, appeared to the Boers to free the Transvaal from any British control. However, Britain certainly felt a responsibility for the rights of the uitlanders – and indeed for the black inhabitants of southern Africa whose treatment by the Boers was another bone of contention. To Britain, the unsatisfactory nature of the different administrations in the southern African states could only be resolved by uniting them under the Empire. To the Boers in Pretoria, under the obstinate and single-minded leadership of their President Paul Kruger (a man steeped in Boer tradition and history, and governed only by the deep, fundamentalist religious faith he derived from the Bible, the only written word he ever read), unity might be a desirable aim but only on their terms as the rightful heirs of the country. Uitlanders could not be considered as citizens until their nationality had been proven by seven years' residence.

These irreconcilable attitudes were inevitably to lead to a clash and positions hardened after the appointment of Sir Alfred Milner as governor of Cape Colony and high commissioner for South Africa in 1897. After a few months studying the situation Milner was able to convince the home government under Lord Salisbury, and the Colonial Secretary Joseph Chamberlain, of his belief that nothing short of war against the Transvaal would resolve the political situation in southern Africa and secure the future of the British (and other uitlander) people. The steps by which Milner and Chamberlain contrived to provoke the Boers into pre-emptive action against the British need not be detailed here, but it should be noted that British military preparations had seriously lagged behind the political steps. Partly this was due to a deliberately passive attitude of the Commander-in-Chief of British forces in South Africa, General Sir William Butler, because of his conviction that 'war between the white races ... would be the greatest calamity that ever occurred in South Africa'.[4] But the War Office seemed to be of like mind because, despite the urging of the Commander-in-Chief, Lord Wolseley, no plan had been drawn up for such a campaign. By the time the Boers declared war on 11 October 1899, the new Commander-in-Chief in South Africa, Lieutenant-General F.W. Forestier-Walker, had only been in the Cape for five weeks, the new commander in Natal, Lieutenant-General Sir George White, VC had been in post less than a month and total British strength in South Africa amounted to only 22,000 men and 60 guns.

Meanwhile all units that could possibly be spared from the widespread and already heavily committed British Army were assembled into a huge force of some 47,000 men under the leadership of the popular and heroic figure of Sir Redvers Buller, VC, and began to arrive in South Africa during November. The sappers, under their Chief Engineer Major-General Elliott Wood, sent a field company with each of the three infantry divisions plus Army Corps Troops of another field company, a field park, a bridging battalion, a telegraph 'division' and the 1st Balloon Section. There were also Lines of Communication units; and a railway company and five fortress companies, the latter for general support of the railway system which was to prove a key factor in the war, and also to run the Steam Road Transport branch. All these added to the two field companies, one fortress company and a railway company that were already in the theatre. By December 1899 there were some 3500 sappers in South Africa and this was eventually to build up to well over 5000 adding more specialities including pontooning, searchlights, survey and photo reconnaissance.

By the time Buller and his force were in the theatre, the Boers had seized the initiative by besieging Mafeking on the Bechuanaland border, the diamond town of Kimberley in the Orange Free State and Ladysmith in Natal. These three sieges were to dictate the course of operations in the early part of the war and each provides a fascinating story in itself – but we are only concerned with the events at Ladysmith.

Ladysmith

Before the Boer invasion of Natal, the general plan had been that on his arrival Buller would advance with his force from Cape Colony along the general line of the Central Railway and move on Bloemfontein (capital of the Free State) and Pretoria while Sir George White's force would hold the border areas of Natal. To that end Ladysmith had been built up into a great military depot more because of its situation on the Natal Railway than for any tactical or strategic reasons. It lay in a bowl overlooked by hills; those to its north might have provided a firm line of defence had a sufficient force been concentrated there from the start, although a far more realistic position lay some 20 miles further back where the railway crossed the Tugela river at Colenso.* Unfortunately, when the Boer invasion took place a large proportion of Buller's force was too absorbed in two early battles at Talana and Elandslaagte to stave off the incursions from the north-east. Although both were British victories, after some particularly doughty fighting in which both sides suffered severely, White was unable to capitalise on them and instead concentrated on Ladysmith and tried to defeat the Boer advance by attacking before they could take up position around the town. Three ill-conceived piecemeal attacks failed and by 2 November the town was surrounded.

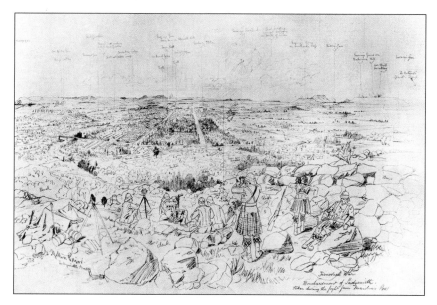

A sketch of Ladysmith by Melton Prior of the Illustrated London News *taken from a point on the Platrand to the east of Wagon Hill.*

From every angle this was a disaster. Morale in the army plummeted as people realised that the Boers had secured a victory fighting on equal terms. Sir George White's own morale deteriorated to the point that he felt unable to show his face more than necessary in the forthcoming siege, let alone undertake offensive action such as was to be so effective at Mafeking. This was a sad come-down for a man with such a record of brilliance in the field. Worst of all, the whole strategic plan had to be recast and Buller decided to take control of events in Natal himself, making the relief of Ladysmith his main strategic aim. Late in November he moved to Frere to take command of the 19,000 troops now concentrated there, leaving 1st Division under Lord Methuen to advance into the Free State towards Kimberley.

Worse was to follow. In the second week of December, the British suffered three appalling defeats: at Magersfontein, where Methuen's division was mauled attempting a frontal assault after a night march on well dug-in Boer positions; at

---

*Only 50 miles west, incidentally, of the point where Chard made his epic stand at Rorke's Drift on the Umzinyati (Buffalo) river, a tributary of the Tugela. See Chapter Four.

Stormberg in the Eastern Cape Colony where General Gatacre also attempted a night march and lost virtually his entire force of about 3000 men; and, lastly and most significantly, at Colenso where Buller's first attempt to move to the relief of Ladysmith was defeated. The most notable casualty of this affair was Lieutenant the Honourable Frederick Roberts, son of the field marshal who at that stage was Commander-in-Chief in Ireland. Young Roberts died a hero's death attempting to save some guns which had been imprudently positioned in a vulnerable position, for which he was awarded the VC. Before Roberts senior had learned of his son's death, the events of this 'Black Week' had decided the home government to invite him, the only senior general with the experience of independent field command, to go to South Africa to take overall command of operations. At 67 it was felt that Roberts should have a younger deputy and the 49-year-old Lord Kitchener, fresh from his triumph at Omdurman, was appointed as Chief of Staff. Roberts also brought with him as Adjutant-General another sapper, Colonel Sir William Nicholson, the future Field Marshal Lord Nicholson of Roundhay.

Back at Ladysmith two aggressive sorties had already taken place despite Sir George White's somewhat negative attitude. Both were designed to take out enemy gun positions and were accompanied by sappers who destroyed the guns

Map II

The Ladysmith area during the siege.

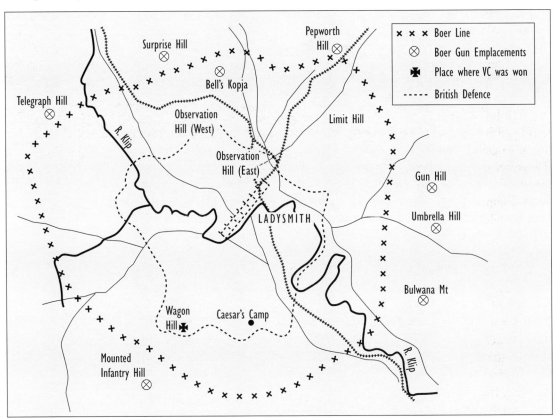

with guncotton charges. But the garrison then became further depressed by the news of Colenso and settled in for a long and passive siege. White's strength was now some 13,500 which included 23 Field Company and No. 2 Balloon Section. The Balloon Section had already made a name for itself in the battles before the siege and now continued to provide useful information to the great discomfort of the Boers – until the supply of gas ran out. The officer commanding 23 Field Company, now Commanding Royal Engineer, concentrated largely on strengthening the defences, preparing gun positions and wire obstacles with a few improvised mines. The key to the defence, which became the scene of much of this work, was a ridge of high ground to the south of the town known as the Platrand (sometimes referred to as Bester's Hill), about three miles in length, with a prominent feature at either end, Caesar's Camp to the east and Wagon Hill to the west.

In general the Boers seemed content to let this continue but early in January they received information that Buller was planning a second attempt to relieve the besieged garrison and decided to try to pre-empt this by a strong attack on the Platrand. It was there that Lieutenant Robert Digby Jones had been detailed to supervise the installation of two naval 12-pounder guns and a 4.7-inch howitzer known as Lady Anne on Wagon Hill.

Lieutenant Robert Digby Jones

Robert Digby Jones was the son of Charles and Aimée Digby Jones. He went to school at Alnmouth and later to Sedbergh in Yorkshire where he had a fine record as a sportsman. He was also academically bright enough to pass sixth into the Royal Engineers Division at the RMA Woolwich and was commissioned in August 1896. After his courses at Chatham, where he again had been active in rugby football and golf, he joined 23 Field Company and with them arrived in Natal in June 1899. The company went straight to Ladysmith where they were employed in camp works and later on the defences. Digby Jones had been the Royal Engineer with the second of the two sorties already mentioned, on 11 December against Surprise Hill, to the north-west of the town. The party, five companies of the Rifle Brigade under the command of their commanding officer, and accompanied by the sappers, had ejected the enemy from the hill, kept them at bay while the sappers blew up the gun, and fought their way back albeit with severe casualties. Digby Jones was mentioned in despatches for his part in the operation.

Then on 5 January Digby Jones was given the task on Wagon Hill. The whole of the Platrand position was under the command of Colonel Ian Hamilton, a survivor of Majuba and later, as General Sir Ian Hamilton, to gain notoriety as Commander-in-Chief of the ill-fated Gallipoli force in 1915. The position had been inadequately prepared for defence. Caesar's Camp was defended by the Manchester Regiment and Wagon Hill by 25 men of the Imperial Light Horse with their two officers. Another Royal Engineer, Second Lieutenant George Denniss, the officer in charge of this section of the defences, was also present. Fortunately the party moving the guns under Digby Jones was in considerable

Robert Digby Jones
(1876–1900)

strength. As well as 33 NCOs and men from 23 Field company there were ten Royal Navy with their working party of 100 infantry for the guns, another working party of 50 with Digby Jones and an escort of 70 Gordon Highlanders.[5] Thomas Pakenham describes the scene at 2.40 am:

> In the chiaroscuro cast by the sappers' lanterns came the usual cheery sounds that accompanied Lady Anne on her progress: the grating of the wagons, the similar eloquence of the British NCOs, the grousing of the men, Africans calling their oxen 'damned Dutchmen'. Suddenly, a new sound. Flip, flop, flip, flop: the sound of rifle bullets splashing on the stones around them. One of the Sappers described it. 'What the hell'? A report of rifles. We kicked the lamps out and dashed for our rifles. Into the sangar we went. Some poor devils panicked – they couldn't find their rifles and began to run. Young Digby Jones jumped on to a rock … drew a revolver and said [to the stampeding sappers] 'The first man that passes me I'll shoot him dead.'
>
> Wagon Hill was now a confused mass of shouting men, and criss-crossed by rifle bullets, striking sparks as they bounced off the rocks. The pickets supposed to protect this vital crest were less than a hundred men of the Imperial Light Horse. They wore the same slouch hats as the Boers, which added to the confusion. Against the glare of a Boer searchlight, somehow brought into action, several Free Staters poured on to the ridge, beating down the pickets. Fortunately for the garrison, the ILH had built one small 'fort': a loop-holed ring of stones, about twenty feet around. This was the sangar into which rushed Digby Jones and some of the sappers. Others took refuge in the gun emplacement prepared for one of the 12-pounders.[6]

If they 'took refuge', they also made a determined enough stand to keep the Boers off the top of Wagon Hill and moved out to a forward ring which they maintained until 5.45 am when reinforcements began to arrive under Major Miller-Wallnutt of the Rifle Brigade – all this under the command of Digby Jones, the two ILH officers having been wounded early in the engagement. Three miles away at Caesar's Camp things had not gone so well. Without the benefit of any force to boost their inadequate strength, the Manchesters' pickets were overrun and soon the enemy were in possession of that end of the ridge. There then followed a series of ill-coordinated events as guns were brought forward to bombard the Boers at Caesar's Camp and more reinforcements ordered up. On Wagon Hill the Boers penalised any movement, including some gallant counter-attacks by men of the 60th Rifles, with accurate and fatal fire from their Mausers but by 11.00 am the shooting died down and Major Robert Spring Rice, commanding 23 Field Company, who had come up to give support to his men, asked that they should pull back for some well-earned lunch.

At about 1.00 pm Digby Jones and Miller-Wallnutt were joined by Hamilton in the gun position they were occupying. Suddenly, Second Corporal Hunt of 23 Company fell dead beside them, victim of a shot from a small party of Boers who had come back over the crest, driven back the line of defenders and arrived unseen at Lady Anne. This very brave attack was led by two senior Free State commanders, Commandant C.J. de Villiers and Field Cornet de Jagers.* There then followed a desperate shoot-out between these two command groups. In Major Rice's version:

> In a moment Digby Jones picked up a rifle, dashed round the end of the epaulment, and killed de Villiers. L.-Corpl. Hockaday R.E., at the same time shot de Jagers dead. Digby Jones was heard to say, 'What's up? The infantry have gone.' A man replied: 'There is an order to retire, sir.' Jones said: 'I have had no order to retire.' A sergeant of the I.L.H. who was near him said 'Don't let's retire, sir; lets give them Elandslaagte again.' … Digby Jones at once ordered bayonets to be fixed, and, calling on his men to follow him, led them (with Denniss) at the charge, re-occupying the firing-line in front of the 4.7-inch emplacement.[7]

Shortly afterwards, Miller-Wallnutt was shot dead. In Conan Doyle's version,[8] it was de Villiers who shot Miller-Wallnutt, Hamilton then fired at de Villiers but missed and de Villiers was then shot by Trooper Albrecht of the Imperial Light Horse. De Jagers then shot Albrecht and Digby Jones shot de Jagers. The confusion of these accounts reflects the confusion of the situation and the lack of surviving witnesses, because almost at once Digby Jones was himself shot. As *The Times* put it: 'It was all the work of a moment, but six brave men lay extended on the ground.' A final tragedy followed when young Denniss went out just to rescue the, as he thought wounded, Digby Jones and was himself killed. Hamilton might

The Wagon Hill memorial to Robert Digby Jones and his fellow sappers, killed in action there on 6 January 1900.

(IWM Q80946)

---

*A field cornet was in charge of the men raised from a particular 'wyk' or ward; a commandant of a commando, the men from a whole district.

reasonably have despaired at this sudden misfortune; however he was able to send a typically up-beat note to Colonel Sir Henry Rawlinson, a key member of Sir George White's staff:

> My dear Rawley. Wot [sic] a day we are having ... Probably the first time the Boers have been outBoered in this way ... I hope you are all fit and cheery ... Thine Ian H.[9]

The fighting continued, even involving yet another advance by the sappers under Major Rice, until, although it seemed probable that the Boers would give up when night fell, Hamilton was given the Devons and ordered to despatch them on a last counter-attack. This, conducted in a torrential thunderstorm and against continuing deadly fire, was finally and heroically successful albeit with the loss of all their company officers, and the Boers did indeed withdraw.

The Boers had made other attacks on the positions around the Ladysmith perimeter but that on the Platrand was by far the most important. Its loss could have led to the collapse of any will to prolong the siege. As it was, neither side took any further aggressive action and the pressures now came on the Boers to raise the siege in order to free forces for elsewhere. They never did and it was to be another two months before, on 28 February 1900, they finally withdrew under pressure from Buller's ponderous advance. For the besieged it was a question of hanging on. White soon accepted that he would never be in a position to break out and this enabled him to agree to the slaughter of cavalry horses to feed the garrison and the population. The diet was thus doubly improved as, by the same decision, the stocks of maize could now be reallocated for human consumption. Thus they eked out their existence until relief came. That they were able to do so was due to the outcome of the only major engagement of the siege which itself had depended so critically on the resolution of one junior sapper officer. In the opinion of the *South African Review* of 24 February 1900, 'So far as can humanly be judged, it was this officer who saved Ladysmith and the British arms from the mortification of defeat and its incalculable consequences.'[10]

Whether or not Digby Jones saved Ladysmith, Hamilton had no doubts about Digby Jones's role or the performance of Trooper Albrecht. The old question of posthumous VCs was again revived. This was a different case from that of the Kashmir Gate where the awards had been provisionally conferred on Home and Salkeld by the GOC. The now established procedure was therefore followed of publishing a memorandum in the *London Gazette* that the VC would have been conferred on Digby Jones and Albrecht had they survived, and the crosses were given to the relatives of both recipients but only after considerable argument had raged between the Commander-in-Chief, the War Office civilian and military, and the Treasury (there were four other cases at the time). Later in the war more cases arose which had the same treatment but the most significant break with precedent came when the King was finally persuaded to allow VCs to be sent to relatives in six cases prior to the South African War, including two from Isandlwana. There was, however, no written change to the rules at this stage and, come the start of the First World War, posthumous awards were made simply on the grounds that there was nothing in the warrant to disallow them. The matter was not finally cleared up until the warrant of 1920.

The joy at the relief of Ladysmith was much tarnished by the cost of the achievement. Colenso, in Black Week, had been only the first of Buller's reverses on the Tugela river. Early in January he had decided to make his second attempt to force the river line, this time by outflanking Colenso some 20 miles further west at Trichardt's Drift. The difficulty of movement in the broken country precluded surprise and the enemy had time to strengthen their defences on Spion Kop, the high ground overlooking Trichardt's Drift. By the failure of the 5th Division to capture it, and for the awful casualties unnecessarily sustained there, Spion Kop has come to exemplify the poor leadership and incompetence of the generals in the Boer War. Sadly, for sappers, the commander of 5th Division was a sapper, Sir Charles Warren, who had acquired a reputation as a field commander in the Cape Frontier Wars, led a successful expedition to Bechuanaland, although he had not been required to fight and, curiously, had held the post of chief commissioner of the Metropolitan Police in which he was much criticised for their failure to track down Jack the Ripper. Between them Buller and Warren displayed, as it turned out, fatal indecision which resulted in a humiliating withdrawal. A further failure at Vaal Krantz to the east completed this sorry tale, the real tragedy of which is that on both occasions the Boers had been within an ace of giving up in the face of the dogged performance of the battalions; hundreds of lives had been lost apparently for lack of enterprise and resolution on the part of the high command. History has gradually cast a more understanding light on these deficiencies and it is apparent that even at the time many of the participants realised what a difficult task faced Buller and Warren. Both can claim some credit for the final, successful crossing of the Tugela at Hlangwane to the east of Colenso where with better use of ground, better co-ordination between arms and better fieldcraft learned from bitter experience, the Boers were finally prised off their positions and the way to Ladysmith lay open.

Lord Roberts in Command

Another strong influence in the Boers' withdrawal from Natal was doubtless the actions of Lord Roberts in the Free State. Roberts had arrived in Cape Town on 10 January, a few days after Digby Jones's exploit on Wagon Hill and two weeks before the disaster on Spion Kop. By 15 January he was in his field headquarters at Waterval Drift just south of the Modder River where his army was concentrated. His main aim was to seize the initiative. To this end he had made the decision to advance towards the Free State capital, Bloemfontein, not by the expected route along the Central Railway which crossed the River Orange at Norval's Pont, but across country from the Modder using wagons rather than the railway for transport. However, he could not ignore three main problems which faced him.

A typical sapper-built rail diversion. Railways were the lifeblood of the British Army in South Africa.

First, Buller in Natal was claiming his share of the reinforcements now pouring into the Cape. Buller could reasonably argue in his support that he was facing by far the largest enemy force of any deployed and was having to operate in the most difficult country. Secondly, Roberts had to accept that something had to be done about Kimberley. The siege there had become something of a public relations matter as among the besieged was Cecil Rhodes, still a powerful influence in the country. Rhodes had fallen out with the military commander in Kimberley, Colonel Robert Kekewich, and made a public fuss both about the position inside the garrison and about the apparent lack of determination in the British Army to come to its relief. Last but not least Roberts had to deal with the problem of the entrenched Boer force under the veteran Piet Cronje at Magersfontein which had so tragically held up Methuen five weeks earlier. Roberts's decisions on these points were, first, to deny any further reinforcement of Natal; if necessary Buller could go on the defensive while his own operations developed from the west. Secondly, he would have to put the relief of Kimberley high on the agenda and this also argued for the River Modder as the springboard for his next moves. Lastly, he would deal with the Magersfontein position by a swift outflanking movement to the east.

The detail of the outcome of these decisions is an intriguing story in itself. Here we need only record that Kimberley was relieved on 15 February by the Cavalry Division under Lieutenant-General John French and that the flanking operation to bypass Magersfontein resulted in Cronje's army, some 5000 strong, being caught, surrounded and forced to surrender at Paardeberg on 27 February. It is worth noting that Paardeberg was the occasion when the balloons, operated by the Royal Engineers, reached a peak of operational efficiency. They were in constant use throughout the investment and significantly contributed to the effectiveness of the artillery and to the identification of the enemy positions and movements. Thus the tide began at last to turn against the Boers and the two Boer capitals, Bloemfontein and Pretoria, now beckoned. Although successful, these moves had not been achieved without some setbacks. This revealed something of the strengths and weaknesses of both sides which were to become increasingly apparent as the war progressed.

The main Boer strengths were their mobility, understanding of the country and flexibility of action. Many times they had proved themselves capable of lightning strikes to the great discomfort of the more pedestrian, baggage-encumbered British Army. The British, for their part, needed their logistics to maintain their vastly superior force. This constrained their operations and, in particular, made the railways a dominating factor in planning. Roberts's determination to press on to Pretoria was going to leave his lines of communication vulnerable to attack by marauding Boer commandos who took many opportunities to exploit this weakness. Thousands of soldiers had to be allocated to the protection of these lines, something which must have seemed all too familiar to Roberts from his Afghan War days.

Roberts entered Bloemfontein on 13 March, reached the River Vaal 200 miles to the north on 24 May and entered Johannesburg on 31 May. This was no triumphal progress. It all had to be fought for and the elusive Boer commandos in the field sought out and dealt with. The main enemy opposition was a force of some 6000 men under the leadership of Christiaan de Wet who remained perhaps the greatest thorn in the British flesh throughout the war. To reach Bloemfontein Roberts had planned a pincer movement of two divisions but with the cavalry division (under Lieutenant-General French) sweeping ahead to cut off the Boer retreat. In contrast to his highly successful dash to the relief of Kimberley, French unfortunately failed to deliver on this occasion and de Wet and his force escaped. He led something of a Boer revival and the British advance was held up at Karee Siding north of Bloemfontein on 29 March and suffered a severe jolt when, in a brilliant guerrilla action at Sanna's Post two days later, de Wet's men trapped an 1800-strong British force killing or wounding 159 and capturing 421 and a large quantity of stores. After crossing the Vaal and as he approached Johannesburg, Roberts sent the cavalry off again on the left flank while Ian Hamilton, now a lieutenant-general in command of one of the columns (Roberts having arranged for his transfer from Buller's command), carried out a successful, if expensive, set-piece attack on the enemy at Doornkop just south of the Rand on 28 May, incidentally, at the very spot at which Dr Jameson had surrendered after his abortive raid in 1896. Only three days later, however, Christiaan de Wet's brother Piet fell on an unsupported battalion of the Imperial Yeomanry and took over 500 prisoners.

These are only examples of the setbacks which attended the British in South Africa as Roberts pursued his main goal. As well as the operational difficulties, the Army was also beginning to suffer severely from the effects of its extended lines of communication. The railways were essential to the progress of the advance but the Boers took every opportunity to deny their use to their enemy by effective demolitions. The sappers were continually stretched to deal with this problem. Overall command of the railway system was in the enlightened hands of the 33-year-old Canadian, Lieutenant-Colonel Percy Girouard, who had made his name in the Sudan in charge of building Kitchener's railway across the Nubian desert. He created a military-led task force for the repair of lines damaged by enemy action which included a Railway Pioneer Regiment recruited from pre-war miners and artisans from the Johannesburg area.* Most serious of all was the overstretch in the medical services which caused something of a scandal evoking memories of Scutari in the Crimean War. Deaths from disease (enteric fever was a particular killer) far outnumbered those from enemy action.

Nevertheless, Roberts's inexorable march on Pretoria continued and he entered the city on 5 June. On the way new tactics were developed all the time by the British. One such was to launch raids behind the enemy lines to cut the railways and so help to close escape routes. This task fell to the Cavalry Division and a leading exponent in the art was the commander of the sapper field troop with the division, Brevet Major Aylmer Hunter-Weston.

Maurice's *The War in South Africa* describes one such incident. A small party of an officer and seven men from his own troop with two guides set out at 1.00 am riding north-east across difficult country 'seamed with deep and steep-banked spruits' – difficult enough in the moonlight but very hazardous after 3.00 am when the moon set. They reached their target at 4.20 am, cutting a telegraph line on the way, blew up a double spanned culvert and headed back as it was getting light. Quite soon they ran into a strong Boer force entrenched in one of the sluits. 'To hesitate meant destruction, for only thirty yards separated the British patrol from the hostile picquet, and there was no cover to be had. Hunter-Weston, therefore, followed by the rest of the party in single file, galloped straight at the donga, and forced his horse to jump down into its bed.'[11] They just got away from the surprised Boers who chased them as they galloped across the broken country in open order. One sapper's horse stumbled in another donga, leaving him in mortal danger. Sergeant Engleheart of the 10th Hussars went back to help him while the rest of the patrol kept on at a slow trot under Lieutenant Charles of the Royal Engineers. Engleheart just managed to rescue the sapper before the Boers caught up with him and for this gallant act he was awarded the VC. The party made it back to base by 6.00 am. By this action valuable railway equipment was caught at Bloemfontein and captured, including 25 engines and 108 coaches and trucks.

---

*This regiment was commanded by Major J.E. Capper (eventually Major-General Sir John Capper, KCB, KCVO) who later gained fame developing airships for the Air Battalion (see Chapter Thirteen) and as a tank specialist in the First World War. His Adjutant was Captain E.D. Swinton (later Major-General Sir Ernest Swinton, KBE, CB, DSO) who was also closely involved in tank development. Swinton was the author of the classic satirical commentary on infantry tactics in the Boer War, *The Defence of Duffer's Drift*.

On 11 May an even more ambitious raid was ordered by French as his cavalry went on to the north of Kroonstad. An expedition moved off under Hunter-Weston at 5.30 pm.

> This time the little party [of sappers] was accompanied by an escort 100 strong, who, however, returned after three hours marching, taking with them three Boer spies, who were captured very shortly after setting out. The party, consisting of 2 officers and 6 N.C.O.s and men, R.E. [including Corporal Frank Kirby], continued their journey, eventually reaching Kronstadt [sic]. Owing to the district being infested with Boer patrols, they experienced great difficulty in reaching the railway line. Disaster was narrowly averted at this point; the party perceived a mounted patrol, and only escaped being challenged by bending down along their horses' necks and letting them graze. Whilst so situated the party was challenged by 3 Boers, who appeared almost directly under their horses' noses; these were promptly disarmed and told to sit down and keep quiet, or be bayoneted. The party now blew up the railway …[12]

They finally regained the main body but not before another narrow escape in which a man was wounded and Kirby's horse killed.

The hazardous nature of these operations can be gauged from these accounts. Corporal Frank Kirby took part in both. On the first occasion he was nearly caught when he left the main body to search for a culvert. On the second his horse was killed during the retirement. Thus he knew what to expect when he set out in a 200-strong column under Hunter-Weston on 1 June 1900. He may even have witnessed the inspiring example of Sergeant Engleheart. However, he had already proved his own courage in March at Bloemfontein where he had won the DCM for showing 'special gallantry in the face of the enemy'. He was soon to find himself in an almost identical predicament to Engleheart's.

Corporal Frank Kirby

Frank Howard Kirby was a south Londoner who had been educated at Alleyn's School. He enlisted in the Royal Engineers in 1892.

Frank Kirby in South Africa

During the last few days before Roberts's arrival in Pretoria on 5 June, there had naturally been some dismay and difference of opinion among the Boer leadership as to what action should now be taken. Any ideas of a last stand were undermined by the quiet departure of President Kruger on 31 May and the removal of all war material from the city under the orders of General Louis Botha, army commandant general. One influence on Kruger's decision may have been his belief that Roberts was planning to send a task force to cut the Delagoa Bay Railway, the vital link to the coast which was now the only remaining escape route for the government. Kruger was correct; Roberts was going to do just that.

At 6.30 pm on 1 June Major Aylmer Hunter-Weston led out his party, this time 200-strong. Their objective was the bridge on the Pretoria–Delagoa Bay Railway at Bronkhorstspruit. They had 50 miles to cover and doubtless it was difficult to conceal the movements of such a large body. Certainly, at 9.00 am the following morning they ran into a very much stronger force of Boers. There was no alternative but to retire although in the process an officer was killed and 13 men wounded, one of whom died later.[13] It was in the course of this action that Corporal Kirby earned his VC. He had attempted to rescue the officer who initially was only wounded, but had had to abandon the attempt when the officer was killed by another shot.

> Kirby then caught a spare horse and took it to a man of the 9th Lancers, whose horse had broken away, thus enabling him to escape. The Boers approaching rapidly, compelled the Lancers to take cover in some Kraals. One of their number, a corporal, was left behind owing to his horse being killed by the enemy. Kirby, seeing this, returned about 400 yards for him and, after great difficulty, under a hot fire, managed to get the thoroughly exhausted man on to his horse and bring him to safety. The Boers at the time were within 200 yards. It was noticeable at the time that two Boers who were near to Kirby did not fire during the actual time he was getting the man on his horse.[14]

Lieutenant-General
Lord Kitchener
of Khartoum,
c. 1900

There now followed some months of consolidation in an attempt to bring the war to a close. Kitchener was despatched south to put the lines of communications under control. Buller's forces moved forward from Natal achieving some notable tactical successes on the way and Roberts and Buller personally met up for the first time in Pretoria in July. Several more major battles were fought and several times the Boers seemed near to defeat, but the most determined managed to slip away and re-form ready to fight again. For example, in July in the Brandwater Basin, 9000 Boers were surrounded and formed themselves into four columns to attempt a breakout through the passes. Only one column got away. By the end of September Lord Roberts reported to the Secretary of State for War that 'organized resistance of the two Republics might be said to have ceased'.[15] Milner was appointed administrator of the two colonies. Buller returned home in October. The same month President Kruger escaped to exile in France and Roberts handed over command to Kitchener, to the chagrin of many generals more senior. In December Roberts returned to England, succeeding Wolseley as Commander-in-Chief.

But the war was not over. There now lay before the British forces in South Africa another 18 months of hard grind before finally bringing the Boers to terms in a bitter guerrilla war often involving draconian, unpopular and controversial methods. More casualties were to be suffered in this period than in the whole of the time up to the occupation of Pretoria. Individually the Afrikaner people had dreadful dilemmas of conscience to resolve. It was clear to most that the British could never be defeated. The realistic choice was to return home to rebuild their shattered lives and the country's economy. To that end many turned over either to open support of the British or at least to passive compliance. But others, who came to be known as the 'bitter-enders', became even more hardened in their resolve to fight on however difficult the struggle. The guerrilla columns that resulted performed prodigies under leaders such as Christiaan de Wet, Jan Smuts (later to become a staunch friend of Britain in two world wars and a field marshal

The network of blockhouses was the key to controlling the movement of the Boers in the guerilla phase of the Boer War.

in the British Army), 'Koos' de la Rey, General P.H. Kritzinger and Judge Barry Hertzog.

Defeating these leaders required special, often harsh, measures. Kitchener formed up independent columns to take on the Boers at their own game. However, most of the army was engaged in more formal cordon and search operations, and fighting patrols were based in a network of static posts. Blockhouses were designed for this purpose and their construction, support and maintenance became a major sapper task. Initially the blockhouses were intended to protect the railways, which would always have to provide the framework for operations, but later they were extended in lines across the open country, each blockhouse about half to three quarters of a mile apart and protected by wire and other obstacles. Some 8000 blockhouses were built, disposed over a total length of about 3000 miles. By the end of 1901 the blockhouse system had developed a more positive role in containing the guerrilla columns and, combined with the work of the British columns such as that with which Captain James Colvin, VC was working, was beginning to pay off.

The guerrillas had to be denied their means of sustenance. Farms were systematically burnt and homeless Boer families accommodated in concentration camps. The alleged mismanagement and deaths from hunger and disease in these camps became a highly contentious political issue but Kitchener pressed on with the remorseless energy and determination for which he had become renowned.

The Boers continued to achieve some remarkable victories but it was not enough. The inevitable end came as their manpower was gradually reduced to a level where continuation was impracticable against the apparently inexhaustible resources of Britain. It was Kitchener who contrived the first step that led to an acceptable conclusion. He arranged for all the Boer commando leaders to be brought in with guarantees against capture to a meeting at Vereeniging on 11 May 1902 where they could first discuss their own position and then negotiate the terms under which the war could be ended. On the British side the struggle was between Milner, standing out for total submission of the Boers, and Kitchener, who wanted the whole miserable affair brought to a respectable conclusion as soon as possible. He had already been selected to serve as Commander-in-Chief in India and the desire to move on may have been uppermost in his mind. But by this stage all the British military had conceived a deep professional respect for the Boer military leaders and saw that these people, and not the uitlanders or other men incarcerated in the camps, now represented the future of South Africa. There was a multitude of differing issues and opinions to be satisfied, but it was Kitchener with his single-minded but lucid vision who ensured that sufficient concessions were granted to the Boers to allow for the restoration of peace and the continuation of the reconstruction process.

Aftermath

Herbert Kitchener duly went to India in 1902 after a brief visit home when he received the honours of a viscountcy and the GCMG. The remainder of his career is well known – he became a field marshal in 1909 and Secretary of State for War in 1914, creating the army which was to form the backbone of the British armed forces in France in the First World War.

At his level, Frank Kirby's progress was no less impressive. The Delagoa Bay Railway raid resulted in promotion to troop sergeant-major, as well as the VC which, incidentally, he only learned about from a newspaper cutting sent to him by a relative from home. He was back in England by the end of 1901 and his homecoming was marked by a colossal party held in the NCOs' Mess at Chatham at which the other guest-of-honour was Sergeant G.E. Nurse, VC of the Royal Field Artillery, who had won his award alongside Lieutenant Frederick Roberts trying to save the guns at Colenso. After a florid speech of welcome to the two heroes from the chairman, Kirby replied in predictable vein.

> He trusted that he did his duty ... He was one of the lucky ones who had had the opportunity ... The good training he received at Chatham had a lot to do with it (hear hear). He was not much of a speaker, so he would call upon Serjt. Nurse to help him out of the difficulty (laughter and cheers).
>
> Serjt. Nurse, who was loudly cheered, said the one thing above another he hated was talking. ... He must stand up and say something, but he would rather shoot CSM Kirby for bringing him there (laughter). It was often said that Engineers were seldom, if ever, in the firing line. Those who talked like that should have seen them as he had seen them. In a hot engagement, at a railway crossing, Engineers came up with sandbags, in the face of death, to save a few men, and he did not know what they wanted more than that for the firing line (cheers) ...[16]

After tours as CSM and QMSI (Quartermaster Sergeant Instructor), Kirby himself became RSM at Chatham in 1906 and was commissioned in 1911 and posted to the Air Battalion. When that unit gave birth to the Royal Flying Corps the following year, he transferred and spent the rest of his career in aviation. He became

Frank Kirby
(1871–1956),
second from right,
standing.

Stores Officer at the central flying school at Upavon and, by now a captain, went to France in 1916 in command of 3rd Army Aircraft Park at Trevent. By December the same year he was back in England as a major, taking over command of No. 1 Stores Depot at Kidbrook. He went on in this burgeoning business to be Inspector of Stores Depots (lieutenant-colonel) in 1917 and to command the Technical Group, Royal Air Force (colonel) in 1918. He served on in the stores and technical side of the Royal Air Force earning an OBE in 1919 and a CBE in 1926. He retired at the age of 55 with permission to retain the rank of Group Captain (colonel). On retirement he turned his talents to the commercial world and became managing director of Sika Limited, Constructional Waterproofing Contractors based in Victoria Street in London. While at Chatham Kirby had married Kate Jolly in 1909; they had two daughters.

The Boer War had been a severe test for both the Army and the nation. It was followed by a series of studies and committees to look at ways of reorganising the Army, culminating in the Haldane reforms of 1906. Much the same ground was covered by these studies as was later to be gone over again in the second half of the 20th century. For the Royal Engineers the arguments have a familiar ring: who was to be responsible for transportation, works services, communications; how should the Royal Engineers fit in to the chain of command and how should the various specialisations be organised; what would be the effect on careers of reorganisation? In the reforms which doubtless placed the Army in a much better position to face wars yet to come, one lesson from South Africa had escaped most of the military thinkers – that the accuracy, range and effectiveness of small arms, and particularly the machine-gun, had swung the balance of advantage on the battlefield from attack to defence. It was the consequence of this that was now to result in the winning of a further 24 sapper VCs.

The lamps are going out all over Europe; we shall not see them lit again in our life-time. (Lord Grey of Fallodon)

By 1914 the Royal Engineers could view with pride the 27 VCs awarded to its members. Doubtless many regular soldiers then setting off to war dreamed of the opportunities for fame that lay ahead. Few could have realised just what that was to mean. The scale of death and suffering was to exceed anything previously experienced. The total number of deaths suffered by the British Army in the whole of the Crimean War was 18,000 (of these only 1761 occurred actually in battle, the remainder in hospital from wounds and sickness). With 22,000 British deaths the Boer War was on the same scale. British dead in the Somme battle alone were 419,000 and at Passchendaele 300,000. Even today it is hard to understand how such apparently mindless slaughter of a whole generation could have come about.

The total number of VCs awarded in the 1914–18 War was 633 (sappers 24), compared with the 522 (sappers 27) in the years which had passed since its inauguration by Queen Victoria. Today, the personal accounts of the fighting in the First World War leave us wondering what singular order of bravery was necessary to qualify for the supreme award when compared with the day-by-day courage demanded of every soldier, particularly the junior leaders whose expectation of life was so notoriously low. To judge by a comparison of the number of men killed in action one might expect many more VCs, but the introduction of the Military Cross (December 1914) and Military Medal (March 1916), and the practice of awarding the Distinguished Service Order more frequently for gallantry, successfully prevented the proliferation of VCs and protected the unique character of this highest award.

In the first week of August 1914 the seething European cauldron finally boiled over. The ingredients of the great brew, thrown into the pot during the previous half century, were the political alliances and the national and imperial ambitions and jealousies, backed by the growing militarism, of the European powers. Irreversible simmering had started a month earlier with a threat to Austro-Hungary's authority in the Balkans and Russia's resultant mobilisation against Austrian intimidation of Serbia. Germany, allied with Austria and ostensibly fearful for the security of her eastern border, attacked France through Belgium in accordance with the long-laid plans evolved by Field Marshal Graf von Schlieffen (although he had died in 1913) which demanded that France be neutralised in swift, decisive action before Russia could be dealt with.

Britain, unable to accept German domination of Europe with all that that meant for imperial security, invoked a treaty of 1839 guaranteeing Belgian independence, and declared war on Germany. Although nowadays the British part in the First World War conjures up images mostly of the gruelling trench warfare on the Western Front, in fact it became a global affair involving imperial troops both in Europe and overseas and significant fighting on land in the Middle East, Africa and even in China as well as the naval battles worldwide. Without the Indian Army formations in the winter of 1914–15, for example, the British contribution to the war in France would have dwindled to an embarrassingly inadequate scale.

However, all but one of the sapper VCs in 1914–18 were won on the Western Front and this account will therefore be largely confined to that theatre. For our purposes the war there can be divided into four main phases. There was the preliminary mobile battle during which the Germans were frustrated in their efforts to accomplish the primary aim of von Schlieffen's Plan, the fall of France. The main battles in this phase were Mons, First Marne, First Aisne and First Ypres. The British Expeditionary Force (BEF), effectively Britain's regular army under Sir John French, organised into I and II Corps, arrived in Belgium on 9 August, made an effective stand at Mons and then withdrew in conformity with the French, to the east of Paris just behind the Marne. The Allied victory there, after heavy casualties on both sides, forced the Germans to retreat to the Aisne where they in turn made a stand. The attempt then by both sides to outflank one another resulted in the so-called Race to the Sea during September and October – in which the BEF was transferred to Flanders to hold a line on the ground to the east of Ypres where the land rises above the sea-level plain lying between Ypres and the Channel coast. Here the British occupied a position which formed a salient into the German line and here was fought not only the final battle of this preliminary mobile phase but also a bitter struggle throughout the war, which was to symbolise the sheer slog of the war and the horrendous conditions which both sides had to overcome. Through October and November 1914 the Germans made increasingly determined efforts to break through the Allied left flank but were held in desperate fighting by the BEF and three corps of the French Army.

This fighting (First Ypres) effectively marked the end of the BEF. Between mid-October and the end of November the British force lost some 58,000 men. In 7th Division, for example, only 44 officers and 2336 men were left from an original complement of 400 and 12,000. It also marked the end of the preliminary mobile phase of the war.

Thereafter the opposing lines of trenches dominated the style of warfare. Both sides sought to break the stalemate, but were unable to find an alternative to launching massive infantry attacks, artillery being employed in ever greater quantity in preliminary bombardment and subsequent creeping barrage. This went on throughout virtually the whole of the three years 1915 to 1917. However, in 1915 the Allies still held to an optimistic view, supported by the diversion of a large proportion of the German Army to the Eastern Front, that a breakthrough was possible. The year 1915 could be regarded as a separate phase called, perhaps, the ill-founded optimism stage (General Joffre, the French commander in the early stages of the war, called it 'the war of stabilisation'[1] – perhaps with some hind-sight) in which it seemed to the Allied commanders that all that was needed was one last effort, albeit with terrible sacrifice of human life, to regain the occupied territory in France and Belgium and force Germany to make peace. Thus occurred the seemingly insanely wasteful Allied attacks in the battles of Neuve-Chapelle, Aubers Ridge, Festubert and Loos, so castigated in Alan Clark's classic *The Donkeys*. The exception to this pattern of Allied attacks was the second German attempt to eliminate the Ypres Salient in March.

This chapter deals with the VCs won in these first two phases of the war. Two more phases were to follow: the attrition phase, in which both sides attempted to break through in such strength and across such a wide front that the results could only be assessed by the degree of success in sapping their enemy's will to carry on the fight. This phase lasted throughout 1916 and 1917 and included the battles of Verdun, the Somme, Arras and Cambrai. It was the Germans who then broke the stalemate for the final phase of the war, the mobile phase, with their Ludendorff offensives in early 1918 striking in turn on three fronts: in the Somme area (threatening Amiens), in Picardy around the River Lys (threatening Calais) and on the Aisne. Finally, there was the Allied counter-offensive in the autumn of 1918 after the Americans had joined the war, which precipitated the German collapse.

Mons to the Aisne

The opening stages of the war may appear to the casual reader as being something of a chaotic shambles. In fact the highly professional contribution of the BEF, derided by the Kaiser as a 'contemptible little army', was crucial to the wrecking of the German plans and thus to the outcome of the war as a whole. If it looked a shambles, we have to remember a number of facts. First, that when they deployed their troops the Allies were unaware that the Schlieffen Plan was in progress, hence they underestimated both the strength and direction of the German attacks. Secondly, the French reaction to the invasion of Belgium was governed by that spirit for offensive action (*attaque à l'outrance*) which underlay all their pre-war training. This was never the approach of the British; nor was it an option, faced as they were by such overwhelming strength. Nevertheless, British actions both at this stage and later were determined by the perceived need either to conform with the French or to demonstrate the resolve of the British Army to meet its obligations.

Thirdly, the BEF, well-trained professional force as it was at unit level, had had no recent experience to test its command, staff and logistic systems in the conditions that it now faced. Lastly, there was no machinery in existence even for co-ordination between the national forces of the Allies other than liaison officers exchanged between formation headquarters, let alone any form of unified command structure as would exist today. Language itself was a major barrier to co-operation.

The Germans invaded Belgium on 9 August 1914, the day on which the BEF under General Sir John French started to arrive in France. Belgian resistance was tougher than the Germans had anticipated, but by the time the BEF had reached its concentration area at Mauberge and had begun to advance into Belgium in conformity with the French, the Germans were preparing to wheel their army in the massive anti-clockwise move that would theoretically outflank the Allies and swiftly threaten Paris. By the night of 22 August it was clear that this massive attack was imminent and at 5.30 am Sir John French issued orders to the BEF to take up positions along the Mons-Condé canal with General Sir Horace Smith-Dorrien's II Corps on the left and Lieutenant-General Sir Douglas Haig's I Corps on the right. Demolitions were to be prepared on the canal bridges but these were not to be fired until later. II Corps bore virtually the entire brunt of the advancing attack by five German corps. The defenders declared themselves as astounded by the massed field grey targets that confronted them as the German defenders of the Somme were to be of their khaki-clad successors two years later.

> 'Poor devils of infantry!' said a Gordon Highlander. 'They advanced in companies of quite 150 men in files five deep, and our rifle has a flat trajectory up to 600 yards. Guess the result. We could steady our rifles on the trench and take deliberate aim. The first company were simply blasted away to Heaven by a volley at 700 yards, and in their insane formation every bullet was almost sure to find two billets. The other companies kept advancing very slowly, using their dead comrades as cover, but they had absolutely no chance …[2]

Map 12
The Mons-Condé canal bridges, 23 August 1914

But it was the BEF that really had no chance of hanging on in this one-sided and bloody affair. The sheer weight of numbers, coupled with the overpowering effi-

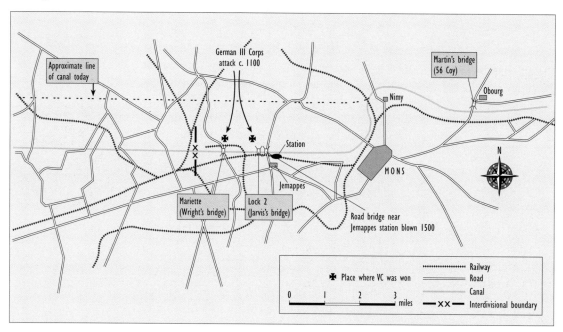

ciency of the German artillery, was bound to prevail. The bridges along the canal soon became the key points in the battle. The honour of the first VC of the war is usually credited to Lieutenant Dease, commanding a machine-gun section of the Royal Fusiliers, who was killed on the bridge at Nimy just to the east of Mons. Private Godley, who survived and was able to tell his story on BBC Radio 40 years later, also won the VC in this gallant action.

The II Corps Sappers (3rd and 5th Divisions) had some ten bridges to deal with; 56 Company were responsible for the sector to the east of Mons. The experiences of Lieutenant Cyril Martin, later to win both the DSO and VC within a few months, on the bridge at Obourg give the flavour of this work.

> During a lull in the firing I dashed across the bridge and got under it and saw that it would take a long time to fix the charges. I dashed back over the bridge and found my toolcart had come up and was under cover about 50 yards away and the explosives were being unpacked. I found a ladder and with five men and all the stuff dashed across the bridge and got under it. By now a few shells were arriving and heavy rifle fire mostly from our side. We found that the ladder was too short and that without a quantity of planks and uprights it was impossible to fix any charges to the underside of the bridge. At this moment the firing above us showed that the Germans were very close so I decided to get back. I semaphored the Middlesex for covering fire and dashed over … I told the men to pack up and return to Mons and as I turned I saw the Germans swarm over the bridge.[3]

To the west of Mons the crossing points were presenting similar problems to 57 Field Company and it was here that the first sapper VCs of the war were won. There were eight bridges to be dealt with but there was only one exploder, so the operation became a nightmare of organisation against the clock – getting permission for blowing, moving stores around, improvising to make up for lack of the proper materials and enduring the increasingly intense enemy fire.[4]

Charles Alfred Jarvis

Charles Jarvis was 33 years old in 1914. He had been born in Fraserburgh, Scotland and had former service with the Black Watch. He had left the Army in 1907 and was recalled as a reservist in 1914.[5]

On their arrival at the Mons-Condé canal Lance-Corporal Jarvis and Sapper Neary were ordered to fix their charges on the bridge at Lock 2 at Jemappes. Along this section a subsidiary canal ran parallel to and south of the main canal. The bridges were of relatively simple construction, usually two I-section girders with cross members. That on the main canal could be lifted by a winch and counterweight mechanism on the north bank to allow for barge traffic. At Lock 2, A company of the Royal Scots Fusiliers was holding a barricade at the north end of the bridge but were driven off to the south, while Jarvis and Neary were working with a boat under the bridge and having to make occasional dashes back across the canal to obtain their materials. The enemy fire was now intense and Jarvis dispatched Neary to obtain the exploder.

Charles Alfred Jarvis
(1881–1948)

By this time the firing on the position had become so violent and the casualties were so numerous that a retirement had been decided on. Corpl. Jarvis was then called upon to destroy the bridge, but was still without the exploder and leads, as the sapper had not returned. He pulled along the lock to a position where no fire was being directed, crawled out over the bank, and got into the street, and was riding towards the market square to find the exploder himself, when he met Capt. F. [sic] Wright, V.C., R.E., ... Capt. Wright told Lance-Corpl. Jarvis to go back to the bridge and be prepared to connect up the leads, as he would fetch them in a motor car, and taking the bicycle from Jarvis, went off to collect the necessary articles. Jarvis returned to his former position ... By this time the infantry had been terribly cut up, and the general order to retire came, which practically meant every man for himself.[6]

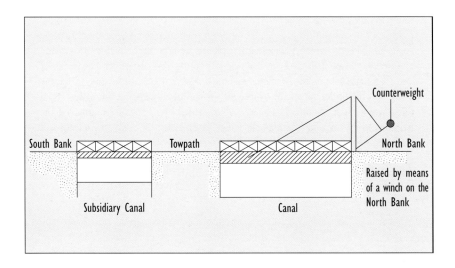

Typical layout of the bridges on the Mons-Condé canal.

From the 1932 article in the *Royal Engineers Journal*[7] it is clear that of the eight bridges allotted to 57 Field Company only the one to the east of Jarvis's bridge, close to Jemappes station, was successfully blown. Jarvis's own account never mentions blowing his bridge nor explains how he might have obtained the exploder which, as will be seen, was the key problem. So, to this extent the citation is inaccurate. Nevertheless, his extraordinary and selfless gallantry had earned the deep respect of the infantry defending the crossing and was duly recognised with the award of the VC.

Theodore Wright

Theodore Wright, known as Dodo, came from the Guildford area in Surrey. He was educated at Clifton College and the RMA Woolwich and commissioned into the Royal Engineers in 1902. After training at Chatham he joined the Balloon Section at Aldershot (see Chapter Thirteen) and served in Gibraltar and Cairo. On his return to England he was posted to Bulford as Adjutant of 3rd Division RE with whom he deployed with the BEF.

Theodore Wright (1883–1914)

As Adjutant, Wright was visiting the eight crossing sites to see what he could do to help. While at Lock 2 he had been wounded on the head but shortly afterwards met the officer in charge of the sector, Lieutenant Boulnois of 57 Company, and they agreed that he, Wright, would take the exploder and leads in his car to the Mariette site while Boulnois dealt as best he could with two bridges further west which had been prepared by Lance-Corporal Halewood.[8] It should be mentioned here for the technically minded that no 'instantaneous fuse' was available. Charges had to be fired either by safety fuse or electrically. If no exploder was available, simultaneous firing of multiple charges could only be achieved approximately by accurate lengths of safety fuse lit on a signal by a man at each charge.

> Captain Wright and Sergeant Smith on reaching Mariette made most gallant attempts to get at the free ends of the leads, which only just reached the towpath. 'B' Company of the Northumberland Fusiliers was still holding out at the barricade on the south side of the canal, but the towpath was separated from the barricade by the subsidiary canal, here spanned by a girder bridge 15 to 20 feet wide … Captain Wright 'bridge-laddered' under this subsidiary canal bridge with extra leads tied on to him, and time and again tried to get at the ends of the leads on the towpath. Each time his hands or head appeared above the level of the towpath he was fired at from about 30 yards off, so eventually he gave up the attempt. In swinging himself back under the girder across the subsidiary canal, he lost his grip owing to exhaustion, and was pulled out of the water by Sergeant Smith.[9]

A witness of this incident later reported:

> Actually B Company … was in the act of withdrawing when Wright made his forlorn hope. Although we did not know it, by that time we had been practically cut off by the Germans who had come in about Mons. Wright's gallantry made a great impression upon the men of B Company of my regiment. Two days later in the early morning, when they were leaving a very chilly bivouac at Bavai, they recognized Wright riding by and cheered him heartily; rather a unique demonstration from Northcountrymen.[10]

The Mons-Condé canal. This picture was taken the day after Corporal Jarvis's VC action and shows the German bridge built under fire from the Northumberland Fusiliers.
(IWM Q70073)

We shall be meeting Theodore Wright again in this account. Charles Jarvis's life story after Mons, however, has a sadly bitter flavour. He wrote a cheerful and lively account of the immediate aftermath of the events on the canal which were mostly narrow escapes from the pursuing Germans but included a night spent in a theatre where his section found some musical instruments and gave an impromptu concert. In due course he was most surprised to be awarded the VC but returned to England for the investiture and was fêted at Woodford Green and Chelmsford 'on the occasion of his homecoming'.[11] In Fraserburgh, the town of his birth, he was credited as 'the first hero who received the Victoria Cross ...'[12]

It is not clear where the rest of Jarvis's service took him but in 1916, much to his disgust, he received his discharge. Although this rebuff to someone of such proven gallantry received some publicity in the national and local press there was no redress and he left the service a somewhat embittered man. It is not known how he earned his living thereafter although he joined the LDV at the beginning of the Second World War and did duty in Portsmouth Dockyard. However, he returned to Scotland and died in Dundee in 1948.[13]

The Retreat

By the end of the dramatic first day, the men of the BEF had shown themselves to be part of an effective and well-trained fighting force and had earned the respect of their enemies. Although the casualties in some units had been severe, overall they were trivial compared with what was to be experienced later in the war. True, they had been forced off the line of the canal but they took up new positions a few miles back ready to fight again the next day. It was not to be. Events on the flanks demanded a withdrawal in conformity with the French armies and thus began the retreat which, apart from one famous and controversial major holding action by II Corps at Le Cateau, continued until the exhausted troops were across the Marne to the east of Paris.

It was at Le Cateau that Lieutenant Cyril Martin of 56 Field Company, whom we have already met on the bridge at Obourg, found himself with his section fighting alongside the infantry (2nd Royal Irish) and persuading them that they must not retire. He directed their fire from a nearby building.

> Suddenly as I was pointing out a target the whole house shook and I found myself on the floor rather dazed. The bed and the back wall of the room had disappeared with all my kit on it. Just under the window out of which I was looking was a round hole about one foot in diameter and I am sure that the shell must have passed between my legs which were about 2 feet apart. It took me a minute or two to collect myself and get out of the house. I opened the front door and found that all the infantry had cleared off and my sappers wondering what was left of me. I told them to go on firing as hard as they could to pretend that we were still a large force. I lay down next to my Sergeant Major who was rather large, he felt awfully unhappy because a machine-gun was firing about 3 inches above him and he could not move. The man on my right lifted his foot for a second and had the heel of his boot taken right off.

The infantry reported that I was dead and that the Germans had captured the village. The infantry mounted a counter attack and found us instead of the Germans holding the village...[14]

For his actions at Le Cateau, Cyril Martin was awarded the DSO.

On 6 September, in a surge of rising morale, the Allies turned and halted the German advance in the Battle of the Marne. The essentials of the Schlieffen Plan had been abandoned when the Germans decided to realign their advance in response to the actions of the French Army. This presented the Allies with the opportunity of the famous flank attack which forced a German retreat to the line of the Aisne where, however, they now took up strong positions. It was in the bitter fighting to break this line that two more sapper VC actions occurred on 14 September.

The Germans had successfully destroyed or severely damaged all the bridges over the Aisne and the main sapper task was therefore to build and man brigade crossing sites.[15] At Vailly, in the 3rd Division area, a pontoon bridge was built overnight on 13/14 September by 56 and 57 Field Companies to back up a rather flimsy single-plank footway over the damaged road bridge. This area came under intense fire as the 5th Cavalry Brigade were crossing and Captain Theodore Wright, who had already won a VC at Mariette near Mons three weeks earlier, was killed while helping wounded men to shelter. This incident was included in his VC citation.

At Moulin des Roches near Missy, a few miles further to the west, even more stirring events were in progress. A ferry had been built by 59 Field Company to

Map 13
The Missy–Vailly sector on the River Aisne, 1914.

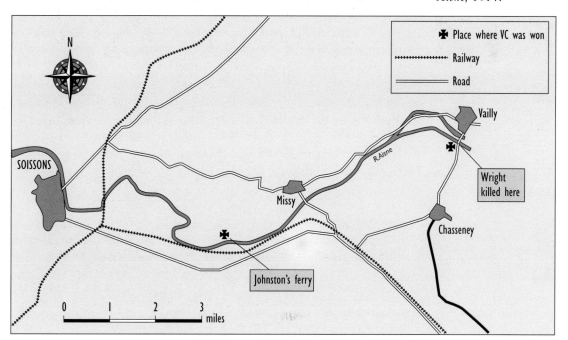

support the 5th Division. It was used to take troops and ammunition forward and to bring back the wounded. The success of 5th Division's operation hung to a great extent on maintaining this fragile link, as it was the only means by which 15th Infantry Brigade could cross, all other crossings having been destroyed. The Germans realised this and subjected it to intense fire. In these conditions Captain William Johnston and Lieutenant R.B. Flint worked the rafts indefatigably all day. Johnston was awarded the VC and Flint the DSO.

William Henry Johnston

William Johnston
(1879–1915)

William Johnston was a fairly senior captain at the time of these events. He had been born in 1879, the son of a Royal Artillery officer, and commissioned into the Royal Engineers in 1899 after attending the RMA at Woolwich. His service before the war had taken him to Gibraltar in 1904 where he was employed in the Intelligence Department. After an attachment to the Survey Department back in England, he was sent to China where he served for three years on the staff, travelling extensively throughout the northern provinces in the course of his intelligence work. He also took part in the survey of the New Territories in Hong Kong and in 1911 was transferred to the South China Command. He went to the Staff College at Camberley in 1913 and joined 59 Field Company in early 1914. He was actively engaged in the Mons battle and in the subsequent retreat.

After the Aisne battle Johnston returned to England for five days' leave. His VC had been gazetted and his reaction is contained in a letter he wrote at the time replying to the congratulations of a family friend. 'I only wish I could feel that your congratulations were honestly earned. As a matter of fact I feel the most awful fraud, someone must have exaggerated badly for it was never worth a V.C. and I don't feel at all comfortable about it.'[16]

Modest man though he may have been it is unlikely this was false modesty – he was further recognised by two mentions in despatches. Such was the intensity of operations, though, that he must have witnessed many acts of bravery which went unrewarded.

On his return to France Johnston was given command of 172 Tunnelling Company. He was then appointed Brigade Major of 15 Brigade on 2 June 1915 but was killed by a sniper a few weeks later when in the trenches near Zwarteleen in the Ypres Salient. In this short time, according to his divisional historian, 'the gallantry and resource constantly displayed by him had earned him great popularity in the Brigade.'[17]

Flanders and Artois

The German stand on the Aisne signalled the start of the long period of trench warfare stalemate that characterises the First World War, for it was from that point that both armies tried to move to outflank each other until the whole line of confrontation was intact from the Channel coast to Switzerland. It was during this process that the BEF was moved from the Aisne area to Flanders, undertaking responsibility for the Ypres Salient and south to Armentières. By the end of

November after First Ypres (as outlined at the beginning of this chapter), the threat to the Channel ports had been averted, the line stabilised and the British force, with all too few men of the original BEF, began its build-up. Most importantly, the Indian Army divisions had also arrived and had been in action building up to two infantry and two cavalry divisions and four field artillery brigades bringing the strength of the BEF to 16 divisions in all.[18]

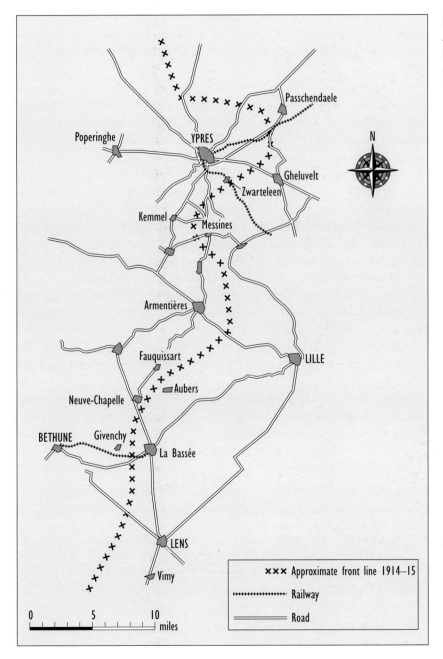

Map 14
Approximate front line in Artois–Flanders, Lens to Ypres, 1914–15.

Although no major battle was now to take place for some months, the winter was a period of intense activity. The sappers, now with a third field company in each division, had to provide the Army with the means to fight the new form of war by producing materials for fieldworks, setting up the mining sections that eventually led to the vast complex of tunnelling in the underground war, establishing roads and railway systems for resupply and devising and producing offensive equipment including bombs (hand grenades).

Bombing became an established technique in trench warfare. It resulted in the award of two more sapper VCs during the operations kept up during the winter to maintain the offensive spirit and domination over the enemy.

Philip Neame

Philip Neame,
on first commissioning

Philip Neame made good use of his privileged background of a Kent landowning family acquiring, in the pursuit of an active country life, a taste for adventurous sport from an early age. He became a proficient horseman and shot and was apparently inured to physical hardship and danger. He was educated at Cheltenham and the RMA Woolwich, having been influenced in his ambition to become a Royal Engineer by the many sapper friends of his family who naturally circulated in county circles from their base in Chatham.

Commissioned in 1908 his first posting was to 56 Field Company at Bulford. His Officer Commanding was Clifford Coffin, whom we shall meet later winning his VC as a brigadier-general, and when Neame left to go to Gibraltar his place was taken by Cyril Martin. Gibraltar provided him with good professional experience and even better hunting (across the border in Spain) and polo, but after less than a year he returned to England with 15 Field Company to prepare for their move to France as part of 8th Division.

Immediately he was in the thick of the first Battle of Ypres and having to solve the problems of erecting wire obstacles at night in front of the infantry lines. His own report in the company's war diary for December gives a good flavour of the operations at this time. The sappers had to crawl out of the trenches in the dark each with two coils of wire and three pickets, locate the line of the obstacle and then erect the fence. They were under fire throughout, sometimes only 30 yards from the enemy. The entry for the night of 19 December, however, is a simple record by another officer.

> 5pm … Lt Neame returns with No 1 Sect and reports that at 8am 2 W Yorks were driven from their captured trench by bombs. They were unable to use the bombs they had made and could make no reply until his arrival. By lighting and throwing bombs himself he managed to check German advance, stop them bomb throwing and cover retreat of our infantry party.[19]

As so often in the war diaries there is little to distinguish this feat from any other normal day's work. It was far from normal and earned Neame the VC.

In his autobiography written 30 years later, Neame's own vivid account of this incident opens matter-of-factly: 'On December 19, 1914, I won the Victoria

Cross.'[20] He then explains how the attacks due to take place in his area on the German trench system around the Rue Tilleloy, Neuve-Chapelle were designed to draw German reserves northwards away from the French sector where a large-scale operation was in progress. His task with 30-odd sappers was to join up the captured German trenches with the British system and to cut away the traverses (the buttresses incorporated into every trench system to prevent the enemy firing down its length) so that any Germans trying to recapture the system could be kept away by small arms fire. In such an operation they would be most likely to use bombs (hand grenades) which had become one of the most effective weapons in trench warfare at the time. At that stage the Germans already had well-manufactured bombs but the British were dependent on designs improvised in the Royal

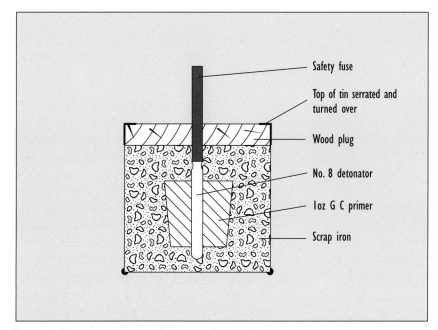

Diagram of the type of home-made bomb in use at the beginning of the First World War, before being superseded by the manufactured hand grenade.

Engineer workshops from such devices as jam tins filled with guncotton and nails and initiated using an awkward-to-light length of safety fuse. For this purpose a special slow-burning match, a fusee, was normally available but sappers were trained to do the job with an ordinary match head if necessary.

Neame was called forward when the infantry battalion, the West Yorks, became severely threatened by a German bomb attack but could not respond in kind having no fusees. Neame obliged and started a bomb fight with the enemy.

> I stood up on the firestep, head and shoulders showing clear above the trench, took a quick look towards the Germans, and threw my first bomb. It hit the parapet near where I could see the Germans, and exploded with a roar. Our bombs, although heavy to throw, were very violent and destructive. I crouched down and quickly prepared another bomb. As I stepped down a rifle bullet cracked past close to my head, and a fraction of a second later there was the stutter of a machine-

gun. From then on every time I showed my head and shoulders a rifle or two cracked and the machine-gun fired. I soon realized that the machine-gunner was a little slow in his reactions, and was always just late, but why I was not hit by a rifle bullet I cannot imagine. While I crouched a German bomb came over, fell right in the crowded trench behind me, and burst with a frightful crash, killing and wounding many of our men. They cleared back out of that bay of the trench, and I withdrew once more behind the next traverse. That was the last bay I gave up: it was here that I held up the enemy. The trench all round me was by this time a dreadful sight, men lying with bodies broken and maimed. A bomb inflicts terrible wounds. I never saw anything worse in the succeeding years of warfare.

I settled down and carried on with the fight. I lit and threw half a dozen bombs as quickly as I could in both directions from which the Germans were bombing me, as they were not only in our trench, but also in one parallel, a little distance off. I was determined to get the upper hand quickly, as this was our only hope. My first bomb landed truly in the trench beyond a traverse where I saw a German moving. It burst with another roar, and I heard screams and groans from the enemy. I must have secured several good shots, as the German bombing slowed down and died away entirely from the direction outside our trench.[21]

And so it went on until the German activity petered out and the infantry withdrawal could be organised. At that point Neame's own supply had dwindled to seven or eight bombs. His own withdrawal was every bit as perilous as the bomb fight and included rescuing numerous wounded under heavy fire, as important in the citation as the bombing.

The rest of Neame's war was scarcely less hazardous than these early days. Even when on the staff he was continually exposed to enemy action and particularly seems to have relished reconnaissance in no-man's-land as a pastime. However, several more hectic months were to pass in command of his section of 15 Field Company, including the Battle of Neuve-Chapelle where he witnessed the destruction of the 2nd Middlesex. He describes this event as 'a dreadful slaughter', a rare comment on the mayhem which he must have witnessed throughout his time in France.

Trenches in the Fauquissart area, looking towards Aubers ridge. A scene similar to that where Lieutenant Philip Neame won his VC.
(IWM Q42145)

By the end of 1915 he had been awarded the DSO for his work with 8th Division and moved on to a series of staff appointments: Brigade Major 168 Infantry Brigade for the Somme battle, GSO2 XVth Corps also on the Somme but moving north to Nieuport where the headquarters was grievously damaged by shelling with many casualties, also as GSO2 in Headquarters First

Army dealing with the hectic troop movements resulting from the German offensives of 1918 and finally, on promotion, as GSO1 30th Division.

In between the two world wars, Neame spent 12 years in India, returning to England in 1938 as a major-general to command the RMA Woolwich. India had offered exploration and hunting galore and Neame's exploits included a brush with armed poachers and a severe mauling by a tigress. The particular outcome of that was marriage in 1934 to Alberta Drew of the Lady Minto Nursing Association, the nurse who had cared for him in the Lansdowne Hospital, Simla.

At the outbreak of the Second World War, Neame was first involved as Deputy Chief of the General Staff in planning for the BEF in France. In 1940 he was appointed to the command of Palestine, Trans-Jordan and Cyprus in the rank of lieutenant-general, followed soon after by his posting in February 1941 to Barce in Cyrenaica as GOC-in-C and military governor. It was an ill-fated turn of events for not only were his forces entirely inadequate for the task, but Rommel's German–Italian offensive towards Egypt was imminent. In the very fluid circumstances of a carefully planned withdrawal Neame was captured by the Germans.

He remained a prisoner-of-war in Italy until 1943 when the Italian capitulation presented him with an opportunity for escape. Fortunately he had not wasted his time while in prison: he played a leading role in helping several prisoners to escape, as well as writing his autobiography.

Sir Philip Neame was Lieutenant-Governor of Guernsey from 1945 to 1953. His extraordinary career in the Army ended when he retired in 1947.

We must now return to 1915 and the man who took over from Philip Neame at Bulford in 1913.

Cyril Martin

We have already met Cyril Martin living dangerously at Mons and Le Cateau; until 1914 his career had been uneventful. Cyril Martin had been born in China where his father was a missionary. He was educated at Clifton College and at the RMA Woolwich, being commissioned into the Royal Engineers in 1911 at the age of 19. From his course at Chatham he went to Bulford, joining 56 Field Company and training with them in the increasingly urgent preparations for war.

Cyril Martin (1891–1980) (IWM Q85889)

After the Battle of the Marne he took part in the operations to cross the Aisne, reconnoitring the bridge at Vailly, making what improvements he could to the single-plank crossing and taking part with his company in the construction of the pontoon bridge where Theodore Wright was killed.

On 1 October, 56 Field Company went into reserve and was redeployed with its brigade to the Ypres area in a ten-day move by train and on foot. On 16 October they took part in the advance towards Neuve-Chapelle[22] but on 24 October Cyril Martin was involved in a desperate hand-to-hand fight at Fauquissart and he was evacuated to England with bayonet and bullet wounds. He returned to France in 1915 rejoining his old company, now in the Salient to the south-east of Ypres, on 28 February for what was to be a sensationally brief appearance. On 12 March

1915 he was detailed to take part in a major raid with the 3rd Worcestershires into the German trenches near Spanbroekmolen, an area that was later to become better known as one of the sites of the vast mine explosion that opened the battle of Messines in 1917. This raid was typical of the operations that were constantly taking place as the two opposing armies fought to improve their relative positions. Martin's task with his section was to lead the infantry to their assembly point and then 'accompanying the assaulting party and rushing and blocking the communication trenches on their right'.[23] In fact the attack failed but despite having been badly wounded in the initial advance, Martin, together with Second Corporal Skinner 'gained a footing in a German trench with their infantry party and held it till 6.30 pm …'[24] – that is, for nearly two and a half hours until the party was withdrawn. For this he was awarded the VC. Corporal Skinner was awarded the DCM. Martin was again evacuated to England and did not recover from his wounds until October when he was posted to Chatham as an Assistant Instructor.

Martin found Chatham uncongenial and sought a posting – which he was granted – to go on secondment to the Egyptian Army. With them he took part in operations in Sinai, the Sudan and in Allenby's campaign in Palestine. Between the wars his career followed the pattern familiar to most sappers, rotating between field, works and training units. He was in the Sudan again in the early 1920s as Assistant Director Military Works and, after a spell at Chatham, went to India in 1928. After two tours on the North-West Frontier and various other appointments, he was Deputy Chief Engineer Northern Command at the beginning of the war. He then went to Iraq as Chief Engineer, responsible among much else for the ports and base infrastructure that was urgently needed to support the resupply of Russia that was then undertaken. Martin returned to India after a short tour as Commandant of the RE OCTU at Newark and remained there until his retirement in 1947.

Ill-founded Optimism

While Cyril Martin was winning his VC at Spanbroekmolen, a battle was being fought further south at Neuve-Chapelle. This was the first in a series of battles by which the Allied commanders felt they could break through with a decisive victory to bring the war to an end. The British force was effectively what remained of the old regular Army which had now been deployed to take the place of the almost liquidated 'Old Contemptibles' of the original BEF, together with the Indian divisions. The start of the attack was carried out on 10 March 1915 by the First British Army under Sir Douglas Haig but the initial successes and colossal fortitude of the soldiers – fighting in the appalling conditions of muddy ground and cold, wet weather – came to naught through the inability of the First Army to exploit their gains, to reinforce quickly their strength on the ground and to follow up before allowing the Germans to reinforce and counter-attack. The opportunity was lost, with some 12,000 casualties on both sides.

Neuve-Chapelle showed that massed frontal infantry attacks across open country could easily be held by well-entrenched forces protected by wire; that artillery could have only a minor effect in opening gaps through wire obstacles; that temporary gains could be made but only at hideous cost; and that without rapidly deployed reserves, attacking forces could not withstand determined counter-attacks. In battle after battle both sides fought each other seemingly constrained by this pattern of action. A conviction grew that the solution lay in an overwhelming use of artillery, and infantry tactics became neglected as a result.

The battles of Aubers Ridge and Festubert followed. The first day of the former was described by Alan Clark[25] as 'a disastrous fifteen hours of squandered heroism, unredeemed by the faintest glimmer of success'; the latter achieved no more. At the same time Sir John French's problems were compounded by the attack of the Germans in the Ypres Salient which became known as Second Ypres. Extraordinary gallantry in a long slog for over a month was displayed by all the British forces but particularly by the Canadians who demonstrated that the new German weapon – gas – used here for the first time, did not have to be overwhelming in its effect. As a result Ypres was saved but the British line in the Salient was much reduced giving the Germans domination over the area for the rest of the war.

Loos

It must be remembered that these events, already reaching apocalyptic proportions in comparison with other wars, were occurring simultaneously with others further afield. By the end of June the protagonists were engaged in bitter struggles in Eastern Europe, Italy, Turkey (Gallipoli), Africa and at sea. By October another front had been added in the Balkans. On the Western Front the need was ever more apparent for the British to co-ordinate with the French, still by far the largest partner.

The Battle of Loos, the scene of two more sapper VCs, was a case in point. Sir John French was persuaded that he should prepare an attack to support French moves in Artois and Champagne. The disappointing, to some tragic, outcome of Loos led to severe acrimony between the Allies and accusations of duplicity. It also led to the replacement of Sir John French by Sir Douglas Haig as Commander-in-Chief. These controversies have been the subject of many accounts and are too long and complex to include in this book, which will confine itself to a summary of the story.

The area chosen for the British attack lay between La Bassée in the north and the village of Loos (just north of Lens) to the south. The ground greatly favoured the defence being largely flat but broken by mineworkings and slight natural undulations. Haig, now Commander of First Army, was in charge of the operation with I Corps under Sir Hubert Gough in the northern sector and IV Corps under Sir Henry Rawlinson in the south. Two divisions from IX Corps were allocated as reserve but, despite Haig's protestations, they were to remain under French's command until committed. All the higher command realised the dangers of the task ahead. However, in response to the German use of gas during Second Ypres, the British had now put together their own equipment for delivering

Map 15
The Loos sector, 1915.

Based on a map in *Loos*
by Philip Warner
(William Kimber, 1976).

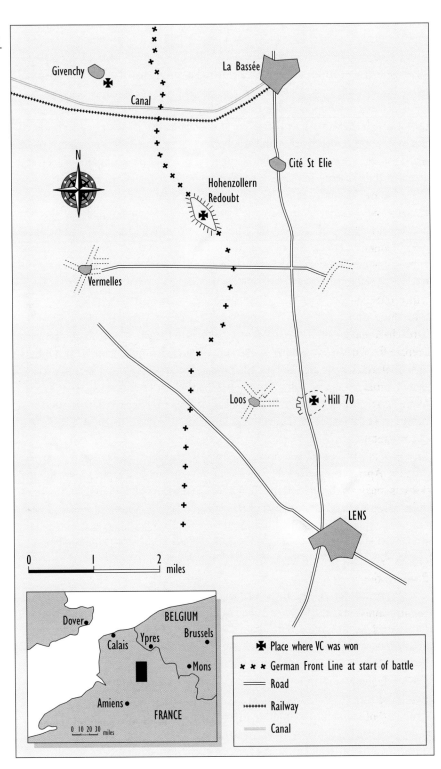

Map 15
The Loos sector, 1915.

Based on a map in *Loos*
by Philip Warner
(William Kimber, 1976).

chlorine offensively. How this came about (the task was given to the Royal Engineers) will be touched on in the next chapter. At this stage, suffice it to state that Haig believed that gas enhanced enormously the opportunity of success for a broad frontal attack. He also realised that this would be suicide should the weather be unsuitable for gas attack on the day; he therefore devised an alternative plan for a narrow frontage attack by two divisions.

In the event the wind only favoured the use of gas over parts of the front. It certainly contributed to some early successes in the I Corps sector and in front of Loos itself but it also caused acute trouble in many of the British units. However, the broad front attack was launched at 6.30 am on 25 September. Despite almost a replay of the awful mauling that had been experienced in the earlier battles of 1915, on this first day, by a display of enormous courage and resolution, the Germans were forced out of their first lines of defence and by the evening the British had made gains of up to two miles including occupying the strongly pre-pared Hohenzollern Redoubt in the north and Hill 70, a point of critical impor-tance about half a mile to the east of Loos.

These accomplishments were at great cost, many battalions were virtually wiped out. The loss in officers and junior leaders meant that exhausted men – even those who had found the protection of a trench (digging their own in the hard chalk was virtually impossible) – were in no position to be rallied and to prepare for the German counter-attacks which began in force by the evening.

In all these activities the sapper field units were generally fighting in an infantry role. Each brigade had its allotted field company from which a 'section' (equivalent to today's field troop) would normally be allocated to a battalion. For example, 44 Brigade had 73 Field Company among whose number was Second Lieutenant Johnson who was to win the VC on this day. 73 Field Company was divided, half to undertake sapper tasks, the remainder to advance with the infantry. Apart from straight infantry combat they would be able to help in such tasks as making crossings over enemy trenches, improving field defences on the objectives and constructing communication trenches.

Frederick Henry Johnson

It was in the bitter fighting for the 'Keep' – the redoubt that dominated the Hill 70 area, that Frederick Johnson won his VC. Just turned 25, Johnson had been commissioned into the Royal Engineers in 1914 from London University OTC. He was a Londoner, the son of Samuel Roger Johnson and Emily, daughter of Henry White of Ewell. He was educated at Middle Whitgift School, St Dunstan's College Catford and Battersea Polytechnic.

The facts of his particular action are clear from the citation and corps history.[26] Eighty years on, the Battle of Loos is often seen as typifying the 'senseless slaughter' of the Western Front. Traumatic experience though it must have been, so many of the accounts of those who took part are remarkable for their unemotional professionalism and lack of criticism of the high command. The

Frederick Johnson (1890–1917)
(IWM Q85886)

handwritten reports, dated 27 September 1915, of three of the section NCOs who took part have survived in the War Diary of 73 Field Company. That of Sergeant E.J. Chapman of No 3 Section is typical, its breathless style and lack of grammar reflecting perhaps the stress of the aftermath of such a holocaust.

Sir,

We left Fosse 7 [one of the mineworkings] at about 5 on the morning of the 25th with No 4 Section and Captain Cardue [sic, Captain E.D. Carden] in charge. We were ordered to put smoke helmets on and proceeded by way of trench 9 to get into trench 6. Here we waited behind 10th Gordons until attack started. Orders were given after attack had started for men with picks, shovels, felling axes and hand axes, to get on top for the purpose of bridging a trench over. At this order Lieut Nolan got on top and the felling axes and hand axes were handed over to No 3 section to find wood etc under charge of Lieut Johnson and No 4 Section was ordered on top to prepare trench for bridging under charge of Lieut Nolan. After working for about 10 minutes one of the numerous shells fell in amongst No 4 Section killing and wounding Lieut Nolan NCO's and men about 14 being put out of action. About 5 minutes later we were given the order to advance by Capt. Cardue myself on the left Capt Cardue centre and Lieut Johnson on right our objective being between Loos towers and the Windmill. We entered the village of Loos at the left hand corner. Here we met the Col of the 10 Gordons and his staff.

After waiting for about 5 minutes he gave us orders to advance and getting well to the left we found ourselves again under the charge of Capt Cardue. We followed the advance to Hill 70. Rifle and machine gun fire was awful [?] crossfire very thick from our left.

About 9.30am we reached the crest of the hill. At this point a sharp rise in the hill gives us good cover and a field of fire about 30 yds. On our left front barbed wire is very thick from this point we had to crawl forming up with the infantry we found they were partly in the Keep. Capt Cardue and Lieut Johnson being on my right they were busy helping to get a machine gun in position about this time. The fire being so hot in the Keep the infantry retired no officers were with them at the time and a Scotch Sergt and myself had a very hard job to keep them together. We got them back to the sharp rise in the ground which I just mentioned. At this point Capt Cardue and Lieut Johnson took charge Lieut Johnson rallying the Engineers which included some of No 1 and 2 Section as well as No 4. Our men got into the Keep and again we had to give up but not after [sic] a very hard struggle in which Lieut Johnson, Capt Cardue, LCpl Millars, Spr Gibson and Cpl Burt quite distinguished themselves here I think we lost Capt Cardue severely wounded and Cpl Burt.

By this time we had collected the infantry and strengthened the position which we held well in the afternoon until reinforcement came. About 9 o'clock in the evening a Captain of the 9th Gordons gave me orders to collect the REs and report to Major Mildred at 44th Brigade Headquarters at Loos this I did, collecting 34 REs in all. Getting the order from Major Mildred to proceed to Mazingarbe we arrived at Headquarters at 11.30pm same day.

Sergt E J Chapman,
No 3 Section 73rd F Coy RE
27/9/15[27]

Frederick Johnson survived the battle and, after recovering from his wounds, was presented with his VC at Buckingham Palace in December. In due course he was appointed to the command of 231 Field Company in 40th Division but was killed in Bourlon Wood at the Battle of Cambrai on 26 November 1917.

The Crux

Gallantry of this order had been displayed throughout the day and had put the Germans in a very awkward situation. Their forward lines were now occupied and there were few reinforcements immediately to hand either to strengthen their line or to recover their lost ground. There is little doubt that this was the moment to reinforce success by the commitment of the reserve divisions. Tragically these were not available having been held back too long. They were eventually deployed into position for a new attack in the middle of the morning of 26 September after a long and exhausting night march that involved the harrowing experience of crossing the previous day's battlefield, littered as it was with the dead and dying, many still entrapped in the wire entanglements, grim evidence of the ineffectiveness of the preliminary bombardment. Despite all this, most accounts bear witness to the determination of the men to get to grips with their enemy. Courage was not lacking on that day.

But no amount of courage could have averted the doom that awaited these two divisions (the 21st and 25th) – nearly 10,000 men. The Germans had made good use of the respite they had been given and what was initially for them a daunting sight eventually became the target for the straightforward business of killing by the most efficient means: the well dug-in machine-guns sited in enfilade across the open ground supported by artillery. Somehow these gallant battalions rallied from time to time but after a few hours they had to give up and those who could had to crawl or stagger back to their lines. At one point on Hill 70 the Germans themselves were so disgusted by the slaughter that 'no shot was fired at them … for the rest of the day, so great was the feeling of compassion and mercy for the enemy after such a victory.'[28] This day had cost the British 385 officers and 7861 men, the volunteers who had answered Kitchener's famous call the previous year.

Despite all this, the Battle of Loos ground on until October as the Germans attempted to regain some of their lost territory and the British made one final effort to improve their situation. Both sides lost heavily, the lines finishing much as they were before the battle although the Allies now occupied Loos and some of the open ground to the north. The recriminations were bitter and controversy remains to this day as to responsibility for this disaster. Some commentators feel that the tragedy was not simply that of the squandered lives of so many fine men, ghastly though that was, but that it lay in the loss of a very real opportunity for that breakthrough which had so far eluded either side and which, had early success been able to be exploited, might have shortened the war dramatically and saved so many more millions of lives.

After Loos the idea of any early end to the war evaporated. The attrition phase was about to begin. In this trench war stalemate neither side seemed able to find an alternative to the idea of an artillery onslaught followed by massed infantry attacks to occupy ground. Even this was no option for the British at the end of 1915 as they had neither the armament production nor, until they could be conscripted, the men to meet their needs. For the sappers, three specialisations now began to take on increasing importance. The next chapter tells of the three VCs won in these specialisations: gas warfare, signalling and tunnelling.

The First World War
The Specialists (1915–1917)

Historically whenever some new technology needed investigation for military purposes, the task was given to the Royal Engineers. Kipling had spotted this:

> *When the Waters were dried an' the Earth did appear,*
> *('It's all one,' says the Sapper),*
> *The Lord he created the Engineer,*
> *Her Majesty's Royal Engineer,*
> *With the rank and pay of a Sapper!*

The 19th century had seen the Royal Engineers giving birth to new technical specialisations many of which were destined to grow into organisations in their own right. In the Boer War, for example, as well as the field companies which provided the main engineer support for the infantry and cavalry divisions, there were specialist units for pontoons, railways, searchlights, balloons, survey, photo-reconnaissance, fortress and telegraph. By 1914 the Royal Engineers had already taken on, developed and then shed responsibility for military flying, for mechanical transport and even for submarine mines. Nevertheless in 1914 the Royal Engineers comprised 59 Regular and 117 Reserve Army companies. The basic units in support of the Army in the field were the 42 field companies and squadrons* but in addition there were 134 specialist companies such as the signallers, searchlights and survey. The outbreak and development of the war led to a huge rise in the number of units and the birth of multifarious specialisations which became known as the War Babies. By 1918 the total number of companies had risen to 1832 of which some 1500 were specialists, increasing the manpower of the Royal Engineers from its pre-war total of 25,000 to 314,300 by November 1918.[1] Three of these specialisations were to produce the VCs who are the subject of this chapter.

The first was a Royal New Zealand Engineer and his appearance in this book, along with another of his countrymen and a Canadian, is a reminder of the extent to which the British war effort was dependent on the Commonwealth countries. As James Morris put it: 'The entire British Empire went to war with Germany and her allies that August, all 450 million subjects of the Crown being bound by a single declaration from the King-Emperor.'[2] The figures given so far for units

---

*Units affiliated to cavalry formations were designated 'squadrons'. This practice continued until after the Second World War when all company-sized units became squadrons.

are only for those raised in Britain. The contribution of the Commonwealth countries was immense in proportion to their populations. We have already seen how without the Indian divisions the outcome of the fighting on the Western Front in the winter of 1914/15 might have been very different. In sappers alone, Canada[3] contributed three battalions in each of their four divisions and a further 30 other units; Australia provided over 50 companies of which 17 were field, 11 signals and six tunnelling.

Signalling

Signalling had been part of the Royal Engineers' responsibilities since the introduction of telegraph in the Crimean War. The telegraph companies had contributed substantially to the development of the international telegraph network as well as to the rapid expansion of the Post Office's telegraph service in Britain. For example, in 1886, the Telegraph Battalion had two divisions of which one was stationed at Aldershot with a section in Egypt; the other had its headquarters in London and was employed on the Post Office telegraph.[4] By 1914, the introduction and rapid increase in the efficiency of the telephone had led to the formal allocation of responsibility for army signals to the Royal Engineers. In 1912 the Signals Service, a largely infantry organisation based in Aldershot, which had developed a very effective system of visual signalling, was amalgamated with the Royal Engineers Telegraph Service, and the new organisation became a separate service within the corps. Wireless telegraphy had been experimented with since the Boer War; in 1914 technically qualified men were enlisted to develop this side of communications but the unreliability of equipment coupled with the problems of security delayed its general acceptability until the closing stages of the war.

Today, with secure wireless communication down to section level, and often to the individual man, it is easy to forget how much communications – or the lack of them – were such an influence on the battlefields of the First World War. Once a major operation was launched it was really extremely difficult for commanders to influence the battle. For example, at Loos, some felt that the attack on 25 September should have been postponed, to await better weather conditions for the use of the gas upon which the whole plan for a wide frontal attack depended. But with six divisions moving forward into their forming up trenches, and a carefully timed artillery and gas plan, the time needed to ensure any change of orders reached the units meant that such plans had an almost unstoppable momentum. Furthermore, the lack of a quick means of communication, which prevented attacking forces from pressing home early gains by appropriate and timely commitment of reserves, accounts for so many of the failures to break through in the big set-piece battles such as the Somme and Cambrai.

Thus it was a matter of life and death that communications were maintained on the battlefield and this meant a complex system of telephones connected by wire through exchanges, all of which had to be deployed from men's backs in an advance and, once deployed, maintained from the depredations of shot, shell, the weather and other myriad accidents that could damage such fragile links. This work was lonely, dangerous and technically challenging. The men who did it knew that on their ability to react swiftly to restore communications – be it in the gas-contaminated, machine-gun swept fields of Loos or the liquid mud of Passchendaele – hung the success of the day and the lives of so many of their comrades.

RE signallers fixing telephone wires in a tree near Fricourt, 1916.
(IWM Q4137)

Such a man was Corporal Cyril Bassett of the Royal New Zealand Engineers. The scene of his exploit was the Gallipoli peninsula. His was the only sapper VC of that campaign, so a brief description of the background must suffice.

Gallipoli

The British Government, urged particularly by the then First Lord of the Admiralty Mr Winston Churchill, attempted to break the stalemate that had gripped the Western Front during the winter of 1914 by striking a blow at Germany's ally Turkey and introducing an element of strategic mobility to the war. First hopes that a naval assault might do the trick sank in the heavily defended straits of the Dardanelles in March 1915. The need for an expeditionary force to land on the peninsula was accepted and this, composed largely of Australians and New Zealanders but including a British and a French division, arrived in April; but the Turks were ready for them and after a severe fight and horrific casualties during the landings, stalemate in a bitter trench war then ensued. The Allies had two footholds, one on the toe of the peninsula* and the second at Anzac Cove some ten miles further up the coast on the western side. Here gallant and determined attempts to cut the peninsula were frustrated by an equally resolute defence on the Sari Bair ridge.

In August a further landing of three British divisions was made at Suvla Bay, two to three miles north of Anzac Cove. This was planned to coincide with a major attack on the Sari Bair ridge on the night of 6 August, by the forces who had already so doggedly established their hold in the Anzac Cove sector, with the Chunuk Bair feature as a key objective. The Suvla attack became bogged down, a matter of bitter recrimination after the campaign, and had no effect on the main attack which developed into one of the most savage hand-to-hand fights of the war. The inevitable counter-attacks in the following days forced the Allies back off the key ground on the ridge.

This disastrous campaign was finally called off in December and the survivors embarked in a brilliant evacuation operation which was completed on 9 January 1916.

Corporal Cyril Bassett

Cyril Royston Guyton Bassett was a bank clerk by trade. He was born at Mount Eden, Auckland and educated at Auckland Grammar and Auckland Technical College. He had been with the bank some six years when the war broke out and had already had some military training with the Auckland College Rifles before volunteering to join the New Zealand Expeditionary Force in which he enlisted in August 1914. In October he embarked for Egypt as a sapper in the divisional signals unit of the Royal New Zealand Engineers.

*Cyril Bassett
(1892–1983)
This photograph was
taken c. 1916.*

*Where, incidentally, the sapper Major-General Aylmer Hunter-Weston was commanding 29th Division (see Chapter Seven).

On 25 April 1915 Cyril Bassett took part in the landings at Anzac Cove. 'When I got ashore at Gallipoli there was a line of dead and wounded as far as the eye could see. Our troops hadn't got far inland and were having a hell of a time from the Turks, who could see everything that was happening and were well entrenched.'[5] In fact excellent progress had been made initially despite the landings having taken place on a much narrower beach than originally intended, but

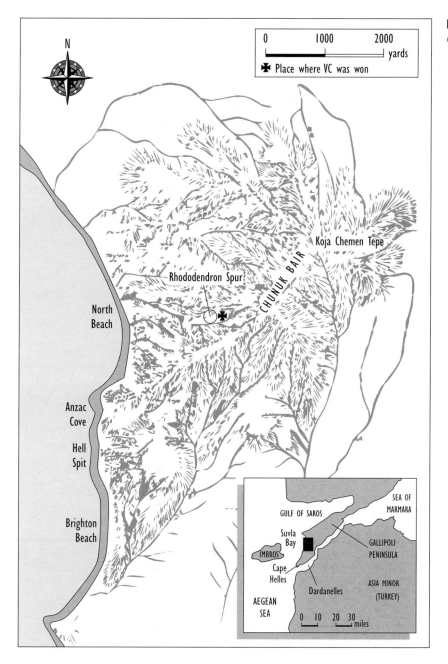

Map 16
Gallipoli, 1915.

the Turks, under the determined leadership of Mustafa Kemal, knew that the position the Anzacs were occupying on the Sari Bair ridge was critical to the whole battle, and launched ferocious counter-attacks which nearly forced an Allied withdrawal. This was not a practicable option, however; instead they were ordered by the overall commander, Sir Ian Hamilton (whom we last met on Wagon Hill in the Boer War), to 'Dig, dig, dig, until you are safe';[6] hence the nickname 'Diggers' for Australian troops.

This modest foothold became the scene of an eerie trench warfare amongst the spurs and ravines that reached down to the coast from the Sari Bair ridge. It exploded into action in mid-May when the Turks tried unsuccessfully to eject the Anzacs. In August it became the springboard for the great attack on Chunuk Bair that was to lead to Cyril Bassett's VC. Bassett was now a corporal in charge of the section of signallers with a brigade-sized column commanded by Brigadier F.E. Johnston. They set off on the morning of 6 August on the right of the attack and worked their way through the deep gullies and up the steep slopes. The initial objectives were achieved with 'a brilliance which was never surpassed, if indeed equalled during the campaign. Almost the entire Turkish defence north of ANZAC was, for the moment, swept aside ...'[7] The column reached a feature called Rhododendron Spur from which they launched their attack on the final objective, Chunuk Bair. On 7 August battalion after battalion, New Zealand, British and Gurkha, fought their way forward against devastating machine-gun fire. Early on the 8th, after a heavy naval bombardment, the Wellington Regiment under Lieutenant-Colonel W.G. Malone with the 7th Gloucesters fought their way up on to a tiny foothold, exposed to the Turkish artillery and machine-guns. Throughout that day wave after wave of Turkish attacks tried to eject Malone and his men.

> The discordant clamour of battle beat back like a message to the thousands of Allied troops who stopped what they were doing to look up toward the ridge under a pall of dust and smoke. On the ridge the din was lifted to a nerve-wracking crescendo by the naval salvos trying to catch the counter-attacking Turks in the valley between the opposing positions.[8]

Brigadier Johnston sent forward more battalions to come to their relief and, at night, after Colonel Malone had been killed, 70 men out of the 760 that had set out that morning marched off the ridge. The next day a mass attack by the Turks finally destroyed the remaining British units on Chunuk Bair.

Some understanding of this inferno is necessary to appreciate the significance of Cyril Bassett's contribution. During these three days innumerable acts of heroism must have been performed and yet Bassett's was the only New Zealand VC awarded in the whole Gallipoli campaign. It is difficult to deduce the heroism involved from his own account.

> I followed our line all the way to a point where I could see some shelling, and I happened to come across three breaks in the line. Two of them were very close together and the other was 12ft to 15ft away ... I eventually found my way back to

brigade ... and the first thing they told me was that the line was not functioning
... so we [Bassett and another of his men called Burkett] decided to go out again
that night. We were out at dusk and we were out until first light the next morning.
Burkett and I located and mended three breaks that night but our activities were
very much hampered by members of the Fifth Reinforcements on their way to the
line and wounded men on the way out. A number of these troops used our lines
as guidelines to their destinations.[9]

From the start of the operation Bassett had clearly appreciated the importance of
his lines. To Malone on the ridge they must have seemed his only hope of support.
To the brigade commander they were critical to his ability to give that support
with reinforcements or artillery fire. As Bassett saw it, while the infantry were
going through their ordeal, he would not be found wanting in his part of the
endeavour. The fact that he had to do his work throughout the three days under
incessant shell fire with which the Turks swamped the approaches to the ridge,
and frequently having to evade the direct fire from small arms, made no difference. His survival was a miracle. Early in the battle a bullet lodged in his boot,
another passed through the neck of his tunic and his right pocket was shot away.

Soon after this Bassett fell ill and was evacuated to England. He learned of his
VC from a newspaper article he read in hospital. In June 1916 he rejoined his unit,
now in France, and was promoted sergeant. The following year he was commissioned and then returned to France where he was twice wounded before the end
of the war. He went back into civilian life and took up his old job again as a clerk
with the National Bank of New Zealand eventually rising to become a manager,
which post he held for some 20 years. Bassett had continued his service with the
Territorial Force until 1929. In 1940 he was mobilised with the New Zealand
Corps of Signals until being retired as a lieutenant-colonel at the end of 1943.

Cyril Bassett was a small modest man – so small he had almost been rejected
for military service. But he was certainly a self-sufficient individual who had
delighted in sailing his own yacht from an early age. Gallipoli doubtless had a
marked effect on his attitudes. In one report in 1918 his company commander
describes him as 'keen and reliable. Inclined to worry himself unduly.'[10] But, as
one newspaper article put it after his death,

he was anything but a tortured introvert. His niece ... describes him as the life and
soul of the party; a small nuggety man, full of bounce, with a dry and often cheeky
wit. In his own words he was forever disappointed to find out 'that I was the only
New Zealander to get [a VC] on Gallipoli, because hundreds of Victoria Crosses
should have been won there.'

Gas

One of the earliest of the special responsibilities that the war brought to the Royal
Engineers was to evolve a response to the German use of gas at the Second Battle
of Ypres, in the same month as the Gallipoli landings. The use of gas in warfare
has always caused repugnance even though injury and death from the effects of
more conventional weapons can be every bit as dreadful. Whatever the niceties of

the operational arguments for or against its use, it was a fact that Germany had subscribed to the Hague treaties of 1899 (proscribing 'the use of all projectiles the sole object of which is the diffusion of asphyxiating or deleterious gases') and of 1907 which added 'poison or poisoned weapons' as well as weapons causing 'unnecessary suffering'.[11] Even so, its use at Second Ypres should not have been the surprise it was, as evidence had existed of German gas attacks on the Eastern Front and there were definite intelligence reports from the Ypres Sector which should have made the Allies more prepared.

The immediate British response from the British Expeditionary Force was the summoning of Major C.H. Foulkes of the Royal Engineers to GHQ from his field company and charging him with 'dealing with this [gas] question as a whole'.[12] His immediate tasks were to explore with British industry how to dispense large clouds of chlorine in the field and to work out the drills for this and for the defensive measures that the British Army must adopt against the German capability. Eventually this was to result in the formation of the Special Brigade (so called for secrecy) whose responsibilities ranged over the whole business of chemical warfare including gas, smoke, flame and other devices. All this is outside the scope of this book but it is worth remembering some of the factors that had to be taken into account. Much had to be learned about the nature, effects, manufacture and delivery of the gases themselves. Chlorine was the immediate concern but phosgene was discovered and used fairly soon afterwards. Mustard gas was first used by the Germans in July 1917 and in Foulkes's view its introduction was 'the sole event in the gas war from which the Germans derived any substantial advantage ...'[13]

Defensive anti-gas measures were instituted immediately after the first German use. The first respirators were simple flannelette bags with celluloid eye-

Gas cylinder in a front line trench ready to be discharged. The infantry are B Company 1st Gloucesters.
(IWM Q57912)

pieces. The bags would be placed over the head and air breathed in through the flannelette and out through a mouthpiece. The bags would be soaked in chemicals, the constituents of which evolved as the threat from differing types of gas developed. Later the box respirator was devised with a much more efficient filtering system in which air was drawn in through a container of carbon granules. Backing up this technology was the essential discipline with which men were trained in its use and the warning systems and alarms devised for units in the trenches. At first, anti-gas defence was the responsibility of the Royal Army Medical Corps but it was transferred to the Royal Engineers in 1916.

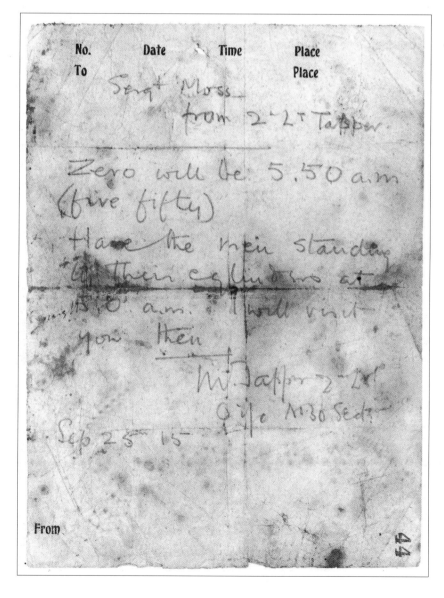

Field message for the first offensive use of gas by the British Army.
(IWM Q56655)

The other main consideration was the means of delivery and tied in with that the logistics and meteorology. Initially both sides used clouds of gas delivered from cylinders located in the front line. The problems of locating these (700 tons were used on the first day of Loos and that was insufficient) and of the infantry having to live with this dangerous and cumbersome equipment in the trenches are obvious. Later the Germans tended to favour artillery delivery in shells but the British found that more effective concentrations could be emplaced by means of mortars. At first the 4-inch version of the Stokes mortar was used but later a unique but remarkably simple device known as the Livens projector was procured – essentially a 9-inch steel tube with a baseplate that could be dug into the ground, delivering a container of substantially more gas (or anything else come to that) than either a mortar bomb or artillery shell could accommodate.

As we have seen, the first British use of gas was at Loos where 5500 cylinders were employed over a frontage of some ten miles (nearly half the total frontage of the attack). Although the wind conditions were far from ideal the effects were devastating to parts of the enemy line, thanks to exceptional measures having been taken to ensure secrecy – necessary because the German respirators were well developed by that time. A by-product of this plan incidentally was that, because of the shortage, smoke was used in considerable quantity instead of gas to deceive the Germans. It was so successful in concealing the movements of units that henceforth it was adopted in its own right as part of normal tactical plans.

In summary, in front of Loos, the gas cloud carried well over the German trenches as it did in the neighbourhood of the Hohenzollern Redoubt (see also Chapter Eight) and 'was to exert a marked influence on the advance of the 47th, 15th and 9th Divisions, only falling short of complete success because it moved too slowly and there was not enough of it.'[14] South of Loos the vapour cloud moved too slowly and in the centre it actually began to float back. The worst sector was that of the 2nd Division where representations were made to abandon the use of gas because of the obviously unfavourable wind. This was initially refused but eventually agreed when casualties to the British troops from their own gas were becoming serious.

Corporal James Dawson

James Dawson (1891–1967). This photograph was taken c. 1916.

The two units responsible for this work on 25 and 26 September 1915 were 186 and 187 Special Companies, RE. Corporal James Dawson was a member of 187 Company but it was not until the very end of the battle, three weeks later on 13 October, that he won undying fame. James Dawson was a well-educated man who had attended Alloa Academy and the Royal Technical College, Glasgow. He was a teacher for a time and enlisted into 5th Cameronians in November 1914. He transferred to the Royal Engineers after going to France in March 1915, no doubt as a direct result of the need to recruit men of good technical education into the Special Brigade. He must have experienced the intensive training and experimental work that the special companies underwent at their base at Helfaut near St Omer.

As we have seen, one of the key points in the Battle of Loos was the Hohenzollern Redoubt, situated on the high ground near Cité St Elic on which the Germans had developed an immensely strong complex of trenches (see Map 15). Although this strongpoint was taken with extraordinary determination on the first day of the battle, it was effectively lost, barring a small foothold, a week or so later. The Germans counter-attacked elsewhere on the battlefield on 8 October thereby upsetting plans for the next British effort to recover the Hohenzollern, which was now postponed to 13 October. The attack was to be made by the 29th Brigade of 9th Division.

Preparing for this, the infantry were crammed in the trenches and having to put up with the unwelcome presence of the gas team with their cumbersome and dangerous equipment. There then occurred one of those crises that had always been feared. Gas started to leak from cylinders situated in the trenches in which the infantry were forming up and from which a gas attack was in progress. The cylinders had to be removed and the infantry led to a safer place. James Dawson climbed out of the trench, as the citation puts it, 'in order to be the better able to give directions to his own sappers, and to clear the infantry out of the sections of the trench that were full of gas. Finding three leaking gas cylinders, he rolled them some sixteen yards away from the trench, again under very heavy fire, and then fired rifle bullets into them to let the gas escape. There is no doubt that the cool gallantry of Corporal Dawson on this occasion saved many men from being gassed.'

Dawson could not have expected to survive long in the hail of fire to which the trench was being subjected but, miraculously, he did and afterwards rose rapidly through the ranks in the rest of his career. He was a WO2 within a few weeks, was commissioned the following February and finished the war as an instructor in the rank of major.[15]

Dawson was demobilised in 1919 and completed his education at Glasgow University obtaining his BSc in 1920. He must have hankered after army life for he obtained his commission in the Army Education Corps in that year and embarked on an extremely impressive career in the Indian Army, transferring to the Indian Army Ordnance Corps in 1931. He was again a major by 1936, attended the Staff College, Quetta in 1938 and reached the acting rank of Colonel in 1943 while serving with the India Supply Commission in North America. After the war he remained in India and stayed on after Independence to assist the Indian Army.

After Loos gas was regularly used by both sides in all major battles as part of the battle plan. On the British side much effort went into improving the means of delivery. Effectiveness was always seen as being proportional to the quantity of material that could be emplaced. However new gases and combinations of them were experimented with. The Germans remained largely dependent on artillery as the means of delivery but put much effort into discovering new gases, mustard being the most significant.

The overall impact of gas as a weapon in the First World War has sometimes been exaggerated. Its effectiveness in causing casualties was always tempered by the weather conditions and the possibility of danger to own troops. Nevertheless there were occasions when gas created that critical breakthrough that led to success. Moreover, by forcing the mandatory wearing of respirators and other counter-measures, the threat of gas greatly hampered offensive operations and inhibited routine in the trenches.

The Tunnellers

In a flash the monsters of destruction lurking below the ground were goaded into wakefulness. With a stupendous paroxysm they shook themselves free, convulsing the earth for miles around … It seemed as if the Messines ridge got up and shook itself. All along its flank belched rows of mushroom-shaped masses of debris, flung high into the air … This was a man-made earthquake, a spectacle out-majestied only by Nature in her most ungovernable moods.[16]

A mine crater.

This florid language aims to convey something of the awesome sense of climax experienced by all the men of General Sir Herbert Plumer's Second Army as they waited for the assault on the heavily fortified Messines ridge on 7 June 1917; none more so than the Royal Engineers' tunnellers who had been preparing for this event for over two years. On the efficiency of their work hung the success or failure of the attack – and the lives of thousands of men. This was the greatest offensive mining* operation of all time. Many of the 19 mines, each containing 20,000 to 100,000 lb of ammonal, laid 50 to 100 feet deep and at the end of galleries some 1500 feet in length, had been emplaced more than a year earlier, their condition being painstakingly maintained against the ravages of the climate, enemy action and accidental falls of earth.

The attack shattered the German defence and by mid-afternoon the ridge was firmly in Allied hands. Adequate measures had been taken for reinforcements and support by artillery and tanks, and the counter-attacks which followed the next

---

*Today the term 'mine' in a military context normally means a manufactured explosive device designed to be set off by a target such as a soldier (anti-personnel) or a tank initiating its fuse mechanism. Such devices did not exist in 1914. Mines were then, as they had been from time immemorial, buried charges fired 'on command' from a distant firing point.

day were successfully beaten off. Regrettably, as is well known, no further exploitation of this triumph took place and the Allied attempt finally to break out of the Ypres Salient struggled on until it finally ground to a halt in November in the mud of Passchendaele.

If Messines was the fulfilment of all that had gone into the tunnelling effort on the Western Front, it was by no means typical. Even the many more modest but successful offensive uses of mining were only part of the great contribution that the tunnellers made to operations as a whole.

It all started at the end of 1914. Mining had, of course, always been one of the military engineer's stocks in trade. In Chapter Two of this book Lucknow is just one example, but since the dawn of time attacking forces have burrowed under the walls of fortifications, their tunnels in their turn being attacked by the defence. However, the sort of siege warfare that had developed by the first winter of the First World War had never been envisaged and the field companies had only the most rudimentary training in the necessary skills. What little equipment existed was hopelessly outdated but the need to develop this specialisation became urgent when the Germans started offensive tunnelling operations. Their first success occurred near Givenchy, a spot destined to play a major part in this story, when they broke through the Sirhind Brigade after devastating their forward fire-trench with ten small mines.

A plea by General Sir Henry Rawlinson, commanding IV Corps for a specialist battalion, happily coincided with an offer made to the War Office by a Major J. Norton Griffiths, MP to provide some expert manpower from his considerable construction empire, to undertake the tunnelling operations which he foresaw would be needed. Griffiths was a colourful, unconventional character who was able to persuade the sappers and field commanders to adopt a radical approach, based on the use of the 'clay-kickers' – specialists in driving narrow tunnels in very restricted conditions. He insisted on the procurement of specialist equipment and the provision of mechanical transport for his units, the latter almost unheard of in those days. From this beginning developed a colossal force of up to 24,000 men who served in 32 tunnelling companies of which 25 were British, three Canadian, three Australian and one from New Zealand.[17]

The 'clay-kicking' technique for tunnelling in confined spaces.

Inside a mine. The galleries where the miners worked would be considerably smaller, seldom permitting a man to stand.

In the way of things, applications were found for these units which far exceeded the original expectations. Initially the need was for defensive measures. The morale of troops in the forward trenches was suffering badly from the prospect of being undermined and buried in some catastrophic explosion, and the lack of any available response. While one of the field companies had done a little mining on the Ypres front on 17 February 1915, the first successful counter-mine was fired shortly afterwards, also in the Ypres area, by a party of 171 Tunnelling Company under Lieutenant Cloutman (the brother of Major B.M. Cloutman who won the VC on the Sambre-Oise canal in November 1914; see Chapter Twelve). Lieutenant W.R. Cloutman was killed in August 1915 in a fall while saving the life of a sergeant in 178 Tunnelling Company.

Offensive mining soon came into its own, both as part and parcel of the defensive measures and, in its own right, integrated with infantry attacks. Philip Neame records one such incident on 9 May 1915 at Fromelles during the Aubers Ridge battle 'a bloody affair for my division. The only real success was the firing of two great mines under the German line, which blew a hundred yards of their trench and its garrison into the air. Our attacking infantry broke through here and went far.'[18]

Thus the underground war developed until the tunnellers became an indispensable arm of the British forces so that, as Grieve and Newman put it, 'Every battle overground had its counterpart below.' To illustrate the intensity of this activity, in June 1916, 227 mines were fired along the whole British front,

101 by the British and 126 by the Germans; 79 and 73 respectively were fired on the First Army front from Laventie to the north end of Vimy Ridge.[19]

Acts of extraordinary courage were performed by these men whose daily life was surrounded by danger from suffocation or crushing in a fall, asphyxiation by mine gases, entombment as a result of an enemy counter-mine or a fight to the death in a three-foot gallery. Tracking of the enemy's tunnels was also crucial and, although this was normally achieved using geophones – large-scale stethoscopes requiring amazing patience and skill to interpret the various sounds – there were many occasions when tunnellers broke through into the enemy's galleries, to explore and destroy them at immense risk to their own lives. Although many decorations were earned in these appalling circumstances, only one VC was awarded.

Sapper William Hackett

William Hackett was a 41-year-old professional miner at the outbreak of war. He never went to school but started work in factories in Nottingham. His father was a travelling brewer who did a considerable business with the country inns. When William Hackett was 18 years of age he started work in the mine at Denaby Main, Mexborough in the South Riding of Yorkshire and stayed there for 23 years. He then went to Manvers Colliery as a 'dataller' – one who was engaged and paid by the day for such work as repairing and making roads or rail tracks, not actually mining. He was a married man with two children. Like so many in his profession he could neither read nor write. He was apparently 'a quiet, unassuming man, typical of the everyday steady-going miner, sparing of speech and philosophical of soul'.[20] His parents, John and Harriet Hackett, lived at Nottingham and in the years up to 1915 William Hackett would occasionally take a few days' leave and walk from Mexborough to Nottingham and back to see them, a distance of some 90 miles. He would need to be fit as it was a hard and dangerous way of life. William Hackett had already survived one roof-fall and, ironically, one of his motives for wanting to join the army was undoubtedly to get away from his unpleasant working conditions. His first attempt to enlist in the York and Lancaster Regiment failed when he was rejected as too old. After three other rejections for age and suspected heart trouble, in October 1915 he was accepted for the Royal Engineer tunnelling companies and less than a month later he was in France as a member of 254 Tunnelling Company after the very rudimentary training and kitting out that the tunnellers received.

Surrounded as he now was by danger and death, at times, for a man of William Hackett's age, the wrench of separation from his family must have been hard to bear. Some of his letters home have survived, including a number of the beautifully worked embroidered postcards that were customarily sent home to wives and sweethearts, treasured until recently by his granddaughter Mrs Freda Warren who kindly donated them to the Royal Engineers Museum in 1996. The inscriptions

*William Hackett
based on a photograph,
c. 1915.*

on these and the ordinary letters that his wife received were written by one of William Hackett's pals, Sapper J.R. Evans. Being subject to censor they reveal very little about the work or conditions but there is a peculiar poignancy in their style:

> We shall have to look on the bright side of things and pray for the best you know because all our lives now is full of troubles and I wish to God they was all over with and the war is only just starting since I have been out here but the young fellow that writes for me says it is only just the same as it was last year but dear Wife there is going to be some bloodshed before so very long I think they don't intend it going on so very much longer and they all seem to think so too and I don't care how soon because we are all fed up … (March 1916)[21]

A particular worry for William Hackett was that his 14-year-old son Arthur, who had already started work in Manvers mine to help with the family livelihood, suffered a bad accident shortly after his father left for France when a train of mine tubs ran off the road. He had only been working in the mine four weeks and now he had to have a leg amputated. It was reported that it had required an effort of will for Mrs Hackett to communicate the distressing intelligence to her husband. He received it 'as he was apt to receive all the troubles of life, with sad resignation.'

> It is very hard to have his leg off but God know best … it's very hard for me to be in this foreign land and have a lad placed in hospital … I cannot help him but I know you will do all you can. (February 1916)[22]

The lack of any substance in these communications may also have worried Sapper Evans who wrote on his own account,

> I hope Mrs Hackett the letters I write for your husband is alright, because he never tells me anything to put in. I know it is not like writing one himself and I know it must be very hard lines if he can't write …[23]

The working conditions in the world in which William Hackett found himself were also very different from those he knew in Denaby and Manvers Main Collieries, hard though those were at that time. The cramped galleries would not permit the swinging of a pick and the ever-present dangers of tunnelling in war would all be new to him. What would be familiar, however, was the legendary pride and *esprit de corps* of the miners, a major factor in their achievements.

254 Company was working at Givenchy when William Hackett displayed the supreme example of this spirit in an extraordinary act of self-sacrifice. The incident is well described in *Tunnellers*.[24]

> The main drive from Shaftesbury Shaft had not proceeded very far, and five men were in it at the time of the blow [from a German counter-mine]. The shock broke some of the timbers near the shaft, causing a fall of roof and cutting off the men. Relays of workers set to work at top speed to release the trapped men. After

twenty-four hours a small opening was made through the soft fallen ground and broken timber. Three men scrambled through it to safety.

It was then discovered that a smaller fall of roof had occurred near the face. Of the two men remaining in the gallery, one, a big man was badly injured by the fall near the face [this was Private T. Collins of the 14th Battalion of the Welch Regiment, one of many tunnellers, often former miners, who had been recruited from within the BEF, at the urging of Norton Griffiths and against the wishes of their commanding officers, so urgent was the demand for professional men]; the other was Sapper William Hackett. The opening which the rescue party had driven through the outby fall was too small to permit the injured man to be passed through, and as there was immediate danger of further falls, Hackett was ordered to come out. Well knowing his fate, he steadfastly refused to leave the injured man saying: 'I am a Tunneller. I must look after my mate.' Scarcely had he finished speaking when both men were overwhelmed by a fall of clay which filled the gallery completely.

The event must have devastated the family, particularly coming so soon after the injuries to their son. Even before his death William Hackett had earned great respect in the unit, no doubt partly because of his age. Sapper Evans wrote to Alice Hackett on 3 July in condolence:

I am most sorry to have to write to you under such circumstances that is to inform you that your husband Sapper Hackett was Killed in Action on 22nd June but I can tell you he died a hero's death as brave as any man as died in this war which I hope before long you will hear more about it. And I can tell you your husband's death is sadly felt as he was respected by all the officers and men of the 254 Company and as for myself I miss him so much as if he was my own Father as you know I used to write all his letters for him ... I only wish I could tell it the way it happen, but if I am spared I will come and see you and let you know all about it ...[25]

Evans's letter is almost prescient in its talk of a 'hero's death' and 'you will hear more about it', almost as if this supreme act of self-sacrifice had created such an upswell of admiration that some sort of recognition must be on the cards. Other than the VC the only posthumous award available would have been a Mention in Despatches – clearly inadequate for the case and so the possibility of a VC must have been discussed, extraordinary as it may have seemed. Nevertheless so it happened, gazetted in August. Sir Evelyn Wood, VC, veteran of the Crimean and many other wars, called William Hackett's 'The most divine-like act of self-sacrifice of which I have ever read.'[26] It is a point of interest that his deed was one of several during this war (see also Carmichael, Chapter Ten) that did not occur strictly 'in the presence of the enemy' and could possibly have been a case for the Albert Medal which had been instituted in 1866, since which date no VCs had been awarded unless in the presence of the enemy. The George Cross, which has now superseded the Albert Medal, could well be considered appropriate for a similar act nowadays.

A collection was made to produce some money for Alice Hackett and her children, including a personal contribution from the Chief Engineer. In a letter to the *Sapper* in May 1917, Mrs Alice Hackett expresses her gratitude for the efforts of her late husband's mates to help with her difficulties:[27]

> I don't know how to thank my kind friends that God has raised up for me in my trouble. He has taken with one hand and given with the other. I am very grateful both to Him and to all my friends. Will you kindly let them know how deeply I appreciate their goodness to me and my children?
>
> I am glad to be able to tell you that I have not had to use the £67 that my husband's comrades sent me, but banked it to use for my children's education, so that if anything should happen to me they would be able to help themselves. They are going to the secondary school here, and my boy is also learning shorthand to fit him for an office. I put him to it as soon as he came out of hospital, and his Dad was so pleased to know that he would not have to go to the pit again. But he knew I should do my best for my chicks, and I trust that they will grow up a credit to their brave father ...

Alice Hackett received her late husband's Victoria Cross from King George V at Buckingham Palace on 29 November 1916. Fifty years later Mrs Mary Hopkins, the only daughter of William and Alice Hackett, presented the Victoria Cross to the Royal Engineers as reported in the *Sapper* of that year:[28]

> [Mrs Hopkins] was insistent that there should be no ceremony... She declined suggestions that the hand-over should take place either at the local TA Drill Hall or at the colliery where her father once worked and is still remembered. As she placed the small bronze cross in Brigadier Inglis' hand she remarked: 'It seems such a little thing in exchange for a life.'

In September the following year Alice Hackett received an invitation from the Manvers Main Colliery, where William Hackett had worked, to a ceremony at which she was to be presented with a gold watch in honour of her husband. Mary Hopkins died in 1974 at the age of 71. Her brother Arthur did manage to make a living but died in 1963, aged 61. The gold watch is still treasured by Mrs Freda Warren and her family.

Both the town of Mexborough and Manvers Main Colliery were justly proud of William Hackett's remarkable sacrifice. He was remembered by the town on a special plaque originally sited on the wall of the former Town Hall but which has now been moved to a more appropriate setting adjacent to the Civic War Memorial. In the grounds of the now closed Manvers Colliery there stands a substantial sandstone memorial to 204 former miners, including William Hackett, who gave their lives in the Great War of 1914–1918. Again in 1996, the Dearne Valley Partnership proposed to clear and re-site this memorial in the course of regenerating the area.

Thus perhaps Wilfred Owen's pessimistic prediction will not come to pass:

William Hackett's memorial in Mexborough. The canny councillors left a space under his name just in case there was a second local VC.

The centuries will burn rich loads
With which we groaned,
Whose warmth shall lull their dreaming lids
While songs are crooned.
But they will not dream of us poor lads
Lost in the ground.[29]

After 1916, with the exception of the Messines Ridge operation, this underground war reduced somewhat in intensity and the tunnellers' skills were sought

in other ways. One was for defusing booby traps at which they had become adept as a result of examining enemy tunnels and bunkers. But possibly their most important contribution was the building of tunnels and subways to enable men in the attack to approach an enemy trench line without being exposed to murderous machine-gun and artillery fire across hundreds of yards of no-man's-land. This technique saved thousands of lives in the Battle of Arras in April 1917, where the subways were linked in with the existing underground cave system lying to the east of the city and provided a two-mile covered approach for the attacking force and its logistic back-up. Although this was on an exceptionally vast scale, lesser tunnel systems did the same in many battles across the front. One of the tragedies of the first day of the Somme was that the Russian saps* which had been laboriously prepared to allow mortar and machine-gun posts to be pushed forward into no-man's-land could have saved thousands of lives if they had been used by the infantry.

Finally, during the great Allied advance in the autumn of 1918, launched by the Battle of Amiens, the tunnellers demonstrated their versatility in many sapper skills from bridging (in which business another sapper VC was to be won) to dealing with booby traps. Field Marshal Haig, Commander-in-Chief of the British Army in France, is reported to have said: 'They are the best unit in the whole army; there is nothing they cannot do'[30] – and wrote a fulsome tribute to them at the end of the war in his own hand.

---

*A Russian sap is a shallow tunnel burrowed forward in such a way that the roof can be broken through and opened up to allow its subsequent use as a trench.

The First World War
The Salient (1917)

By universal consent the Third Battle of Ypres represents the utmost that war has so far achieved in the way of horrors.[1]

Four days after William Hackett had made his lonely sacrifice in the depths of Shaftesbury Shaft, Givenchy, 20,000 British soldiers died in a single day* out in the open fields of the Somme. That battle has become notorious for the apparent misappreciation of the German strength after the preliminary bombardment, the most massive of the war to that point, which resulted in the tragic loss of the citizen army, raised with such energy and foresight by Kitchener since the early days of the war. There are many criticisms of Haig's generalship and of the fact that in four more months of battle and 400,000 British casualties later, only a few miles of territory had been gained. In fact, in two essentials – choice of ground and timing of the assault – Haig's plans had been constrained by the need to co-ordinate with the French. After the first day, much more success was achieved albeit in a fight of growing ferocity, as lessons were learned from the early disasters.

Nowadays the main features of the Somme battle to the general public are the personal tragedies of the casualties and a general bafflement as to how such apparent waste could have been allowed to occur and continue. The other side of the coin is the fundamental determination to prevail that is reflected in so many contemporary accounts and the courage and professionalism with which men, both regulars and volunteers, undertook the job. It is also worthwhile to view the Somme battle in the context of the whole war in 1916. By the time it was launched the French were still engaged in their greatest test of the war at Verdun, where defeating the German attempts to bleed their army to death was absorbing all available manpower and matériel. To the French, the Somme was a mere diversion, albeit one which contributed to their final success at Verdun. On a wider scene, in 1916 there had already been much bad news for the British. In the Middle East Kut had fallen to the Turks in April after a protracted siege. Closer to home, only a few days before Kut, the Easter Rising had occurred in Dublin which had threatened the internal security of the United Kingdom with implications for the loyalty and commitment of the thousands of Irishmen who were fighting in the ranks of the British Army. At sea there was better news; the Battle of Jutland in May had caused the German battle fleet to withdraw from active

---

*Overall casualties were 57,000 and another 2000 missing. Although 19,000 were killed on the first day, many more died from their wounds later. Of the 2000 missing a large proportion would have been recorded on the Thiepval memorial, their names appearing among the 73,412 whose bodies were never found.

participation in the war although the Royal Navy had come off worse numerically. In another event at sea in June, Kitchener had lost his life when HMS *Hampshire*, in which he was travelling to Russia, struck a mine off Scapa Flow.

In retrospect there is little doubt that the Somme was a turning point for Germany in the war. Between the Somme and Verdun they lost over a million men. The experience caused them to build a new line further back, the Hindenburg Line, from which they were to launch their great offensives in 1918. Germany even made some peace proposals at this stage but they were unaccept-

Map 17
*The Salient in 1917
showing Westhoek
ridge and Hill 60.*

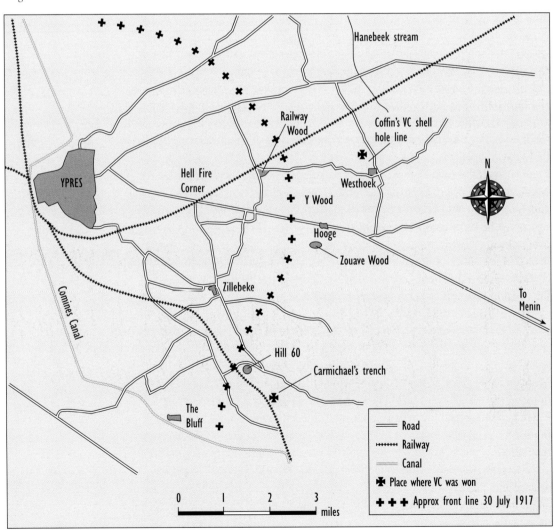

able to the Allies and the war continued. After the war many believed that it was their losses in the Somme battles that struck the fatal blow that finally forced them to give up, even though there was still much life in the body in 1916. Be that as it may, the whole story of the Somme belongs elsewhere, as despite the close support given by the sapper field companies in the deteriorating terrain as the battle progressed, and the high toll taken of men necessarily working in the open on the vital business of keeping the supply routes in order, no sapper VCs resulted.

Notwithstanding these massive battles at Verdun and on the Somme, things were by no means quiet elsewhere on the front and our particular story moves further north back to the Salient at Ypres, scene of the bitter struggles in the winter of 1914–15 for possession of the best tactical ground culminating in the Second Ypres battle mentioned in Chapter Eight. Early in 1916 the Germans broke through the British lines in the northern part of the Salient and captured a feature known as The Bluff which gave excellent observation to which ever side was in possession. It was recaptured later in the year at the cost of thousands of casualties. Haig had always believed that the best area for a successful break through the German lines was from the Salient through Belgium. However, he was distracted from this possibility by the need to conform with the French. After Verdun, Joffre had been replaced by General Robert Nivelle who managed to persuade the British politicians that a further assault by the French in the centre, from the Aisne valley, would achieve the longed-for success. An indispensable part of his plan was a British diversionary attack from Arras to Vimy which would draw off the Germans from the Aisne. The British part succeeded gloriously but Nivelle's attack failed disastrously with dire consequences to the French Army and, as a result, Haig's plans for his attack in the north had to be postponed. Moreover, he had the greatest difficulty convincing Lloyd George, who had taken over as Prime Minister from Asquith at the end of 1916, that any more manpower should be provided for this purpose. Nevertheless, the plans went ahead.

The precursor to the Third Ypres battle, now generally known as Passchendaele, was the assault on Messines Ridge to the south of Ypres in June 1917. From this ground the Germans could bring fire down along the length of the British trench system and launching Third Ypres would have been impossible so long as they remained in possession. The story of mining, and the British attack on Messines in particular, have already been touched on in Chapter Nine. Messines was a resounding success, thanks to the firing of the greatest series of mines in the whole war – in fact in the whole of warfare. The ridge was in British hands by the afternoon of 7 June and Second Army was able to dig in sufficiently to repel the German counter-attacks which, amazingly, they were able to mount the following day.

The gains were limited if measured in miles but the Germans were now off balance and, had a rapid follow-up been possible, the story of the First World War might have been very different. That it was not is characteristic of the war. Such flexibility either of mind or of the sheer mechanics of the movement of formations simply did not exist. So Haig's great plan of attack, largely by Sir Hubert Gough's Fifth Army towards the Passchendaele ridge, did not materialise until late July. By then not only had the Germans had time to recover from the disaster of Messines and improve their defences by building new trench lines in depth, but the weather had begun to deteriorate so that, after the massive bombardment that preceded the attack, the battlefield was reduced to the terrible morass which the name Passchendaele has come to symbolise. Something of the sapper problem is described in the unpublished company history of 409 (Lowland) Field Company, there through October and November 1917, and whom we shall be meeting again later in the final battle of the war:

> the country a brown sea of mud for miles on end pitted with shell holes from 5 to 20 feet across with their lips nearly touching. Hedges disappeared, woods a few shattered stumps. The roads that had been, had ceased to exist except here and there a stump of a tree indicating where it had once been, in their shell-holes brim full of water, green with gas or red with blood, such was the setting for our work. In the devastation one problem stood paramount, how to get food and ammunition over this sea of mud. Roads were shelled to pieces as soon as made, light railways suffered much the same and so their forward progress was small, pack mules nightly were left behind bogged and the edges of what had been roads were strewn with carcases. The only way was duck-boards and so we laid duck-boards and enabled our infantry to get up and be relieved and get their food and many were helped to stick it out by the thought of easing the passage of the many laden stretchers ...
>
> Yet in the midst of all the danger and desolation, there is a certain fascination out there on patrol taping out a new line not quite knowing in the dark where the flounder in the mud has led you until some recognisable land mark is identified; the shells drop in some places not in others, if that track passes in the wrong place ill luck to those who lay it and use it ...[2]

Neither side was spared the agonies of what followed. The German historian, Kuhl, a former Chief of the German General Staff, wrote:

> The sufferings, privations and exertions which the soldiers had to bear were inexpressible. Terrible was the spiritual burden for the lonely man in the shell hole and terrible the strain on the nerves which continued day and night. The 'Hell of Verdun' was exceeded by Flanders. The Battle of Flanders [the German name for Passchendaele] has been called 'The greatest martyrdom of the World War'.
>
> No division could last more than a fortnight in this hell. Then it had to be relieved by new troops. Looking back it seems that that which was borne here was superhuman. With respect and thankfulness the German people will always remember the heroes of Flanders.[3]

This was the background to the scene into which Brigadier-General Clifford Coffin led his brigade on 31 July 1917.

Brigadier-General Clifford Coffin

Clifford Coffin was born in Blackheath, the son of an Indian Army officer, Lieutenant-General Sir Isaac Campbell Coffin. Clifford was educated at Haileybury College and the RMA Woolwich and commissioned into the Royal Engineers in 1888. His elder brother, Campbell, had already joined the Royal Engineers in February 1886.

*Clifford Coffin
(1870–1959)*

Clifford's first overseas posting was to Jamaica with the Submarine Miners. The submarine mines were never engaged in any form of action either in Jamaica or elsewhere, and on his return home in 1894 he married Helen Douglas, elder daughter of Admiral Sir Thomas Sturges Jackson.

In 1899 Coffin was sent to South Africa to participate in the Boer War. He saw action in the relief of Kimberley, at Paardeberg, in Cape Colony and in the Transvaal where he commanded a composite field company in Roberts's final operations after the fall of Pretoria. He took part in Kitchener's anti-guerrilla war and returned to England in 1904 with both war medals, six clasps and a mention in despatches.

Soon after the beginning of the First World War, Coffin was appointed CRE 21st Division, one of the new divisions being raised by Kitchener for the New Army. As we have seen in Chapter Eight, this was one of the two divisions thrown belatedly straight into the Battle of Loos only a fortnight after their arrival in France and which were destroyed by German machine-gun fire on 26 September. 21st Division, on the right flank, were attacking Hill 70 where Captain Frederick Johnson was winning his VC. Coffin's men were largely employed rescuing and collecting men struggling back from the battle and in repairing the trenches. For the Somme battles, 21st Division was part of XV Corps in Fourth Army, and Coffin's contribution was sufficient to earn him a DSO in the 1917 New Year's Honours. The following March he was appointed to command 25th Brigade in 8th Division. 8th Division had been in France since November 1914 and was Philip Neame's division when he won his VC. It had taken part in the battles of Neuve-Chapelle and the Somme, where it had suffered grievously. Shortly after Clifford Coffin took over 25th Infantry Brigade he made an early impression in the advances beyond Bouchavesnes in March 1917 as the Germans withdrew to the Hindenburg Line. The brigade moved into the Salient with 8th Division in June.

Third Ypres

The opening attack for the Third Battle of Ypres started at 3.10 am on 31 July after ten days of heavy bombardment which destroyed the drainage system in the area and created the fields of mud. The Division's initial objectives seemed modest enough, known as Blue and Black Line, respectively some 1000 and 2000 yards ahead. The general intention was to occupy the relatively high ground from which the Germans had observation over Ypres itself, to secure the north-east sector of the Salient in the area of Pilckem Ridge, consolidate there and then move on. 8th Division's sector was well to the south of Pilckem Ridge and lay between Railway Wood on the left and Zouave Wood on the right, the centre line of the attack to be roughly in a north-north-easterly direction. The initial assault was to be by 23rd Infantry Brigade on the left and 24th Infantry Brigade on the right. 25th Infantry Brigade was to remain in reserve. They set off in a downpour and at first met with considerable success. By mid-morning on 31 July:

> The Germans were now [9.30 am on 31 July] deprived almost entirely of observation over the Ypres district. The menace which every British soldier in the Salient had felt for over two years was at an end, and the situation reversed. While men and traffic could now move about the Ypres Salient in daylight with comparative impunity, British ground observers could see deep into the German position.[4]

The decision was now made to carry on with the advance, and it is at this point that Clifford Coffin and 25th Infantry Brigade come into the story. They were ordered forward to Westhoek ridge to carry on the attack to the third objective (Red Line). By now the German resistance was becoming well organised and, within an hour of their advance, 25th Brigade was thoroughly bogged down. The War Diary reports two lines held up on Westhoek ridge at 11.00 am and that the centre company of 1st Battalion the Royal Irish Rifles had reached Hanebeek but then had given ground. At this critical point Coffin moved forward up the ridge with his Senior Artillery Liaison Officer and nothing more relevant is recorded in the War Diary until 2.30 pm when German counter-attacks were noted and at 2.40 pm when consolidation was ordered. In fact, as can be seen from his citation, Brigadier General Coffin was rallying his men while under murderous fire:

> Though under the heaviest fire from both machine-guns and rifles, and in full view of the enemy, he showed an utter disregard of personal danger, walking quietly from shell-hole to shell-hole, giving advice generally, and cheering the men by his presence. His very gallant conduct had the greatest effect on all ranks, and it was largely owing to his personal courage and example that the shell-hole line was held … Throughout the day his calm courage and cheerfulness exercised the greatest influence over all with whom he came in contact, and it is generally agreed that Brigadier General Coffin's splendid example saved the situation, and had it not been for his action the line would certainly have been driven back.

By evening the troops were 'holding with tenacity caused by the failure of the German attacks.'[5] They were relieved overnight.

When it is remembered that on that day some 80 infantry brigades were launched against the German positions and unquestionable heroism had been displayed along the whole length of the front, the nature of Clifford Coffin's contribution to the battle becomes apparent. That he should be singled out for recognition suggests quite exceptional bravery in quite exceptional circumstances from which he could not reasonably have expected to survive. His VC for this action was the first occasion on which one had been awarded to so senior an officer. Not that there was anything in the rules to prevent this. The spirit of the original proposals had been for a reward for bravery regardless of rank and there had been no change to this, merely an almost subconscious feeling that this was a reward for junior ranks. There had even been earlier specific cases where submissions had been rejected on these grounds, for example for Colonel Ian Hamilton when he was commanding a brigade in South Africa.[6]

Westhoek ridge. This picture was taken during the September offensive some six weeks after Clifford Coffin's battle.
(IWM E(AUS)981)

In fact the first day of the battle had gone quite well for the British and in many places the advances exceeded expectations. The next main attack two weeks later achieved some progress after superhuman efforts* but by then the situation had deteriorated into the conditions with which Passchendaele is always connected: the sea of mud into which men and horses were drawn down with little hope of rescue, the duckboard 'roads' forward which became death-traps for reinforcements, reliefs and supplies moving forward and for the walking wounded and stretcher bearers struggling back. On 16 August 8th Division, now in a sector north of the Menin road, launched their next attack, across the Hanebeek stream. Again Coffin was to the fore in the desperate struggle to move forward in the frightful conditions. The divisional history describes how he went forward him-

---

*One of the most vivid accounts of this is contained in *Some Desperate Glory*, the diaries of Edwin Campion Vaughan, published by Leo Cooper in 1981.

self to reconnoitre and to rally the retiring line to check the advance of the enemy counter-attack. Later in the day he decided to put Brigade Headquarters personnel into the line where the Brigade Commander then found the Brigade Signalling Officer, Lieutenant Cohen, RE, 'shooting away very happily and putting carefully into his pocket the empty cases of cartridges with which he had scored a hit.'[7]

In fact the weather did improve and in late September two more big attacks were made after a period of hectic consolidation and work throughout the battlefield to build roads, strengthen positions and move up supplies of ammunition. Much of this was achieved, under relentless fire from the enemy artillery, by the sappers and the infantry parties working with them. Lyn Macdonald notes that of more than 10,000 casualties in the first two weeks of September, 6000 were sustained by the engineers and another 3000 by the infantry.[8]

The battle finally came to an end after the Canadians had captured Passchendaele itself in November. As with the Somme, Third Ypres, for all that 250,000 casualties were incurred on either side for small territorial gain, has to be judged for what it achieved in the overall conduct of the war. The Germans saw it as an opportunity to break the British and Allied armies once and for all. They concentrated all their effort there and this diverted them from their greatest opportunity where great gaps existed in the French line after the mutinies on the Aisne front following Nivelle's unsuccessful offensive. That the Germans failed, despite their improved position as a result of the collapse of the Russian front, must be seen as a success for the British initiative even though Haig's ambition of forcing them back into Belgium was never achieved.

As to Clifford Coffin, the war had much action still in store for him. After Passchendaele the brigade was transferred to the Fifth Army in front of Amiens and became embroiled in the great German onslaught which is the subject of the next chapter. During the retreat south of the Somme he conducted a rearguard action in which at one time he had command of the entire infantry of his division. In May he gained a bar to his DSO for this achievement and was given command of 36th (Ulster) Division which he led during the final victorious but hard-fought advance to Courtrai and beyond.

After the Armistice, Coffin was given a brigade in the Rhine Army and, in 1919, was posted to command 16th Brigade in Northern Ireland. His final appointment in the Army was as commander of the British troops in Ceylon. He retired in 1924 and undertook work on behalf of the British Commonwealth Ex-Service League, becoming its chairman during the Second World War. He died in February 1959, ten years after his wife. A tribute was written to him by Field Marshal Lord Milne in the March issue of *Empire and Commonwealth*:

> In whatever he did he excelled because he put his whole heart in the job without worrying about himself – on the Staff, in the field and in civil life afterwards it was the same as the BCEL, the Diocese of Chichester, the Society of St George and many other worthy cause can abundantly testify …
>
> To carry out his work … he had to leave at a very early hour from his home

Opposite

An aerial photo looking south-east from Ypres in August 1914 which gives some idea of the devastation in the city and the surrounding desolation. Hill 60 is out of the picture to the left, along the line of the railway.

after attending to the many tasks he did there. He was amazingly good at reducing page after page of legal briefs and opinions into one sheet of foolscap. 'You forget,' he said, 'I am a trained staff officer!'

But we must return to the Salient where Clifford Coffin's talents had been a long way removed from staff work.

Hill 60

During the preparations for the September push, the 9th Battalion the Staffordshire Regiment were in occupation of the trenches in the area of Hill 60, one of the most important landmarks in the Salient because of its elevation above the surrounding ground and the observation it gave as far as Ypres. It lay just four kilometres from the Westhoek ridge where Clifford Coffin had fought his battle six weeks earlier. Hill 60 had been the scene of bitter fighting ever since First Ypres, but particularly in 1915 when the British wrested it out of the hands of the Germans in April after the successful blowing of two mines for which tunnelling had been in progress for several months. The Germans recovered the hill after overwhelming gas attacks in May and remained in possession for two years. It then became the scene of some of the most intense underground warfare culminating in the Battle of Messines when two mines laid under Hill 60 and its adjacent position known as the Caterpillar became the most northerly of the Messines ridge mines. In the explosion of those, the German 204th Division lost 10 officers and 677 men.[9]

The 9th Staffords' priority in September was to strengthen the trench system which they were occupying forward of Hill 60. Among their number, supervising the work in a trench called Imperial Avenue, was Sergeant John Carmichael of A Company.

Sergeant John Carmichael

John Carmichael (1893–1977)

John Carmichael was a Scot born at Glenmavis near Airdrie, Lanarkshire. His father, a Highlander, was a quarryman who moved down from Oban for work and John followed his father into the quarries. He enlisted into the Royal Engineers in June 1915, joining 415 (Lowland) Field Company, and was promoted lance-corporal before deciding that his chances of more active service lay in transferring to the infantry. He was sent to join the 8th Sherwood Foresters and served with them in France from the Battle of Loos until early in 1917, when he was transferred to the 9th Staffords, 'presumably because his quarrying experience would be most valuable in a pioneer unit'.[10] On 8 September:

> We were on Hill 60, digging a communication trench, and I was detailed off with a party of men to get it done quick. I was supervising the job. We had men working in the trench and men working outside of it as well. One of the chaps was deepening the trench when his spade struck an unexploded grenade, just lodged there in the side of the trench, and it started to fizz. I was an instructor in bombing, so, knowing a bit about explosives, I knew it would be seven seconds before it

went off unless I did something. I couldn't throw it out, because there were men working outside the trench as well as the blokes in it. So I shouted at them to get clear and I had some idea of smothering it, to get the thing covered, keep it down until they were out of range. All I had was my steel helmet. So I took it off my head, put it over the grenade as it was fizzing away, and I stood on it. It was the only way to do it. There was no thought of bravery or anything like that. I was there with the men to do the job, and that's what mattered.

Well, it *did* go off. They tell me it blew me right out of the trench, but I don't remember that. The next thing I remember is being carried away. That's how I got this thing …[11]

'This thing', as Lyn Macdonald remarks, was the Victoria Cross.

Carmichael was evacuated with shattered legs and a damaged arm which put him in hospital for two years and thus he saw no more active service. In due course he went home to Airdrie to a great welcome and received a cheque for £1000 with which he bought a chicken farm. Later he ran a highly successful public transport business, building up a fleet of over 40 buses operating in the Lowlands of Scotland. He was back in uniform again in the Home Guard as a lieutenant in the Second World War. In 1930 he married Margaret Aitken; there were no children.

However, as we have seen, while Carmichael was on his way home down the casualty evacuation chain, back in the Salient the struggle continued until November. With such a full commitment on its hands it seems extraordinary that Haig's British Expeditionary Force was in any position to undertake another major offensive. Yet this was so. The Battle of Cambrai was launched just a few days after the Canadians entered Passchendaele. This was not a sapper VC battle but needs to be noted because it was a significant step towards the next great confrontation three months later. Cambrai offered the prospect of a breakthrough to the north from the Somme area and hence the cutting off of a large proportion of the German Army in Flanders. It was mounted for this reason and also because the British Army had evolved two new techniques which pointed to success. The first is well known: tanks and the belief of those who had developed them[*] that they should be used in concentrated mass and over country which suited them, unlike the mud of the Somme and the Salient where many felt their special characteristics had been wasted. The other technique, less well known, was predicted artillery shooting under a system worked out through close co-operation between the Royal Artillery and Royal Engineer survey units.[12]

Once again the hoped-for breakthrough remained elusive and yet another new technique, this time on the German side, was employed in the massive counter-attacks which pushed Sir Julian Byng's Third Army back almost to their original starting positions. Although they had broken through the Hindenburg Line, and Third Army units remained in occupation of parts of it throughout the winter, this small advantage was not to remain for long, as we shall see. It was in this

[*]Including the commander of the Tank Corps, the sapper Brigadier-General H.J. Elles, later General Sir Hugh Elles, KCB, KCMG, KCVO, DSO.

desperate fighting that Major Frederick Johnson, VC was killed at Bourlon Wood while in command of 231 Field Company (see Chapter Eight). The new German technique was to infiltrate fast-moving groups between the main enemy positions following a short but intense artillery concentration including gas. It had recently brought spectacular results on the Russian front where defeat at the Battle of Riga finally brought Russia to its knees. In Italy it led to the catastrophic defeat of the Italian Army at the Battle of Caporetto, after which they were only able to hold on because the British and French both sent two divisions, which they could scarcely spare. However, the new German tactics were shortly to be used again in what now became the climax of the war.

The First World War
The Kaiserschlacht (1918)

With one great crash there opened a tremendous bombardment, of trench mortars by the hundred and every calibre of artillery save the 77mm field gun. Its continuous roar was punctuated, to those a little distance from the line, by the explosions of huge single shells upon objectives in the rear.[1]

This is how Cyril Falls describes the opening bombardment, early in the morning of 21 March 1918, of the 'Kaiserschlacht' (Emperor Battle) in the *History of the 36th (Ulster) Division*. John Terraine[2] calls it 'one of the great dramatic moments of the war; for the British Army a tragedy comparable to 1 July 1916.'[*] Following Cambrai, Sir Douglas Haig ordered a period of organisation of the defensive zones occupied by the formations under his command. It soon became clear that the German High Command, now effectively driving government policy and concentrated in the personalities of Field Marshal von Hindenburg and General von Ludendorff, were planning a major offensive. Despite the apparent failures of the Allied offensives in 1917, the German position was deteriorating seriously. Their losses had been severe, and the Allied blockade enforced with such success by the Royal Navy was causing shortages of food at home and supplies of all sorts for the armies in the field. Most serious, however, was the imminent prospect of American involvement in the war which made it necessary for Germany to force an early decision. Unable to mount a general offensive across the whole front, Ludendorff decided on a piecemeal approach, the first step in which was to be the destruction of the British Expeditionary Force by an attack aimed primarily at its junction with the French along and to the north of the River Oise, after which the French would be in no position to maintain the fight. British Intelligence was aware that this would be the objective of the German strategy and even predicted the date with remarkable accuracy.[†]

The Royal Engineers were therefore at full stretch in January and February 1918 supporting the strengthening of the defences and bringing some order to the shambles into which the area had been reduced after the earlier battles there. A major complication was that General Sir Hubert Gough's Fifth Army, occupying the sector in which the blow was to fall, was ordered to take over part of the front of their neighbouring French army. The defences were to be in three zones (Forward, Battle and Rear), all to be laid out in depth with trench lines either

---

[*]The first day of the Somme battle in which the British Army sustained 57,000 casualties.

[†]The sapper, Brigadier-General E.W. Cox, was head of the Intelligence Section at GHQ at the time.

Map 18
*The German advance
in the Fifth Army
area from 21 March
1918.*

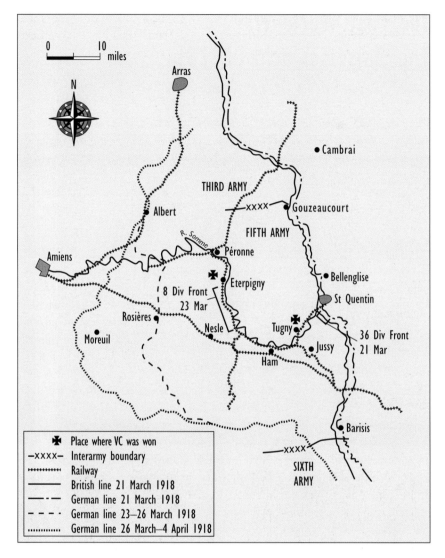

continuous or in groups. Demolitions were to be an important feature, and measures included the preparation of all bridges and the storing of charges carefully parcelled and numbered for their allotted place on their targets. Explosives were in short supply and the results would be limited and, in any case, effective only if the gaps were adequately integrated into the infantry and artillery defensive plan.

The British line in the Fifth Army area lay from roughly Gouzeaucourt (opposite Cambrai), along the general line of the St Quentin canal (St Quentin itself being in German hands) south to across the River Oise at Barisis. 36th (Ulster) Division was responsible for the sector between the St Quentin canal at Oestres to Sphinx Farm just south of Neuville St Amand, a distance of some two-

and-a-half miles. Eight or so miles further back lay the headwaters of the Somme running in parallel at that point with the canal and there Second Lieutenant Cecil Knox was responsible for preparing 13 bridges for demolition.

Second Lieutenant Cecil Leonard Knox

Cecil Leonard Knox came from a large family. He was the second youngest of nine brothers, six of whom served in the 1914–18 War. Two gave their lives: Andrew, killed in action in December 1915 while serving with 185 Tunnelling Company Royal Engineers; and James (DSO and Bar), who died in September 1918 of wounds received while in command of 1/7th Warwickshires, fighting on the Asiago plateau in Italy. There was another sapper, Kenneth, who won an MC; Alec, a Lieutenant RNR; and a gunner, Cedric. Their father, James Knox, was an industrialist in Nuneaton who founded the Haunchwood Brick and Tile Company and was on the board of several other companies.

Cecil Knox
(1888–1943)

Cecil was educated at King Edward VI Grammar School, Nuneaton and Oundle School and, when war broke out, he and his brother Kenneth were working as civil engineers on the Canadian Pacific Railway in Alberta. Cecil was commissioned in June 1917 and, after training, posted to 150 Field Company. The company had taken part in the Battle of Cambrai in November and December and moved into their new sector in the former French area in January.

According to his own account, Knox was responsible for 13 bridges. On his left, Lieutenant J.B. Stapylton-Smith had another 12. The course of events was described by Knox in a letter home:

> When the Boche attacked, my job was to go to a certain place and prepare 13 bridges for demolition in case he broke through. We expected the Boche on the night of the 20th, and in the early morning of the 21st a terrific bombardment started at 4.45am. I said to the other officer with me 'That's it', so we got up and roused the Sergeants and men.
>
> At 5.30 we got orders to 'Man Battle Stations', so I started off for my bridges, and by 10.30am had them all ready to demolish. Of course I had been working on them for some weeks, and had all the charges made up in boxes ready to slip into place. I was then about 6 miles from the front line. All that day the bombardment continued. It turned frightfully cold and foggy at night, and I posted sentries at each bridge, and visited them frequently through the night. I could get no information as to the whereabouts of the Boche, and was supposed to demolish bridges when orders came through from Division, or on my own initiative if necessary. Very foggy through the next night, and in the early morning without any warning the Boche appeared at two of the bridges through the fog, and I exploded the charges as he was on the bridge, and demolished the remaining 11 in a few minutes. He managed to shoot one of my sentries. ... as soon as I had fired the first bridge the Boche started to shell the others to stop me blowing them up. He must have had wonderful communication with his guns...[3]

In fact the forward brigades had been having a fierce struggle throughout the 24 hours in which Knox and his men had to wait. The brigade line actually ran virtually east–west at that point and so when the Germans attacked in a due westerly direction they ran straight into the flank of the brigade Forward and Battle Zones. The foggy weather meant that in every position the Germans were right on top of the British trenches before they were spotted. They were using a tactic new to the Western Front but which had been successful in the east and in Italy. Their troops advanced close behind a massive barrage of high explosive and gas. They moved in small groups, bypassing strong points for mopping up by follow-up forces. The fog and the overstretch across the front added to the difficulties of the defence. Many gallant battles were fought but nothing could prevent the enveloping flow of the enemy. According to the *History of 36th (Ulster) Division*, by the evening when their retirement across the river line began, 'each Brigade had by now one battalion almost completely destroyed, and [it must be remembered] that the Battle Zone battalions were at an average strength of about two hundred and fifty men. ...'[4]

Cecil Knox's laconic account gives nothing away about the deed of incredible self-sacrifice that he performed which was to lead to the award of his VC. Cyril Falls is more forthcoming.

> At Tugny, the Germans were advancing on the main steel-girder bridge when the time-fuse [sic] failed. The night dew or the mist had spoiled it. As Lieutenant Knox rushed forward the foremost of the enemy were upon the bridge, a long one. He tore away the useless time-fuse, clambered under the framework of the bridge, and lit the instantaneous fuse. The bridge was destroyed, and, by some miracle, Lieutenant Knox was uninjured.[5]

For the 36th Division and all British troops along this part of the front, the next few days became a nightmare of improvisation as they desperately tried to stem the German onrush. Knox's letter home gives a few ideas of what this must have been like although, unless he is sparing his parents some of the nastier detail, his field company fared reasonably well compared with the infantry.

> rejoined the Coy. some miles back, and we trekked all day, and lay down in the field at night. So cold and foggy could not sleep ...

> We dug some bits of trenches, and I was in a farmhouse which I loopholed, and prepared to give him some stick.

> Bitterly cold and foggy all night, and we were not at all sure where the Boche was ...

> He appeared on the scene about 2 o'clock in the afternoon and we managed to drive him off with the assistance of some French artillery.

> Hadn't been there five minutes when we had orders to move as Boche had got round us, so marched all night until 7am.

> The next day we moved on to a village for about two hours which was deserted, and had a lot of chickens and rabbits in it, but they did not remain long, our chaps were experts at dispatching them, it was no good leaving them for the Boche ...

> We had no shovels, so scraped holes in the ground with our hands and bayonets. Most bitter cold wind, and freezing hard.[6]

During this time his brother, Ken, was in the adjoining unit. No doubt similar stories were to be told throughout the whole area in which this first onslaught of the Kaiserschlacht took place. To the south of XVIII Corps (36th Division's parent formation) III Corps had been forced back to the canal line at Jussy, close to the boundary with the French. To the north, around St Quentin itself, the fighting was particularly severe. This was the XIX Corps area and, according to the *Viking Atlas of World War I*,[7] in one area, of eight British battalions only 50 men survived to retire and regroup. General Sir Hubert Gough decided that it was time for a withdrawal behind the line of the Somme, and to commit what reserves he had to the defence of that line to enable his exhausted troops to pull back further in the hope of recovering to form a further reserve. One of the reserve formations now ordered to the line of the Somme was 8th Division, whom we last met in the Salient, where, even after the bitter struggle of Third Ypres, they had spent a grim four months in and out of the line. With classic understatement the division's historians described the weather there as continuing to be 'very trying'.

> Many men collapsed from exposure and exhaustion; several were partially buried in mud and shell holes and were extracted with great difficulty. Even Divisional Headquarters itself was not immune. It was located on the Canal Bank, and … [the water] flooded all the lower dug-outs and was endangering the bank, which showed signs of landslide in several places. Some of the dug-outs were entirely destroyed and others were much damaged. The whole division found once more, as it had found in the first winter of the war, that life in Flanders trenches in mid-winter could be dangerous (let alone discomfortable) enough, even if the enemy were left entirely out of account.[8]

The division handed over their line at Ypres on 8 March and 'Before a fortnight had passed it was summoned South – to the greatest episode of its career in France.'[9]

They arrived, in fact at various railway stations some 9–12 miles behind the line they were to take up, during the evening of 22 March, went under the command of XIX Corps and marched forward to the river line between Nesle and Eterpigny. The distance to be covered was rather more than two-and-a-half times a normal divisional frontage. They had had no time to concentrate and shake out into formation. Also, in keeping with the whole of the BEF, because of the acute manpower shortage, they had had to reorganise at the end of December into three-battalion brigades. One of these, 25th Infantry Brigade, was still under the command of Brigadier-General Clifford Coffin, VC, although he had been away temporarily in command of 50th Division. 25th Infantry Brigade was responsible for the right of the line. In the centre was 24th Infantry Brigade and, on the left, covering the northern sector up to Eterpigny, was 23rd Infantry Brigade. Commanding C Company of 2nd Middlesex in that brigade was the other personality forming part of this story, Captain Maurice Toye.

Maurice Toye
(1897–1955)

Alfred Maurice Toye

Maurice Toye was the son of Sergeant-Major James Toye, Chief Clerk of the General Registry, Aldershot Command. In 1911, at the age of 14, he enlisted in the Royal Engineers as a trumpeter. After a tour in Ireland he went to France in August 1915 just after his eighteenth birthday. A year later he applied successfully for a commission and, after attending Cadet School at Blendecques, near St Omer, he was granted a permanent commission in the Middlesex Regiment in February 1917 'as a reward for conspicuous gallantry'.[10] He won the MC in the Third Ypres battle 'when in charge of communications he went to a most forward position and carried out his duties under heavy and continuous fire of every kind with great ability and fearlessness...'[11] This 21-year-old hardened warrior was about to face the greatest test of his life.

With the disadvantages under which the 8th Division deployed to battle, the wonder is they were able to make any stand at all. Before they were in position the elements of the retreating forward units were trickling across the bridges and at 4.00 pm on 23 March all was reckoned ready for the bridges to be blown. Not surprisingly, much went wrong; not all the charges were fully effective and passable crossings remained. In any case, further south the enemy was already across the river and thrusting north in an attempt to roll up the British line from that direction. By early on 24 March Clifford Coffin's brigade was in dire trouble as his right flank was being pushed back and his left was also under attack from a crossing the enemy managed to force over the river. Into this desperate situation reinforcements were brought forward but too few to affect the issue. An expected counter-attack by a French formation never materialised and by first light on 25 March, the right flank had to give way even further. Nevertheless the river line was still being staunchly held by the 1st Sherwood Foresters in the 24th Brigade area (they were still there in the afternoon) and by the 2nd Middlesex at

Eterpigny 1996, close to the place where Maurice Toye won his VC.

Eterpigny. There, however, early in the morning, the Germans managed to cross the river and surround the battalion.

> Capt. A. M. Toye, leading a forlorn hope, succeeded in cutting his way out with a mere handful of men. Out of all the four platoons [in C Company] only ten individuals succeeded in getting away. The rest either perished at their posts or were captured. Having got clear of the village, Capt. Toye successfully rallied some 70 men of the 7/D.L.I. (Pioneers), 50th Division, led them in a brave and bold counter-attack and held on across the Eterpigny-Villers Carbonnel road until assistance came. But for his prompt and energetic action the whole of our remaining positions along the river would have been turned.[12]

The battalion fought on to the evening. A few scraps of messages have survived in the War Diary files (not from C Company).[13]

> 9.15 am. For 23 Inf Bde. The enemy is breaking through at Eterpigny.

> 11.20 am. Line of the Somme will be held at all costs.

> 1.25 pm. I have 2 other officers and 25 rifles and 1 Lewis gun and 1 Vickers on the ridge overlooking Eterpigny.

> Please give bearer on his return journey some more ammunition. We could do with some water later on. Our morale – Excellent.

At 6.30 pm the 25th Brigade issued the order for withdrawal. Unfortunately, few of the companies received it and most stuck to their orders to hold out at all costs. Eleven platoons were thus written off and the commanding officer made arrangements for the remnants to leave, firing the last defiant rounds himself at 7.25 pm.

By this time, Clifford Coffin had led the remnants of his brigade back to their next location at Rosières but soon this was to be outflanked as well and, as the division worked its way to a blocking position in the area of Moreuil, 10 miles to the south-east of Amiens, the entire divisional infantry was placed under Coffin's command. There the situation was stabilised by a well-timed counter-attack and on 2 April the division was relieved. In his message to the troops after the battle the divisional commander pointed out that 'every day and every hour was full of heroic deeds ...'[14] but felt he should record certain outstanding ones. Prominent among these were the actions of the field companies, Royal Engineers, 'thrown into the fight as infantry',[15] the Signal Service [Royal Engineers] and, in person, Brigadier-General Clifford Coffin, VC, DSO, for his skilful command of the infantry during the latter part of the fighting. The division had but a week to receive the 11 officers and 700 other ranks allocated to replace their 250 officers and 4693 other rank casualties suffered in this fighting before they were stood by to move back to the Ypres area to meet the next of Ludendorff's onslaughts. In fact they were spared this but had returned to the line to the east of Amiens when they took part in the last major flare up in defence of the Amiens area from 24 to 27 April at Villers-Bretonneux. This successful fight became famous as the first tank versus tank battle in history.

Later Careers

It remains to record how Cecil Knox and Maurice Toye fared later. Both survived the war. Cecil Knox then went into the family business and, with his brother Kenneth, became a director of the Haunchwood Brick and Tile Company. He continued to lead an active life and served in 605 (County of Warwick) (Bombing) Squadron Royal Auxiliary Air Force at Castle Bromwich from 1926 to 1932. However, he suffered a serious parachute accident while training at Manston and had to retire temporarily from service life. In his late 40s he married Eileen Baylor and they had a daughter, Katrina, born in 1941. He was in the Home Guard, commanding the Nuneaton Company during the Second World War, but died in 1943 as a result of a motor cycling accident at Bucks Hill.

Cecil Knox with his daughter Katrina.

Maurice Toye was evacuated soon after the action at Eterpigny and managed to fit in both his investiture (by King George V at Aldershot) and marriage in the month of June. His wife was the former Flora Robertson and in due course they had two daughters. By the end of the war on the Western Front, as well as his VC and MC, Toye had been mentioned in despatches and thrice wounded. But his war was not over, as he was then sent to northern Russia, where he served from May to October 1919. Later he transferred to the Oxfordshire and Buckinghamshire Light Infantry and went to Egypt where he served for ten years as an instructor at the Royal Egyptian Military College. Promoted major in 1938 and brevet lieutenant-colonel the following year, Maurice Toye then spent the Second World War in a variety of staff, command and instructor posts in the United Kingdom and returned to the Middle East in 1945 where he finished up as Brigadier AG at GHQ Middle East. He retired in 1945 and took up the appointment of Commandant Home Office Civil Defence School at Falfield in Gloucestershire where he remained until his death in 1955, aged only 58.

Aftermath

In this brief account of the Kaiserschlacht, it has been worth following the fortunes of the 8th Division both because of their particular relevance to our story and because they illustrate the manner in which this critical battle was fought by all the divisions engaged. Their achievement at the cost of 163,000 casualties in the Fifth and Third Army sectors was decisive, for the Germans were unable to press on their attacks against such a resolute defence. For all their aggressiveness in this last desperate fling, however, the German Army was showing the fatal flaws that were eventually to be its undoing. One manifestation was the amazement of their soldiers at the relative plenty they found as they broke into the British lines – food, ammunition and general supplies – compared with their own circumstances which were severely spartan. The resultant looting has been said to be a major factor in the slowing down of their attack. A more realistic explanation however may be their lack of follow-up capacity in the face of the resistance which they met here and in the other fronts on which the so-called Ludendorff offensives were launched, combined with a decline in that mental conviction required of a would-be occupying power fighting in a country whose very way of life is at stake.

The Kaiserschlacht battles went on until July. In the British sector the most critical came on 9 April: the Battle of the Lys in which Flanders and the Channel ports were more seriously threatened than at any time, and for which Haig had issued his famous order of the day:

> There is no other course open to us but to fight it out! Every position must be held to the last man: there must be no retirement. With our backs to the wall, and believing in the justice of our cause, each one of us must fight on to the end. The safety of our homes and the freedom of mankind alike depend on the conduct of each one of us at this critical moment.[16]

Later in June and July came three successive attacks on the Aisne front against the French Sixth Army. Tragically, several British divisions which had been so badly mauled in the March and April defensive battles had been sent down to this supposedly quiet area to recover. They suffered even more terribly than they had earlier. 8th Division was one of them, and it is possible that Clifford Coffin's life was saved by his promotion in May to the command of 36th (Ulster) Division as his successor in command of 25th Infantry Brigade died from the effects of the dreadful bombardment of mixed high explosive and gas to which they were subjected. By the end of July the former line of trenches from which both sides had confronted each other had ballooned out into three salients; in the south as far as and across the Marne; in the centre, as we have seen, almost to Amiens; and, in the north, well to the west of the Ypres Salient although the city itself remained in Allied hands. All the ground fought for in 1916 and 1917, at such enormous cost, was back in German hands.

This territorial gain was, however, the only credit the Germans now held. Ludendorff knew he could not break the Allied line, a conviction that had been held by much of the German nation for some months. Although both sides had intractable manpower problems, the Americans were now in theatre in strength. The supplies situation was in every way in the Allies' favour. Above all, the will to win was deserting the German nation. Haig knew this as did Marshal Foch, the leader of the newly established Allied Supreme War Council. The scene was set for the final stages of the war. That the fighting was to be as severe a test as any is reflected in the awards of a further eight sapper VCs.

The First World War
The Last Hundred Days (1918)

It's death or glory work which must be done for the sake of our patrol on the other side.[1]

These were the words of Corporal James McPhie to his men as he was about to earn both death and glory on the Canal de la Sensée on 14 October 1918. Ludendorff's three great offensives of March, April and May had exhausted their momentum by mid-summer and the Allies realised that the opportunity now lay within their grasp to deliver the *coup de grâce* before the end of the year. The Germans too sought peace but, although fundamentally demoralised and looking for ways to bring the war to an end, were still hoping to enter any negotiations for an armistice from a position of strength, hence their dogged resistance to the end. The great advance that the Allies now took across north-eastern France into Belgium was no walk-over. Some measure of the scale of the fighting is that, during the final months of struggle, the Allies lost some 350,000 men, the Germans an even more terrible 500,000.[2]

In this final act it is simplest to follow the story of what John Terraine has called 'the greatest succession of victories in the British Army's whole history ...'[3] in the context of each of the Allied armies that were now lined up to confront their enemy. In the north, King Albert of the Belgians commanded his army, the recovery of their homeland now in their sights. To their south was Sir Herbert Plumer's Second Army, facing very much the area where they had so famously shattered the Germans at the Battle of Messines in the summer of 1917. On Plumer's right was the newly constituted Fifth Army under Sir William Birdwood of Gallipoli fame. Next was Sir Henry Horne's First Army whose sector embraced Arras and Vimy, scene of their great battles in 1917. Sir Julian Byng's Third Army faced the area centred on Bapaume which included the desolate wastes of the 1916 Somme battlefield. On the British right was Sir Henry Rawlinson's Fourth Army, backs to the wall in front of Amiens. (Rawlinson's Fourth Army was the old Fifth Army in all but name. Rawlinson had replaced Sir Hubert Gough who was made scapegoat for the disasters on 21 March. Rawlinson, a former commander of Fourth Army, made it a condition of acceptance that the Fifth and Fourth Armies should swap titles.) The remainder of the line stretching to Switzerland was covered by three French army groups and sandwiched between them, the all-important American army under John Pershing, in the rugged broken country of the Argonne forest and the area to its east where they had recently successfully ejected the Germans from the St Mihiel salient.

In the British sector, a framework for the Germans' fight to hold on to their gains was provided by the canals and rivers of northern France. These were now to become the setting for some of the British Army's, and the Royal Engineers', greatest achievements and the scene of the last eight sapper VCs of the war.

Map 19

The main canals and rivers in the area of the British counter-offensives, 1918.

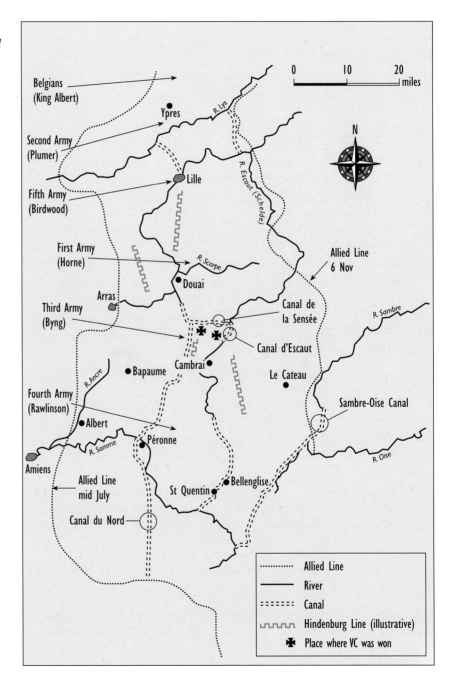

The first of the canal obstacles, although not a sapper VC site, was the St Quentin canal from which Fifth Army had been so unceremoniously swept on 21 March. The St Quentin canal guarded the front of the formidable Hindenburg Line, the name given by the Allies to the series of fortifications which the Germans had built in depth stretching roughly from Lille to Metz. We noted in Chapter Ten that the building of these followed the 1916 Somme battle and resulted in the Germans being able to shorten their line (freeing some 16 divisions for reserve) and in the Allies advancing forward to a new line in March 1917. The Hindenburg 'Line' was not a line at all but a number of defensive positions or 'stellungen' with interlocking arcs of fire and deep networks of barbed wire: 'They were often arranged in intricate patterns, so that the angles could be swept by machine-gun fire, and there were in places, as many as eight or nine belts of barbed wire in front of the trenches.'[4] Each position contained deep concrete bunkers, proof against artillery, laid out to a depth of some ten miles.

The first blow finally to turn the tide was struck by Haig on 8 August 1918, command having been entrusted to him by Foch, leader of the Allied Supreme War Council. The formation chosen was Fourth Army under Sir Henry Rawlinson. The Battle of Amiens was a brilliant success, achieving total surprise in foggy weather, not unlike that in March which had helped the Germans so much. As well as the infantry and cavalry divisions, prominent among them the Canadians and Australians, over 400 tanks advanced and German losses were severe – 27,000 men and 400 guns. Ludendorff called it 'the black day of the German Army ...'[5] It was not just the size of the setback but the manner of the fighting that brought him to this despairing mood. 'Our war machine was no longer efficient. Our fighting power had suffered, even though the great majority of divisions still fought heroically ...'

Fourth Army broke into the Hindenburg Line at the end of September in a carefully prepared operation at Bellenglise, where one battalion was able to make use of an almost dry section of the St Quentin canal. Others had to swim across. Royal Engineers Corps history records factually that 'three thousand life-belts had been sent up, and a number of rafts and light portable boats were prepared ...'[6] John Terraine is more dramatic about the role of the corps:[7]

> It was on the Royal Engineers that the final responsibility for success or failure would fall: it was their job to devise the means for crossing the canal. There was no lack of ingenuity in the corps ... They made wooden rafts, supported by empty petrol tins or bundles of cork mats. They provided collapsible boats, mud-mats made of canvas rolls reinforced by reeds, life-lines and scaling ladders for climbing the steep canal banks. 'Finally some genius hit on the novel idea of using life-belts on a considerable scale ...' All these contraptions were tested on the eve of the attack ... It was found that the collapsible boats could be opened and launched in twenty seconds; fully loaded men discovered that they could swim across forty yards of deep water in the life-belts without any danger of drowning; a man who could not swim was hauled across by a life-line, similarly supported and equally safe ...

This comment on the Hindenburg Line operation is worth inclusion because, give or take a few details, it reflects the approach used in the deliberate attacks on all the water obstacles in these final hectic months. All involved a combination of careful preparation and rehearsal, imaginative improvisation and a nice balance between proficient technical judgement and acceptance of risk. In all there was also the need for courageous resolution under fire, sometimes exercised, as we shall see, beyond the call of duty.

By the time of this battle all the other armies were engaged in one way or other. In the south, the Americans, with the French Fourth Army on their left, had launched their great Argonne offensive, a hard and costly struggle which was to last to the end of the war. Shortly after the Battle of Amiens had achieved its aims, the rest of the line moved forward in response. On Rawlinson's right the French Tenth Army attacked between Soissons and the River Oise, taking Noyon and 8000 prisoners on 22 August. Our story now moves to Byng's Third Army whose 'limited' operation started on 21 August. His IV Corps, in the centre, was given the task of capturing Bapaume by 26 August and the night of 23/24 August found the New Zealand Division, flanked by the British 42nd and 37th Divisions, formed up on the line of the Albert–Arras railway which ran along the valley of the River Ancre, scene of so much tragedy in July 1916. The New Zealanders' 1st Brigade with the 1st Wellingtons on their right and 2nd Auckland Regiment on their left edged their way forward at 1.30 am to their assembly area in the angle between the Albert line and the branch to Bapaume. Attached to the 2nd Aucklands was the 27-year-old sapper, Sergeant Samuel Forsyth.

Sergeant Samuel Forsyth

*Samuel Forsyth
(1891–1918)*

Samuel Forsyth was a gold-mining amalgamator[*] by peace-time trade, born at Wellington. He had enlisted in the Expeditionary Force in August 1914 and embarked for Egypt as a sapper in October. He served in Gallipoli from May to July 1915 and again from August to November when he was evacuated sick to England. In April 1916 he joined 3 New Zealand Field Company in France. The company had formed up in Egypt after Gallipoli and served thereafter on the Somme, at Messines and in Third Ypres. They were back in the Somme area at Bray, for the Kaiserschlacht, moving from there to Third Army.

Forsyth must have impressed, as he rose to the rank of sergeant and applied for a commission. It was normal for such applicants from arms other than infantry to have a spell of attachment to a battalion to test their suitability, and this was the reason for Forsyth's presence in the 2nd Aucklands.

A necessary preliminary step to the capture of Bapaume was the securing of the line of relatively high ground that lay between Loupart Wood on the right, through Grévillers to Biefvillers on the left. After an unpleasant wet night 1st Brigade launched their attack at 4.15 am, once again in the helpful mist that had

[*]Amalgamation is the process by which a metal is extracted from the material containing particles of it by dissolving it in mercury.

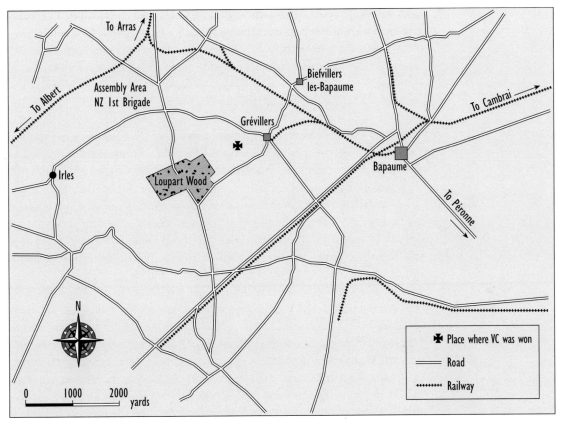

Map 20
Grévillers and
Bapaume.

benefited many of the attacks since 8 August. Eight tanks had been allotted in support. Initial objectives were quickly achieved in the poor visibility but as soon as daylight broke through, the leading companies started getting into difficulties from well-concealed machine-gun posts. In the Wellingtons' sector on the right, Loupart Wood was surrounded by 8.30 am but it was noon before it was cleared. 2nd Auckland had a similar experience around the village, to the south of which lay the very strongly prepared line of defences protecting Bapaume. Sergeant Forsyth now came to the fore. As the citation for his VC states, he had already led successful attacks on three machine-gun positions, been wounded trying to bring forward one of two tanks that were approaching to tackle two more, had his wound dressed, returned to the tank and tried to bring it forward 'with magnificent coolness, to a favourable position …' The tank was put out of action so he rescued the crew and then organised them and some of his men into a section to outflank the machine-guns at which point he was shot dead by a sniper. 'The other tank was also destroyed, but thanks largely to Forsyth's heroism, the high ground about the village passed securely into our possession.'[8]

The New Zealand Division's gallant work was crowned with success when the Germans evacuated Bapaume on 29 August. Then, after a two-week pause, they, along with three British divisions of IV and VI Corps, made another significant advance taking objectives 7 miles to the south-west of Cambrai. This effectively outflanked the Canal du Nord, a major obstacle which nevertheless the Germans held in strength further north. By 27 September Third Army, in conjunction with Horne's First Army, had succeeded in crossing this great obstacle and exploiting forward close to Cambrai, and to the lines of the Canal d'Escaut (Schelde) and the Canal de la Sensée that barred their further progress.

During Third Army's battle, their left flank had been protected by the operations of First Army to their north. Five days after the assault towards Bapaume had begun, First Army had launched their attack in the Battle of the Scarpe. The Scarpe valley runs east–west from Arras in the direction of Douai and so on to the Schelde, and the major obstacle that confronted it was the Canal de la Sensée running south from Douai to Palleul and then swinging east to join the Canal d'Escaut to the north of Cambrai, forming an awkward elbow – the area in which two sapper VCs were to be won. In the plan to envelop Cambrai, the Canadian Corps on the right wing of First Army had the task of forcing a crossing over the Canal d'Escaut.

As mentioned in Chapter Nine, the Canadian contribution to operations on the Western Front had been immense, most famously in the assault on Vimy Ridge in 1917. The corps had taken part in the Battle of Amiens as part of Fourth Army and in July had been relieved and moved to the Arras sector. A particularly valuable element of the Canadian Engineers had been their tunnelling squadrons who had achieved so much at Vimy and elsewhere. Now the mobile war had made tunnelling less of a priority and the tunnellers' skills were being put to use in other fields. Many of the units became specialists in the equally dangerous work of dealing with the mines and booby traps with which the Germans were now attempting to slow the Allied progress; others acquired new talents as bridging experts. Some individuals were redeployed to field units. One such was Captain Coulson Mitchell who originally crossed the Atlantic as a member of the Canadian Overseas Railway Construction Corps (made up largely from the employees of the Canadian Pacific Railway and not part of the Canadian Engineers).

Coulson Norman Mitchell

Coulson ('Mike') Mitchell (1889–1978)

Coulson Norman Mitchell (known as 'Mike') was a native of Winnipeg, Manitoba where he had attended Mulvey Public School and graduated from the University of Manitoba in 1912. He joined a Canadian company working on projects in Manitoba and British Columbia. He enlisted as a sapper in November 1914 and, after a spell in 2nd Division Signal Company, went to Britain with the Canadian Overseas Railway Construction Corps. With them he spent three months in Belgium in the autumn of 1915, building a narrow gauge track and receiving his first taste of enemy fire. In April 1916 he was commissioned and in July joined 1st Canadian Tunnelling Company Canadian Engineers, in France. Their work was concentrated on the area known as The Bluff, lying to the south-east of Ypres alongside the Ypres–Comines canal. Like Hill 60, this was a key observation point in the area and was bitterly fought for both above and below ground. In December 1916 Mitchell won the MC during an operation in which all the enemy tunnels were either captured or destroyed. 'He displayed great courage and skill in countermining against enemy galleries. On one occasion he was cut off from our own lines for twelve hours …'[9] Remaining with the 1st Tunnelling Company, he took part in the preparation of the mines that were to be blown in the Battle of Messines. After a period on Vimy Ridge early in 1918, he was posted to the 4th Battalion, Canadian Engineers in July 1918 as an explosives specialist.

The Task of the Canadian Corps

As we have seen the Canadian Corps had crossed the Canal du Nord at the end of September. In this right wing of First Army they were therefore well to the east of the Army formations on their left, who still had a substantial sector of the Hindenburg Line defences to break through before they could reach the northern section of the Canal de la Sensée. Nevertheless, in the overall plan, Third Army was to resume the advance on 8 October, with First Army co-operating on their left with the Canadian Corps who were then to attack across the Canal d'Escaut just to the north of Cambrai the following day. General Currie now gave orders for this attack at 1.30 am.

> Across the Third Army and First Army fronts, the Escaut Canal-River system promised to be a difficult barrier to force if the enemy made a determined defence. The Canal, 90 to 100 feet wide, was too deep for the infantry to cross without assistance. The paralleling rivers, although troops could ford them in most places, formed a barrier to guns and vehicles. Much of the canal bank was above 'country' level, consequently ramps would have to be built. Crossings could best be made at the locks and these were critically examined by the sappers, using maps, air-photographs and, wherever possible, ground reconnaissance.[10]

What follows is based on the account which the Canadian Engineers put together on the acquisition of Mitchell's VC and his personal collection of documents after his death.[11] Quotations are from Mitchell's own notes. The attack was planned for midnight, over the bridge, Pont d'Aire, leading to the village of Escaudoeuvres, north-west Cambrai. 'This approach was complicated by the fact that in addition to the main bridge over the canal there were two mill streams about 20 feet wide to the west of the canal, about 500 feet and 1000 feet respectively.' If possible, demolition of these bridges must be prevented and Captain Coulson Mitchell was given this task by his brigade commander with the cheering words 'Well, Mitchell, this is one time the Engineers go over ahead of the infantry.' Zero hour was postponed, adding to the nervous strain of the party of Mitchell, his sergeant and four sappers. Then:

> At 1.00am the barrage started and we followed it closely and were fortunate enough to arrive at the right point in good time. It was a spectacular night, many buildings in Cambrai were on fire and the sky was red over the city …
> At the first stream we found the bridge destroyed, leaving a 20 foot gap, so

sent two runners back to the bridging train with information. It was Lloyd [Sapper] Brewer who, meanwhile had located a plank footbridge across the stream about 100 feet to our left which we crossed and found that it ended at a door in a brick wall. When we opened the door we found no enemy but only a large warehouse full of bales of wool. It was a scary place and we were glad to get out on the road again and ran for the second mill stream. Here a stone arch was intact and a quick examination showed no signs of it being mined, so sent two runners back to inform the infantry and bridging train and to act as guides to the infantry to the second bridge.

Lieutenant-Colonel 'Mike' Mitchell revisiting the Pont d'Aire site with his wife Gertrude in 1956.

They ran the 500 feet to the main bridge, a double span steel girder resting on two abutments with a pier and locks in the centre of the stream. They felt their way across looking for wire for electric firing circuits until, on reaching the other side and posting a sentry at either end, Mitchell and his sergeant (Jackson) slid down the bank to the towpath about 15 feet below and began to examine the underside of the bridge with flashlights.

Sure enough we saw a large box of explosives attached to the girder … with the fuzes entering the box … While Jackson held the flashlight, I separated the bundle of fuzes in search of the electric wire … It was there and we cut it, then greatly relieved started to cut the fuzes when we heard Brewer firing and yelling 'Stand to.' We ran down the ladder, up the bank, to find Brewer in a shell hole and he told us that he had shot two men who had come from the back of the building, to the left of the bridge. It was now about 4.00am and light enough to see dimly a short distance. We found the bodies lying about 30 feet away.

Another man appeared whom Mitchell shot ('although I hated doing it').

Suddenly a large party came from behind the same building and ran for the bridge, where we met them. I'll never forget those few minutes – the only way I can describe my feelings is that it was like being in the crucial moment of an exciting game of football or hockey and you don't feel the kicks or bumps, just excited. Teddy Jackson and Brewer were grand, their guns blazing and bayonets flashing in and out. All three of us yelling like madmen, which is probably what saved us as the Germans must have thought they were up against a whole battalion for they suddenly disappeared and we were alone again.

Some anxious moments then followed while the small party awaited a possible counter-attack until the infantry came up with a Lewis gun and they then, under heavy fire, continued their task of removing the charges (four in all) and leads and

we discovered twelve very scared Germans of their demolition party, which had suddenly disappeared, standing on the tow path with their backs against the abutment and their hands full of watches, etc., as peace offerings. They were taken prisoner and handed over to the infantry. The bodies of eight more of their party were found on the road above …

By this time troops of 5th Infantry Brigade were moving across the canal using footbridges, some left by the Germans plus three new cork-float ones, and establishing themselves in Escaudoeuvres. Further to their south, Cambrai was being entered by two battalions of infantry accompanied by the large sapper parties required to deal with the fires and demolitions.

As well as Mitchell's VC, the only one awarded to a Canadian Engineer in the war, DCMs were awarded to Sergeant Jackson and Sapper Brewer and the MM to Sapper Murphy. Among the documents found in Mitchell's effects after his death was a 'rather glowing newspaper account of his action …' to which had been appended a hand-written note: 'Too much poetic license! Re-write more accurate description of action at bridge, giving credit to my six men.'

The Canal de la Sensée and the 56th Division

We may leave Mitchell and his men for a while and focus now on the Canal de la Sensée where, notwithstanding the success of the Canadian Corps at Cambrai, much of the ground to the west and south of the Sensée still lay in German hands. They were making the most of a strong defensive line and complicating matters by carrying out inundations, a simple and effective expedient in this low-lying country intersected by waterways. Aggressive patrolling was as much as could be managed by First Army in the cause of making progress. One such patrol was mounted by 1/2nd Londons of the British 56th Division, now under the command of the Canadian Corps who were now responsible for the whole area within the Sensée/Escaut canal elbow, at the village of Aubencheul-au-Bac on the main route north towards Douai. 416 Field Company was in support and at 7.30 pm on 13 October, Corporal James McPhie arrived on the canal with five sappers detailed to take over as maintenance party for a cork-float bridge which had been constructed earlier for the patrol.

James McPhie
(1894–1918)

James McPhie

James McPhie had joined the Territorial Force at the beginning of 1912 at the age of 18. He was the son of Allan and Elizabeth McPhie of 21 Salisbury Place, Edinburgh and had been educated at South Bridge School. 416 Field Company had arrived in France from Egypt at the end of April 1916 joining 56th Division as the field company for 169th Brigade. The division had fought on the Somme, at Third Ypres, Cambrai and Arras, before joining the operations forming this part of our story.

Operations of the 56th Division

Following the Canadian action to cross the Canal d'Escaut on 8/9 October, the enemy position inside the canal triangle was becoming increasingly untenable. The 56th Division harried the enemy along the south bank of the Canal de la Sensée and by 11 October Fressies was captured. During the night of 12/13 October: 'A clever and daring enterprise to capture Aubigny-au-Bac was then undertaken.'[12] 169th Brigade made a surprise and silent crossing of the canal with two companies of 2nd London Regiment using a cork-float footbridge constructed in the night by 416 Field Company. In the original plan this was to have been preceded by some rafts for a preliminary patrol of the Queen's Westminsters but Lieutenant A.E. Arnold decided to proceed with the bridge at once and the patrol crossed. 'One cannot give higher praise to the Engineers than this: on landing, the patrol found that they could not proceed more than ten paces in any direction without being challenged by German sentries – there appeared to be three posts in the immediate vicinity of the bridge.'[13] Arnold led the patrol across his bridge and then reported to the battalion headquarters where he was informed that another bridge would be required nearer the village. He sent back for more men for this task, knowing that those who had built the first bridge were now exhausted, while he carried on with the reconnaissance with his runner, Sapper Hart. At this point they were heavily shelled; Arnold was wounded twice and, while he and Hart took shelter, died from his wounds. Some slight satisfaction for his family might have been derived from the award of the MC for his work, the citation recording that 'it was due to his determination and energy that the attack was able to take place successfully …'[14]

The 2nd Londons nevertheless now passed two platoons over the canal and, in a brilliant operation, surprised the enemy and took prisoners. By morning they had, however, been pressed back to a small stream just 300 yards from the canal bank. A further patrol now crossed over and the story is then taken up by the 416 Field Company War Diary:

> Corporal McPhie's party stood by to help them cross, as the enemy shellfire which at this time commenced, threatened to damage the bridge. Corporal McPhie himself crossed to the enemy bank …
>
> During the passage of this patrol and owing to the fact that they now crowded on the bridge, the raft was broken and Sapper Cox thrown into the water. In spite of being in the canal Sapper Cox continued to hold the bridge together

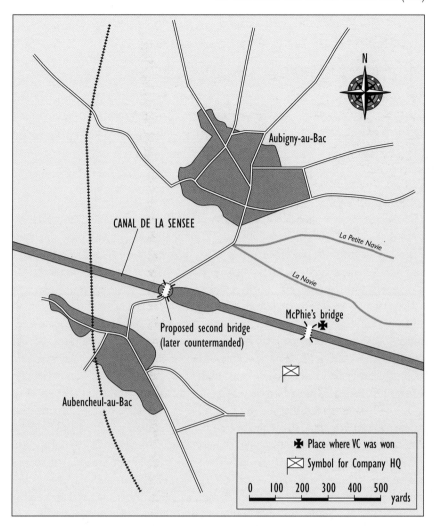

Map 21
McPhie's crossing at
Aubencheul-au-Bac.

until his hands were so badly trodden upon that he was forced to let go. Corporal McPhie and Sapper Cox swam ashore and Corporal McPhie reported to the CO 2nd London Regiment that the bridge was broken, when the latter gave the order that the bridge must be maintained. Thereupon Corporal McPhie and his party commenced to carry material from Aubencheul-au-Bac but it was daylight before sufficient material was on site, and the enemy could be seen on the other bank. Corporal McPhie informed his men that the re-erection of the bridge was a matter of life and death to the infantry who remained on the north bank of the canal and then led on to the bridge with Sapper Cox and commenced to cut away the broken cleats. Corporal McPhie was immediately shot in the face by a sniper in a house about 80 yards distant, and fell into the water.

At the same time Sapper Cox received wounds in the arms and leg but nevertheless he managed to draw Corporal McPhie partly on to the bridge and to hold him. The enemy immediately opened machine gun fire from close range and Corporal McPhie was hit again in the back and Sapper Cox received four or five additional wounds in the thigh. Sapper Cox continued to hold on to Corporal McPhie until he saw the latter was dead.

Sapper Hawkins then went out at considerable risk to himself and threw a rope to Sapper Cox and drew him to the shore.[15]

As the history of the 56th Division puts it, 'this wonderful man still had the strength to hold on to it ...' but Cox died two days later. McPhie was awarded the VC, and the medal was presented to his widowed mother at Buckingham Palace the following April.

Second Army Sector

The investiture of Second Lieutenant Cecil Knox by George V at Oxelaere, northern France, 6 August 1918.

Only ten days later another VC was won in the Second Army sector to which we must make at least passing reference since the remarkable winner was an infantry-man who became a sapper later in life. Second Army was the most northerly of the BEF's armies and was advancing into Belgium across the devastation of the old Third Ypres battlefield. In this story we are again concerned with 36th (Ulster) Division, whom we last met on the St Quentin canal and the Somme in the story of Cecil Knox's VC. Knox was still with 150 Field Company and, indeed, during the division's period of reorganisation in the Ypres area, he had received his VC from the King at a ceremony at Oxelaere, a small village on Cassel Hill. By now, also, the division was under the command of Major-General Clifford Coffin, VC, fresh from his escapades in front of Amiens.

The Second Army advance had begun on 28 September as part of a general offensive into Flanders under the overall command of the King of the Belgians whose national army was on the left. The first stage of this had cleared the old battlefield and on 14 October the second stage began. 36th (Ulster) Division had the task of crossing the River Lys to the north-east of Courtrai and advancing over the ridge that lay between it and the River Schelde running parallel and to the south. The Lys crossing entailed preliminary rafting and bridging under fire and the leading battalions only crossed after considerable casualties. They advanced with leap-frogging brigades down their axis through hilly open country in which the enemy took full advantage of the network of small hamlets which were strong-ly fortified with machine-gun posts.

On 25 October, on 36th Division's right, the 9th Division had captured the high ground at Ingoyghem and Ooteghem and, to secure the ridge, 109th Brigade of 36th Division had now to capture Kleineberg. A hasty operation was laid launched late in the afternoon by the 1st and 2nd Inniskillings. These battalions were now so thin on the ground, however, that only three companies were available, two of the 1st and one of the 2nd, each only some 50 strong after the losses from the recent fighting. In the evening light 1st Royal Inniskilling Fusiliers were badly held up by machine-gun fire from a farm but, thanks largely to a most remarkable solo performance by Private Norman Harvey, were able to press on.

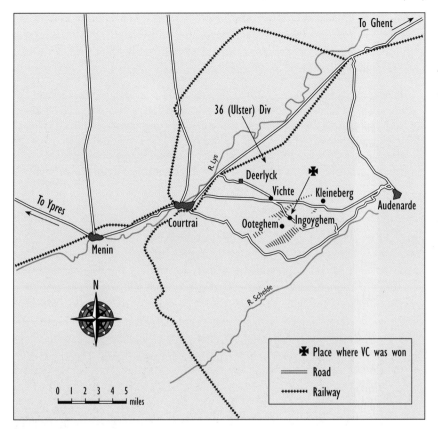

Map 22
36th (Ulster)
Division's advance
from the River Lys
in which Norman
Harvey won his VC.

Private Norman Harvey

Norman Harvey had joined the battalion only the previous spring by which time he was a 19-year-old veteran. He had originally enlisted in the Lancashire Regiment but omitted to mention his true age, only 15½. He was twice wounded in France and his actual age was only discovered in hospital. He remained in England doing various courses until the chance came to volunteer as a reinforcement, hence his arrival in 1st Inniskillings. The occasion on which he won his VC at Ingoyghem is described by his platoon sergeant:

Norman Harvey
(1899–1942)

> On the 25th October 1918, my platoon was attacking. Suddenly very heavy machine-gun fire was opened on us from a farm about forty yards from my left front. It held my platoon up, and we all got down to fire. Five of my men were wounded, and I saw Private Harvey bring about a dozen Bosches from the farm. I went forward to the farm and found two dead Bosches and one badly wounded with the bayonet. There were two machine-guns there. He was doing awfully fine work all day and seemed to bear a charmed life, because he was running about under heavy machine-gun fire all the time. He went forward to another farmhouse where machine-gun fire was coming from, and was away about fifteen minutes, and when he came back he was laughing and told me the Bosches beat it when he went for them.[16]

Although the Inniskillings clung on to Harvey's farm, the last objective on the ridge fell only two days later when the Germans withdrew to the Escaut. This was 36th Division's last act of the war as it was relieved that night by 34th Division.

The 36th (Ulster) Division's history sums up this period as one of:

> brilliant co-operation of every arm … amid many achievements, perhaps the most satisfactory of all had been that of the Engineers. For once their work, always so hard, but generally so obscure and thankless, had stood out in the foreground. Upon it had hinged the whole attack across the Lys. They had carried out, with supreme skill, devotion, and success, what is perhaps the sapper's first task in warfare, of which he is popularly supposed to dream, that of putting the infantry across a great river, to be launched to victory from the further bank.[17]

This comment could have been repeated again and again across the whole front of Haig's force over those weeks. Magnificent though the fighting of the battalions was, in all such operations all hung on the logistics of getting them to battle and supplying them and their supporting artillery in the field. The countryside over which that had to be achieved had been occupied and deliberately engineered to prevent movement over the past four years. The old battle areas were a shambles where cross-country movement was rarely possible. On top of this, in retreat, the Germans had taken every opportunity to block routes with demolitions and their skill in laying mines and traps to hold up the advancing Allies was taking its toll.

The Sambre-Oise Canal – Fourth Army

This was particularly the experience on the Fourth Army front to which we now return for the last action of the war. On 17 October, the day that 36th Division had started their advance from the Lys to the Escaut, XIII Corps of Fourth Army was forcing the crossing of the River Selle which runs from the high plateau round Le Cateau northwards into the Escaut near Valenciennes. In itself the Selle was not much of an obstacle but the surrounding countryside offered excellent cover for the German machine-guns, and the high ground to the east gave them good observation for artillery. By the time XIII Corps had established a bridgehead over the Selle, a pause in the general advance across the army front had become essential in order to reconstruct the new routes and bring up supplies for what was to be the final act of the war, the crossing of the Sambre-Oise Canal. The German reverses on the Western Front since 8 August were also having their effect worldwide; indeed, it is sometimes argued that it was the collapse of the 'props' of its allies, the Austrians in Italy, the Bulgarians in the Balkans and the Turks in Palestine, that undermined the Western Front. In fact, the failure of Ludendorff's offensives and the success of Haig's attacks starting with the Battle of Amiens, combined with the Allied blockade which was making life in Germany itself intolerable, were the real issues.

The Germans had already begun the peace process on 4 October by indicating their acceptance of President Wilson's Fourteen Points. Their continued resistance on the Western Front was in the cause of rescuing as good a negotiating position as possible from their dire circumstances. With no hope of further support, resistance in the 'sideshows' was doomed. In Palestine the Turks had been on the run since Gaza had fallen in October 1917, but Allenby had had to give up divisions to bolster up the Western Front and was not able to bring his business to a conclusion until the autumn of 1918. The Turks surrendered on 30 October. In the Balkans, the Allied advances in September had forced the Bulgarians to submit on the 29 September. In Italy, the Italian army, despite their catastrophic losses at Caporetto the previous autumn, had in June defeated an Austrian effort to match Ludendorff's Kaiserschlacht. They now took the offensive against the Austrians and forced them to ask for an armistice on 30 October, which they signed on 3 November.

Therefore, for the doughty men of Haig's army the sweet scent of peace was in the air. The paradox they had to face was that only by continuing their exertions and conducting operations with the utmost resolution and selfless courage could that peace be achieved. All were aware of this reality. Although letters of condolence after death in action are notorious for their economy with the truth, those written to Lieutenant Arnold's next-of-kin (his aunt) reflect something of the mood. Three weeks before the war actually ended, his CRE had said: 'He was so cheery and full of enthusiasm. I can hardly believe we have lost him. It is to such as him that England owes the happy outcome of the war'; and a brother officer, 'I cannot tell you how sorry we all are about it. He was most popular with us and with his men and we are dreadfully sorry to lose him, the more especially when things seem nearly over.'[18]

It was on 29 October that Haig issued his orders for a general attack in the direction of Mauberge and Mons. The Allied attack had to be in this area, as the only hope left to the Germans was to hang on through the winter for a better bargaining position for their dwindling gains in northern France and Belgium. Conversely, the Allies' hope for forcing the issue lay in breaking the Sambre-Oise canal defence line and striking out towards the remaining all-important German supply lines.

The Fourth Army area of responsibility lay between its junction with the Third Army just south of Englefontaine, seven miles from Le Cateau on the Mons road in the north, to the canal line just north of Oisy in the south, a total frontage of about 12 miles. XIII Corps had the northern sector with the responsibility of crossing at Landrecies and IX Corps the south, to cross at Catillon and Ors. In general the canal was a considerable obstacle, some 70 feet wide between banks and 35–50 feet wide at water-level. The crossing areas were selected because of the prospect they offered of bridging the 17-foot-wide locks at Catillon, Ors and Landrecies. However, large quantities of materials would also be required to make rafts and floating footbridges for infantry crossings and for bridging for follow-up formations and supplies once bridgeheads had been established. Collecting the material for these (much of it captured from the Germans), preparing the equipment and rehearsing the various operations with the infantry formed a major part of sapper work at this time. A foretaste of the likely German resistance was experienced by 15th Lancashire Fusiliers who had been launched on 2 November, to capture the high ground of the Happegarbes Spur which overlooks the canal west of Landrecies, as a preliminary to the main attack which was planned for 4 November. They succeeded after heavy fighting but were driven off

Map 23
The Sambre-Oise canal crossings in the IX Corps area, November 1918.

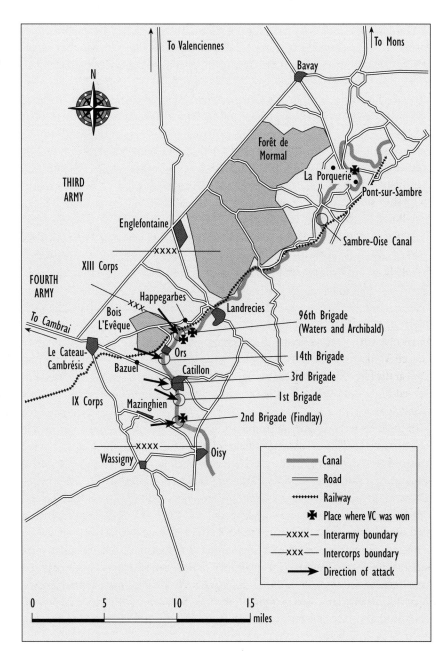

To Valenciennes

To Mons

Bavay

N

Forêt de Mormal

La Porquerie

Pont-sur-Sambre

THIRD ARMY

Englefontaine

Sambre-Oise Canal

XXXX

XIII Corps

FOURTH ARMY

Happegarbes

Bois L'Evêque

Landrecies

96th Brigade (Waters and Archibald)

To Cambrai

XXX

Le Cateau-Cambrésis

Ors

14th Brigade

Bazuel

Catillon

3rd Brigade

IX Corps

1st Brigade

Mazinghien

2nd Brigade (Findlay)

XXXX

Wassigny

Oisy

	Canal
	Road
	Railway
✸	Place where VC was won
—XXXX—	Interarmy boundary
—XXX—	Intercorps boundary
→	Direction of attack

0   5   10   15
miles

by determined counter-attacks and the decision was made to leave this feature in enemy hands to be dealt with as part of the main plan.

In the early morning of 4 November, First, Third and Fourth Armies attacked. Apart from a brief return to Third Army later, we are primarily concerned with IX Corps sector of Fourth Army. However, it is worth noting that in the XIII Corps, on IX Corps' left, the operation to cross at Landrecies met with full success despite the trials and tribulations that inevitably attend such an intricately planned affair. To put the infantry across quickly, their sappers had pre-prepared a large number of rafts improvised from petrol-tin floats, experience on the St Quentin crossing having shown that the more commonly used cork floats would be too heavy and cumbersome for carrying parties over the approach distance of one-and-a-half miles. The rafts went in 20 yards apart along the front, manned by sappers, and when sufficient infantry were across were formed into bridges. All this occurred in thick fog which made for some confusion on the move forward although it greatly reduced the casualties on the crossing. Mid-morning the bridge in Landrecies was blown by the German garrison but shortly afterwards the locks were reached and more footbridges put across there. As soon as the situation allowed, the heavier bridging equipment moved forward, albeit held up by shell fire, and by 8.30 pm a pontoon and trestle bridge was taking traffic to be followed by another two hours later.

However, the real dramas were in progress further south in the IX Corps sector and were to result in VCs for Major Arnold Waters, Sapper Adam Archibald and Major George Findlay.

Major Arnold Waters

Arnold Horace Santo Waters was the son of a Plymouth United Methodist Free Church Minister, the Reverend Richard Waters, and his wife Abigail. He was educated at the Hoe Grammar School and then worked on projects in Plymouth while articled to the Borough Surveyor there. He qualified in 1905 and worked with a contractor for four years before joining the firm of Wilcox and Raikes in 1910. With them he was engaged on major works in the Rhymney Valley and Eastern Valleys in South Wales. He was commissioned into the Royal Engineers in January 1915 and joined 90 Field Company. His record before the Sambre-Oise crossing was quite outstanding. He won an MC on 30 June 1917 for a most determined performance near Nieuport, by then with 206 Field Company, when he volunteered to lead a party to blow a gap through two successive belts of enemy wire to allow an infantry raid to enter the enemy trenches. The citation called the task of getting all the stores across no-man's-land 'a particularly trying and dangerous one and could not have been carried out without a determined leader.' The party was attacked and fired on in the process but they carried on and achieved their objective. Shortly after this he joined 218 Field Company with whom he was to serve until after the end of the war. He was awarded the DSO in the Birthday Honours in June 1918.

Arnold Waters
(1886–1981)

Adam Archibald
(1879–1957)

Sapper Adam Archibald

Arnold Waters's collaborator was the 39-year-old Adam Archibald. Born in Leith, the son of Rennie and Christina Anderson Archibald, Adam was educated at Leith Walk Public School. He served his apprenticeship with a plastering firm in Leith but joined the Edinburgh branch of Stuart's Granolithic Company in July 1900 and worked there until he joined the Royal Engineers in November 1916. He had married in 1902, Margaret Sinclair, and by the time he joined up he was father of four children.

218 Field Company was in support of 96th Brigade in 32nd Division who had been allocated the sector of canal between Catillon and the eastern end of the Bois L'Evêque. At the time of writing the canal is a tranquil rural locality, where nothing more violent than fishing and bird-watching occurs to break the peace other

The canal bend north of Ors just south of which Arnold Waters and Adam Archibald built their bridge. Taken from the north, 1997.

than the occasional low murmur of the barges which slip respectfully along its waters. On 4 November 1918 it was a scene of death and destruction.

> Only through the heroism of Major Waters and Sapper Archibald of the 218th Field Company was it possible to get a bridge across. The whole area was swept with shell and machine-gun fire, and it seemed impossible for anyone to live on the bank of the canal. All the rest of the party were killed or disabled, yet these two gallant engineers carried on the work, while bullets splintered the wood they were holding and struck sparks from the wire binding the floats.[19]

The floats mentioned were cork floats for two infantry footbridges. The point at which this attempt was made was just to the south of the elbow in the canal to the north of Ors. Two of 218 Company's officers were killed and Arnold Waters now took charge of the remnants. A third hero, Second Lieutenant Kirk of the 2nd Manchester, managed to get across the canal on a raft and to engage the enemy with a Lewis gun. He was killed and the bridge made by Waters and Archibald was destroyed by artillery fire after only two platoons had crossed. All further efforts to repair it were to no avail. VCs were awarded to Kirk, Waters and Archibald for this action. The infantry, too, displayed extraordinary gallantry and also suffered severe casualties in their efforts to cross. It was also here that the poet, Wilfred Owen, then a lieutenant in the 2nd Manchester, was killed. Another bridge was attempted just below the canal elbow for a crossing by the 16th Lancashire Fusiliers, with the same result: 31-year-old Lieutenant Colonel John Neville Marshall of the Irish Guards who was commanding this battalion organised parties of volunteers to repair the bridge but was killed trying to rush across at the head of his battalion. He was awarded a posthumous VC.

Fortunately 206 Field Company, working with 14th Brigade just south of Ors, managed to get two petrol-tin bridges across within 25 minutes of zero hour. The brigade infantry were able to cross, and in due course, to save further loss of life in 96th Brigade, they too were diverted to cross at this point at 8.30 am. 206 Field Company also built a horse-transport bridge by 10.00 am.

Further south at Catillon the enemy put up equally stiff resistance to 1st Division's attempts to breach the canal. Here there were three brigade crossings planned. The northernmost, at Catillon itself where the enemy was occupying the village to the west of the canal, involved 3rd Brigade with only a section of sappers, attacking the village from the south, clearing and holding it until the main bridgeheads had developed. The attack was successfully accomplished and even succeeded, with the help of two tanks, in capturing the canal bridge and other German-built bridges in the area.

However, the main bridgehead was to be developed from two crossings further south where in most places the enemy had been pushed back to the eastern canal bank. The most promising route lay over the Lock No. 1, nearly two miles south of Catillon and this was allocated to 2nd Brigade, while 1st Brigade were given a site about 1200 yards further north. In the event, this crossing, the responsibility of 23 Field Company, was relatively straightforward.

> Their bridges reached the canal five minutes after zero. There was no enemy shelling, and practically no resistance except from one machine-gun post on the west bank. Sergeant E. Cook, of the 23rd Company, with Sapper G. F. Daycock, rushed this post, killing three Germans and capturing two. The sergeant then laid his bridge nine minutes after zero, and the 1st Cameron Highlanders began to cross. A minute later, the three remaining first-wave bridges were in position.[20]

Things went nothing like so smoothly at the lock where Major George Findlay, in command of 409 (Lowland) Field Company, was to earn his VC – in a display surpassing the gallantry for which he had already won a considerable reputation and two MCs.

The 1st Brigade crossing on the Sambre-Oise canal, 1918.

The 1st Brigade crossing on the Sambre-Oise canal, 1918.

George Findlay as a young officer at Chatham.

Major George Findlay

George de Cardonnel Findlay, at 6ft 4in a man of impressive build, came from a well-connected family whose home was at Boturich Castle, Balloch in Dunbartonshire. He was the third son of Major R.E. Findlay, a director of the Glasgow firm of East India merchants, Findlay, Richardson and Company, an intensely loyal man who had strong opinions about duty and commanded Glasgow Yeomanry units during the war. All four sons were in the services. The eldest was a gunner lieutenant-colonel with an MC, the second served in the Argyll and Sutherland Highlanders in Second Ypres but was tragically killed in the troop train accident at Gretna in May 1915, and George's younger brother served in the Royal Navy. George was educated at St Ninian's preparatory school at Moffat, going on to Harrow and the RMA Woolwich. In 1908 he had won the Spencer Cup at Bisley as the best schoolboy shot of the year. He was commissioned into the Royal Engineers in January 1910, attended the usual courses at Chatham and then remained there until the beginning of the war as Assistant Adjutant for Musketry. The outbreak of war found him training recruits while recovering from two broken legs following a riding accident.

Findlay went to France in March 1915 and a year later joined the staff of Chief Engineer V Corps. In June 1917 he took command of 409 (Lowland) Field Company, a territorial company which, with the regular 23 and 26 Field Companies, made up the 1st Divisional Engineers. He was mentioned in despatches in February 1917 and awarded an MC for gallantry at Passchendaele for working 'for hours in heavily shelled areas and deep mud to establish communications. His ability in reconnaissance by night over difficult ground was invaluable in assisting the infantry …'[21] – perhaps this explains the quotation from his company history in Chapter Ten: 'Yet in the midst of all this danger and desolation, there is a certain fascination out there on patrol ...'[22] A bar to that award

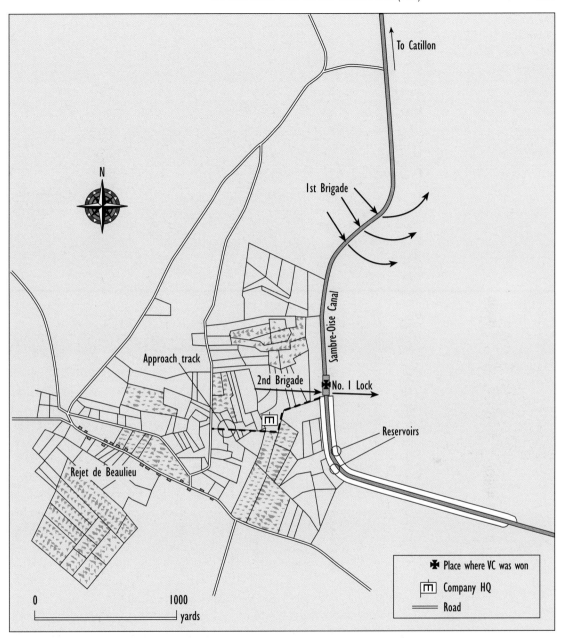

To Catillon

1st Brigade

Sambre-Oise Canal

Approach track

2nd Brigade

No. 1 Lock

Reservoirs

Rejet de Beaulieu

✳	Place where VC was won
🗠	Company HQ
═══	Road

0   1000
yards

Map 24
Lock No. 1,
Sambre-Oise canal.

followed in October 1918 for his work during an attack in the area of Wassigny, just a few miles short of and barely two weeks before he was to win the VC. 'He made reconnaissances both before and during the fighting under heavy machine-gun fire. He set a fine example and largely contributed to the success in that area.'

He and his company now began to plan for the most demanding challenge they had yet met, due to take place in the early morning of 4 November. Only four days

No. 1 Lock south of Catillon on the Sambre-Oise canal 1918, seen from the west.

Findlay's design for the footbridge which was to be manhandled into position on Lock No. 1 (based on the original drawing).

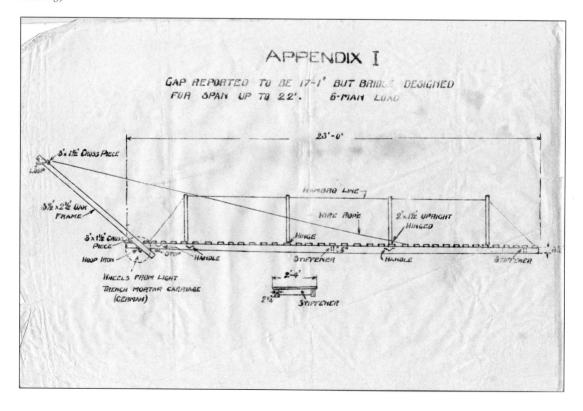

were available for these preparations which included reconnaissance, collection of stores, the design and construction of 30 bridges, rehearsal and briefing. The quotations that follow come from the War Diary, recorded with marvellous detail and clarity in Findlay's own hand;[23] and from the company history, almost certainly also written by him.[24] Any re-interpretation of the immediacy of the language in these two documents seems heresy. War Diary extracts are shown in italics.

> *Reconnaissance. The problem of the lock was different from other portions as here we did not hold the near bank* [there were three enemy posts on the near bank, one of which was cleared before the operation, the other two during it] *and consequently exact information was difficult to obtain. – In all 6 close reconnaissances were carried out, 3 by officers, 3 by NCOs – the information obtained from these was sufficiently definite to decide on the bridges required and the plan of action –*

What they found was a 17-foot gap at the lock for which they designed a special 23-foot lightweight bridge with a set of wheels and a lever so that it could be man-handled forward and dropped over the gap. Four more supplementary bridges without wheels were required for the lock. Eight 12-foot and eight 16-foot foot-bridges were also prepared for crossing the streams that ran parallel to the canal on either side. In addition two heavier pack transport bridges were needed for each of the gaps, six in all.

> *(1) Transport of Bridges to site*
> *Four wagons left under Capt RHIND at 3.30pm 3/11/18 with unloading party. The bridges were dumped … by 6pm*
>
> *(2) HQ & remainder of Sappers*
> *(a) Paraded at 7 pm with 1 toolcart, 1 limber, 2 wagons with BERTHON boats. Marched to near Bn H.Q. … arrived dump 9.30pm*
>
> *(b) Offloaded BERTHON boats & carried them to site, this threw an unforeseen [delay] on the assembly … infantry bridges carried to assembly position by 12.30pm … mule bridges by 1.30pm …*
>
> *(c) Gaps cut in wire* [at this point the history adds ' … and we lay down in the ditch for a well earned rest knowing that the morrow at dawn one of the proudest tasks of the war lay before us.']
>
> *(d) 5am Capt RHIND reported and took charge of 4 [?] bridges*

Then came the reveille: no noisy awakening and bustle but a sergeant here and a corporal there slipping quietly round announcing breakfast ready … Five minutes to go, memories of waiting for the whistle to blow for the kick off of a football match … and it is the spirit of working as one whole for the common good imbued by these games that helped many that day to play their last great game; all helping, each man doing his share and filling the gap when a comrade fell without waiting for orders.

> *(e) Hot soup Rum and Breakfast until 5.30 …*

05.44 One minute from Zero the Machine Gun Barrage from South opened up followed by MG further North.

05.45 Artillery barrage opened punctually and fell on line of canal and near bank ... the Southern party under Sergt McLaren and the 4 span 23-ft bridges under Capt RHIND were well away at Zero and were 50 to 100 yds away from the infantry ... Northern Group ... under Lt Elmslie RE ... also moved out punctually at Zero. They had to cross a small stream & Lt Elmslie had arranged to temporarily utilise two of his light bridges to expedite passage of 23-ft bridge. ... the second bridge was on the point of crossing when an ENEMY shell passing over the heads of the leading team put out of action the whole section, officer (Lt Elmslie), Sergt and the whole team except one man ... thus demobilising [sic] half the bridges from the Northern Group.

In the half light up to twenty or thirty yards away shadowy forms could be discovered through the veil of smoke and mist and it was not till the enemy bank of the stream was gained that the extent of the wire could be seen, but it was there right up to the top and foretold untold delays. A hurried search and a place 50 yards further north was found clear except for stumps of trees and debris and a few loose strands, more the top was clear and the lock walls intact. It seemed too good to be true. Meanwhile the long bridges with the gaps in their crews filled by men who had already placed the light bridges and by helping Infantry were plodding forward but had not had time to get up but the shells were falling fast and the ground was covered with dead and dying while our two medical orderlies already had their hands full giving first aid to the wounded.

There then followed a period of not more than ten minutes when both infantry and sappers struggled to get forward in the fog, smoke and devastating shell-fire. More casualties. At this stage the commanding officer of the 2nd Sussex, Lieutenant-Colonel Dudley Johnson, came up to the bridge and urged his men on helping the sappers and then on into the attack. Findlay comments that their determination to get over seemed to be largely due to Johnson's personal influence.

06.00 By the time the first 23' bridge was across the first stream [this was one of those intended for the lock but had to be used here], *the 2nd swing bridge was dragged across and up the bank during which time infantry assisted – Its team, assisted by other Sappers carried it across placing it parallel to the lock, fixed swinging gear – only one guy was left the other having been severed – it was gently raised and swung*

06.10 <u>and lowered successfully across</u> – The bridge was twisted almost to breaking point and a jerk would have meant failure – A party of RE went over first and opened fire on the enemy – During the crossing Spr Wells (a Lewis Gunner) saw the necessity of heavier covering fire and asked the loan of a gun, this was refused but the Lewis Gunner came right forward on the lock and firing from the hip sprayed the top of the opposite bank, he continued to do so till hit when his No. 2 carried on. This very valuable act may have decided the success of the crossing ...

Or, as the history puts it:

> Back for a second bridge is our job. But no! The place of honour is left and so the Lowlands on the spot take it and lead the way over and open fire on the nearest enemy while a few rush toward the building which is still held. The first platoon is over on their heels and the lock buildings are ours and prisoners are coming in. That one narrow strip. Stop that firing – back for the other bridge – through the barrage to where it lay 150 yards back surrounded by the men who fell at their post. Meanwhile another bridge has arrived across the stream and up the bank. ...
>
> But the first success must be confirmed by ensuring the ammunition supply. Back for the mule bridges past where we had lain that morning, yes it was well we were early clear, the road had its tale to tell. By this time more than a third were down and the bridges were where the shells were falling but not so thick. A crew had to be found, a spare driver here, a party detailed for heavy bridge, a few German prisoners. All lent a hand and the bridges were got up and over, screens and all, the mules and ammunition over within a few minutes of completion.

And so the brigades moved forward to consolidate this success. 409 Field Company stood by to maintain the crossing and bury their dead, one officer and nine men. Twenty soldiers were wounded and three officers including Findlay himself, although he carried on with his duties. As well as George Findlay's VC (originally gazetted as a DSO but later replaced with the VC), 16 MMs, two bars to MMs, three DCMs and an MC were awarded for this operation. Colonel Dudley Johnson was also awarded the VC. On 6 November, the Division went into reserve where they remained until the Armistice.

The memorial at Lock No. 1.

Sambre-Oise Canal — Third Army

But there was one final episode to the story of the First World War sapper VCs. On the same day as 1st Division retired to lick their wounds a further crossing of the canal was being planned in the Third Army area. Third Army had taken part in Haig's great 4 November attack but at that stage their front line lay considerably to the west of the Sambre-Oise canal. Between them and that objective lay several miles of occupied territory including the great Mormal forest. It was an awkward and untidy task in which route clearance was the major problem until they reached the canal. There the 5th Division was to have the responsibility for the crossing in the area of the Pont des Quartes at Pont-sur-Sambre. The officer who went forward for a preliminary reconnaissance was Major Brett Cloutman.

Major Brett Cloutman

Brett Cloutman
(1891–1971)

Brett McKay Cloutman was the son of Alfred Benjamin Cloutman, a governor of the furnishing company, Maples. He was educated at Berkhamsted School, Stanley House School, Bishop Stortford College and London University from which he graduated in 1913 in modern languages. He enlisted in the Territorial 12th Battalion The London Regiment (Rangers) but was initially rejected for a commission because of his poor eyesight. Eventually he was accepted for a commission in the Royal Engineers and joined the Kent Fortress Royal Engineers at Gillingham. He was married in February 1916 and went to France the following year, first seeing action at Vimy Ridge and later in the fierce fighting at Passchendaele. By this time Cloutman's brother, a lieutenant in 178 Tunnelling Company, had died, overcome by poisonous fumes while attempting to rescue a sergeant from some old trench workings near Albert (see Chapter Nine).

In December 1917 5th Division, with 59 Field Company, went to Italy, part of the reinforcements that the Allies had squeezed out of their thinning ranks after the Italians had nearly collapsed at the Battle of Caporetto, and Cloutman spent the winter on the Piave, returning the following spring. As part of Third Army, it then participated in the Allied advance after the Battle of Amiens. On 30 September 1918, only six weeks before the crossing of the Sambre-Oise canal, he undertook an extremely dangerous reconnaissance for a possible crossing of the Canal d'Escaut at Banteux, in the wasteland of the old Cambrai battlefield, for which he was awarded the MC.

The modern bridge, Pont des Quartes, at Pont-sur-Sambre, spanning the canal which Brett Cloutman swam across on his reconnaissance on 6 November 1918.

Now he was to face an even more dangerous situation in the dying days of the war. In the 4 November attack in which Findlay, Waters and Archibald were so momentously engaged on the canal, 5th Division was still some ten miles to its west. The town of Pont-sur-Sambre was among the objectives of the corps attack which was to take place through the Forêt de Mormal. By 5 November, in torrential rain, 5th Division was fighting its way forward and by the evening was close enough to be able to send patrols down to the canal. The 59 Field Company War Diary entry for 6 November, written in Cloutman's own neat hand, reads:

> SAMBRE R is reconnoitred for crossings – and opposite bank found strongly held – and 1 Girder bridge [the Quartes bridge at Pont-sur-Sambre] is found not destroyed, but with charges on – leads to these charges are cut, – but after nightfall and bridgehead was formed, fresh charges were set and bridge blown up. Coy moves to La Porquerie [about one mile west of the village].[25]

A reader could be forgiven for not realising that the writer of this gem of understatement had just won a VC. Even the citation for Cloutman's VC is considered by Creagh and Humphris to give 'but slight an idea of the incident'.

> The bridge was a single-span structure on stone abutments, situated in quiet country surroundings. Close by was a cottage, and a lock and another building just beyond. The infantry were to advance after the retiring Germans, and it was most desirable to save this bridge from the destruction which would have hindered the progress of our men. The enemy had placed charges at his end, and Major Cloutman made it his business to destroy these. The cottage was full of machine-gunners and the banks of the river also concealed some of the enemy. Major Cloutman managed to reach the river unseen, swam across, and crept along the bank, taking cover as best he could towards the bridge, where he accomplished his object on one side. On his way to the other side, however, the enemy in the lock-keeper's cottage perceived him and directed machine-gun fire at him. He managed to complete his work and set out by the way he had come. He succeeded in dodging the fire which was directed at the bank by which the enemy knew he must return, and swam across the river once more, but on landing and making his way back to the British the lock-house gunners once more did their best to hit him. He reached our lines in safety nevertheless.[26]

Cloutman's was the last VC to be won in the war.

And so 'at the eleventh hour of the eleventh day of the eleventh month'[27] the great contest came to its end. Contemporary accounts of the event run the whole gamut of emotion from ecstatic joy, through simple relief, to grief and guilt that such a monstrous ordeal should ever have had to be endured. For the sappers there was work to do and doubtless this suppressed any tendency to introspection. For us it remains only to follow the fortunes of the survivors of the acts of valour so selflessly performed in these final few months.

Later Careers

Of Norman Harvey, the young infantryman so keen to go to war, there is a sad tale to tell. He was duly fêted in his home town and his words in response to his reception reflect the attitude of so many of those who were rewarded. After thanking the people of Newton-le-Willows he said, 'The only thing I did was not bravery but was what my conscience bade me do. Many more lads have done more and never been seen – have never got so much as a "thank you" for what they have done …'[28] He left the Army and obtained employment on the railways. He was married in 1919, to Nora Treadwell, and they had two daughters and a son. In 1939, then nearly 40, he re-enlisted in the Royal Engineers joining 199 Railway Workshop Company. He quickly rose through the ranks becoming a Company Quartermaster-Sergeant in April 1941. Then, ten months later, he tragically and inexplicably ended his life with a rifle shot – another casualty, perhaps, of the First World War?

Coulson 'Mike' Mitchell returned to Canada after his investiture at Buckingham Palace in April 1919 and rejoined the civilian company he had been with at the start of the war. Three years later he married Gertrude Bishop; they had two daughters. In 1926 Mitchell became General Superintendent for the Construction and Development of Steam and Hydro-Electric Power Plants of the Power Corporation for their subsidiary companies and associates in every province from Newfoundland to the Yukon. The Second World War found him back in uniform and, in the rank of major, he took C Company 2nd Pioneer Battalion RCE to Britain in 1940. Promoted lieutenant-colonel he then commanded No. 1 Training Wing of the Canadian Engineers Reinforcement Unit until returning to Canada in October 1943. In April 1944 he took over command of A6 The Western Canadian Engineer Training Centre which in due course became the present Canadian Forces School of Military Engineering. The war over, 'Mike' Mitchell once again returned to civilian life becoming Construction Manager of the Power Corporation until retiring to live in Beaurepaire, Quebec, in 1957. He died at Mount Royal Quebec in 1978 at the age of 89.

Arnold Waters likewise had a very distinguished career in engineering. He had his own practice in Birmingham specialising mainly in water supply and sewerage projects. He was twice President of the Institution of Structural Engineers, in 1933 and 1943, and an Honorary Member of the Institution of Royal Engineers. On the outbreak of the Second World War, now 53, he was turned down for any active military service but became Divisional Food Officer for the West Midlands.

In 1952, he was appointed as Honorary Colonel of 127 Construction Regiment TA (later 48th Divisional Engineers (Volunteers)), a post which he held until 1958. The commanding officer at the time described him as 'the most unassuming great man that I have had the good fortune to know. Not only did he have a magnificent war record, he was undoubtedly one of the most distinguished civil engineers in the country yet he could spend long periods talking to the men, not only looking as though he was enjoying the experience but, in fact, was entirely happy in the role he played.'[29] A teetotaller himself, he always insisted that at mess dinners the Loyal Toast should be drunk either in port or water – nothing else – and the provision of Sir Arnold's jug of water became an agreeable regimental custom on these occasions.

In 1929 Arnold Waters was appointed JP on the Sutton Coldfield Bench and he became Chairman after the Second World War. He was made CBE in 1949 and was knighted in 1954 for services to the Ministry of Housing and Local Government. He married in 1924, Gladys Barriball, and they made their home in Sutton Coldfield. They had three sons. Sir Arnold Waters died at Four Oaks, Sutton Coldfield on 22 January 1981.

Adam Archibald returned to his peacetime employment with the Edinburgh branch of Stuart's Granolithic, in the appointment of Superintendent of the Edinburgh branch. On 29 May 1919 the Board of Stuart's noted that Archibald was to be invested with the VC at Buckingham Palace on 31 May, minuted their congratulations and resolved that he be given a cheque for £50. He retired in February 1949 with a pension of £15 per month and died at Leith eight years later.

George Findlay's post-war career in the Royal Engineers alternated between regimental and works appointments. He was Adjutant of the 52nd (Lowland) Division Engineers until 1924 when he was given command of 59 Field Company (in command of which his fellow VC, Brett Cloutman, had won his award on the Sambre-Oise Canal). From there he was posted to Liverpool as DCRE (Works). He then went out to India; first to further works appointments in Dehra Dun and at Karachi and then, returning to regimental duty, joining the Queen Victoria's Own Madras Sappers and Miners at Bangalore as Assistant Commandant and later in command of the Training Battalion.

*George Findlay
(1889–1967)*

In 1934 Findlay returned home on sick leave and later that year was appointed CRE Highland Area with his headquarters at Perth. He retired in 1938 but on the outbreak of war was re-employed in the rank of colonel and became Chief Engineer Northern Ireland District in 1940. After a second retirement that year due to ill-health he was again re-employed and served with the Allied Military Government in Italy from 1943 to 1946.

Findlay had always been a very active member of the community in his native Dunbartonshire. He was a County Councillor from 1941 to 1964 and in 1957 he was appointed a Deputy-Lieutenant. In 1921 Findlay had married Dorothy Gordon but the marriage was later annulled. He married again, Constance Clark, in 1959. There were no children from either marriage. He died at Helensburgh, Dunbartonshire in June 1967.

Brett Cloutman, the last of the First World War sapper VCs, also returned to his pre-war employment with his family firm, Maples, but later took up law, joining Gray's Inn and being called to the Bar in 1926. His distinguished career thereafter was well portrayed in the memoir published in the *Royal Engineers Journal* after his death upon which the following account is based.[30]

Brett Cloutman joined the Western Circuit where he built up a considerable practice and also frequently appeared in the North London Sessions.

Recalled for service in 1940, he arrived at the RE Mess Aldershot, then temporarily housing a number of sapper officers each of whom had undergone some shattering experiences during the evacuation from Dunkirk and other places. Cloutman's remarkably serene composure and unshakeable optimism were an inspiration to those whose morale was at an all-time low. Shortly afterwards he was posted as Second-in-Command 26 Field Company, which was reforming at Dumfries after most of the unit had been made prisoner at St Valéry. He later served in Syria and commanded the RE Training and Reinforcement Depot in Egypt. He became CRE Levant Engineer Battalion, which consisted of one road construction company and two artisan works companies. The personnel of this volatile, multiracial unit comprised Arabic-speaking Syrians and Lebanese, Greek-speaking Cypriots, and British officers and senior NCOs. An account by Cloutman of how these men 'of little education and less manners' were welded into a relatively well-behaved body of men' and the sterling work they did in Italy was published in the June 1950 issue of the *Royal Engineers Journal*. What the author left unstated was his own great powers of leadership that brought about this metamorphosis.

After the war Brett Cloutman returned to the legal profession and became a Divorce Commissioner and took silk. He was knighted in 1957. Sir Brett Cloutman died in London in August 1971. Before his death he made two arrangements which harked back to his time in the First World War and perhaps reflected the deep feeling of loss he experienced when his brother was killed. He made a Deed of Gift handing over all his brother's and his own medals to the Royal Engineers Museum; and he stipulated that on his death he should be cremated and his ashes scattered at his brother's grave in Norfolk Cemetery near Albert.

Thus, of the six survivors of these events in the last months of the war, four were able to return to the colours and gain some satisfaction in seeing finished the job which they had begun even if, at the time, not one could have expected to survive the ordeal. None could have been in any doubt as the portents manifested themselves in the 1920s and 1930s as to what had to be faced. In their own way they passed on the wisdom of their experience to the next generation of heroes whose achievements in very different circumstances is the subject of Chapter Fourteen. But first we tell of a very particular variety of courage in a new element, the mastering of which had its origins in the Royal Engineers.

The First World War
The New Arm

Flying will be the most important and decisive element in the coming war with Germany and it will begin in that unit [the Balloon Company in Aldershot].[1]

So, with prophetic foresight, believed Second Lieutenant Rex Cammell on commissioning into the Royal Engineers in July 1906. He was explaining to his sister why he had elected to join the Balloon Company (formed from the former Balloon Sections) at Aldershot. His view of the future was not one universally held and even those who did foresee the importance of air power in war did not all agree as to the means by which it might be applied. The first Army balloon unit had been formed by the Royal Engineers in 1878. Aided by the energies of various slightly eccentric enthusiasts (by no means all of them sappers) who were prepared to swim against the tide of scepticism, the sapper balloonists had notched up a fine record of operational success culminating in the Boer War, where the balloons had significantly affected several battles to the discomfiture of the Boers.

By the time Cammell reached Aldershot he would have found planning there well advanced for the launch of the first British military airship *Nulli Secundus*, which in fact flew the next year. Airships with their great lift and endurance seemed to some the best prospect for a military craft but Blériot's Channel flight in 1909 convinced most people otherwise; particularly Cammell who, in 1910, became the first man to fly a military aircraft in Britain after volunteering to bring back from France a Blériot XII which had been donated to the Army by the Duke of Westminster.

The next year, 1911, the Air Battalion Royal Engineers was created with two companies, one for airships at Aldershot and the other for aeroplanes at Larkhill. If this was indicative of the approaching fulfilment of Rex Cammell's prophecy five years earlier, he never lived to see it. He was killed in September while trying out a new French aircraft of unfamiliar design. It was a great loss of a man who had already done much to move aviation forward from an adventurous sport towards its military potential. He had experimented with signalling, designed a form of gyroscopic control and made a special study of air photography and the evolution of bomb sights.[2]

By April 1912 the Air Battalion was ready to leave the apron strings of its parent corps and acquire an existence in its own right as the Royal Flying Corps (RFC). Two years later it was ready to fly no less than 63 aeroplanes across the Channel to concentrate with the BEF at Mauberge. The French had done even better starting the war with 138 aeroplanes, and the Germans deployed 198 into the field.[3] Considering that the Wright brothers had taken their first faltering

Lieutenant Rex Cammell, Royal Engineers, who made the first military flight in an aeroplane; killed in a flying accident in 1911.

hop barely ten years before, these figures reflect a quite remarkable rate of development. It was nothing to the explosion that was about to occur.

Growing Up

At once the new corps set about proving itself. It had already developed a character of its own, rooted in the experience shared by officers and men of being part of a new and exhilarating enterprise. By definition it attracted the unconventional and high-spirited but there was also a self-discipline that derived from the inherent risks and what today would be called a steep learning curve. This applied equally amongst allies and enemy so that:

> Those who brought these frail contraptions to war … met their opponents in a new kind of combat and formed with them an empathy, shared a gallantry, that transcended national animosity … This new breed, airmen, created a unique brand of good manners in mortal conflict and of wry, sardonic, understated fortitude that was to distinguish their successors in every war.[4]

Initially, by general agreement, the only suitable tasks for the new arm were to be reconnaissance and artillery observation. Very soon, however, offensive operations were required and the plea went back to the War Office for aeroplanes which could carry machine-guns rather than just bombs or grenades. By the time of the Battle of the Marne in September 1914, the RFC was already earning accolades for its contribution to operations and for the manner in which this was accomplished.

In March 1915 the intensity of the RFC's operations began to pick up with the Battle of Neuve-Chapelle. By this time there was a Wing of two squadrons allocated to each of First and Second Army. At Neuve-Chapelle, aerial bombing had for the first time been integrated into the operational plan and some successes had been achieved although with modest overall effect on the battle. The enormous advantages that were obtainable from aerial reconnaissance and artillery observation were now proven, however, and the objective for the future was dominance by means of air-to-air combat. The Germans sought this through the introduction of the Fokker single-seater monoplane armed with a forward firing machine-gun synchronised to fire through the propeller disc. The latter they had developed from a French system acquired from a shot-down Morane flown by the inventor of the system, Roland Garros. To this technical advance the Germans added tactical and aeronautical innovation and training under such famous names as Max Immelmann, Oswald Boelcke and Ritter Manfred von Richthofen, and soon began to achieve a psychological dominance which took root in the public imagination. British aircraft, weaponry and pilots were by no means incapable of meeting this threat, but it was to be a whole year before a specialised squadron with a purpose-designed aircraft was to break the 'Fokker menace'.

It is easy to get carried away by the romance of this early flying when tales of derring-do can obscure the reality of the experience. Flying itself was still fraught with danger. Spins had to be avoided because the technique for recovering from them was not yet understood. Navigation depended almost entirely on eye and map observation with a compass to help. Communications initially were by hand signals or Aldis lamp using Morse code. Wireless was eventually introduced but absorbed considerable payload. Bickers's book *The First Great Air War* gives some idea of the adverse physical conditions.

> It was intensely cold and now [1916] that patrols at heights of 14,000 feet and higher were becoming standard the low temperature was painful and incapacitating. Pilots and observers came close to suffering hypothermia. Frostbite was a common affliction. More dangerous and a greater physical handicap was lack of oxygen. In the 1939–45 war, when all aircraft were fitted with oxygen 'bottles', it was compulsory in the RAF to switch them on at 10,000 feet … Oxygen starvation causes hallucinations … headache, nausea, lack of strength and energy. On top of these handicaps was the nauseating effect of castor oil as an engine lubricant. The fumes caused vomiting and diarrhoea. A rotary tractor engine sent oil spraying back over pilot and observer reducing vision …[5]

– and, of course, there was the perpetual noise and bone-shaking vibration. The courage and endurance required by men to go out and fight in these conditions, often two or three sorties a day, was of a special order even if the conditions on their return were more agreeable than in the trenches. The nature of this fighting tended to result in decorations being awarded for repeated and consistent bravery more than for a single outstanding act of valour, and so it was with the VC awarded to Captain Lanoe Hawker, the first of the former sappers to be so honoured and the second RFC VC of the war.

Lanoe George Hawker

Lanoe Hawker, the son of a comfortably off naval captain, initially followed his father into the Navy but later joined the Royal Military Academy at Woolwich in 1910. He had conceived an early passion for flying and an aptitude and interest in technical invention. While at the RMA he joined the Royal Aeronautical Club and took flying lessons at Hendon. Fortunately he abandoned these, as the aircraft was the unreliable Valkyrie which was to kill Rex Cammell the following year. He was commissioned into the Royal Engineers in July 1911, gained experience in things mechanical by driving and experimenting with cars and took further flying lessons at the Deperdussin school, gaining his licence in March 1913. On completing his courses at Chatham, Hawker was posted to Cork to join 33 Fortress Company whose main role was searchlight operating. But flying remained his true ambition and he applied to join the RFC. His work in Cork was somewhat mundane, and no doubt a frustration while a revolution was then in progress with the growth of aviation on Salisbury Plain.* But the summons from the Central Flying School finally came, in a telegram on 30 July 1914.

Lanoe Hawker (1890–1916)
(IWM Q61077)

---

*The Central Flying School containing naval and military wings had been established at Upavon in 1912 and became the focus for all military flying.

At Upavon Hawker learned to fly the Maurice Farman Shorthorn and the RFC's main aeroplane, the BE2. Also while there he learned of the death in action on 22 August of Lieutenant C.G.G. Bayly, his closest friend of his Woolwich and sapper days. Bayly was the first RFC casualty of the war and is buried in Tournai Commonwealth Graves Commission Cemetery.*

Hawker flew to France on 6 October with No. 6 Squadron and was immediately swept into the routine of strategic and tactical reconnaissance, taking part in First Ypres. It was not long before Hawker's exceptional powers of leadership became noticed. By all accounts he was an engaging character with a huge sense of fun and *joie de vivre*. His biographer brother, commissioned into the Royal Artillery and whom Lanoe took every opportunity to visit when they were both in France, clearly looked up to him even before he became celebrated by his exploits. But Lanoe's leadership powers derived also from the example of courage he set, his standards of efficiency, his endless search for improved operational performance from men and machines and his selfless concern for his subordinates. He developed a motto 'attack everything' which became a tactical axiom as well as an inspiring war cry.

Hawker was awarded the DSO for a particularly resolute bombing attack on a Zeppelin shed at Gontrode near Ghent on 18 April 1915. The Zeppelins were beginning to have a serious effect on morale at home where they were able to do much damage with little risk of reprisal. Some of their sheds were in Belgium – just within range. Hawker's raid was intended as an initial reconnaissance but he took three bombs 'on spec'. He reported:

> I dropped a couple from about 4,000 feet. It was a huge mark and I thought no one could miss it, but different bombs vary so and I let fly too soon. ... There was a silly captive sausage balloon there that annoyed me so I spiralled at it dropping hand grenades, he had a machine gun on board, the brute, so deserves no sympathy, but it must have been horrid to see a mad aeroplane circling down at it, ... I shut off and dived down at the shed, the anti-aircraft battery had no chance as I must have been moving at over 120 m.p.h. but the machine-guns were unpleasant Zip-zip-zip-zip-zip-thud as they struck something. I think I got down to about 200 feet and flew across the shed ... and let fly with No. 3, again just too soon, as I looked back when circling away and saw the smoke up alongside the shed.[6]

In fact he was more successful than he thought, and two bombs hit. Unfortunately there was no Zeppelin inside but the vulnerability of these forward sheds had been exposed by this daring raid and in due course the Zeppelins were forced to abandon the sheds in Belgium.[7]

Lanoe Hawker's performance during Second Ypres drew particular admiration. Time and again he would set out on reconnaissances of two hours or so duration, flying slow and low to ensure his reported observations were accurate

---

*Hawker formed a deep friendship with Bayly's sister Beatrice although initially she did not respond with the same ardour. Nevertheless Beatrice remained an important emotional focus for Hawker and they corresponded regularly.

and relevant. His Wing Commander wrote of him: 'During the critical period after April 22nd, he often flew low over the enemy rather than fail to get the required information. His machine was hit by a variety of missiles and it was only a question of time until he himself was at least wounded. While things were still critical he was hit in the leg but remained on flying duty until matters settled down. He then went sick.'[8] Hawker was still keeping a journal at this time and his entry for 24 April gives some flavour of the operations.

> That evening about 5 p.m. I set out again on the same reconnaissance, a job for which I had been reserved. This one was far more difficult than the morning reconnaissance owing to the poor light, low clouds and hazy mist. Urged to be cautious, I tried at first to work above the clouds, but found that impossible.
>
> I had orders to specially note the ground from St. Julien wood eastwards … The firing was particularly heavy that afternoon. Above 4,000 feet all noise from the ground is drowned by the roar of the engine. At the height I was working rifle fire was audible and the noise made by the guns firing and the bursting of the bigger shells was very marked …
>
> We still clung to that part of St. Julien S. E. of the stream which seemed to be forming our line of resistance at the moment. From here the line went N. E. again and I had a very careful look at that bit of ground, circling and going over it again and again till I could make sure of the exact positions we held. It was while flying low over a big farm to the north of this bit that I received a bullet just above my left ankle that solved the problem as to who held the farm! It was remarkably painful at first and I headed for home but as I could use my foot I turned back to deny the Germans the satisfaction of having driven me off, placed the farm carefully on the map and went home … [9]

He returned to England to recuperate and was back in France on 20 May. In mid-July he was in command of both A and B Flights and flying the newly arrived Bristol Scout.

On 25 July Hawker was on patrol flying a single-seater Bristol Scout* at 10,000 feet when, according to his own report, 'The Bristol attacked two machines behind the lines, one at Passchendaele at about 6 p.m. and one over Houtholst Forest about 6.20 p.m. Both machines dived and the Bristol loosed a drum at each at about 400 yards before returning [one made a forced landing behind enemy lines].'[10]

The Bristol climbed to 11,000 feet and about 7.00 pm saw a hostile machine being fired at by anti-aircraft guns at about 10,000 feet over Hooge. The Bristol approached down-sun and opened fire at about 100 yards range. The hostile machine burst into flames, turned upside down, and crashed east of Zillebeke.[11]

This incident is the one quoted in Lanoe Hawker's VC citation though doubtless his exemplary work on patrol up to that point had as much an influence on the submission as this episode itself.

---

*Confusingly the term 'Scout' was used to describe aeroplanes designed for fighting as opposed to reconnaissance, as one might suppose.

A model of a De
Havilland Scout, single-
seater pusher biplane.
(IWM Q60921)

The trend to specialised fighter squadrons now led to Hawker being given command of the first such squadron composed of one type of single-seater. This was No. 24 Squadron and the machine was the new DH2, specifically designed for the role. Superficially it compared badly with the Fokker. To a modern eye it looks like a return to the older type of stick-and-string biplane with a pusher engine. It also quickly acquired a reputation for uncontrolled spinning and the nickname 'spinning incinerator'. After two pilots had been killed in this way, Hawker took a DH2 up to 8,000 feet and deliberately spun it and successfully evolved a procedure for recovery. This was a huge boost to morale and meant that his pilots, who immediately went out to practise, would be free from the restraint of always having to avoid a spin.

This was not the only innovation for which Hawker was responsible. The discomforts of high altitude flying had concerned him for some time and he designed some boots which he christened 'fug boots' to overcome that problem. He had designed a machine-gun mounting and ring sight that was adopted throughout the service. He experimented with a double ammunition drum and practised his squadron exhaustively in their gunnery.

In fact in performance the DH2 was no slouch and began to get results. The reward for all this commitment came on 24 April 1916 when four of Hawker's aircraft, escorting a reconnaissance mission, saw off an attack by 12 Fokkers by turning on them with determination and an agility which caught the Germans by surprise. This event marked the end of the Fokkers' grip on the British Sector.

Two months later the Battle of the Somme was to see the Germans in the ascendant again. The newly formed Jagdstaffeln ('Jastas') were specialist fighter units which could fly faster than most of the British aircraft and had the advantage of a force in defence in that they could wait for the enemy to come to them. However, Hawker's DH2s struck one deadly blow on 28 October when two of them, engaged by ten German aircraft well behind enemy lines, forced Boelcke into a fatal collision with one of his own Jasta. Dire revenge was to come within a month.

There is no doubt that this intensity of operations was an immense strain on Hawker. He had to struggle to keep his squadron's performance and morale up in the face of the German successes and the toll this was taking on his pilots. He was also flying regular missions at the same time. On one of these he came up against possibly the only man with a matching reputation – von Richthofen (Immelmann had been killed in July). On 23 November the two fought a 35-minute duel over the German lines in which Hawker's superior flying skills in an inferior and limping machine were pitted against von Richthofen's cold-blooded temperament and the endurance of his Albatros. Almost out of fuel Hawker finally made a zigzag dash for home but one of von Richthofen's shots caught him in the head.

Gloom and despondency settled over the squadron as they realised Hawker would never return. The German ascendancy remained although the intensity of operations slackened with the dying days of the Somme battle and the onset of winter weather. It was not until the arrival of the highly successful SE5a that No. 24 Squadron was back in contention and scoring the successes for which Hawker had laid the foundations.

The foreword to Lanoe Hawker's biography was written by Air Marshal Sir Robert Saundby, KCB, KBE, MC, DFC who had joined No. 24 Squadron in 1916 as a 20-year-old pilot. In it he describes Hawker as 'a leader of men who combined modesty with great courage, gentleness with a steely determination, and unselfishness with a most human understanding … Hawker taught me the meaning of leadership … He died young, at the height of his glory, and his death cast a shadow far and wide.'[12]

James Thomas Byford McCudden

On the face of it there is even less reason to treat James McCudden as a sapper than Lanoe Hawker, even though both men's VCs were 'credited' to the Army after the war. James McCudden's only actual service in the Royal Engineers was as a bugler from 1910 to 1913. However, not only was this an extremely formative experience, which included a tour in Gibraltar, but the McCudden family were steeped in the Royal Engineers through and through. James (normally Jimmy) was the second son of Corporal (later Sergeant-Major) W.H. McCudden of the Royal Engineers, an Irishman from County Carlow but of Northern Ireland descent. The three eldest sons all started their careers as boy buglers and, obsessed with flying, all transferred to the RFC. Only the fourth son, Maurice, survived the war, being too young for active service. The family's medals, including their father's – he died tragically in a railway accident in 1920 – were eventually entrusted to the Royal Engineers Museum.

James McCudden (1895–1918)
(IWM Q46099)

Jimmy McCudden joined the RFC Depot at Farnborough in April 1913 as an air mechanic. He already had a wide theoretical understanding of aviation having read everything he could lay his hands on about the subject. He spent 15 months at Farnborough before joining No. 3 Squadron at Netheravon from where he went to France on the outbreak of war detailed, to his disgust, to move with the ground party. After the Mons battle the squadron moved south-west, took part in the Aisne battle and, on the redeployment of the BEF, moved north to settle at Gonneham to the north of Béthune in November.

By this time McCudden had flown as a passenger many times and made his first operational sortie. He was also gaining an intimate knowledge of the aircraft in which he was to become such an expert pilot. The unit was equipped with the SE5a[*] and Bristol Scout and shortly received the Morane Parasol. By April 1915

James McCudden in an SE5a.

(IWM Q46099)

he was a sergeant with a reputation for mechanical expertise and thoroughness. It was at this time that he learned of the death of the elder brother to whom he had looked up with respect and affection all his life. Bill's career dated back to the Royal Engineers' Balloon Section which he had joined in 1910 and with whom he had trained as a mechanic. In 1912, now transferred to the new Royal Flying Corps from the Air Battalion Royal Engineers, he became the fourth NCO to be trained as a pilot. Initially on the outbreak of war, his skills as a mechanic were more in demand and he remained grounded until, in April 1915, he returned to

---

[*]SE stands for 'Scouting Experimental'. SEs were single-seater tractor biplanes designed by the Royal Aircraft Factory. Others were 'BE', Blériot Experimental; and 'FE', Farman Experimental, named after the original designs on which they were based.

flying as an instructor in No. 13 Squadron at Gosport. Taking off for a flight in a Blériot trainer on 1 May he was forced by a faulty engine to turn back but, with insufficient height, the aircraft stalled and crashed.

Throughout his first 11 months Jimmy McCudden had become a shrewd judge of the capabilities of the various pilots he had seen. He had flown with many as observer, now an official category of aircrew with its own badge, and had even reported sick on one occasion to avoid flying with a pilot he deemed risky.[13] He did not care for the 'dashing and enterprising kind'.[14] However, he had immense confidence in his new squadron commander, Major Edgar Ludlow-Hewitt.*

> By now, having flown a good deal with Major Hewitt, I intensely disliked ever going up with anyone else, for I can assure you that I knew when I was flying with a safe pilot, and I now had so much faith in him that if he had said 'Come to Berlin', I should have gone like a shot.[15]

The feeling was clearly mutual as it was Ludlow-Hewitt who eventually approved his application for training as an NCO pilot.

McCudden returned to England for pilot training in January 1916 and was successful enough to be retained as a 'student instructor' until July when he returned to France as a flight sergeant and, after a short spell with No. 20 Squadron flying FEs, he joined No. 29 Squadron at Abeele about 20 miles east of St Omer. This was the second of the dedicated DH2 squadrons similar to that in which Lanoe Hawker was engaged in the Somme battle. No. 29 Squadron's area was much quieter and it was 6 September before he achieved his first combat victory, shooting down a two-seater to the north of Messines.

One of the inevitable results of the creation of the specialist fighter units was the practice of individual pilots acquiring victory scores or kills. The term 'ace' had first been coined by the French whose press took a particularly excited interest in the exploits of their military aviators. The RFC had resisted the hero-cult that had grown up in the German and French air arms, maintaining that results came about by teamwork and insisting on anonymity. Concentration on the feats of the fighters also tended to diminish the importance of the achievements of the bomber, artillery-spotting and reconnaissance airmen whose work required equal nerve and whose effect on operations was every bit as important.

However, McCudden, in his steady professional way, reported the action of his first without any claim to a kill. This was confirmed later from a ground report. The difficulty over claims and confirmation was highlighted by the citation for his MM which was awarded in October 'for consistent gallantry, courage and dash during September 1916, in attacking and destroying an enemy machine, and forcing two others to land ...' Probably these two were countable victories but they never appeared in his final tally of credits.

His MM was timely recognition of his contribution as an NCO pilot as he was commissioned on New Year's Day 1917. With three more enemy planes to his

---

*Later Air Chief Marshal Sir Edgar Ludlow-Hewitt, GCB, GBE, CMG, DSO, MC.

credit, he was posted to England as an instructor at 6th Training Wing at Maidstone on 23 February and attached to the Reserve Squadrons at Joyce Green. Two weeks later his MC was gazetted for 'conspicuous gallantry in action'. Among those he encountered at Joyce Green was Edward Mannock, the third subject of this chapter. The two formed a mutual respect for each other's skills. McCudden records how Mannock, in his intense way, had come up to his instructor and credited him with saving his life: 'He had just had his first spin and had remembered my advice, which I think at the time was to put all controls central and offer up a very short and quick prayer.'[16]

McCudden received his captaincy on 1 June and it was about this time that the raids by Gotha bombers took place over the south-east of England. He made several frustrating attempts to get to grips with this menace which was resulting in numerous fatal casualties among the civilian population. This invasion of the homeland particularly enraged the normally unruffled McCudden but despite numerous sorties, he was unable to deter them. In the last raid, on 7 July, he engaged the bombers on their return journey over Tilbury, but even though he used a whole drum of ammunition fired at 100 yards range, he failed to make the required impression.

> I remained above again and now thought of a different way to attack the Gotha. I put on a new drum and dived from the Hun's right rear to within 300 feet, when I suddenly swerved, and changing over to his left rear, closed to 50 yards and finished my drum before the enemy gunner could swing his gun from the side at which I had first dived. I zoomed away but the Hun still appeared to be O.K.
>
> Then I put on my third and last drum and made up my mind that I should have a good go at getting him. ... and had the satisfaction of seeing my tracer bullets strike all about his fuselage and wings, but beyond causing the Gotha to push his nose down a little, it had not the desired effect.[17]

In August McCudden returned to France as a flight commander in No. 56 Squadron flying the very successful SE5s, having applied to join this elite unit. As Bickers puts it, the day of the lone hunter, the fighter pilot dodging in and out of cloud, climbing as high as possible to position himself up-sun from the enemy, was not quite done. McCudden and Mannock were among its continuing practitioners. But the trend near the end of 1917 was towards offensive patrols in formation. 'Air fighting had entered the era of what was then called dogfighting, when twenty or more aircraft mixed it in a brawl that spread over a large area of sky and several thousand feet of altitude.'[18] McCudden's own account of this period conveys the intensity of the operations but is recorded with the factual calm of the professional.

> September 28th, I led my patrol over the lines at 11,000 feet over Boessinghe, and before crossing the lines I saw a patrol of Albatroses going south ... I signalled to my patrol, who understood what I wanted, and down went our noses, and although I thought I was going down fairly slowly, my comrades afterwards said they were recording 180 m.p.h. to keep up with me. I picked out the Albatros who was on the east of this formation and, opening fire at 200 yards, released my

triggers about 50 yards short of the Albatros, whose left wings at once fell off, and then the whole machine fell to pieces at about 9,000 feet. The enemy pilot also fell out and went down much quicker than his machine.

> I then flew onto the leader … My opponent and I continued to circle round from 8,000 feet down to 4,000 feet, when, as the German passed directly below me in the opposite direction, I did a steep Immelman turn to get on his tail, but in doing so I lost a good deal of height and now I found the German above me. I continued to circle, but at last the German got behind me and commenced to shoot …[19]

At first McCudden had experienced a frustrating lack of success but, persevering, the results then began to flow in. In the four months from September to the end of 1917 his tally was 28 kills compared with a single one for the same period the previous year. Many of these were spectacular, such as on 28 December when during a solo patrol he brought down three enemy planes between 11.30 am and 12.20 pm. Much of his initial frustration was due to technical problems with both aircraft and guns. McCudden soon established a reputation for meticulous attention to technical detail (for which his early experience as a mechanic was paying off); and for dogged persistence in stripping his weapons and examining them for possible faults and insisting on personally loading his ammunition belts and drums. 'For two whole days I tested my guns, and could not get them to my liking. All my comrades and "Grandpa", our dear old Recording Officer, simply chaffed me to death, and suggested that why my guns did not go when I got into the air was because I wore them out first on the ground.'[20]

McCudden was not all heartless efficiency. He, like so many other pilots, was imbued with the spirit of chivalrous admiration for the bravery and skill of his enemies and frequently joined in toasts to them after dinner in the Mess. In his book he records an incident where he landed beside a Rumpler that he had shot down inside British lines and remarks that 'Shooting Huns is very good fun while we have to do it, but at the same time it makes one think, as I say, when one views such an object as I was doing then.'[21] And, again, agreeing with his OC that 'it was a pity we could not down Huns without this happening' – alluding to the dead occupants – '…but I suppose I am getting too sentimental, and one cannot afford to be so when one has to do one's job of killing and going on killing.'[22]

In November 1917 No. 56 Squadron moved to Lavieville, some 15 miles north-east of Amiens, to take part in the forthcoming Battle of Cambrai. Poor weather limited the air activity initially but it soon picked up to an unprecedented intensity, December bringing McCudden 14 victories until the battle petered out. Both of his DSOs were earned in this period. His philosophy for fighting air battles becomes clear at this stage:

> My system was to always attack the Hun at his disadvantage if possible, and if I were attacked at my disadvantage I usually broke off the combat, for in my opinion the Hun in the air must be beaten at his own game, which is cunning. I think that the correct way to wage war is to down as many as possible of the enemy at the least risk, expense and casualties to one's own side.[23]

– but he adds that as far as fighting the Hun in the air is concerned, nothing succeeds like boldness. The DSO and bar were gazetted on 4 and 18 February respectively and the details appeared on 5 and 18 July. The following extract refers to the DSO itself.

> He attacked and brought down an enemy two-seater machine inside our lines, both the occupants being taken prisoner. In another operation he encountered an enemy two-seater machine at 2,000 feet. He continued the fight down to 100 feet, in very bad weather conditions and destroyed the enemy machine. He came down to within a few feet of the line on the enemy side of the lines and finally crossed the lines at a very low altitude. He has recently destroyed seven enemy machines, two of which fell within our lines, and has set a splendid example of pluck and determination to his squadron.[24]

It was also at this time that the whole question of public recognition came to a head. For some months the press had been demanding a change in the policy, contrary to German and French practice, under which successful British airmen remained anonymous. On the whole the public learned of their feats only when awards were gazetted – but this could be six months after the deed and heroes tended to be identified only after they were dead. The *Daily Mail*, which had been particularly active in this matter, succeeded in breaching the protocol with a photograph of McCudden and another pilot under the caption 'Our Wonderful Airmen – Names at Last'. He was greatly embarrassed by this and, rather too late, wrote to his family in strong terms, telling them not to communicate with the press on his private affairs.

Second Lieutenant Anthony McCudden, MC, James's younger brother, killed in action on 20 March 1918.

(IWM Q68599)

McCudden returned to Britain in March having brought his score up to 57 with 20 more victims in the new year, completing his time in No. 56 Squadron in a frenzy of activity despite symptoms of battle fatigue and some days of actual sickness. He was posted to No. 1 School of Aerial Fighting at Ayr. By the time he joined them in April he had learned of the loss of his younger brother, Anthony, shot down over enemy territory on 20 March. A week later his own VC was gazetted exposing him to a further bout of publicity, including a furious argument between the mayors of Chatham and Gillingham each claiming the hero as their own. McCudden himself arbitrated, declaring himself a Gillingham man and accepting his appointment as an Honorary Freeman of the Borough.

The ceremony granting this honour never came about as McCudden had to make a short return trip to France on an urgent aircraft delivery mission, the reasons for which have never been clear. There he visited his old squadron and undertook what were to become his last operational sorties. Back in Ayr he received his next posting – to take over No. 60 Squadron in France in the rank of major. He set out for Boffles from Hounslow on 9 July, putting down twice in France en route. The second stop was at Auxi-le-Château, simply to obtain directions to his destination. Taking off again he seemed to perform a stunt manoeuvre which went tragically wrong and he crashed to his death in the surrounding woods.

*Part of the letter
written by Captain
James McCudden, VC,
DSO, MC, MM, RAF,
on the occasion of being
offered the Freedom of
Gillingham.*

9/6/18.   No 1 School of Fighting & Gunnery.
                              Turnberry, Scotland

Dear Sir.

I have received your letter dated the 6th inst. and feel very honoured indeed that you have decided to present me with the freedom of the borough, and am sure that I shall ever be very proud of such a distinction.

With regard to the public [...]
[...] again [...] you.

I Remain.
          Yours Faithfully
                J. B. McCudden.
                      Capt. R.A.F.

It will remain a mystery how such a perfectionist could meet his end in such a way. Technical failure seems almost impossible as the aircraft was brand new and prepared to immaculate condition for its distinguished pilot. Human error seems an equally unlikely explanation. McCudden was no show-off but even had he been, there was no one at Auxi-le-Château to whom to show off. The visit was entirely unscheduled and he had not been recognised. Perhaps he was attempting to demonstrate to his own satisfaction flawless precision in a tricky manoeuvre. Perhaps it was just a courteous gesture of farewell and thanks for help given. The matter has been fully explored in his biography but with no definite conclusion.[25]

James McCudden was one of the RFC's highest scorers, with 57 victories but, whatever the statistics, many commentators feel that his early experience as mechanic and observer, his contribution as tactician and trainer and his influence at home as a result of his efforts against the Gothas, make him the outstanding all-round airman of the war.

For an independent personal assessment of the man we have Edgar Ludlow-Hewitt's contemporary view:

> Although McCudden was a quiet, unassuming, essentially modest person, he was nonetheless one of those people who are not easily forgotten. He was far from being the glamorous, fire-eating hero of fiction, and yet there was about him an elusive distinction which somehow arose out of his naturally self-assured and serene disposition ... High principled, tolerant and very generous in his judgments of others, he had a natural modesty which I am sure remained untouched by his subsequent fame and success.[26]

Edward Mannock

Edward ('Mick')
Mannock
(1887–1918)
(IWM Q60800)

The contrast in the upbringings of Hawker and McCudden are sharp enough: the comfortable, well-educated middle-class, property-owning Hawkers versus the modest, sergeants' mess-based, local school educated and relatively subservient McCuddens. But at least both families had values which gave their children a stable start in life with some sense of purpose. Edward Mannock, on the other hand, suffered a poverty-stricken childhood in which the strongest influence was his violent, drink-sodden father, an Irish corporal in the cavalry until, after discharge following the Boer War, he abandoned his family to scrape a living on their own. The boy, known universally in his eventual army service as 'Mick' from his Irish parentage, earned some cash in menial jobs until joining the National Telegraph Company at the age of 16, initially as a clerk but later as a labourer. He also acquired his first military experience in the Royal Army Medical Corps, Territorial Army, in which he rose to the rank of sergeant.

He seems to have been a highly emotional man holding and proclaiming deeply entrenched socialist views while at the same time being a rabid British nationalist. In February 1914 Mannock took up an opportunity to go to Turkey on a cable-laying contract but, along with all British expatriates, was imprisoned as soon as the Turks declared their allegiance to the German cause. Mannock made a complete nuisance of himself to his captors, leading demonstrations and organising a system whereby he was able to break out by night to buy provisions to ease the plight of his compatriot prisoners. He was caught at this and placed in solitary confinement.

Repatriated in January 1915 and in very poor physical shape, Mannock rejoined the RAMC but, not relishing the idea that in this role he might have to treat German battle casualties, he applied for a commission in the Royal Engineers. He achieved this ambition in June 1916 despite, as he saw it from a position of openly declared class hatred, having to work doubly hard to overcome the prejudice and attitudes of his better-educated competitors. While on leave he had met a friend who was a pilot in the RFC and now saw flying as the best way of satisfying the other main obsession in his life – to kill Germans.

He transferred to the RFC and, after his pilot training, Mannock joined No. 40 Squadron at Bruay, north-west of Arras on 6 April 1917 and made an extremely unpromising start. His bumptious and self-important manner, probably a mask for the social insecurity from which he suffered, went down badly among his fellow officers.

His first efforts on operations were no less awkward. His clumsy performance on his first few sorties led to suspicions of cowardice and he became snubbed in the Mess, adding insult to injury with his attempts to foist his views on his colleagues, guilty even of the ultimate Mess solecism of political discussion.

However, his was not a spirit to admit defeat. Despite some ridicule he took immense pains to improve his gunnery, spending much time diving at targets from different angles and at different speeds and, like McCudden, loading his ammunition drums himself. In May he recorded his first success by destroying a balloon. Observation balloons had become an important factor in the air war, principally for artillery spotting. The RFC took on the responsibility of manning them and the equipment used was the French Caquot kite balloon looking much like the Second World War barrage balloon. The German Drachen was similar. The observer crews led a perilous life being obvious targets for enemy aircraft and there were frequent unpleasant deaths. It was the vulnerability of these crews that led to the first use of parachutes. The balloons themselves were not as easy to destroy as they looked and special techniques and weaponry had to be evolved. Also pilots tended to despise balloon hunting as if it were an unsporting activity. Nevertheless it was a necessary and often dangerous task, the balloons being well protected by artillery, and doubtless Mannock gained confidence from this first blood.

Despite this, as well as a growing sense of commitment and a more relaxed attitude coaxed out by a wise squadron commander, Mannock was having no luck at all against enemy planes. However, in June things improved and by mid-July he had achieved his fourth kill even though he had been away for two weeks' leave.

After a spell in England instructing and testing FE2s with wireless, Mannock asked to return to the Front and was back in France as a flight commander in No. 74 Squadron on 1 April 1918. At that stage he had an MC and bar. By the end of September a DSO and two bars had been gazetted.

In the intensity of operations that led to this extraordinary tally, Mannock was beginning to display many of the symptoms of a manic-depressive. He subjected his pilots to the most thorough analysis of all their engagements. His manner towards them was earnest and exacting although constructive. He himself began to be obsessed with the manner of pilots' deaths, particularly by burning, the most feared fate, and did what he could to alleviate the anxieties of his own subordinates in this matter. He would be deeply upset by the death of a friend and recover overnight to a state of hearty joviality.

In June Mannock was promoted major and appointed to the command of No. 85 Squadron, taking over from Billy Bishop, perhaps the most distinguished pilot of the war, but a loner who had not developed the squadron as a unit. Mannock was in his element as a commander. He purged the squadron of pilots he felt he could not trust; he taught the unit to fight as a team; he devised tactics which inspired them with enthusiasm and brought success; and he made a speciality of encouraging inexperienced pilots by taking them out on 'let's catch a Hun' missions when often the tyro would add to his score a kill which could equally have been credited to Mannock.

However his own introspectiveness and fatalistic outlook took a turn for the worse when he learned of James McCudden's death. In response he indulged in an orgy of solo sorties for a week attacking everything he could find. His score rose to 73, passing Bishop's 72, but there it stayed (it was never exceeded in the RAF) as he was shot down and killed on 26 July. As with Hawker and McCudden, the news was hardly credible when it came through, but he had been caught by machine-gun fire from the ground on his way back from yet another successful mission. It was a year later before his VC was gazetted, the result, it is said, of pressure from those in the Royal Air Force who knew his qualities and achievements.

Mick Mannock has sometimes been described as the most decorated man of the First World War. Although he had one more DSO than James McCudden, McCudden had an MM and Croix de Guerre to add. However, such considerations are academic in the light of the overall attainments of these magnificent men.

All three sapper/RFC VCs lie in honour in France. Lanoe Hawker's body was never found but he is remembered on the Arras memorial. James McCudden was buried at the Wavans British Military Cemetery. Mystery still surrounds the location of Mick Mannock's remains. Despite a fairly accurate report of his burial place and several further enquiries by the Imperial War Graves Commission, the only clue was of the grave of 'an unknown British airman' in the neighbourhood of but some distance from the reported spot. An article in the *Sunday Telegraph* dated 7 November 1993 claims that evidence subsequently gathered indicates that a grave in Lavantie Cemetery inscribed 'An unknown British aviator' must indeed be Mannock's, but evidence for this is entirely circumstantial.

The Second World War (1939–1945)

In all, 633 VCs had been awarded in the First World War, 20 of them to men serving as sappers at the time. The introduction of the MC and the allocation of the DSO to actions of extreme gallantry, meant that the VC had become statistically much harder to earn than ever in its history. If the number of deaths in a war can be taken as the criterion, the Crimean War in which 18,000 died and for which 111 VCs were awarded was far more generously treated than the Boer War (22,000 deaths, 78 VCs). Even on the latter scale the First World War (736,000 deaths) would have merited something like 2500.

Whatever the worth of such crude statistical comparisons, there is little question that by the time of the Second World War, the VC had acquired an almost mystical status which put it beyond the realistic aspirations of most reasonable servicemen. In Queen Victoria's day it was quite normal to try openly to win a VC. The matter was freely discussed and, while it might not have been particularly good form to say so, actively seeking out a VC-earning situation was not unknown.

By 1939 the hope of a VC could only be an ambitious soldier's pipedream. Statistically the Second World War (350,000 British and Commonwealth deaths in battle) might have been expected to produce about 300, using the First World War scale. In fact only 182 were awarded, of which three were earned by sappers. Of these only one was for valour in a specifically sapper role. Its winner was Premindra Singh Bhagat of the Indian Engineers and there is surely no more appropriate symbol of the historic contribution of the Indian Army to the Royal Engineers' operations. The second was won at sea, awarded posthumously to Sergeant Thomas Durrant, in the famous commando attack on St Nazaire, the first (and possibly only) occasion on which a VC was earned by a soldier in a ship of the Royal Navy. The third was won, and again the award was posthumous, by Lieutenant Claud Raymond in Burma in an action away from the mainstream battles. He was fighting as an infantryman albeit in pursuit of a sapper cause. A fourth VC winner will appear in this story. Lieutenant-Colonel Charles Newman, the commander of the army element of the St Nazaire operation, became a sapper after the war when, by virtue of his distinguished career in the construction industry, he was enlisted into the Engineer and Railway Staff Corps (TAVR), a unique unit almost as elite – although for different reasons – as the commando which he had directed so famously during the war.

The three operations with which we are concerned are so dispersed in time and space that the only common thread is the pattern of the war itself: the rise and eventual defeat of fascism with its arch-priest Adolf Hitler and the simultaneous battle to deny Japan the far eastern empire it wished to create on the back of the perceived weakness of Britain's hold on its own.

In the autumn of 1940 when our story starts, Britain still had few successes to show for its lonely stand against Hitler. Germany was now master of continental Europe from the south of France to the Vistula and north to the Arctic Circle. France, bar a small Free French force, was out of the war. Italy had declared war on Britain in June, invading British Somaliland in August and Egypt in September. The Battle of Britain was in full swing with the looming threat of invasion from across the Channel. In the Atlantic, although there had been the success of the Battle of the River Plate at the end of 1940, losses in merchant ship-ping were reaching serious proportions (217 in the four months July to October 1940),[1] while the Royal Navy had to concentrate on the prevention of invasion. However, by December some successes were beginning to show in the Western

Map 25

The invasion of Italian-held East Africa, 1940–1.

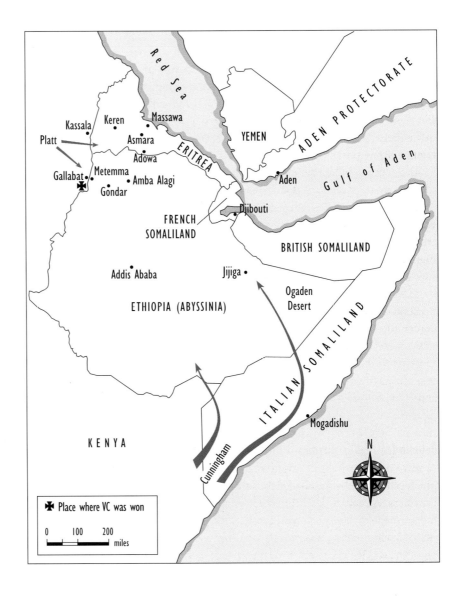

Desert as the Italians were pushed back into Libya and the Commander-in-Chief General Sir Archibald Wavell had begun to formulate the plan for evicting them from East Africa.

The Italian empire in Ethiopia and Somaliland had had its origins in the 'scramble for Africa' of the late 19th century but a severe setback to expansion had occurred in 1896 when an Italian army invading Abyssinia had been annihilated at Adowa. As Winston Churchill put it, 'this tragic episode bit deep into Italian memories'[2] and when Mussolini came to power he saw the acquisition of Abyssinia both as an appropriate aggrandisement for his country and necessary revenge for national humiliation at Adowa. The seizure of the territory and its pacification had entailed brutal and inhumane acts, including the use of poison gas, which had earned the condemnation of the non-fascist world but had brought no reprisals. This, and the perceived weakness of Britain and its empire, encouraged Mussolini, after allying his country with Germany, to swallow up British Somaliland and threaten the Sudan and British East Africa. With these territories and Egypt, Italy would certainly have gained the imperial status which it sought.

Allied action to thwart these ambitions by forcibly removing the Italians from Abyssinia was worked out in conjunction with the South Africans who, under their leader Jan Smuts, whom we last met as a guerrilla leader fighting the British in the Boer War, had a vested interest in keeping the area free of the fascist menace. An important element was to be a popular uprising generated by a small irregular force of a Sudanese battalion under Brigadier D.A. Sandford. Eventually there were to be two main thrusts. One, under Lieutenant-General William Platt would be from Sudan into Eritrea with 4th and 5th Indian Divisions. The other, under Lieutenant-General Alan Cunningham, setting off some weeks later with two African divisions and a South African brigade, would advance into Italian Somaliland from Kenya, occupy Mogadishu and then turn north to free Addis Ababa and allow the reinstatement of the Emperor Haile Selassie.

However, at the end of 1940 these troops were not in place and there was no question of offensive action. On 4 July, the Italians had struck across the Sudanese border and occupied Kassala in the north and Gallabat 120 miles to the southwest. With British forces then fully engaged in the Western Desert the only response to these incursions was observation by the Sudan Defence Force while reinforcements were brought in from India. 5th Indian Division was despatched and arrived in October. With them was Second Lieutenant Premindra Singh Bhagat.

Premindra Singh Bhagat

Premindra Singh Bhagat, hereinafter referred to as 'Prem', was the product of a privileged Indian background. His father was an executive engineer in the United Provinces. Although they were Sikhs from the Punjab, Prem and his two older brothers were launched into a school career at the Royal Indian Military College (RIMC) whose ethos and structure had its origins in the British public school system. The RIMC was essentially a feeder for the Indian Military Academy (IMA)

Premindra Singh
Bhagat
(1918–1975)

to which all three brothers duly went. Until the IMA was opened in 1932, the only route for an Indian to a King's Commission in the Indian Army was through the Royal Military College at Sandhurst which did not offer the appropriate training for officers destined for the sappers or gunners.

At school Prem was above average academically and showed signs of leadership but with a restless temperament. He was following in the footsteps of two elder brothers, the oldest of whom, N.S. Bhagat (Tony), had been outstanding in almost every field. It was much the same story at the IMA from which Prem followed Tony into the Royal Bombay Sappers and Miners, forerunner of the present Bombay Engineer Group, gaining his commission two months before the outbreak of war. His base for the next 14 months was Poona, headquarters of the Bombay Sappers and destined to become Prem's spiritual home: he would spend some 15 years of his life there and it would become his final resting place. He joined 21 Field Company and, in September 1940, embarked for East Africa. He was the only Indian officer in the company. It has often been suggested that his outstanding performance in the months of action that followed had much to do with the desire of a politically aware Indian officer to prove himself and his race in the eyes both of his British superiors and of the Indian soldiers under his command.

5th Indian Division landed in Port Sudan in late October two brigades strong (9th and 10th), a third (7th) being sent on to reinforce the meagre British force in Egypt, which the Italians had now invaded. It was not until December that, following the first stage of Major-General Richard O'Connor's brilliant desert campaign, Wavell was able to spare any troops to make offensive action into Abyssinia a feasible proposition. Meanwhile General Platt turned his attention to the possibility of recapturing Gallabat using Brigadier Bill Slim's 10th Brigade with 21 Field Company (OC, Major G.E.H. Philbrick) under command. Gallabat lay on the southernmost of the two possible routes into the country from the Sudan. Platt's main thrust was eventually to follow the northern route, from Kassala towards Asmara and so to the Red Sea port of Massawa, with diversionary operations around Gallabat, but at this stage the northern route was far too strongly held.

Prem's first test came on 5 November when 3/18 Royal Garhwal Rifles under Lieutenant-Colonel S.E. Tayler advanced on Gallabat. The incident is recorded in the *History of the Royal Bombay Sappers and Miners 1939-47*.[3]

> Lieutenant Patterson, the section commander, was mortally wounded when his carrier hit a mine. Second Lieutenant Bhagat, his section officer, took over command of the section. The enemy was well dug in and the final assault was held up by intense defensive fire and some troops started to retreat, but one Garhwal company and the Sapper section hung on. Lieutenant Colonel Tayler, standing firm where he could be seen by his men, although vulnerable to enemy fire, stopped the rot. He was joined by Second Lieutenant Bhagat who saw that Tayler's arm had been wounded by shrapnel and reached out to help him, but the Colonel ordered him to stay put and not let the men know that he (Tayler) had

been wounded. He kept standing until order was restored and only then did he seek first aid assistance. Bhagat, in his own words, was '… stunned with such cool bravery and total dedication.' It undoubtedly had an influence on Bhagat's subsequent actions.

Although the fort was captured, further advance across the gorge known as the Boundary Khor to the next occupied position on the route, the village of Metemma, proved impossible; indeed, such was the intensity of the counterattacks and sustained bombing that casualties began to mount and, with no possibility of digging in in the rocky ground, the Gallabat ridge itself became untenable. A withdrawal to the fort's outpost line took place on the evening of 7 November after the sappers had destroyed as many of the usable buildings and stores as they could.

> Next day the enemy, closely following up, had to be delayed at a culvert bottleneck. Two derelict tanks packed with explosive were fired but only one detonated leaving the culvert partly intact. Under small arms fire and air strafing Second Lieutenant Bhagat broke cover to reignite the failed charge and completed the destruction of the culvert. Major Philbrick witnessed this incident and recommended him for an MC, but it seems that it was subsequently revised to a mention in despatches which was notified after Second Lieutenant Bhagat's immediate VC award two months later.[4]

10th Brigade was now relieved by 9th Brigade (Brigadier A.G.O.M. Mayne) but 21 Field Company remained in the area. As well as this dramatic work in support of their brigades in the field, the sappers had their normal tasks of route maintenance and development to cope with and the ever-present problem of water supply. The latter depended on their either finding existing wells or digging new ones after first locating sources by dowsing. But on the operational side, Prem again came to notice in December when he accompanied a raid by the 3rd Frontier Force Regiment on an enemy airfield near Metemma. 'Much damage was done and [he] … distinguished himself in carrying out the demolitions regardless of personal danger.'[5]

In mid-January General Platt, now reinforced by 4th Indian Division and a third infantry brigade in 5th Division, launched his invasion of Eritrea. This began the series of intense and mostly bitterly fought operations that took Platt's force through the massive escarpment close to the town of Keren and eventually to Massawa. Although this was Platt's main axis of advance he had ordered 9th Brigade to maintain the pressure on the enemy at Gallabat with the intention of deceiving them into thinking that this might be the main point of attack. Throughout December and early January the Italians hung on stubbornly but on 30 January, conforming to the withdrawal of their force on the Massawa route, they vacated Gallabat and its twin, Metemma. 3/12 Frontier Rifles, with a detachment of 21 Field Company under Prem, were despatched in pursuit. The route was heavily mined and it was now that Prem was to rise to the occasion with a display of such sustained gallantry that he was to earn the first VC of the war to be won by an Indian Commissioned Officer. As the citation records, for four days he never let up while clearing the way through 15 minefields over a distance of 55 miles.

> On two occasions when his carrier was blown up with casualties to others, and on a third occasion when ambushed and under close enemy fire he himself carried straight on with his task. He refused relief when worn out with strain and fatigue and with one eardrum punctured by an explosion, on the grounds that he was now better qualified to continue his task to the end.
>
> His coolness, persistence over a period of 96 hours, and gallantry, not only in battle, but throughout the long period when the safety of the Column and the speed at which it could advance were dependent on his personal efforts, were of the highest order.

Eventually the column commander ordered Prem back for medical treatment and, after completing a successful pursuit raid, the column returned to Gallabat. Sappers Balakrishna and Ananda Padalkar, who were with Prem, were awarded the IDSM and a Jangi Inam (a traditional reward in kind for distinguished service, normally a plot of land), respectively. In February, 21 Field Company moved with 9th Brigade and Prem, now restored to fitness albeit with permanent damage to his ears, arrived back in March in time to take part in the battle for Keren. It took 53 days and many casualties, including the death in action of Lieutenant-Colonel Tayler whom Prem had admired so much, before Keren fell on 27 March. Massawa was then entered on 8 April.

Although Platt's objectives in Eritrea had been effectively accomplished by early April, there was still some way to go before the Italians were ejected from East Africa. While Platt was struggling in the Keren gorge, Lieutenant-General Alan Cunningham was advancing from Kenya into Italian Somaliland. Mogadishu fell on 25 February and by mid-March Nigerian troops had crossed the Ogaden desert and entered Jijiga. Cunningham's force then closed in on Addis Ababa from the east and south as the Italians evacuated the city in order to concentrate against Platt's force in northern Abyssinia. There they held out in the mountain stronghold of Amba Alagi until Cunningham's force reached them from the south and further resistance became impracticable. The war in East Africa was still not over, however. It was to take another eight months and cost more casualties than had been incurred to date finally to evict the Italians from East Africa.[6]

As to Premindra Singh Bhagat, his great achievement was not gazetted until June 1941. In the same month he was presented with the ribbon of his VC by General Wavell at a victory parade in Asmara. His company embarked at Massawa to continue their war in the Mediterranean area, not returning to India until well after the end of the war. Prem himself returned to India

> to a hero's welcome. He was lionised and feted by everybody. The laurels that he had won stood for far more than recognition of an act of rare courage. To his family, friends, and indeed, to the people of India it meant that a 'native' son of the soil was second to none. He was invited to speak to the nation over All India Radio and the talk was billed 'Our Hero'. To the Government in power, an alien

government, he was useful as a means of living propaganda in the recruitment drive for more troops for the war effort in the new critical theatre of war – South East Asia.[7]

Two months after Prem had been presented with his VC, he married Mohini Bhandari, daughter of a colonel in the Indian Medical Service. He remained in India almost to the end of the war, where he raised a new company, 484 Field Company, at Dighi near Kirkee. In his time with 484 Field Company he developed the military personality that characterised his highly successful career in the post-Independence Indian Army. Two British officers serving under his command at the time testified to his strong personality ('The adjective "charismatic" could have been invented to describe his leadership').[8] Prem was selected to attend the last wartime Staff College course at Camberley. He was nearly two years in England and while still there wrote the first of his books, *My Land Divided*, reflecting his hope for a reconciliation between the religious groupings: 'What greatness and power there is in store for us, the four hundred million people of India, if only we unite, yet we keep apart.'[9]

Prem returned to India in time for Independence and its terrible immediate aftermath. He was appointed Commander Royal Indian Engineers in 4th Infantry Division, East Punjab Area where they were in the thick of controlling the vast movements of population – later estimated at some 8.5 million – across the new border. The Division was soon involved in the operations in Jammu and Kashmir to evict incursions of Pakistanis and stabilise the border area. In July 1948 Prem had a brief eight-month tour as GSO1 at the headquarters of the Armed Forces Academy at Dehra Dun and was then posted as commandant of what was eventually to be, after India became a republic in November 1949, the Bombay Engineer Group and Centre, dropping its former Royal title. It was a seminal time both for the Group and for Prem during which he set the standards of training and established permanent traditions for the Bombay Sappers. He himself retained immense pride in his Bombay Sapper origins and a fierce loyalty for the Corps.

However, his future lay in the wider Army and in March 1957, he was appointed to command 165 Infantry Brigade at Ramgarh. The steps in the rest of his career can be summarised: 1959, Director of Military Intelligence (DMI); 1961, National Defence College Course; 1962, Commandant Indian Military Academy; 1963, Chief of Staff to Army Commander Eastern Command; 1964, GOC 9th Mountain Division; 1966, Commander XI Corps, Western Command; 1970, Army Commander, Central Command; 1972, Army Commander Northern Command; 1974, retirement from the Army, appointed Chairman Damodar Valley Corporation.

During his time in Central Command in the 1970s, Prem was presented with a major sapper challenge when the River Gumti flooded near Lucknow. His personal involvement in this affair and the energy with which he marshalled all available resources substantially contributed to the prevention of total disaster.

For this work he was awarded the Param Vashist Seva Medal, the highest military decoration for distinguished service outside the battlefield. When Prem left Central Command to take over the newly created Northern Command, many people thought that would be only a short tour, and that he would be appointed to the ultimate prize, Army Chief.

It was not to be. For whatever reason, following an inevitably political shuffling of the top appointments, he was offered nothing after Northern Command. Instead, he was appointed to head the Damodar Valley Corporation. The Corporation had been set up by Nehru as a showpiece development project in Bihar and West Bengal and had become the victim of paralysing bureaucracy and mismanagement. Prem, still with a few months to run as a serving general and with the moral authority that carried, swept in with all ceremony in July 1974. Within months he had, through the application of the principles of personal example, delegation of responsibility and trust of subordinates, turned the whole outlook of the organisation round and positive results were being obtained. Tragically, after barely a year in the job he contracted some virulent fever and died in Calcutta military hospital on 23 May 1975 at the age of 56. The funeral was held in Calcutta and among the rituals that attended his death was, extraordinarily, a Requiem Mass held by Mother Teresa's Missionaries of Charity. The ashes were taken to Poona and ceremonially consigned to the River Moola.

St Nazaire

Returning now to 1941, the defeat of the Italians in East Africa, together with the other reverses that were overcoming Mussolini in the Western Desert, in his ill-starred invasion of Greece and the loss of many of his fleet at Taranto and Matapan, were certainly something to cheer the success-starved British public. But in the Mediterranean the tables were soon turned on the British by the arrival of Rommel and the Afrika Korps while so many of their resources were tied up in the doomed expedition to hold the Germans in Greece. Also in June the Germans had launched their fateful attack on Russia in Operation Barbarossa. Churchill rejoiced: 'That Germany should at this stage, and before clearing the Balkan scene, open another major war with Russia seemed to me to be too good to be true.'[10] Nevertheless the awesome accomplishment of the German blitzkrieg across the vast spaces of the Soviet Union was an alarming demonstration of German power.

The main strategic menace to Britain in 1941 was, however, closer to home, in the Atlantic, where Hitler's attempted blockade was still taking a severe toll on the British convoys. The U-boats, operating from French ports, remained elusive and had refined their tactics. The Luftwaffe had joined this fight with some success. In February five ships in a single convoy had been sunk by Focke-Wolf 200 long-range bombers. Possibly more threatening than anything were the surface ships. The battlecruisers *Scharnhorst* and *Gneisenau* had sunk 22 merchantmen in the north Atlantic earlier in the year. On 18 May the battleship *Bismarck* sailed from the Baltic with the heavy cruiser *Prinz Eugen* in support. The British battleships

Hood and *Prince of Wales* intercepted but in an action to the east of Iceland HMS *Hood* was sunk and 1400 of her crew died. As is well known, this depressing blow was avenged on 27 May with the sinking of *Bismarck* and the loss of over 2000 German lives. *Bismarck* had been damaged in her brush with *Hood* and *Prince of Wales* and when she was finally caught had been making for the only dock on the German-occupied Atlantic coast big enough to take her, the great Forme Ecluse at St Nazaire, more commonly know as the Normandie Dock after the ship for which she was built, the French liner *Normandie*, the largest ship in the world. Only one other German battleship carried the same single threat as *Bismarck* – and the same limitation that she would depend on the Normandie Dock as a base for any operations in the Atlantic – *Bismarck*'s sister ship *Tirpitz*, and by early 1942 she would be ready to move out of the Norwegian waters in which she was undergoing her sea trials.

Thus it was that when Combined Operations Headquarters were looking for a suitable target for a major offensive operation that would strike hard at the Germans and raise morale at home, their attention was drawn to St Nazaire.

Combined Operations was the inter-service organisation set up in June 1940 to co-ordinate operations involving all three services. Much of its work so far had been in launching reconnaissance and raids along the enemy coastline – for example near Boulogne (June 1940), Guernsey (July 1940), southern Italy (February 1941), the Lofoten Islands (March 1941) and Spitzbergen (August 1941) – using the Army's commandos, the units of volunteers specially equipped and trained for this role. They had already established a reputation for physical and mental toughness, preparedness to take risks and undergo exceptional privations, unorthodoxy and *esprit de corps*. They were elite units – that had not only to live up to expectations, but also to bear the criticism tinged with envy of the more conventional bulk of the Army who often felt the diversion of resources, and the glamour that accrued to elite units, was not justified by their results.

By October 1941 Churchill saw Combined Operations as the focus for preparations for the eventual invasion of the continent and appointed the then Captain Lord Louis Mountbatten as its chief. Under him the plan for the attack on St Nazaire grew with astonishing speed. The central prize was to be the destruction of the Normandie Dock, to be achieved by ramming the vast steel gate (or caisson) with an obsolescent destroyer, the *Campbeltown*, loaded in her bows with a three-ton charge designed to explode some hours after the raiding party were clear. The inner gate of the dock would be attacked by a torpedo if the *Campbeltown* succeeded in breaching the outer gate. If not, it would become one of the targets of the commando raiding party who would also attack the complex subterranean pumping system on which the operation of the dock depended, as well as some 14 other targets.

St Nazaire lies six miles into the estuary of the River Loire and it was guarded by the heaviest defences of any of the German bases with the possible exception of Brest. Surprise was essential. It was therefore decided that the approach would avoid the main channel, and be made by shallow-draft vessels at a time when the tide was high and there was little moon. This fixed the date for the end of March 1942. Part of the commando force would be carried in *Campbeltown* herself, the rest in 18 small craft of which 16 were wooden motor launches armed only with twin Lewis guns for air defence and three-pounder Hotchkisses, relics of the Boer War; four were also armed with torpedoes. A motor gun boat and motor torpedo boat made up the total. The overall complement to embark was to be 611 including the navy crews (345), the commando force (257), a medical team, three liaison officers and two press representatives.[11]

The commando force was to be in three groups. The main party in *Campbeltown* would land as soon as she had successfully come to rest against the dock gate. They would be responsible for all the demolitions connected with the dock. A second party would go ashore at the old harbour entrance which lay to port of the dock gate and would have a number of demolition and protection tasks. The third party, with similar targets for attack, was to land at the Old Mole which the other two parties would have passed, leaving it to port, as they made their approach to their objectives. Once the mission had been accomplished, the whole force was to withdraw downriver in the small craft. The details of this part of the plan were inevitably less explicit and it was clear to all that the chances of many returning were very low. For the outward and return journeys the force would be escorted by the destroyers *Atherstone* and *Tynedale*. A diversionary bombing raid would be made on the new town of St Nazaire. The operation was timed to put *Campbeltown* against the dock gate at 1.30 am on 28 March 1942.

In command of the naval force was Commander Robert Ryder. The captain of HMS *Campbeltown* was Lieutenant-Commander S.H. Beattie. The commando force was in the charge of Lieutenant-Colonel Charles Newman.

Charles Augustus Newman

Charles Newman was 38 years old, married with a young family, when he was appointed to command the St Nazaire operation. A civil engineering contractor by profession, he had been a territorial officer in the Essex Regiment for 16 years. In Lucas Phillips's view: 'Few commanding officers can have enjoyed so much as Newman, not only the regard, but also the warm affection of all who served under him.'[12]

Newman was commanding No. 2 Commando which had evolved from 3 Independent Company (the latter had taken part in the Norway campaign in 1940) and 1 Special Service Battalion of which he was second-in-command until it was split up into smaller units. He had put his men through the rigorous training which is now the hallmark of special forces units: long arduous marches, gruelling night exercises and familiarity with the sea by swimming in full kit in icy waters and going to sea in any form of naval craft on which he could scrounge lifts, to say nothing of professional skills with weapons and radio. Newman struck up a close working relationship with Ryder as soon as they met. Together they worked out the detail of the plan for Operation 'Charioteer' and foregathered in Falmouth in mid-March for the final preparations.

This brief account of the operation, told fully and most vividly in C.E. Lucas Phillips's *The Greatest Raid of All*, would be incomplete without a mention of the key sappers who took part. Leaving Sergeant Tom Durrant's astonishing feat until later in the story, we must note the roles of Captains R.K. Montgomery and W.H. Pritchard, MC. The two had worked together on the problem of dockyard demolitions long before Charioteer was planned. Bill Pritchard was the son of the Dock Master of Cardiff and had won the MC carrying out demolitions in the Dunkirk withdrawal. He and Montgomery realised from first hand the ineffectiveness of aerial bombardment on docks and, at the instigation of the Transportation branch of the War Office, were instructed to study the matter. From this developed what Lucas Phillips calls Pritchard's 'consuming purpose [for the] destruction of dockyards.' By an extraordinary fluke, the plans they were given as an example to work on were those of St Nazaire, a port of which, by another fluke, Montgomery had some knowledge. Both officers were extracted from other employment to go on Charioteer.

Lieutenant-Colonel Charles Newman (third from left) seen here with Lord Gort (in mackintosh on left).
(IWM H8195)

The technical details of the demolitions are fascinating and covered in essence in Lucas Phillips's book though out of place in this narrative. Suffice it to mention the work of the naval demolition expert, Lieutenant Nigel Tibbits, who devised the means by which the charge within *Campbeltown* was to be fired: 'To him and to Pritchard the splendour of the Charioteer's achievement is largely due.'

The expedition left Falmouth at 2.00 pm on 26 March in good weather with a clear outlook, and it must have been strange for the crews to be forced to enjoy such a peaceful cruise with the prospect ahead of them of extreme violence from which it was clear many would never return. All was well, however, until 7.00 am on 27 March when a U-boat was sighted at some distance and engaged but not sunk by HMS *Tynedale*. It turned out later that although the U-boat had reported the flotilla, its mission was misinterpreted as a minelaying operation as a result of which a group of five destroyers located in St Nazaire put to sea using the main navigation channel; hence the Charioteers slipping in over the mudflats that night were not spotted. As we shall see, this event led directly to the incident in which Sergeant Tom Durrant was to win his VC.

The little armada continued on its course amid growing tension. There were two anxious moments when *Campbeltown* grounded but managed to force her way through the mud. Otherwise they were not spotted until 1.15 am, 15 minutes short of their goal and even then, thanks to a clever piece of deception, were not fired upon seriously for a further 13 precious minutes. Then, retaliating with everything she had, *Campbeltown* began to take casualties but Beattie, with dead and dying around him in the wheelhouse, concentrated on the critical last few minutes of his course and struck home on the dock gate at 1.34 am, four minutes late.

The commando parties leaped ashore and began to tackle their various targets. Those who had been based on *Campbeltown* met with brilliant success, despite severe casualties as the German defence force went into action. The two most important targets, the subterranean pumping equipment and the inner dock gate, were dealt with. Both huts containing the winding mechanism for the dock gates were likewise destroyed and their gear badly damaged. This group was under the general direction of Bob Montgomery and within about half an hour they were reporting in, albeit sadly depleted in numbers, to take part in the withdrawal plan. The long training and sheer courage and determination of the commandos had borne fruit but, for success, these qualities alone are not enough. In Lucas Phillips's words: 'The achievement was not only the visible record of the daring of the men who performed it; it was also a triumph for the man, now at this moment about to die on the doorstep of fulfilment, who had planned it. It was Pritchard whose imagination, invention and fanatical persistence had built the way to this technical achievement, it was his midnight assiduity that had calculated every charge and written out every item of each man's task and load to the last fusee and it was his meticulous training that had taught each man precisely what to do. In the honours and memorials of the Charioteers his name, denied by death the award of any decoration, stands among the highest in the bright light of its devotion and sacrifice.'[13]

Charles Newman himself had gone ashore in the old harbour entrance a few minutes after his men from *Campbeltown* had rushed off to their demolition targets. According to his obituary in the *Royal Engineers Journal* 'during the ensuing fighting [he] personally entered several houses and shot up the occupants and supervised the operations in the town regardless of his own safety. He directed fire to put out of action enemy gun positions and to compel an armed trawler in the harbour to withdraw. Under Newman's brilliant leadership the troops held superior enemy forces at bay while the demolition parties got to work.'[14] Positioned centrally to be able to exercise control over the other landings from the old harbour entrance and the Old Mole, he was unaware how these had fared when Bob Montgomery reported success at the dock. Very shortly, however, the awful truth became clear. Both these landings had been met with a maelstrom of fire. Few of the launches had been able to land and the majority had been so badly hit that they were now full of casualties and blazing fiercely offshore. There was no longer any question of a withdrawal for those who had succeeded in landing, and Newman gave orders for a breakout battle which eventually boiled down to small parties trying to evade capture and make it overland to Gibraltar, a mere 900 miles to the south-west. The extraordinary thing was that five of them actually succeeded. The rest were either killed or captured within 24 hours. However, there were two more dramatic events still to unfold.

Most of the land party were in German hands by 10.00 am and they were deeply concerned not to have heard the explosion from *Campbeltown*'s carefully prepared charge which had been timed for between 7.00 and 9.00 am. Some, including Beattie, were in process of being interrogated by Germans who were pouring scorn on the feeble effect of *Campbeltown*'s ramming of the dock gate when at 10.35 am a mighty roar shook the whole area. The ship and surrounding dock area were crowded with German navy personnel and numerous sightseers, including many women. Many hundreds died, blown to smithereens.

The Forme Ecluse at St Nazaire ten months after the commando raid in March 1941. The remains of HMS Campbeltown, *her bows blown off, lie half-way down the dock. The outer end of the dock has been sealed with sand to prevent flooding.*

(IWM C3317a)

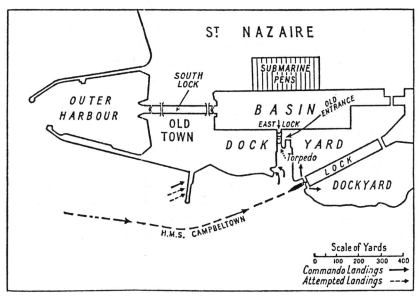

The layout of St Nazaire.

Of the 18 small craft that had accompanied *Campbeltown*, ten were sufficiently seaworthy to attempt the return journey, the first leg of which was to rendezvous with *Tynedale* and *Atherstone* outside the estuary. Two more were to be caught in the murderous fire from shore batteries and sunk with many casualties. A third, ML 306, among whose complement was Sergeant Tom Durrant Royal Engineers, met an extraordinary fate.

*Tom Durrant
(1918–1942)*

Thomas Frank Durrant

Sergeant Tom Durrant came from Green Street Green in Kent. He had been a butcher's boy and a builder's labourer before enlisting in the Royal Engineers on 1 February 1937, joining Recruit Party 219. In 1939 he was a member of No. 7 War Party, 2nd Training Battalion RE at Shorncliffe and a year later was posted to 555 (Welsh) Field Company, 53rd (Welsh) Divisional Engineers. He joined the company at Lurgan in Northern Ireland travelling there as one of two acting lance-corporals in charge of a draft of a hundred or so recruits. His NCO qualities and professional attitude made an immediate impression and earned him his substantive promotion. Soon afterwards there was a call for volunteers from the divisional units for service with the special service independent companies. Lance-Corporal Tom Durrant was accepted and went to Norway with No. 2 Independent Company (commander Major Hugh Stockwell), in the sapper section which was under Second Lieutenant Logan Scott-Bowden. In the operations which took place to the south of Bodo to hold up the German advance to the relief of their beleaguered garrison in Narvik, the sapper sergeant became a casualty. His place was taken by Lance-Corporal Durrant whose steadiness and courage had justified his rapid promotion in the field.

After their evacuation from Norway in April 1940, No. 2 Independent Company went initially to Lochailort in Scotland for intensive commando training and was then sent back to Northern Ireland. About this time Tom accompanied his brother Jack to the investiture at Buckingham Palace where Jack was to be presented with the Military Medal he had won for bravery, by chance close to St Nazaire,

> when the Cunard liner *Lancastria*, in which nearly all the crew and more than three thousand soldiers had met a ghastly death from burning oil [several thousand more were drowned], had been sunk by bombs while evacuating our troops from the surrender of France. ... and there is ... a relish of prophecy in the words of Tom when he accompanied Jack to Buckingham Palace to see him decorated by the King. When his brother had told him the tragic story, Tom said nothing for a moment and then burst out:
>
> 'Jack, tell them when we go back to St Nazaire we are going to knock seven hells out of them.' That was a year and a half before the Raid.[15]

At this stage the special service independent companies were disbanded to form the special service battalions which then developed into Nos 1 and 2 Commandos, based at Dartmouth. Tom's unit was No. 1 Commando but as a sergeant in the Demolition Section he was attached to No. 2 Commando who were to be strengthened for the raid. During the preparations for Charioteer, he was placed in the group under the command of Lieutenant Ronald Swayne who described him as 'without doubt the most loyal and efficient NCO I ever encountered' and 'a formidable character [who] was treated carefully by all ranks, yet his charm and good-humour were evident to everyone in his infectious smile.' Lucas Phillips adds: 'His whole inner self burned with the dedicated zeal of a crusader and he would burst out violently against any man who faltered in zeal and against anyone who criticized those to whom he owed loyalty. He had a granite-like determination, was himself a very fine technician and was steeped in that high code of soldierly integrity which is the hallmark of his Corps. But he had also a strong strain of independence and self-reliance and when his opinion was asked by an officer answered like an equal.'[16] The day before their departure Tom Durrant wrote to his mother: 'My Dear Mum, I have enclosed £20.10.0 as I shan't be needing it where I am going. I hope everything is O.K. at home. I can't tell you where I am but if anything happens you will be notified. Give my love to Reg, Ivy, Ruth, David and take care of yourself. Lots of love, Ever your Loving Son Tom.'[17]

HM ML 306 was commanded by Lieutenant Ian Henderson, an RNVR officer, and he had found it impossible to bring the ship alongside either at the Old Mole, their originally planned landing point, or at the old harbour entrance so heavy was the enemy fire at the time they arrived. The vessel having been hit many times and suffered several casualties, Henderson reluctantly made the decision to withdraw to the rendezvous. The frustration of the team of commandos was intense and morale very low as they were carried away from the scene for which they had prepared so hard; but there was no alternative.

They set course and headed out to sea at 18 knots. At about 5.30 am they were horrified to sight the five enemy light destroyers* that had set out from St Nazaire, as a consequence of the U-boat sighting of the force the previous day, to search for any mines that they believed may have been laid. This powerful small flotilla was heading back having been recalled because of the raid. As the enemy ships drew closer, Henderson decided that the only course was to hope they would remain unnoticed but that, if not, they would fight it out although the odds of such a puny wooden craft surviving against a steel 800-ton destroyer were negligible. They nearly got away with it as two of the enemy ships slipped by but a third, *Jaguar*, swung round and its searchlight suddenly lit them up in all their vulnerability.

In the ensuing battle ML 306 fired defiantly with everything she had but was for her part raked severely with heavy machine-gun fire and casualties began to mount. Durrant was initially manning one of four Bren guns but when Able Seaman Alder on the twin Lewis guns was too badly wounded to carry on,

ML 217, similar to ML 306 in which Tom Durrant fought his last battle.
(IWM HU1287A)

Durrant, already badly wounded himself, took over from Alder on the high exposed anti-aircraft mounting. Meanwhile *Jaguar* manoeuvred round the motor launch, anxious to take her as a prize rather than resort to her own heavy 4.1-inch armament, the Germans spraying their prey with small arms and eventually ramming her beam-to-beam with sufficient shock for one man to be lost overboard. Henderson, who had avoided a direct ramming by turning hard to port, continued his manoeuvre but was mortally wounded by a shot believed to have come from the enemy 4.1-inch gun which wrecked the bridge. Ronald Swayne

---

*In his book *The Attack on St. Nazaire*, Ryder describes these vessels as torpedo boats of the Möwe class, similar to the British 'Hunt' class destroyers of that time.

was now the only unwounded officer and came up on deck at the moment ML 306 was hailed from *Jaguar*, now some 30 yards away, to surrender and not to shoot. Durrant immediately replied with a burst from his Lewis guns, supported by the Bren guns. *Jaguar* now came alongside. Another call to surrender received the same response from Durrant, this time aimed at the bridge and just missing the captain. *Jaguar* pulled away to resume a better firing position. Durrant was hit again; desperately wounded he collapsed on deck.

With only eight men unwounded out of the original 28, Swayne decided the time had come to surrender. The German crew under Kapitänleutnant Paul treated the Charioteers with respect and honour. He called Swayne into his cabin, gave him a drink and congratulated him on their fight. The wounded were cared for, though Durrant and Henderson died shortly after they and the gallant survivors had been lifted from the bloodstained wreckage of HM ML 306. 'About a week later a German officer called on Newman in the prison camp at Rennes and said that he wished to bring to his notice the gallant conduct of a sergeant in a captured motor boat, "as you may wish to recommend him for a high award".'[18] In fact, neither Newman's nor Durrant's VCs were gazetted until after the war.

Three of the motor launches made it to the rendezvous together with the gunboat Ryder was using as his headquarters, the latter the last to leave the scene and having had a desperate fight to extricate itself. (Able Seaman Savage, its gunner, was later awarded a posthumous VC for an incredibly brave and selfless performance, not only for his gallantry 'but also for the valour shown by many others' of coastal forces.) In the interests of making sufficient speed to avoid the retribution that was undoubtedly on its way, the three small boats were scuttled; but three more which had missed the rendezvous made it home, even succeeding in shooting down a Heinkel 111 on the way.

Of the 630 navy and army men who took part, 144 lost their lives, 215 became prisoners-of-war and 215 returned to England, including five who succeeded in breaking out of St Nazaire and making it, after many adventures, through Spain to Gibraltar.[19] Though costly, it was a significant step forward on Combined Operations' road to the eventual return to continental Europe. 'German propaganda reactions alone were significant evidence that the impact of the raid made deep inroads upon enemy morale.'[20] But its success was far more than just morale-building; it achieved a strategic triumph as well. The Normandie Dock was out of action for the rest of the war and *Tirpitz* was never able to leave Norwegian waters.

Ryder and Beattie were both also awarded VCs, the latter 'in recognition not only of his own valour but also that of the unnamed officers and men of a very gallant ship's company'. Ryder and Newman led the march past at the memorial ceremony in St Nazaire on 2 August 1947 at which the French Prime Minister, M. Ramadier, remarked: 'In all the towns and villages of France your coming brought us a renewal of confidence and hope.'[21]

After the war Charles Newman returned to his old company W. & C. French Ltd, civil engineering and public works contractors, which he had originally joined in 1922. It was in that capacity that he became a member of the Engineer and Railway Staff Corps, a territorial unit whose origins lay in the 19th century, whose membership was by invitation only and normally drawn from chartered engineers or directors of leading engineering companies, and whose role was to provide expert advice to the War Office. He retired in 1969 and died on 26 April 1972.

The Far East Theatre

The events at St Nazaire coincided with one of the grimmest episodes of the whole war, the fall of Malaya and Singapore to the Japanese. However, from Britain's point of view things were soon to take on a better aspect. The very fact of Japanese entry into the war brought America in, thus assuring eventual victory for the Allies. Before the end of the year, the tide had begun to turn irreversibly with the Battle of El Alamein – 'the end of the beginning' as Churchill conceded in his speech at the Lord Mayor's Day luncheon on 10 November 1942. The Soviet counter-offensive at Stalingrad began in December. In the Pacific the Americans had begun to dominate the seas after the Battles of the Coral Sea and Midway. Even in Burma, from which British forces had been unceremoniously ejected, the Japanese had reached the limit of their resources although there was still a long struggle ahead. It is to that theatre that we must turn for the last of the Second World War sapper VCs – though not until the end of June 1945 by which time the war in Europe was over.

Claud Raymond (1923–1945)

Lieutenant Claud Raymond

Claud Raymond was born in 1923, the son of an Indian Army officer, Lieutenant-Colonel Maurice Raymond, CIE, MC and Margaret Lilias Nancy Raymond (née Brown) of Fulham, London. Claud was educated at Wellington College and Trinity Hall, Cambridge and commissioned into the Royal Engineers in May 1943. Tributes in the national press after his death dwelt on the non-heroic side of his nature at school. The *Daily Herald* called him 'a quiet studious boy'. A contributor to *The Times* from Wellington College wrote:

> Like so many of his generation he believed that war was not the best way of reaching decisions and he went to join up with no sense of heroics. He was not outstanding at school except for his gift for friendship. ... He was genuinely fond of contemporary literature and a great admirer of the poetry of Auden ... Claud's sense of discipline was erratic and he was always disinclined to accept rules at their face value. In the JTC [Junior Training Corps] he showed more ingenuity than he did efficiency. However, his affection for outdoor life and his love of horses seemed to give him an independent attitude and a natural, charming roguishness which endeared him to his many friends.[22]

A more realistic picture of Claud is drawn by his Cambridge contemporary and friend Robin Williams who shared a room with him.

> From the word go it was obvious that he was destined to great things and who knows what he would have done if his life had not been cut short in such a

heroic manner? He was in a number of scrapes and was always up to something agin authority. He was in a cinema in Brighton when it was demolished by a bomb; he was not hurt but spent the night succouring the wounded. Only one bomb fell on Cambridge during the entire war and this landed on the 'Blue Boar' public house just as he was coming out of it. He was blown into the air and when he came to he stretched out his hand and reached into the crater. He was again unhurt. This information was never divulged as he was not supposed to be there.

Claud Raymond was one of the night climbers of Cambridge and did the Senate House leap in the dark. He climbed the spire of King's College Chapel by night. He had an illicit motorcycle. I never knew much about his love life but it was hectic. He used to climb into College well after hours and I would put him to bed sometimes the worse for wear. He had a particular friend … not a student at Cambridge but who lived locally; he claimed to be a hypnotist and they used to practise on their girlfriends. To make certain they had been properly put to sleep they used to stick pins in their bosoms.[23]

Robin Williams later remarked: 'I liked him, but I can understand that he was not an easy person. He had a very strong personality and knew what he wanted to do and what he wanted anyone else to do. He was, I think, what is termed a "born leader" and he certainly led me at Cambridge.'[24]

After Cambridge Claud Raymond completed his training and eventually found his way to the Far East theatre in an occupation that seems appropriate to his special talents, requiring 'more ingenuity than efficiency'. He joined a unit called D Force whose business was deception. The unit had a counterpart in north-west Europe, R Force, which had proved sufficiently successful to try replication in Burma. There they 'fought with fireworks and compressed air, duping the Japanese into pouring gunfire on to positions that didn't exist and countering attacks that never came from where they were expected.'[25] D Force started life in Iraq as Force X whose business was dummy tanks. It went through several metamorphoses but after the completion of the desert war was sent to India and redesignated 303 Indian Brigade. By the end of 1943 the Force's six 'observation squadrons' were in action, one at Imphal, three in the Arakan and two with the second Chindit expedition.

their role largely was to set up feint attacks and to draw enemy fire. Their main deceptive weapon was the linked crackers known as Bicat sausages. But these bangers failed miserably. Their bangs weren't loud enough, there were more duds than thuds; jungle weather ruined them; and they were totally incapable of simulating convincing light machinegun fire. In fact, the deceivers were only able to produce sounds of a company-strength attack by using their real Bren guns to simulate the noise of the (un)sound effects![26]

Early in the summer of 1944 these units were all withdrawn, and amalgamated with two other units known as 4 and 5 Light Scout Car companies. In reality they were sound deception units equipped with amplifier systems, known as Poplin, using film sound tracks and capable of producing more realistic battle noises including the movement of vehicles to and fro.

The resulting unit had eight subunits, now called companies, six of them Indian and two British, and was redesignated D Force. It was commanded by Peter Fleming, the explorer and brother of author Ian, creator of James Bond. In command of Claud's squadron was Major Ronald Norman, a Parachute Regiment officer who many years later was to remark that 'if it were not for Claud, I would not be here now.'[27]

A brief résumé of the war in Burma is necessary for an understanding of D Force's operations in the Arakan. The Japanese had invaded Burma in December 1941 and by the following May the two divisions, 17th Indian and 1st Burma, had been pushed out of Burma as had their Chinese allies, to the borders of India and China respectively. Considering the superiority of the enemy forces and the political pressure to hold out as long as possible, not much more could have been expected. Burma Corps returned to India having lost over 13,000 men. Regrouping, some reinforcement and changes in command then followed. In an attempt to recover the Arakan, a premature offensive was launched in September 1942 using 14th Indian Division and, after a fair amount of muddle, the invading force was outmanoeuvred by the Japanese and withdrew to India the following May, 5000 men the fewer. Nevertheless the Indian Army was by then being trained and equipped for a more realistic offensive and, in the meantime, the Chindit deep-penetration operations were beginning to have a positive effect, at least on morale. In October 1943 Fourteenth Army was formed and General Bill Slim (last seen in this narrative as the brigade commander at Gallabat), who had been in the theatre in various roles since early 1942, was appointed to its command.

Early in 1944, the next offensive into the Arakan with the British, Indian and West African troops of XV Corps was launched, in conjunction with a combined Chinese and American operation into northern Burma under the command of the American Lieutenant-General Joe Stilwell. These operations now made progress which was not to be reversed, but only after fierce fighting as the Japanese tried to surround and destroy both. Allied success also hung on the ability of Fourteenth Army to hold off a Japanese onslaught into Assam, where an epic struggle at Kohima and Imphal broke the impetus of the now desperately over-extended Japanese Fifteenth Army. By June the enemy were in retreat to the Chindwin and by November Fourteenth Army were poised for an offensive into central Burma – achieved by one of the great masterstrokes of deception of the war. Slim switched IV Corps from its planned line of advance into the central plain to a flanking offensive to cross the Irrawaddy 100 miles downstream of Mandalay, so as to strike at the nerve centre and main logistic base of the Japanese army at Meiktila. The secrecy with which this move of over 300 miles through daunting terrain was achieved meant that the enemy never realised until too late that the XXIII Corps thrust downriver to Mandalay was not their principal concern. In the north the Irrawaddy was crossed in mid-January; in the centre and on the IV Corps front, four weeks later. Meiktila had been occupied in the first week of March but a furious counter-attack was then mounted so that towards the end of the month two mighty battles were in progress; one to hold on to Meiktila and destroy the Japanese forces there, and the other to take Mandalay.

Map 26
*Burma and its
neighbours, 1945.*

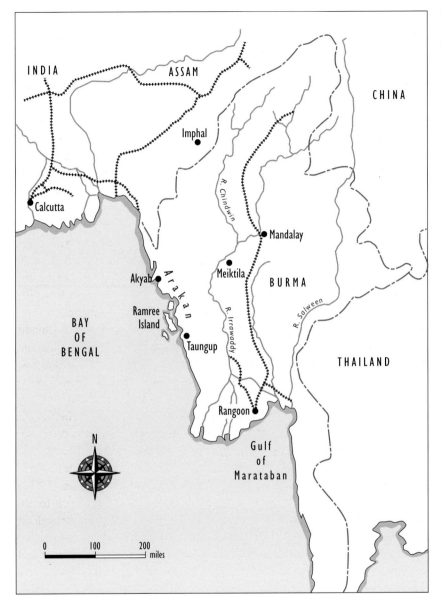

There had been two important elements in Slim's plan for the crossing of the Irrawaddy and the advance to Meiktila. The first was that a sufficient proportion of the Japanese force in Burma would be drawn into battle in the north against the Chinese and in the Arakan against XV Corps. In his *Defeat into Victory*, Slim records his reliance on 'our deception schemes, with their threat of amphibious attack, to tie down a further one and a third [divisions] in the south.'[28] The second element was the need for forward air bases from which to support the central Burma battle. The number of troops that Fourteenth Army could deploy into its sector was limited by its tenuous supply lines, of which a 200–250-mile air-lift was

Map 27
*Thinganet Creek,
scene of Second
Lieutenant Claud
Raymond's VC
action.*

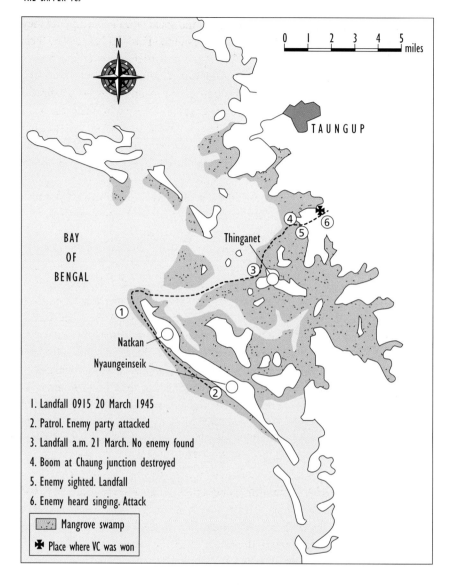

BAY
OF
BENGAL

Thinganet

TAUNGUP

Natkan

Nyaungeinseik

I. Landfall 0915 20 March 1945

2. Patrol. Enemy party attacked

3. Landfall a.m. 21 March. No enemy found

4. Boom at Chaung junction destroyed

5. Enemy sighted. Landfall

6. Enemy heard singing. Attack

Mangrove swamp

Place where VC was won

a critical part. If this could be reduced, it would not only help the immediate battle but would allow further exploitation into southern Burma. To this end XV Corps had carried out successful assault landings on the islands of Akyab (which had in fact been left undefended) and Ramree, which had fallen by the end of February, although its airfield in the north was in operation within a week of the landing on 21 January.

At this stage of events D Force had three squadrons operating down the Arakan coast. One of them was Claud Raymond's 58 Squadron which had sailed from India on 18 October. An example of D Force in action was when, in early February, 71st Brigade had been held up at a 'chaung' – waterway – during the advance on Ramree Island. While manoeuvring to outflank the Japanese position the brigade had the use of D Force to deceive the enemy into believing that they were still in position on the far bank. In this situation D Force had to provide their own defence as infantry as well as producing the battlefield deception noises. Poplin was successfully used on this occasion. It was then planned that XV Corps would make further assault landings, this time on the mainland, so as to maintain pressure on the enemy and discourage any diversion of these forces to the main Fourteenth Army battle; and also to cut a possible line of retreat that existed from the Irrawaddy to the coast and the south. The southernmost of these assaults was conducted by a brigade of 26th Indian Division by landing craft from Ramree, to land and advance towards Taungup. These operations were fraught with difficulty as there were practically no beaches and the coastline was shrouded in mangrove jungle intersected by muddy tidal inlets. Detailed reconnaissance was essential and D Force's deception skills were often highly beneficial.

In connection with the advance towards Taungup, a detachment of D Force was sent to land ahead of the main body 'to gain information about the enemy's disposition and movements and to create a diversion in the Taungup area.'[29] Between 20 and 22 March 1945 the detachment explored the coastline at the entrance to Thinganet Chaung, sending patrols southwards to Natkan and Nyaungeinseik. They had found footprints on the beach and eventually a party of Japanese whom they attacked but who ran away. On 22 March a patrol, of which Second Lieutenant Claud Raymond was second-in-command, was sent inland up the chaung. Their first landfall was on Thinganet Island which they found clear of enemy. They re-embarked in the assault craft and carried on in the direction of Taungup, destroying a bamboo and wire floating boom on their way. At that point a Japanese soldier was spotted running away. The patrol landed and found recently occupied bunkers and foxholes overlooking the chaung. Moving on they learned from locals of an enemy detachment a few miles further to the north-east. They went in pursuit and at 2.30 pm heard some singing from a basha (hut). With one officer and two British soldiers giving covering fire, Claud Raymond led the remainder of the patrol in a charge uphill. The Japanese defended themselves with rifle fire and grenades and in the course of the operation one soldier was hit in the leg but Raymond was grievously wounded.[30]

> Lieutenant Raymond immediately charged in the direction of the fire. As he began to climb the hill he was wounded in the right shoulder, but he ignored this wound and continued up the slope firing his rifle from the hip. He had advanced only a few yards further, when a Japanese threw a grenade which burst in his face and most severely wounded him. He fell, but almost immediately picked himself up again, and, in spite of loss of blood from his wounds, which later were to prove fatal, he still continued on, leading his section under intense fire. He was hit yet a third time, his wrist being shattered by what appeared to have been an explosive bullet. In spite of this third wound he never wavered, but carried on into the enemy position itself, and, in the sharp action that followed, was largely responsible for the killing of two Japanese and the wounding of a third.
>
> The remaining Japanese then fled in panic into the jungle, thus leaving the position in our hands, together with much equipment.

The position itself was strongly fortified by foxholes and small bunkers and would have proved extremely formidable had not the attack been pressed home with great determination under the courageous leadership of Lieutenant Raymond.

Several other men were wounded during the action and Lieutenant Raymond refused all treatment until they had been attended to, insisting despite the gravity of his injuries, on walking back towards the landing craft in case the delay in treating his wounds should endanger the withdrawal of the patrol.

It was not until he had walked nearly a mile that he collapsed and had to allow himself to be carried on an improvised stretcher. Even then he was continually encouraging the other wounded by giving the thumbs up sign and thus undoubtedly helping them to keep cheerful and minimise the extent of their injuries until the landing craft was reached. Soon after he died of his wounds.

The outstanding gallantry, remarkable endurance and fortitude of Lieutenant Raymond, which refused to allow him to collapse, although mortally wounded, was an inspiration to everyone and a major factor in the capture of the strong point. His self-sacrifice in refusing attention to his wounds undoubtedly saved the patrol, by allowing it to withdraw in time before the Japanese could bring up fresh forces from neighbouring positions for a counter attack.[31]

With the victories at Meiktila and Mandalay the opportunity now opened up for the advance on Rangoon. It fell on 3 May without resistance, in fact to an assault landing operation by XV Corps, and was reached by Fourteenth Army, after a hectic dash to beat the monsoon, two days later.

By that date the war in Europe was effectively over. Hitler had killed himself in his Berlin bunker on 30 April after the desperate fighting which cost the Russians some 100,000 casualties. There was still much to be accomplished in the war against Japan, however. It took another three months to flush the Japanese army out of Burma. Further afield, the Americans had invaded the Philippines in January but, although Manila fell in early March after a bitter fight, resistance continued on Luzon and on some of the outlying islands until the end of the war. The capture of Iwo Jima in February/March and Okinawa in April/May, at colossal cost to both sides, paved the way for the bombing of mainland Japan but even the resulting devastation failed to provoke a Japanese surrender. Finally, the prospect of costly seaborne landings taking the war to the Japanese homeland persuaded the American President Harry S. Truman to use the newly developed atomic bombs on Hiroshima and Nagasaki. Japan surrendered on 15 August 1945.

Some are born great, some achieve greatness, and some have greatness thrust upon them. (Shakespeare, Twelfth Night, Act II, Scene v)

Claud Raymond's astonishing act of gallantry and deliberate self-sacrifice perhaps exemplifies the final bench-mark of courage which now must be attained before the honour of a Victoria Cross can be granted. It is this high standard which endows the decoration with its unique prestige. But such prestige could not have been acquired overnight; it has been built up over the years of its existence by that select band of heroes whose actions have been deemed beyond normal praise. In the early days, selection for such a signal honour was bound to give rise to anomalies and controversy about the relative merits of a particular recipient in comparison with his comrades. For two similar acts one adjudged slightly more brave than the other, there was effectively a borderline between undying fame and obscurity. Nowadays, for the Army, there are at least three borderlines separating out four levels of gallantry earned for acts in the face of the enemy: the Victoria Cross, the Conspicuous Gallantry Cross, the Military Cross and a mention in despatches. The nature of the qualifying deed has also become more clearly defined. The most obvious distinction to have been drawn since the inception of the Victoria Cross is that between humanitarian acts – even when 'in action' such as rescues and bomb disposal, which are often now recognised by civil awards (such as a George Cross, George Medal or Queen's Gallantry Medal) – and heroism while engaged with the enemy. There have been 11 awards of the Victoria Cross since 1945 – four in Korea, one in Borneo, two in the Falklands, and four in Vietnam to members of the Australian Training Team. All illustrate this refining process and the extraordinary level of gallantry now required.[1]

The 55 sapper VCs covered in this book are a good sample of the total 1354 awarded since its inception. Part of the fascination of the honour lies in the nature of supreme heroism displayed in the different cases, prompting the question as to whether, for example, it is more meritorious to perform a heroic act on the spur of the moment in the heat of battle, as in Claud Raymond's case and the near-suicidal rescues by Goodfellow, Hart and Kirby; or whether sustained, premeditated courage is more to be admired, such as in the cases of the Kashmir Gate VCs of Home, Salkeld and Smith and those VCs won at the crossings of the Sambre-Oise canal by Waters, Archibald, Findlay and Cloutman? There is then the incentive element. Who can deny that the chance of achieving glory in battle lurks in the back of the mind of most professional soldiers and what better mark of glory than a gallantry award; even though nowadays we speak less of glory and more of professional competence and duty performed with honour? Another angle much discussed is the extent to which such a reward as the Victoria Cross should be made simply for performing a soldier's duty, which is, after all, to risk his life for the cause to which he has signed up. In many instances, the man chosen for the award had no choice but to perform the deed concerned. Chard at Rorke's Drift had little; there was even less choice for those at the Kashmir Gate and the Sambre-Oise canal: they were carrying out their orders.

Thus individual heroes begin to fall into Shakespeare's three categories quoted at the beginning of this chapter. There seem to be those whose nature is to perform acts of heroism, who thrive on danger and challenge. They are *born* great. There is a sort of inevitability about the awards which came to such as Graham, Prendergast, Aylmer, Martin, Neame, Coffin, Durrant and Raymond. Give them a war and they will win glory. Those who *achieve* greatness are more calculatingly ambitious, such as Leach and Bell and possibly the RFC VCs, but no less brave. What is significant is the large number of those who have greatness *thrust upon them*, who are ordinary people who manage to respond when the supreme call comes. Chard is the obvious case – presented in Colonel Vetch's comment in the *Royal Engineers Journal* as a young subaltern of engineers of no very conspicuous ability who rose to the occasion and was the hero of the gallant defence of the post, so doing the Corps honour. But then most of the true sapper VCs, those won in the course of a military engineering task, fall into this category.

Could this be the reason for so few sapper VCs in the Second World War? Could it be that even then, let alone now when official definitions of gallantry have been even more refined, only supermen (and women) would qualify? Maybe this is desirable. We need our Valhalla, our breed of heroes whose deeds are so meritorious that they bring honour to the title, as defined by Machiavelli in the quotation on page vi of this book. On the other hand, the ultimate prize should always lie within the aspirations of the ordinary person, however unrealistic their dreams – and should we deny entry to those who display that special brand of courage in performing their duty under fire ('much annoyed by the enemy' as the Victorians would have put it) but unable to shoot back?

There is, of course, the luck factor and the manner in which citations are presented. Two cases from the Second World War stood out during the research for this book. In the first, in August 1944, an officer of 53 Divisional Engineers was caught up in a battle when he was accompanying 1st Oxfordshire and Buckinghamshire Light Infantry for the purposes of a bridge reconnaissance. The platoon position was being broken into by enemy tanks when the sapper officer (Lieutenant Donald Harvey) rallied the platoon and led them out to break up the attack with machine-guns and PIATs. He was killed at the moment of success. The subsequent glowing reports by the infantry NCOs carried all the flavour of Digby Jones's affair at Ladysmith. One said: 'I remember thinking to myself at the time, "this chap should have been in the infantry".' The VC citation was unsuccessful. The second case was that of a sapper of 77 Indian Field Company, one of a party of a Viceroy Commissioned Officer (VCO) and four or five sappers, detailed to destroy a Japanese bunker whose occupants had caused many casualties during repeated attacks by 33 Indian Brigade in the furious fighting for the relief of Kohima in May 1944. The sapper concerned was badly wounded while the charges were being laid and almost unable to move. Waving aside orders from the VCO to crawl off the bunker to allow someone else to detonate the charge, he pulled the pin. The bunker, its occupants and the sapper were blown to bits and the subsequent attack by the infantry was successful. A citation was written, not for a VC but for the Indian Order of Merit which could also be awarded posthumously. In the end a mention in despatches was granted, although it is difficult to think of a more deliberately heroic and self-sacrificing act.

Doubtless those with experience of such battles would have many similar tales to tell of the fortunes of war. From that fact emerges the final impression gained during the research for this book. In so many of the cases the recipients, if they had the chance to think about the matter at all, seldom saw themselves worthy of being placed on such an exclusive pedestal in comparison with their comrades. One of the commonest themes that has emerged is the honest bafflement of those honoured that they should have been selected when others had been equally brave and many killed. It is no dishonour to those who gained the ultimate reward for their valour, and it would probably be their own wish, to remember that victory in battle is the outcome of endeavour by all; and that the same experiences, often scarcely endurable, have been shared by the rewarded and unrewarded alike.

The following notes are presented using the author–title system. Full details of all titles may be found in the Bibliography on pp.299–304.

Introduction

1 PRO WO 98/1 quoted in Crook, *The Evolution of the Victoria Cross.*
2 Ibid., p.29.
3 Ibid., pp.34, 35.

Chapter 1

 1 Letter from Lieutenant G. Graham to his father, June 1855, Royal Engineers Museum, Accession No. 6707.04.
 2 Porter, *History ... Royal Engineers*, Vol. 1, p.418.
 3 Ibid., p.425.
 4 Ibid., pp.423–4.
 5 James, *The Journal of My Life.*
 6 Cecil Woodham Smith's *The Reason Why* is the classic account of the grotesque feud between Lucan and Cardigan which reached its climax at Balaclava. As well as describing the events vividly, the book throws much light on the nature of the British Army in the years after Waterloo.
 7 Adkin, *The Charge*, p.217.
 8 Porter, *History ... Royal Engineers*, Vol. 1, p.434.
 9 Letter from Lieutenant G. Graham to his sister, January 1855, Royal Engineers Museum.
10 Lennox, W., *Royal Engineers Journal*, 1 April 1898, p.84.
11 Conolly, *History of the Royal Sappers and Miners*, p.282.
12 Ibid., pp.282, 283.
13 Pemberton, *Battles of the Crimean War*, p.195.
14 Conolly, *History of the Royal Sappers and Miners*, p.350.
15 Ibid., p.347.
16 McClintock, *The Queen Thanks Sir Howard*, p.23.
17 Pemberton, *Battles of the Crimean War*, p.200.
18 Letter from Lieutenant G. Graham to his father, June 1855, Royal Engineers Museum.
19 Vetch, *Life of Lieut-General Sir Gerald Graham*, p.108.
20 Pemberton, *Battles of the Crimean War*, p.223.
21 Ranken, *Six Months at Sebastopol*, p.53.
22 Conolly, *History of the Royal Sappers and Miners*, p.435.
23 Crook, *The Evolution of the Victoria Cross*, p.92.
24 *Sapper*, September 1898, p.22.
25 PRO WO 97/1361.

26 Riordan, T.M.J., MM, *Sergeant-Major W J Lendrim VC*, Royal Engineers Historical Society Occasional Paper No. 8, January 1987.

27 Kinglake, *Invasion of the Crimea*, p.167.

28 *Royal Engineers Journal*, 1 February 1900, p.28.

29 Crook, *The Evolution of the Victoria Cross*, p.224.

30 McClintock, *The Queen Thanks Sir Howard*, p.265.

Chapter 2

1 Porter, *History ... Royal Engineers*, Vol. 2, p.403.

2 Philip Mason's *A Matter of Honour* gives a full account of this issue and the whole of the origins of the Uprising.

3 Sandes, *The Military Engineer in India*, Vol. 1, p.326.

4 Perkins, *The Kashmir Gate – Lieutenant Home and the Delhi VCs*. Strongly recommended source.

5 Kingston, *Memoir of Lieut Charles Duncan Home*, p.8.

6 Ibid., p.15.

7 Blomfield, *Indian Mutiny Journal of Arthur Moffat Lang*, p.84.

8 Sandes, *The Indian Sappers and Miners*, p.232. Subadar Toola (Tula Ram), Jemadar Bis Ram, Jemadar Ramteroz (elsewhere Havildar Ramtaroy or Ramtarai or Ramdulari), Havildar Mahdoo (Madhoo), Havildar Tilok Singh (Tillok or Tiluk Singh), Havildar (elsewhere Naik) Harpal Singh, Havildar (some say Sepoy) Ajudhya Pershad Pathak, Naiks Devi Deen (Debi Singh), Sheik Abdulla (Sheik Abdul) and Nihal Khan; and Sepoys Ram Heth (Heth Ram) Thakurdin Tiwari, Ramsaful Upadhya and Sahib Singh. All received the Indian Order of Merit and were rewarded with grants of land.

9 Thackeray, *The Royal (Bengal) Engineers*, p.264.

10 Sandes, *The Military Engineer in India*, Vol. 1, pp.343, 344.

11 Ibid., p.344.

12 Crook, *The Evolution of the Victoria Cross*, p.70.

13 Blomfield, *Indian Mutiny Journal of Arthur Moffat Lang*, p.107.

14 Sandes, *The Military Engineer in India*, Vol. 1, p.345.

15 Thackeray, *A Subaltern in the Indian Mutiny*, p.599.

16 Ibid., p.600.

17 Ibid.

18 Ibid., p.601.

19 Innes, General J.J. McL., typescript article 'The Defence of the Residency of Lucknow' in the possession of Mrs Sue Smithson, Innes's great-granddaughter, possibly a draft for the lecture of that name given to the United Service Institution of India on 28 August 1883, the published transcript of which does not, however, mention Duncan Macleod's connection with the Iron Bridge.

20 *Royal Engineers Journal*, Vol. 7, 1908, p.384, quoting General Franks's report.

21 Original letter from Innes to his wife in the Royal Engineers Museum (courtesy of his granddaughter Mrs C. Morley).

22 Royal Engineers Museum, copied from the report in the *Bengal Hurkaru*, 1 July 1859.

23 Sandes, *The Military Engineer in India*, Vol. 1, p.361.

24 Ibid., p.364.

25 *Fermanagh Times*, 28 August 1902, copy provided by Mr John Cunningham.
26 *Bombay Gazette*, from Lummis files, National Army Museum.
27 Royal Engineers Museum file M3/16.13.
28 PRO WO 97/1856.
29 Letter from Neil Roberts of the Victorian Military Society's India and Burma Study Group, quoting Cadell's *History of the Bombay Army*, Low's *History of the Indian Navy*, *Soldiers of the Queen*, issue 78 (September 1994), Bancroft's *Deeds of Valour* and A.G. Stone's pamphlet *Indian Campaigns 1778–1914*.

Chapter 3

1 Snelling, Forlorn Hope at Dewangiri, p.16.
2 *Royal Engineers Journal*, Vol. 7, February 1908, p.79.
3 Rhodes, An Officer Not Only of Great Talent But of Rare Coolness and Courage. Major General W.S. Trevor VC Royal (Bengal) Engineers 1831 to 1937, p.132.
4 *Royal Engineers Journal*, Vol. 7, February 1908, p.81.
5 Letter from Captain W.S. Trevor to his brother Salusbury, held in the Royal Engineers Museum.
6 Vibart, *Addiscombe; Its Heroes and Men of Note*, p.372.
7 Snelling, Forlorn Hope at Dewangiri, p.18.
8 Letter from Captain W.S. Trevor.
9 Ibid.
10 Ibid.
11 Snelling, Forlorn Hope at Dewangiri, p.18.
12 Ibid., p.19.
13 Letter from Captain W.S. Trevor.
14 Rhodes, An Officer Not Only of Great Talent But of Rare Coolness and Courage, p.137.
15 *Royal Engineers Journal*, 2 February 1880, p.40.
16 Dundas family memorial book, sold at Spinks with the medal set on 18 March 1997.
17 Ibid.
18 Creagh and Humphris, *The Victoria Cross*, p.84.
19 Letter from Captain W.S. Trevor.
20 Sandes, *The Indian Sappers and Miners*, p.408.

Chapter 4

1 Morris, *Heaven's Command*, p.393, quoting a speech to Cambridge undergraduates by David Livingstone.
2 Ibid., p.393.
3 Porter, *History ... Royal Engineers*, Vol. 2, p.10.
4 Lloyd, *The Drums of Kumasi*, p.44.
5 Ibid., p.24.
6 Ibid., p.15, quoting Major Home's report.
7 Ibid., pp.15, 16.
8 Home, Lieutenant-Colonel R., Engineer Operations on the Gold Coast, published in the *Professional Papers of the Royal Engineers*, New Series, Vol. XXIII.

9   Lloyd, *The Drums of Kumasi*, p.106.

10   Unidentified newspaper cutting in the Lummis files, National Army Museum.

11   Lloyd, *The Drums of Kumasi*, p.149.

12   *Royal Engineers Journal*, November 1888, p.244.

13   Statement of Mehlo-ka-Zulu, son of Sirayo, one of Ketchwayo's Chiefs, *Royal Engineers Journal*, February 1880, p.24.

14   Knight, *Brave Men's Blood*, p.47.

15   Droogleever, *The Road to Isandhlwana. Colonel Anthony Durnford in Natal and Zululand*, pp.26 *et seq.*

16   Knight, *Brave Men's Blood*, p.70.

17   Royal Engineers Museum and Library Information Sheet No 3: *Lieut J R M Chard VC RE and the Defence of Rorke's Drift*.

18   Chard, J.R.M., Account of the Defence of Rorke's Drift submitted to Queen Victoria on 21 February 1880, Royal Archives, Windsor Castle.

19   Wilkins, *History of the VC*, pp.396–8, quoted in the Lummis files, National Army Museum.

20   Parke Jones, letters and transcripts, Royal Engineers Library.

21   Ibid.

22   Knight, *Nothing Remains but to Fight*, p.132.

23   *Royal Engineers Journal*, 1 August 1899.

Chapter 5

1   G.K. Chesterton, quoted in Giddings, *Imperial Echoes*, p.xx.

2   Heathcote, *The Afghan Wars 1839–1919*, p.32.

3   Robson, *The Road to Kabul*, p.32.

4   Sandes, *The Military Engineer in India*, Vol. I, p.376.

5   Ibid., p.380.

6   Jackson, Memories of Afghanistan in 1879, p.97.

7   Ibid., p.98.

8   Ibid., pp.98–100.

9   Lummis papers, quoting Court News, *Illustrated London News*, 13 December 1879.

10   Sandes, *The Military Engineer in India*, Vol. I, p.380.

11   Leach, Brigadier-General H.P., author of memoir of E.P. Leach in *Royal Engineers Journal*, Vol. 18, 1913, p.303.

12   Ibid.

13   *Royal Engineers Journal*, 1 May 1879, p.87.

14   Confidential letter held by the Royal Engineers Museum.

15   Hensman, *The Afghan War, 1870–80*, quoted in Sandes, *The Military Engineer in India*, Vol. I, p.386.

16   Leach, Brevet Major E.P., Operations on the Halmand and Battle of Maiwand, p.265.

17   Porter, *History ... Royal Engineers*, Vol. 2, pp.58–9.

18   Robson, *The Road to Kabul*, p.297.

19   Quoted in *Royal Engineers Journal*, March 1932, p.123.

Chapter 6

1   Knight, *Where Three Empires Meet*, p.398.

2 Sandes, *The Miltary Engineer in India*, Vol. 1, p.424.

3 Ibid., p.421, quoting Paget and Mason, *Record of Expeditions against the North-West Tribes*.

4 Hopkirk, *The Great Game: On Secret Service in High Asia*, pp.356 *et seq.*

5 Sandes, *The Military Engineer in India*, Vol. 1, p.435.

6 Ibid., p.434.

7 Ibid., p.436.

8 Knight, *Where Three Empires Meet*, pp.398–400.

9 Sandes, *The Military Engineer in India*, Vol. 1, p.438.

10 Crook, *The Evolution of the Victoria Cross*, p.167.

11 Younghusband, Captains G.J. and F.E., *The Relief of Chitral*, quoted in Lummis files, National Army Museum.

12 Sandes, *The Military Engineer in India*, Vol. I, p.446.

13 Churchill, *The Story of the Malakand Field Force*, p.189.

14 Ibid., p.194.

15 Sandes, *The Military Engineer in India*, Vol. I, footnote, p.448.

16 Churchill, *The Story of the Malakand Field Force*, p.204.

17 Transcript of Colvin family private correspondence dated 18 September 1897.

18 Ibid., dated 3 June 1895.

19 Ibid., dated 2 January 1898.

20 Ibid., dated 2 September 1903.

21 Ibid., dated 25 September 1903.

Chapter 7

1 Swinton, *The Defence of Duffer's Drift*, p.52.

2 Morris, *Farewell the Trumpets. An Imperial Retreat*, p.21.

3 Morris, *Heaven's Command*, p.446.

4 Farwell, *The Great Boer War*, p.37.

5 Creagh and Humphris, *The Victoria Cross*, p.133.

6 Pakenham, *The Boer War*, p.272.

7 Creagh and Humphris, *The Victoria Cross*, p.133.

8 Conan Doyle, *The Great Boer War*, p.230.

9 Pakenham, *The Boer War*, p.275.

10 *Royal Engineers Journal*, 2 April 1900, p.86.

11 Maurice, *History of the War in South Africa 1899–1902*, Vol. 1, p.236.

12 *Sapper*, August 1906, p.4.

13 Ibid., Vol. 3, p.94.

14 Ibid.

15 Farwell, *The Great Boer War*, p.312, quoting Worsfold, *Lord Milner's Role in South Africa*, p.322.

16 *Sapper*, November 1901, p.100.

Chapter 8

1 Holt, *Battlefields of the First World War – A Traveller's Guide*, p.43.

2 Terraine, *Mons: The Retreat to Victory*, p.91.

3 Diary of Lieutenant C.G. Martin, lent by his daughter, Miss Mabyn Martin.

4 Buckland, Demolitions Carried Out at Mons, p.18.

5 Gliddon, *VCs of the First World War – 1914*, p.19.
6 *Sapper*, February 1915, p.174.
7 Buckland, Demolitions Carried Out at Mons, p.28.
8 Gliddon, *VCs of the First World War – 1914*, p.14.
9 Buckland, Demolitions Carried Out at Mons, p.29.
10 Ibid., p.23.
11 Wilson (ed.), *The Great War*, p.370. A caption in this source describes Jarvis as 'the first VC of the War'.
12 *Fraserburgh Herald*, quoted in Gliddon, *VCs of the First World War – 1914*, p.18.
13 Gliddon, ibid., p.19.
14 Diary of Lieutenant C.G. Martin, lent by his daughter, Miss Mabyn Martin.
15 Pritchard (ed.), *History of the Corps of Royal Engineers*, Vol. 5, p.194.
16 Letter from William Johnston, copy held in the Royal Engineers Museum.
17 Hussey and Inman, *The Fifth Division in the Great War*, p.80.
18 Mason, *A Matter of Honour*, p.412.
19 War Diary of 26 Field Company, Royal Engineers Museum.
20 Neame, *Playing With Strife*, p.41.
21 Ibid.
22 PRO WO 95/1403.
23 Ibid.
24 Ibid.
25 Clark, *The Donkeys*, p.126.
26 Pritchard, *History of the Corps of Royal Engineers*, Vol. 5, pp.234–9.
27 War Diary of 73 Field Company, Royal Engineers Museum.
28 Clark, *The Donkeys*, p.173.

Chapter 9

1 Pritchard (ed.), *History of the Corps of Royal Engineers*, Vol. 5, p.27, quoting *Work of the Royal Engineers in the European War 1914–1918*, pp.61–71.
2 Morris, *Farewell the Trumpets*, p.158.
3 Kerry and McDill, *The History of the Corps of the Royal Canadian Engineers. Vol. 1. 1749–1939*, p.329.
4 Watson, *History of the Corps of Royal Engineers*, Vol. 3, p.35.
5 *New Zealand Herald*, 12 August 1978.
6 Moorehead, *Gallipoli*, p.155.
7 Bryant, *Where the Prize is Highest*, p.38 quoting Bean, *The Official History of Australia in the War*.
8 Ibid., p.40.
9 *New Zealand Herald*, 12 August 1978.
10 New Zealand Expeditionary Force Confidential Report dated 19 January 1918 supplied to author by Mr Howard Chamberlain.
11 Richter, *Chemical Soliders. British Gas Warfare in World War I*, p.7.
12 Foulkes, *"Gas!" – The Story of the Special Brigade*, p.17.
13 Ibid., p.271.
14 Clark, *The Donkeys*, p.149.
15 Oldfield, Lieutenant-Colonel P.J., research notes.
16 Grieve and Newman, *Tunnellers*, p.166.

17 Ibid., p.110.
18 Neame, *Playing With Strife*, p.59.
19 Grieve and Newman, *Tunnellers*, p.110.
20 Press release *Mexborough and Swinton Times* dated August 1916.
21 Hackett papers, RE Museum Accession No. 9603.10.4.
22 Ibid.
23 Ibid.
24 Grieve and Newman, *Tunnellers*, p.243.
25 Hackett papers, RE Museum Accession No. 9603.10.4.
26 Crook, *The Evolution of the Victoria Cross*, p.148.
27 *Sapper*, November 1916.
28 Ibid., May 1966.
29 Blunden (ed.), *The Poems of Wilfred Owen*, p.99.
30 Grieve and Newman, *Tunnellers*, p.323.

Chapter 10

1 Terraine, *The Road to Passchendaele*, quoting Gillon, *The Story of the 29th Division*, p.122.
2 Unpublished *Company History 409th Lowland Field Company*, Royal Engineers Library, Chatham.
3 Warner, *Passchendaele*, pp.1–2.
4 Edmonds, *History of the Great War Based on Official Documents*, 1917, Vol. 2, p.164.
5 PRO WO 95/1727.
6 Crook, *The Evolution of the Victoria Cross*, pp.37, 38.
7 Boraston and Bax, *The Eighth Division in War, 1914–1918*, p.149.
8 Macdonald, *They Called it Passchendaele*, p.166.
9 Coombs, *Before Endeavours Fade*, p.50.
10 *The Staffordshire Knot*, Journal of the Staffordshire Regiment, 1971.
11 Macdonald, *They Called it Passchendaele*, p.167.
12 Pritchard (ed.), *History of the Corps of Royal Engineers*, Vol. 5, Chapter 21.

Chapter 11

1 Falls, *The History of the 36th (Ulster) Division*, p.194.
2 Terraine, *To Win a War. 1918: The Year of Victory*, p.59.
3 Transcript of letter from Second Lieutenant C.L. Knox, supplied by his daughter, Mrs Katrina Barling.
4 Falls, *The History of the 36th (Ulster) Division*, p.202.
5 Ibid., p.203.
6 Letter from Second Lieutenant Knox, supplied by his daughter, Mrs Katrina Barling.
7 Livesey, *The Viking Atlas of World War I*, p.151.
8 Boraston and Bax, *The Eighth Division in War, 1914–1918*, p.169.
9 Ibid., p.171.
10 *Sapper*, June 1918, p.201.
11 *London Gazette*, 26 September 1917.
12 Boraston and Bax, *The Eighth Division in War, 1914–1918*, p.184.
13 PRO WO 95/1713.

14 Boraston and Bax, *The Eighth Division in War, 1914–1918*, p.197.
15 Ibid.
16 Terraine, *To Win a War. 1918: The Year of Victory*, p.66.

Chapter 12

1   McPhie, James, VC citation, *London Gazette*, 31 January 1919.
2   Livesey, *The Viking Atlas of World War I*, p.172.
3   Terraine, *To Win a War. 1918: The Year of Victory*, p.141.
4   Ibid., quoting Maurice, *The Last Four Months*, p.137.
5   Ibid., p.114, quoting Ludendorff, *My War Memories*, p.679.
6   Pritchard (ed.), *History of the Corps of Royal Engineers*, Vol. 5, p.388.
7   Terraine, *To Win a War. 1918: The Year of Victory*, p.167.
8   Stewart, *Official History of New Zealand's Effort in the Great War. Vol. II. France*, p.432.
9   Citation for Coulson Norman Mitchell's MC, supplied by the Military Engineers Museum Association of Canada.
10 Kerry and McDill, *The History of the Corps of the Royal Canadian Engineers, Vol. 1. 1749–1939*, p.196.
11 Documents relating to Coulson Mitchell are held by the Military Engineers Museum Association of Canada.
12 Ward, *The 56th Division*, p.292.
13 Ibid.
14 Papers in the possession of Derrick Martin, son of Lieutenant Arnold's first cousin.
15 416 Field Company War Diary, PRO WO 95/242.
16 Records of the Royal Inniskilling Regimental Museum, Enniskillen. A fuller account of the incident and the reactions in Harvey's home town of Newton-le-Willows is given in Creagh and Humphris, *The Victoria Cross*, p.319.
17 Falls, *The History of the 36th (Ulster) Division*, p.290.
18 Papers in the possession of Derrick Martin, son of Lieutenant Arnold's first cousin.
19 Montgomery, *The Story of the Fourth Army in the Battles of the Hundred Days, August 8th to November 11th, 1918*, p.251.
20 Pritchard (ed.), *History of the Corps of Royal Engineers*, Vol. 5, p.398.
21 Citations for MC and bar supplied by Lieutenant-Colonel P.J. Oldfield.
22 Unpublished *Company History of the 409th Lowland Field Company*, Royal Engineers Library, Chatham.
23 409 (Lowland) Field Company War Diary, Royal Engineers Library.
24 Unpublished *Company History of the 409th Lowland Field Company*, Royal Engineers Library, Chatham.
25 59 Field Company War Diary, Royal Engineers Museum.
26 Creagh and Humphris, *The Victoria Cross*, p.321.
27 Falls, *The First World War*, p.395.
28 Report held by the Royal Inniskilling Fusiliers Regimental Association.
29 Information supplied to the author by Colonel J.L. Osborne.
30 *Royal Engineers Journal*, 1971, p.277.

Chapter 13

1   Quoted by his sister, Maud Beach, in a letter dated 18 February 1951, giving her memories of her brother and early military flying, Royal Engineers Museum.

2 Broke-Smith, *The History of Early British Aeronautics*, Chapter 6.
3 Bickers, *The First Great Air War*, p.3.
4 Ibid., p.4.
5 Ibid., p.119.
6 Hawker, *Hawker, VC*, p.74.
7 Ibid., p.76.
8 Ibid., p.89.
9 Ibid., pp.84, 85.
10 Ibid., p.103.
11 Bickers, *The First Great Air War*, p.79.
12 Hawker, *Hawker, VC*, p.v.
13 Cole, *McCudden VC*, p.34.
14 Bickers, *The First Great Air War*, p.90.
15 McCudden, *Five Years in the Royal Flying Corps*, p.107.
16 Ibid., p.174.
17 Ibid., p.192.
18 Bickers, *The First Great Air War*, p.211.
19 McCudden, *Five Years in the Royal Flying Corps*, p.245.
20 Ibid., p.232.
21 Ibid., p.264.
22 Ibid., p.265.
23 Ibid., p.291.
24 Citation for the DSO for James McCudden, *London Gazette* 5 July 1918.
25 Cole, *McCudden VC*, p.194.
26 Ibid., p.49.

Chapter 14

1 Pimlott, *The Viking Atlas of World War II*, p.62.
2 Churchill, *The Second World War. Volume 3. The Grand Alliance*, p.75.
3 *History of the Royal Bombay Sappers and Miners 1939–47* (under compilation by Brigadier D.A. Barker-Wyatt at time of writing).
4 Ibid.
5 Mackenzie, *Eastern Epic*, p.44.
6 See Biggs, The End of Mussolini's East African Empire, p.144, for a full account of this often forgotten campaign.
7 Thomas and Mansingh, *Lt Gen P S Bhagat, PVSM, VC*, p.94.
8 Ibid., pp.103–4.
9 Ibid., p.141.
10 Churchill, *The Second World War. Volume 3. The Grand Alliance*, p.288.
11 Phillips, *The Greatest Raid of All*, p.105.
12 Ibid., p.52.
13 Ibid., p.163.
14 *Royal Engineers Journal*, Vol. 86, No. 3, September 1972, p.222.
15 Phillips, *The Greatest Raid of All*, p.75.
16 Ibid.
17 Family letter lent to author by Reg Durrant.
18 Ibid., p.233.
19 Ryder, *The Attack on St Nazaire*, p.71.

20 *Combined Operations, 1940–1942*, HMSO, 1943, p.96.
21 Lummis files, National Army Museum, quoting *The Times*, 4 August 1947.
22 Lummis files, National Army Museum.
23 Williams, Robin, *A Time in my Life*, unpublished memoir held in the Royal Engineers Library.
24 Letter to author, dated 13 February 1995.
25 Whittaker, *Some Talk of Private Armies*, p.76.
26 Ibid., pp.76–7.
27 Remark made to author by friend of Major Norman.
28 Slim, *Defeat into Victory*, p.381.
29 Pakenham-Walsh, *The History of the Royal Engineers*, Vol. 9, p.279.
30 PRO WO 172/7200, 58 Company's War Diary gives the factual detail from which this account is drawn.
31 Supplement to *London Gazette*, 28 June 1945.

Chapter 15

1 Adkin, *The Last Eleven? Winners of the Victoria Cross Since the Second World War.*

Books

Adkin, Mark, *The Charge*, Pen & Sword, 1996.
    The Last Eleven? Winners of the Victoria Cross Since the Second World War, Leo Cooper, 1991.

Bean, C.E.W., *The Official History of Australia in the War*, Angus and Robertson, 1921.
Bickers, Richard Townshend, *The First Great Air War*, Hodder & Stoughton, 1988.
Blomfield, David (ed.), *Lahore to Lucknow. The Indian Mutiny Journal of Arthur Moffat Lang*, Leo Cooper, 1992.
Blunden, Edmund (ed.), *The Poems of Wilfred Owen*, Chatto & Windus, 1955.
Boraston, Lieutenant-Colonel J.H., CB, OBE and Bax, Captain Cyril E.O., *The Eighth Division in War, 1914–1918*, The Medici Society, 1926.
Broke-Smith, Brigadier P.W.L., *The History of Early British Aeronautics*, Institution of Royal Engineers, Chatham.
Bryant, George, *Where the Prize is Highest*, Collins Brothers, Auckland, New Zealand, 1972.
Buzzell, Nora (compiler), *The Register of the Victoria Cross*, This England, 1988.

Carter, G.B., *Porton Down. 75 Years of Chemical and Biological Research*, HMSO, 1992.
Churchill, W.S., *The Story of the Malakand Field Force*, Longmans Green, 1901.
    The Second World War. Volume 3. The Grand Alliance, Reprint Society, 1952.
Clark, Alan, *The Donkeys*, Pimlico edition 1991 (first published Hutchinson, 1961).
Cole, Christopher, *McCudden VC*, William Kimber, 1967.
Conan Doyle, Arthur, *The Great Boer War*, Smith Elder, 1902.
Conolly, Captain T.W.J., *History of the Royal Sappers and Miners*, 2nd edition, Institution of Royal Engineers, 1887.
Coombs, Rose E.B., MBE, *Before Endeavours Fade*, After the Battle, 1983.
Creagh, Sir O'Moore, VC and Humphris, E.M., *The VC and DSO. Vol. 1. The Victoria Cross*, The Standard Art Book Co. Ltd., 1920.
Crook, M.J., *The Evolution of the Victoria Cross*, Midas Books in association with the Ogilby Trusts, 1975.

Droogleever, R.W.F., *The Road to Isandhlwana. Colonel Anthony Durnford in Natal and Zululand*, Greenhill Books, 1992.

Edmonds, Brigadier Sir James E., CB, CMG, *History of the Great War Based on Official Documents*, Macmillan, 1921–6.

Falls, Cyril, *The History of the 36th (Ulster) Division*, M'Caw, Stevenson and Orr, 1922.
The First World War, Longmans,1960.
Farwell, Byron, *The Great Boer War*, Allen Lane, 1976.
Fergusson, Bernard, *The Watery Maze*, Collins, 1961.
Foulkes, Major-General C.H., *"Gas!" – The Story of the Special Brigade*, Blackwood, 1934.
French, Patrick, *Younghusband. The Last Great Imperial Adventurer*, Harper Collins, 1994.

Giddings, Robert, *Imperial Echoes*, Leo Cooper, 1996.
Gillon, Captain Stair, *The Story of the 29th Division*, Thomas Nelson, 1925.
Gliddon, Gerald, *VCs of the First World War – 1914*, Alan Sutton, 1994.
Grieve, Captain W. Grant and Newman, Bernard, *Tunnellers*, Herbert Jenkins Ltd, 1936.

Hawker, Tyrrel M., *Hawker, VC*, Mitre Press, 1965.
Heathcote, T.A., *The Afghan Wars 1839–1919*, Osprey, 1980.
Hensman, Howard, *The Afghan War, 1870–80*.
Holme, Norman, *The Silver Wreath*, London, 1979.
Holt, Tonie and Valmai, *Battlefields of the First World War – A Traveller's Guide*, Pavilion Books, 1995.
Hopkirk, Peter, *The Great Game. On Secret Service in High Asia*, OUP paperback edition, 1990.
Hussey, Brigadier-General A.H. and Inman, Major D.S., *The Fifth Division in the Great War*, Nisbet, 1921.

James, Major-General E.R., *The Journal of My Life*, Royal Engineers Corps Library (undated).
Judd, Dennis, *The Crimean War*, Granada/William Clowes, 1975.

Kerry, Colonel A.J. and McDill, W.A., *The History of the Corps of the Royal Canadian Engineers. Vol. 1. 1749–1939*, Military Engineers Association of Canada, 1962.
Kinglake, A.W., *The Invasion of the Crimea*, Blackwood, 1877.
Kingston, William H.G., *Memoir of Lieut Charles Duncan Home*, Griffith and Farran, 1863.
Knight, E.F., *Where Three Empires Meet*, Longmans, Green and Company, 1919.
Knight, Ian, *Nothing Remains but to Fight. The Defence of Rorke's Drift 1879*, Greenhill, 1993.
Brave Men's Blood. The Epic of the Zulu War, 1879, Guild Publishing, 1990.

Livesey, Anthony, *The Viking Atlas of World War I*, Penguin, 1994.

Lloyd, Alan, *The Drums of Kumasi*, Longmans, 1964.

Ludendorff, Erich von, *My War Memories*, Hutchinson, 1919.

Macdonald, Lyn, *They Called it Passchendaele*, Michael Joseph, 1978.

Mackenzie, Compton, *Eastern Epic*, Chatto & Windus, 1951.

Mason, Philip, *A Matter of Honour*, Jonathan Cape, 1974.

Maurice, Major-General Sir Frederick, KCB, *History of the War in South Africa 1899–1902*, Vol. 1, Hurst & Blackett, 1906.
  The Last Four Months, Cassell, 1919.

McClintock, Mary Howard, *The Queen Thanks Sir Howard. The Life of Major-General Sir Howard Elphinstone, VC, KCB, CMG*, John Murray, 1945.

McCudden, James, VC, *Five Years in the Royal Flying Corps*, London, 1918.

Montgomery, Major-General Sir Archibald, KCMG, CB, *The Story of the Fourth Army in the Battles of the Hundred Days, August 8th to November 11th, 1918*, Hodder and Stoughton, 1919.

Moorehead, Alan, *Gallipoli*, Hamish Hamilton, 1958.

Morris, Donald R., *The Washing of the Spears*, Jonathan Cape, 1966.

Morris, James, *Heaven's Command*, Faber & Faber, 1973.
  Farewell the Trumpets. An Imperial Retreat, Penguin, 1979 (first published Faber, 1978).

Neame, Philip, *Playing With Strife*, Harrap, 1947.

Oughton, Frederick and Smyth, Commander Vernon, *Ace with One Eye*, Frederick Muller, 1963.

Paget, Lieutenant-Colonel W.H. and Mason, Lieutenant A.H., *Record of Expeditions against the North-West Tribes*, (official), 1884.

Pakenham, Thomas, *The Boer War*, Cardinal, 1991 (first published Weidenfeld and Nicolson, 1979).

Pakenham-Walsh, Major-General R.P., *The History of the Royal Engineers*, Vol. 9, Institution of Royal Engineers, 1958.

Pemberton, W. Baring, *Battles of the Crimean War*, Batsford, 1962.

Perkins, Roger, *The Kashmir Gate – Lieutenant Home and the Delhi VCs*, Picton Publishing, 1983.

Phillips, C.E. Lucas, *The Greatest Raid of All*, The Companion Book Club, 1959 (originally published by Heinemann).

Pimlott, John, *The Viking Atlas of World War II*, Penguin, 1995.

Pollock, John, *Gordon – The Man Behind the Legend*, Constable, 1993.

Porter, Major-General Whitworth, *The History of the Corps of Royal Engineers*, Vols 1 and 2, Institution of Royal Engineers, 1889.

Pritchard, Major-General H.L. (ed.), *History of the Corps of Royal Engineers*, Vol. 5, Institution of Royal Engineers, 1952.

Ranken, G., *Six Months at Sebastopol*, Westerton, 1857.

Richter, Donald, *Chemical Soldiers. British Gas Warfare in World War I*, University Press of Kansas, 1992.

Robson, Brian, *The Road to Kabul. The Second Afghan War, 1878–1881*, Arms and Armour Press, 1986.

Ryder, Commander R.E.D., *The Attack on St Nazaire*, John Murray, 1947.

Sandes, Lieutenant-Colonel E.W.C., *The Military Engineer in India*, Vols 1 and 2, Institution of Royal Engineers, 1933.
    The Indian Sappers and Miners, Institution of Royal Engineers, 1948.

Slim, Field Marshal Sir William, *Defeat into Victory*, Cassell, 1956.

Smyth, Sir John, VC, *The Story of the Victoria Cross, 1856–1963*, Frederick Muller, 1963.

Stewart, Lieutenant-Colonel H., CMG, DSO, MC, *Official History of New Zealand's Effort in the Great War. Vol II. France*, Whitcombe & Tombs Ltd, New Zealand, 1921.

Swinton, Captain E.D., *The Defence of Duffer's Drift*, Leo Cooper, 1990 (first published 1907).

Taylor, A. Cameron, *General Sir Alexander Taylor, G.C.B., RE.: His Times, His Friends, and His Work*, Williams and Norgate, 1913.

Terraine, John, *Mons: The Retreat to Victory*, Batsford, 1960.
    The Road to Passchendaele, Leo Cooper, 1977.
    To Win a War. 1918: The Year of Victory, Papermac, 1986 (first published Sidgwick and Jackson, 1978).

Thackeray, Colonel C.B. (ed.), *A Subaltern in the Indian Mutiny*, reprinted in the *Royal Engineers Journal*, December 1931.

Thackeray, Sir E.T., *The Royal (Bengal) Engineers*, London, 1900.

Thomas, Lieutenant-General Mathew, PVSM, AVSM, VSM and Mansingh, Jasjit, *Lt Gen P S Bhagat, PVSM, VC*, Lancer International, New Delhi, 1994.

Toomey, T.E., *Heroes of the Victoria Cross*, Newnes, 1895.

Vaughan, Edwin Campion, *Some Desperate Glory*, Leo Cooper, 1981.

Vetch, Colonel R.H., CB, *Life, Letters, and Diaries of Lieut-General Sir Gerald Graham VC, GCB, RE*, Blackwood, 1901.

Vibart, Colonel H. M., *Addiscombe. Its Heroes and Men of Note*, Constable, 1894.

Ward, Major C.H., DSO, MC, *The 56th Division*, John Murray, 1921.

Warner, Philip, *Passchendaele*, Sidgwick and Jackson, 1987.
    Loos, William Kimber, 1976.

Watson, Colonel C.M., *History of the Corps of Royal Engineers*, Vol. 3, Royal Engineers Institute, Chatham, 1915.

Whittaker, Len, *Some Talk of Private Armies*, Albanium Publishing, 1984.

Wilkins, Philip, *History of the VC*, Constable, 1904.

Wilson, H.W. (ed.), *The Great War*, Vol. 4, Amalgamated Press, 1914–18.
Woodham Smith, Cecil, *The Reason Why*, Constable, 1953.

Articles
Biggs, Brigadier M.W., The End of Mussolini's East African Empire, *Royal Engineers Journal*, August 1992.
Buckland, Major-General Sir Reginald, Demolitions Carried Out at Mons and During the Retreat, 1914, *Royal Engineers Journal*, Vol. 46, March 1932.

Elphinstone, Captain H.C., VC and Jones, Major-General Harry D., Siege of Sebastopol, 1845–1855, *Journal of the Operations Conducted by the Corps of Royal Engineers*, 1859.

Home, Lieutenant-Colonel R., Engineer Operations on the Gold Coast, *Professional Papers of the Royal Engineers*, New Series, Vol. XXIII.

Jackson, Major-General Sir Louis, Memories of Afghanistan in 1879, *Royal Engineers Journal* Vol. 52, 1938.

Leach, Brevet Major E.P., VC, Operations on the Halmand and Battle of Maiwand, *Royal Engineers Journal*, December 1880.
Leach, Brigadier-General H.P., CB, CBE, DSO, author of memoir of E.P. Leach in the *Royal Engineers Journal*, Vol. 18, 1913.

Rhodes, Dr John N., An Officer Not Only of Great Talent But of Rare Coolness and Courage – Major General W.S. Trevor VC Royal (Bengal) Engineers 1831 to 1937, *Royal Engineers Journal*, Vol. 110, No. 2, August 1996.
Royal Engineers Museum and Library Information Sheet No. 3: *J R M Chard VC RE and the Defence of Rorke's Drift*.

Snelling, Stephen J., Forlorn Hope at Dewangiri, *Medal News*, October 1989.
Statement of Mehlo-ka-Zulu, son of Sirayo, one of Ketchwayo's Chiefs, *Royal Engineers Journal*, February 1880.

Journals and Periodicals
Fermanagh Times
Medal News
Professional Papers of the Royal Engineers: New Series
Royal Engineers Journal
Sapper magazine
Soldiers of the Queen

Official, Library and Museum Sources
Combined Operations, 1940–1942, HMSO, 1943.
Company History 409th Lowland Field Company (unpublished), Royal Engineers Library, Chatham.

Frontier and Overseas Expeditions from India, Army Headquarters, Simla, 1907.

Gerald Graham letters, Royal Engineers Museum and Library.

Information Sheet No 3: *Lieut J R M Chard VC RE and the Defence of Rorke's Drift*, Royal Engineers Museum and Library.

National Army Museum, Lummis files.

Parke Jones letters, Royal Engineers Museum and Library.

PRO WO 97/1361

PRO WO 95/1403

PRO WO 95/1727

PRO WO 95/1713

PRO WO 172/7200

Royal Engineers Historical Society Occasional Paper No. 8, *Sergeant-Major W.J. Lendrim VC* (T.M.J. Riordan MM, January 1987).

Williams, Robin, *A Time in my Life*, unpublished memoir held in the Royal Engineers Library, 1994.

Work of the Royal Engineers in the European War 1914–1918, Institution of Royal Engineers, Chatham.

Alphabetical List of the Sapper VCs with Citations

Note: Decorations shown with an asterisk indicate a bar, i.e. subsequent award of the decoration.

Sapper Adam ARCHIBALD

(Eventually Mr A. Archibald, VC)
Born 14 January 1879, died 11 March 1957.
Won VC on the Sambre-Oise canal at Ors on 4 November 1918. Unit: 218 Field Company.
VC presented by King George V at Buckingham Palace on 31 May 1919.
Grave or cremation details: Warriston Crematorium, Edinburgh.
Location of VC: not publicly held.

Citation: *For most conspicuous bravery and self-sacrifice on 4 November 1918, near Ors, when with a party building a floating bridge across the canal. He was foremost in the work under a heavy artillery barrage and machine-gun fire. The latter was directed at him from a few yards' distance while he was working on the cork floats; nevertheless he persevered in his task, and his example and efforts were such that the bridge, which was essential to the success of the operations, was very quickly completed. The supreme devotion to duty of this gallant sapper, who collapsed from gas-poisoning on completion of his work, was beyond all praise.*
(*London Gazette*: 6 January 1919)

Captain Fenton John AYLMER

(Eventually Lieutenant-General Sir Fenton Aylmer, Bart, VC, KCB)
Born 5 April 1862, died 3 September 1935.
Won VC at Hunza-Nagar on 2 December 1891. Unit: 4th Company, Bengal Sappers and Miners.
VC presented by GOC Rawalpindi District at Rawalpindi on 28 October 1892.
Grave or cremation details: cremated at Golders Green (CC 33382).
Location of VC: Royal Engineers Museum.

Citation: *For his conspicuous bravery in the assault and capture of the Nilt Fort, on 2 December 1891. This officer accompanied the storming party, burst open the inner gate with gun-cotton, which he placed and ignited, and though severely wounded, once in the leg and twice in the right hand, fired nineteen shots with his revolver, killing several of the enemy, and remained fighting, until, fainting from loss of blood, he was carried out of the action.*
(*London Gazette*: 12 July 1892)

Corporal Cyril Royston Guyton BASSETT

(Eventually Colonel C.R.G. Bassett, VC)
Born 3 January 1892, died 9 January 1983.
Won VC at Chunuk Bair ridge, Gallipoli, on 7 August 1915. Unit: New Zealand
Divisional Signal Company.
VC presented by King George V at Buckingham Palace on 3 February 1916.
Grave or cremation details: North Shore Crematorium, Albany, New Zealand.
Location of VC: not publicly held.

Citation: *For most conspicuous bravery and devotion to duty on the Chunuk Bair ridge in the
Gallipoli Peninsula on 7 August 1915. After the New Zealand Infantry Brigade had attacked
and established itself on the ridge, Corporal Bassett, in full daylight and under a continuous fire,
succeeded in laying a telephone line from the old position to the new one on Chunuk Bair. He has
subsequently been brought to notice for further excellent and most gallant work connected with
the repair of telephone lines by day and night under heavy fire.*
(*London Gazette*: 15 October 1915)

Lieutenant Mark Sever BELL

(Eventually Colonel M.S. Bell, VC, CB, ADC)
Born 15 May 1843, died 26 June 1906.
Won VC at Ordahsu, Gold Coast (now Ghana), on 4 February 1874.
VC presented by Queen Victoria at Windsor Castle on 26 November 1874.
Grave or cremation details: All Souls' Church, All Souls Road, South Ascot.
Location of VC: Royal Engineers Museum.

Citation: *For his distinguished bravery and zealous, resolute and self-devoted conduct at the
battle of Ordahsu on the 4 February 1874, whilst serving under the immediate orders of
Colonel Sir John Chetham McLeod, KCB, of the 42nd Regiment, who commanded the
Advanced Guard. Sir John McLeod was an eye witness of his gallant and distinguished conduct on the occasion, and considers that this officer's fearless and resolute bearing, being always
in the front, urging on and encouraging an unarmed working party of Fantee labourers, who
were exposed not only to the fire of the enemy, but to the wild and irregular fire of the Native
Troops in the rear, contributed very materially to the success of the day. By his example, he
made these men do what no European party was ever required to do in warfare, namely, to work
under fire in the face of the enemy without a covering party.*
(*London Gazette*: 20 November 1874)

Second Lieutenant Premindra Singh BHAGAT

(Eventually Lieutenant-General Premindra Singh Bhagat, PVSM, VC)
Born 14 October 1918, died 23 May 1975.
Won VC near Metemma, Abyssinia, on 31 January–1 February 1941. Unit: 21
Field Company, Bombay Sappers and Miners.
VC presented by the Viceroy, HE the Marquess of Linlithgow KT, GCSI,
GCIE at Delhi on 10 November 1941.

Grave or cremation details: cremated; ashes consigned to River Moola, Poona.
Location of VC: Bombay Sappers Group Museum, Kirkee, Poona.

Citation: *For most conspicuous gallantry on active service in the Middle East. During the pursuit of the enemy following the capture of Metemma on the night 31 January–1 February 1941, Second-Lieutenant Bhagat was in command of a section of a Field Company, Sappers and Miners, detailed to accompany the leading mobile troops (Bren Carriers) to clear the road and adjacent areas of mines. For a period of four days and over a distance of 55 miles this officer in the leading carrier led the Column. He detected and supervised the clearing of fifteen minefields. Speed being essential, he worked at high pressure from dawn to dusk each day. On two occasions when his carrier was blown up with casualties to others, and on a third occasion when ambushed and under close enemy fire he himself carried straight on with his task. He refused relief when worn out with strain and fatigue and with one eardrum punctured by an explosion, on the grounds that he was now better qualified to continue his task to the end.*

His coolness, persistence over a period of 96 hours, and gallantry, not only in battle, but throughout the long period when the safety of the Column and the speed at which it could advance were dependent on his personal efforts, were of the highest order.
(*London Gazette*: 10 June 1941)

Sergeant John CARMICHAEL

(Eventually Lieutenant J. Carmichael, VC)
Born 1 April 1893, died 26 December 1977.
Won VC at Hill 60, Zwarteleen, Belgium, on 8 September 1917. Unit: 9th
Battalion The North Staffordshire Regiment (The Prince of Wales's).
VC presented by King George V at Buckingham Palace on 22 June 1918.
Grave or cremation details: Landward Cemetery, New Monkland.
Location of VC: Staffordshire Regiment Museum, Lichfield.

Citation: *For most conspicuous bravery. When excavating a trench, Sergeant Carmichael saw that a grenade had been unearthed and had started to burn. He immediately rushed to the spot, and shouting to his men to get clear, placed his steel helmet over the grenade and stood on the helmet. The grenade exploded and blew him out of the trench. Sergeant Carmichael could have thrown the bomb out of this trench, but he realised that by doing so he would have endangered the lives of the men working on the top. By this act of resource and self-sacrifice Sergeant Carmichael undoubtedly saved many men from injury, but it resulted in serious injury to himself.*
(*London Gazette*: 17 October 1917)

Lieutenant John Rouse Merriott CHARD

(Eventually Colonel J.R.M. Chard, VC)
Born 21 December 1847, died 1 November 1897.
Won VC at Rorke's Drift, Natal, on 22/23 January 1879. Unit: 5 Field Company.
VC presented by Lord Wolseley at St Paul's Mission Station, near Inkwenken
Camp, Zululand, on 15 July 1879.
Grave or cremation details: Parish Church of St John the Baptist, Hatch
Beauchamp.

Location of VC: not publicly held. In 1972 Chard's South Africa Medal 1877–1879 with 1879 clasp and a replica VC were purchased by Stanley Baker, the actor who took the part of Chard in the film *Zulu*. The medals changed hands again on Baker's death and were lodged with Spink and Son who had the metal analysed. The analysis showed that the bronze was identical to bronze from the source from which all VCs are struck. Spinks therefore believe the 'replica' to be Chard's original.

Citation (to be read in conjunction with Lieutenant Bromhead): *For their gallant conduct at the defence of Rorke's Drift, on the occasion of the attack by the Zulus, on 22 and 23 January 1879. The Lieutenant-General commanding the troops reports that had it not been for the fine example and excellent behaviour of these two officers under the most trying circumstances, the defence of Rorke's Drift post would not have been conducted with that intelligence and tenacity which so successfully characterised it.*

The Lieutenant-General adds that its success must, in a great degree, be attributed to the two young officers who exercised the chief command on the occasion in question.
(*London Gazette*: 2 May 1879)

Major Brett Mackay CLOUTMAN

(Eventually His Honour Lieutenant-Colonel Sir Brett Cloutman, VC, MC)
Born 7 November 1891, died 15 August 1971.
Won VC at Quartes Bridge at Pont-sur-Sambre on 6 November 1918. Unit: 59 Field Company.
VC presented by King George V at Buckingham Palace on 13 February 1919.
Grave or cremation details: cremated at Golders Green; ashes spread near his brother's grave in Norfolk Cemetery, Albert, France.
Location of VC: Royal Engineers Museum.

Citation: *For most conspicuous bravery on 6 November 1918, at Pont-sur-Sambre, Major Cloutman, after reconnoitring the river crossings, found the Quartes Bridge almost intact, but prepared for demolition. Leaving his party under cover, he went forward alone, swam across the river, and having cut the 'leads' from the charges, returned the same way despite the fact that the bridge and all approaches thereto were swept by enemy shells and machine-gun fire at close range. Although the bridge was blown up later in the day by other means, the abutments remained intact.*
(*London Gazette*: 31 January 1919)

Brigadier-General Clifford COFFIN

(Eventually Major-General C. Coffin, VC, CB, DSO*)
Born 10 February 1870, died 4 February 1959.
Won VC at Westhoek Ridge, Ypres, on 31 July 1917. Unit: 25 Infantry Brigade.
VC presented by King George V at Buckingham Palace on 2 January 1918.
Grave or cremation details: Holy Trinity Churchyard, Coleman's Hatch, Kent.
Location of VC: Royal Engineers Museum.

Citation: *For most conspicuous bravery and devotion to duty. On 31 July when his command was held up in attack owing to heavy machine-gun and rifle fire from front and right flank, and was establishing itself in a forward shell-hole line, he went forward and made an inspection of his front posts. Though under the heaviest fire from both machine-guns and rifles, and in full view of the enemy, he showed an utter disregard of personal danger, walking quietly from shell-hole to shell-hole, giving advice generally, and cheering the men by his presence. His very gallant conduct had the greatest effect on all ranks, and it was largely owing to his personal courage and example that the shell-hole line was held in spite of the very heaviest fire. Throughout the day his calm courage and cheerfulness exercised the greatest influence over all with whom he came in contact, and it is generally agreed that Brigadier-General Coffin's splendid example saved the situation, and had it not been for his action the line would certainly have been driven back.*
(*London Gazette*: 14 September 1917)

Lieutenant James Morris Colquhoun COLVIN

(Eventually Colonel J.M.C. Colvin, VC)
Born 26 August 1870, died 7 December 1945.
Won VC at Bilot, Mamund Valley, India (now Pakistan), on 16 September 1897.
Unit: 4th Company Bengal Sappers and Miners.
VC presented by Queen Victoria at Windsor Castle on 19 July 1898.
Grave or cremation details: cremated at Ipswich; buried at Copford Green, near Colchester.
Location of VC: not publicly held.

Citation (to be read in conjunction with Lieutenant Watson): *On the same occasion, after Lieutenant Watson had been incapacitated by his wounds from further effort, Lieutenant Colvin continued the fight and persisted in two more attempts to clear the enemy out of the dark and still burning village. He was conspicuous during the whole night for his devotion to duty to his men in the most exposed positions under heavy fire from the enemy.*
(*London Gazette*: 20 May 1898)

Corporal James Lennox DAWSON

(Eventually Colonel J.L. Dawson, VC)
Born 25 December 1891, died 15 February 1967.
Won VC at Loos on 13 October 1915. Unit: 187 Field Company.
VC presented by King George V at Buckingham Palace on 15 December 1915.
Grave or cremation details: Eastbourne Crematorium, Sussex, Area AL/4.
Location of VC: Glasgow University.

Citation: *For most conspicuous bravery and devotion to duty on 13 October 1915, at Hohenzollern Redoubt. During a gas attack, when the trenches were full of men, he walked backwards and forwards along the parados, fully exposed to a very heavy fire, in order to be the better able to give directions to his own sappers, and to clear the infantry out of the sections of the trench that were full of gas. Finding three leaking gas cylinders, he rolled them some sixteen*

yards away from the trench, again under very heavy fire, and then fired rifle bullets into them to let the gas escape. There is no doubt that the cool gallantry of Corporal Dawson on this occasion saved many men from being gassed.
(*London Gazette*: 7 December 1915)

Lieutenant Robert James Thomas DIGBY JONES

Born 27 September 1876, died 6 January 1900.
Won VC at Wagon Hill, Ladysmith, South Africa, on 6 January 1900. Unit: 23 Field Company.
VC sent to parents by post on order of King Edward VII on 30 August 1902.
Grave or cremation details: Ladysmith Cemetery.
Location of VC: Royal Engineers Museum.

Citation (to be read in conjunction with Trooper Albrecht, VC): *Would have been recommended for the Victoria Cross had they survived, on account of their having, during the attack on Wagon Hill (Ladysmith) on 6 January 1900, displayed conspicuous bravery and gallant conduct in leading the force which reoccupied the top of the hill at a critical moment just as the three foremost attacking Boers reached it, the leader being shot by Lieutenant Jones and the two others by Albrecht.*
(*London Gazette*: 8 August 1902)

Lieutenant James DUNDAS

(Eventually Captain J. Dundas, VC)
Born 10 September 1842, died 23 December 1879.
Won VC at Dewangiri, Bhutan, on 30 April 1865.
VC presented by Major-General Fordyce, commanding the Presidency Division, at The Maidan, Calcutta on 23 March 1868.
Grave or cremation details: Seah Sang, Afghanistan.
Location of VC: not publicly held.

Citation (to be read in conjunction with Lieutenant Trevor): *For their gallant conduct at the attack on the blockhouse at Dewan-Giri, in Bhootan on 30 April 1865.*

Major-General Tombs, VC, CB, the officer in command at the time, reports that a party of the enemy, from 180 to 200 in number, had barricaded themselves in the blockhouse in question, which they continued to defend after the rest of the position had been carried, and the main body was in retreat. The blockhouse, which was loopholed, was the key of the enemy's position. Seeing no officer of the storming party near him, and being anxious that the place should be taken immediately, as any protracted resistance might have caused the main body of the Bhooteas to rally, the British force having been fighting in a broiling sun on a very steep and difficult ground for upwards of three hours, the General in command ordered these two officers to show the way into the blockhouse. They had to climb a wall which was 14 feet high, and then to enter a house occupied by some 200 desperate men, head foremost through an opening not more than two feet wide between the top of the wall and the roof of the blockhouse. Major-General Tombs states that on speaking to the Sikh soldiers around him, and telling them in Hindoostani to swarm up

the wall, none of them responded to the call until these two officers had shown them the way, when they followed with the greatest alacrity. Both of them were wounded.
(*London Gazette*: 31 December 1867)

Sergeant Thomas Frank DURRANT

Born 17 October 1918, died 28 March 1942.
Won VC off St Nazaire, France, on 27/28 March 1942. Unit: No 1 Commando.
VC presented by King George VI to Sergeant Durrant's mother at Buckingham Palace on 29 October 1946.
Grave or cremation details: Escoublac-la-Baule War Cemetery, France, Plot I, Row D, Grave 11.
Location of VC: Royal Engineers Museum.

Citation: *For great gallantry, skill and devotion to duty when in charge of a Lewis gun in HM Motor Launch 306 in the St Nazaire raid on 28 March 1942.*

Motor Launch 306 came under heavy fire while proceeding up the River Loire towards the port. Sergeant Durrant, in his position abaft the bridge, where he had no cover or protection, engaged enemy gun positions and searchlights ashore. During this engagement he was severely wounded in the arm but refused to leave his gun. The Motor Launch subsequently went down the river and was attacked by a German destroyer at 50–60 yards range, and often closer. In this action Sergeant Durrant continued to fire at the destroyer's bridge with the greatest of coolness and with complete disregard of the enemy's fire. The Motor Launch was illuminated by the enemy searchlight, and Sergeant Durrant drew on himself the individual attention of the enemy guns, and was again wounded in many places. Despite these further wounds he stayed in his exposed position, still firing his gun, although after a time only able to support himself by holding on to the gun mounting.

After a running fight, the Commander of the German destroyer called on the Motor Launch to surrender. Sergeant Durrant's answer was a further burst of fire at the destroyer's bridge. Although now very weak, he went on firing, using drums of ammunition as fast as they could be replaced. A renewed attack by the enemy vessel eventually silenced the fire of the Motor Launch, but Sergeant Durrant refused to give up until the destroyer came alongside, grappled the Motor Launch and took prisoner those who remained alive.

Sergeant Durrant's gallant fight was commended by the German officers on boarding the Motor Launch. This very gallant non-commissioned officer later died of the many wounds received in action.
(*London Gazette*: 19 June 1945)

Lieutenant Howard Crawfurd ELPHINSTONE

(Eventually Major-General Sir Howard Elphinstone, VC, KCB, CMG)
Born 12 December 1829, died 8 March 1890.
Won VC at Sebastopol, Crimea, on 18 June 1855.
VC presented by Queen Victoria at Southsea Common, Hampshire, on 2 August 1858.
Grave or cremation details: lost at sea.
Location of VC: not publicly held.

Citation: *For fearless conduct, in having, on the night after the unsuccessful attack on the Redan, volunteered to command a party of volunteers, who proceeded to search for and bring back the scaling ladders left behind after the repulse; and while successfully performing this task of rescuing trophies from the Russians, conducted a persevering search close to the enemy, for wounded men, twenty of whom he rescued and brought back to the Trenches.*
(*London Gazette*: 2 June 1858)

Major George de Cardonnel Elmsall FINDLAY

(Eventually Colonel G. de C.E. Findlay, VC, MC*)
Born 20 August 1889, died 26 June 1967.
Won VC on the Sambre-Oise canal, near Catillon, on 4 November 1918. Unit: 409 (Lowland) Field Company.
VC presented by King George V at Buckingham Palace on 27 November 1919.
Grave or cremation details: Kilmaronock, Gartocharn, Nr Balloch, Dunbartonshire.
Location of VC: Royal Engineers Museum.

Citation: *For conspicuous bravery and devotion to duty during the forcing of the Sambre-Oise canal at the Lock, two miles from Catillon, on 4 November 1918, when in charge of the bridging operations at this crossing. Major Findlay was with the leading bridging and assaulting parties which came under heavy fire while trying to cross the dyke between the forming-up line and the Lock. The casualties were severe and the advance was stopped. Nevertheless, under heavy and incessant fire he collected what men he could and repaired the bridges, in spite of heavy casualties in officers and other ranks. Although wounded, Major Findlay continued his task and after two unsuccessful efforts, owing to his men being swept down, he eventually placed the bridge in position across the Lock, and was the first man across, subsequently remaining at this post of danger till further work was completed. His cool and gallant behaviour inspired volunteers from different units at a critical time when men became casualties almost as soon as they joined him in the fire-swept zone, and it was due to Major Findlay's gallantry and devotion to duty that this most important crossing was effected.*
(*London Gazette*: 15 May 1919)

Sergeant Samuel FORSYTH

Born 3 April 1891, died 24 August 1918.
Won VC at Grévillers, France, on 24 August 1918. Unit: New Zealand Engineers attached to 2nd Battalion Auckland Regiment.
VC presented by King George V to next-of-kin at Buckingham Palace on 23 November 1918.
Grave or cremation details: Plot I, Row 1, Grave 39, Adanac Military Cemetery, France.
Location of VC: not publicly held.

Citation: *For most conspicuous bravery and devotion to duty in attack. On nearing the objective, his company came under heavy machine-gun fire. Through Sergeant Forsyth's dashing leadership and total disregard of danger, three machine-gun positions were rushed, and the crews*

taken prisoner before they could inflict many casualties on our troops. During the subsequent advance his company came under heavy fire from several machine-guns, two of which he located by a daring reconnaissance. In his endeavour to gain support from a Tank, he was wounded, but after having the wound bandaged, he again got in touch with the Tank, which, in the face of very heavy fire from machine-guns and anti-Tank guns, he endeavoured to lead with magnificent coolness, to a favourable position. The Tank, however, was put out of action. Sergeant Forsyth then organised the Tank crew and several of his men into a section, and led them to a position where the machine-guns could be outflanked. Always under heavy fire, he directed them into positions which brought about a retirement of the enemy machine-guns and enabled the advance to continue. This gallant NCO was at this moment killed by a sniper. From the commencement of the attack until the time of his death Sergeant Forsyth's courage and coolness, combined with great power of initiative, proved an invaluable incentive to all who were with him, and he undoubtedly saved many casualties among his comrades.
(*London Gazette*: 22 October 1918)

Lieutenant Charles Augustus GOODFELLOW

(Eventually Lieutenant-General C.A. Goodfellow, VC, CB)
Born 27 November 1836, died 1 September 1915.
Won VC at Kathiawar, India, on 6 October 1859. Unit: Bombay Engineers (with 4th Company Bombay Sappers and Miners).
VC presented by Major-General Green, commanding Mhow Division at Mhow, India, on 11 September 1863.
Grave or cremation details: Leamington Spa Cemetery.
Location of VC: Royal Engineers Museum.

Citation: *For gallant conduct at the attack on the Fort of Beyt on 6 October 1859. On that occasion a soldier of the 28th Regiment was shot under the walls, under a sharp fire of matchlocks, and he bore off the body of the soldier who was then dead, but whom he at first supposed to be wounded only.*
(*London Gazette*: 16 April 1863)

Lieutenant Gerald GRAHAM

(Eventually Lieutenant-General Sir Gerald Graham, VC, GCB, GCMG)
Born 27 June 1831, died 17 December 1899.
Won VC at Sebastopol, Crimea on 18 June 1855.
VC presented by Queen Victoria at Hyde Park, London, on 26 June 1857.
Grave or cremation details: East-the-Water Cemetery, Bideford, grave C#523.
Location of VC: Royal Engineers Museum.

Citation: *Determined gallantry at the head of the ladder-party, at the assault of the Redan, on 18 June 1855. Devoted heroism in sallying out of the trenches on numerous occasions, and bringing in wounded officers and men.*
(*London Gazette*: 24 February 1857)

Sapper William HACKETT

Born 11 June 1873, died 27 June 1916.
Won VC at Givenchy, France, on 22 June 1916. Unit: 254 Tunnelling Company.
VC presented by King George V to his widow at Buckingham Palace on 29
November 1916.
Grave or cremation details: Givenchy, France (body not recovered).
Commemorated on Ploegsteert Memorial, Belgium, Town Memorial,
Mexborough (special plaque), Manvers Colliery Memorial, Yorkshire.
Location of VC: Royal Engineers Museum.

Citation: *For most conspicuous bravery when entombed with four others in a gallery owing to
the explosion of an enemy mine. After working for twenty hours a hole was made through the
fallen earth and broken timber, and the outside party was met. Sapper Hackett helped three of
them through the hole and could easily have followed, but refused to leave the fourth, who had
been seriously injured, saying, 'I am a tunneller and must look after the others first'. Meantime
the hole was getting smaller, yet he still refused to leave his injured comrade. Finally the gallery
collapsed, and though the rescue party worked desperately for four days, the attempt to reach the
two men failed. Sapper Hackett, well knowing the nature of sliding earth, and the chances
against him, deliberately gave his life for his comrade.*
(*London Gazette*: 5 August 1916)

Lieutenant Reginald Clare HART

(Eventually General Sir Reginald Hart, VC, GCB, KCVO)
Born 11 June 1848, died 19 October 1931.
Won VC in the Bazar Valley, Afghanistan, on 31 January 1879.
VC presented by Queen Victoria at Windsor Castle on 9 December 1879.
Grave or cremation details: Netherbury Cemetery, Dorset.
Location of VC: not publicly held.

Citation: *For his gallant conduct in risking his own life in endeavouring to save the life of a private soldier. The Lieutenant-General commanding the 2nd Division, Peshawar Field Force,
reports that when on convoy duty with that Force on the 31 January 1879, Lieutenant Hart of
the Royal Engineers took the initiative in running some 1,200 yards to the rescue of a wounded Sowar of the 13th Bengal Lancers in a river-bed exposed to the fire of the enemy, of
unknown strength, from both flanks, and also from a party in the river-bed. Lieutenant Hart
reached the wounded Sowar, drove off the enemy and brought him under cover with the aid of
some soldiers who accompanied him on the way.*
(*London Gazette*: 6 June 1879)

Private Norman HARVEY

(Eventually Company Quartermaster-Sergeant N. Harvey, VC)
Born 6 April 1899, died 16 February 1942.
Won VC at Ingoyghem, Belgium on 25 October 1918. Unit: 1st Battalion, The
Royal Inniskilling Fusiliers.
VC presented by King George V at Buckingham Palace on 15 May 1919.

Grave or cremation details: Khayat Beach War Cemetery, Haifa.
Location of VC: Royal Inniskilling Fusiliers' Museum, Enniskillen.

Citation: *For most conspicuous bravery and devotion to duty near Ingoyghem on 25 October 1918, when his battalion was held up and suffered heavy losses from enemy machine guns. On his own initiative he rushed forward and engaged the enemy single-handed, disposing of twenty enemy and capturing two guns. Later, when his company was checked by another enemy strong point, he again rushed forward alone and put the enemy to flight. Subsequently after dark he voluntarily carried out 'single-handed' an important reconnaissance and gained valuable information. Private Harvey throughout the day displayed the greatest valour, and his several actions enabled the line to advance, saved many casualties, and inspired all.*
(*London Gazette*: 6 January 1919)

Captain Lanoe George HAWKER

(Eventually Major L.G. Hawker, VC, DSO)
Born 30 December 1890, died 23 November 1916.
Won VC on 25 July 1915. Unit: 6 Squadron, Royal Flying Corps.
VC presented by King George V at Buckingham Palace on 5 October 1915.
Grave or cremation details: no grave. Commemorated on Arras Memorial
(Faubourg d'Amiens Cemetery and Memorials to the Missing), France, and in
Longparish Church, Hampshire.
Location of VC: RAF Museum, Hendon.

Citation: *For most conspicuous bravery and very great ability on 25 July 1915. When flying alone he attacked three German aeroplanes in succession. The first managed eventually to escape, the second was driven to ground damaged, and the third, which he attacked at a height of about 10,000 feet, was driven to earth in our lines, the pilot and observer being killed. The personal bravery shown by this Officer was of the very highest order, as the enemy's aircraft were armed with machine guns, and all carried a passenger as well as the pilot.*
(*London Gazette*: 24 August 1915)

Lieutenant Duncan Charles HOME

Born 10 June 1828, died 1 October 1857.
Won VC at Delhi on 14 September 1857. Unit: Bengal Engineers.
VC sent by post to father on 7 July 1858.
Grave or cremation details: Bolandshah, India.
Location of VC: not publicly held. Home's medals were sold at Sotheby's in
December 1990. The catalogue recorded: 'The original Cross, unfortunately, was
lost in the 1920s. The children took it out of the house while "playing soldiers"
and it was lost in a field. Intensive searches then and later failed to locate it.'

Citation: (*MEMORANDUM. Lieutenants Duncan Charles Home and Philip Salkeld, upon whom the Victoria Cross was provisionally conferred by Major-General Sir Archdale Wilson, Bart, KCB) For their conspicuous bravery in the performance of the desperate duty of blowing in the Cashmere Gate of the Fortress of Delhi in broad daylight, under a heavy fire of*

musketry, on the morning of 14 September 1857, preparatory to the assault, would have been recommended to Her Majesty for confirmation in that distinction had they survived.
(*London Gazette*: 18 June 1858)

Lieutenant James John McLeod INNES

(Eventually Lieutenant-General J.J. McLeod Innes, VC, CB)
Born 5 February 1830, died 13 December 1907.
Won VC at Sultanpore, India, on 23 February 1858. Unit: Bengal Engineers.
VC presented by the Governor General, Lord Canning, at Fort William, Calcutta, on 1 July 1859.
Grave or cremation details: New Cambridge Cemetery, Cambridge.
Location of VC: Royal Engineers Museum.

Citation: *At the action of Sultanpore, Lieutenant Innes, far in advance of the leading skirmishers, was the first to secure a gun which the enemy were abandoning. Retiring from this, they rallied round another gun further back, from which the shot would, in another instant, have ploughed through our advancing columns, when Lieutenant Innes rode up, unsupported, shot the gunner who was about to apply the match, and, remaining undaunted at his post, the mark for a hundred matchlock men, who were sheltered in some adjoining huts, kept the artillerymen at bay until assistance reached him.*
(*London Gazette*: 24 December 1858)

Lance-Corporal Charles Alfred JARVIS

(Eventually Corporal C.A. Jarvis, VC)
Born 29 March 1881, died 19 November 1948.
Won VC at Jemappes on 23 August 1914. Unit: 57 Field Company.
VC presented by King George V at Buckingham Palace on 13 January 1915.
Grave or cremation details: Cupar Cemetery, Fife.
Location of VC: Birmingham Museum.

Citation: *For great gallantry at Jemappes on 23 August, in working for one and a half hours under heavy fire in full view of the enemy, and in successfully firing charges for the demolition of a bridge.*
(*London Gazette*: 16 November 1914)

Second Lieutenant Frederick Henry JOHNSON

(Eventually Major F.H. Johnson, VC)
Born 15 August 1890, died 26 November 1917.
Won VC at Loos on 25 September 1915. Unit: 73 Field Company.
VC presented by King George V at Buckingham Palace on 22 December 1915.
Grave or cremation details: no grave. Commemorated on Cambrai Memorial.
Location of VC: not publicly held.

Citation: *For most conspicuous bravery and devotion to duty in the attack on Hill 70, on 25 September 1915. Second Lieutenant Johnson was with a section of his company of the Royal Engineers. Although wounded in the leg, he stuck to his duty throughout the attack, led several charges on the German redoubt, and at a very critical time, under heavy fire, repeatedly rallied the men who were near him. By his splendid example and cool courage he was mainly instrumental in saving the situation and in establishing firmly his part of the position which had been taken. He remained at his post until relieved in the evening.*
(*London Gazette*: 18 November 1915)

Captain William Henry JOHNSTON

(Eventually Major W.H. Johnston, VC)
Born 21 December 1879, died 8 June 1915.
Won VC at Missy, near Moulin des Roches, River Aisne, France, on 14 September 1914. Unit: 59 Field Company.
VC presented by King George V at General Headquarters, France, on 3 December 1914.
Grave or cremation details: Perth Cemetery (China Wall), Zillebeke, Plot III, Row C, Grave 12.
Location of VC: Royal Engineers Museum.

Citation: *At Missy on 14 September, under a heavy fire all day until 7 p.m. worked with his own hands two rafts, bringing back wounded and returning with ammunition, thus enabling advanced Brigade to maintain its position across the river.*
(*London Gazette*: 25 November 1914)

Corporal Frank Howard KIRBY

(Eventually Group Captain F.H. Kirby, VC, CBE, DCM)
Born 12 November 1871, died 8 July 1956.
Won VC near Bronkhorstspruit, Delagoa Bay Railway, Pretoria, South Africa, on 2 June 1900. Unit: No. 1 Field Troop, 1st Division.
VC presented by the Duke of York at Cape Town on 19 August 1901.
Grave or cremation details: cremated South London.
Location of VC: not publicly held.

Citation: *On the morning of 2 June 1900 a party sent to try to cut the Delagoa Bay Railway were retiring, hotly pressed by very superior numbers. During one of the successive retirements of the rearguard, a man, whose horse had been shot, was seen running after his comrades. He was a long way behind the rest of his troop and was under a brisk fire. From among the retiring troop Corporal Kirby turned and rode back to the man's assistance. Although by the time he reached him they were under heavy fire at close range, Corporal Kirby managed to get the dismounted man up behind him and to take him clear of the next rise held by our rearguard. This is the third occasion on which Corporal Kirby has displayed gallantry in the face of the enemy.*
(*London Gazette*: 5 October 1900)

Second Lieutenant Cecil Leonard KNOX

(Eventually Major C.L. Knox, VC)
Born 9 May 1888, died 4 February 1943.
Won VC at Tugny, France, on 22 March 1918. Unit: 150 Field Company.
VC presented by King George V at Oxelaere, northern France, on 6 August 1918.
Grave or cremation details: cremated at Leicester; ashes scattered in home at Fyves Court, Caldecote, Nuneaton.
Location of VC: not publicly held.

Citation: *For most conspicuous bravery and devotion to duty. Twelve bridges were entrusted to this officer for demolition, and all of them were successfully destroyed. In the case of one steel girder bridge, the destruction of which he personally supervised, the time fuse failed to act. Without hesitation, Second Lieutenant Knox ran to the bridge, under heavy fire and machine-gun fire, and when the enemy were actually on the bridge he tore away the time fuse and lit the instantaneous fuse, to do which he had to get under the bridge. This was an act of the highest devotion to duty, entailing the greatest risks, which as a practical civil engineer, he fully realised.*
(*London Gazette*: 4 June 1918)

Captain Edward Pemberton LEACH

(Eventually General Sir Edward Leach, VC, KCB, KCVO)
Born 2 April 1847, died 27 January 1913.
Won VC at Maidanak, Afghanistan, on 17 March 1879.
VC presented by Queen Victoria at Windsor Castle on 9 December 1879.
Grave or cremation details: Lake Como, Italy.
Location of VC: Royal Engineers Museum.

Citation: *For having an action with the Shinwarris near Maidanak, Afghanistan, on 17 March 1879, when covering the retirement of the Survey Escort who were carrying Lieutenant Barclay, 45th Sikhs, mortally wounded, he behaved with utmost gallantry in charging, with some men of the 45th Sikhs, a very much larger number of the enemy. In this encounter Captain Leach killed two or three of the enemy himself, and he received a severe wound from an Afghan knife in the left arm. Captain Leach's determination and gallantry in this affair, in attacking and driving back the enemy from the last position, saved the whole party from annihilation.*
(*London Gazette*: 6 December 1879)

Colour Sergeant Peter LEITCH

(Eventually Colour Sergeant P. Leitch, VC)
Born August 1820, died 6 December 1892.
Won VC at Sebastopol, Crimea on 18 June 1855. Unit: 2 Company Royal Sappers and Miners.
VC presented by Lieutenant-General Sir James Jackson, KCB at King William's Town, Natal, Cape Colony, on 2 November 1858.

Grave or cremation details: Hammersmith Cemetery (Margravine Road), now levelled.
Location of VC: Royal Engineers Museum.

Citation: *For conspicuous gallantry in the assault on the Redan, when, after approaching it with the leading ladders, he formed a caponnière across the ditch, as well as a ramp, by fearlessly tearing down gabions from the parapet, and placing them and filling them until he was disabled from wounds.*
(*London Gazette*: 2 June 1858)

Corporal William James LENDRIM (or LENDRUM)

(Eventually Sergeant-Major W.J. Lendrim, VC)
Born 1 January 1830, died 28 November 1891.
Won VC at Sebastopol, Crimea, on 14 February 1855. Unit: 7th Company, Royal Sappers and Miners.
VC presented by Queen Victoria at Hyde Park, London, on 26 June 1857.
Grave or cremation details: Royal Military Academy, Grave No. 182.
Location of VC: Royal Engineers Museum.

Citation: *Recommended for intrepidity – getting on top of a magazine and extinguishing sandbags which were burning, and making a breach under fire, on 11 April 1855. For courage and praiseworthy example in superintending 150 French Chasseurs, on 14 February 1855, in building No. 9 Battery, left attack,* and replacing the whole of the capsized gabions under a heavy fire. Was one of four volunteers for destroying the farthest rifle-pit on 20 April.*
*The citation must be mistaken here. All other sources indicate that Lendrim was in the Right Attack on this occasion.
(*London Gazette*: 24 February 1857)

Lieutenant Wilbraham Oates LENNOX

(Eventually Lieutenant-General Sir Wilbraham Lennox, VC, KCB)
Born 4 May 1830, died 7 February 1897.
Won VC at Sebastopol, Crimea, on 20 November 1855.
VC sent out by War Office to Hong Kong on 26 June 1857, probably presented in England on his return from India.
Grave or cremation details: Woodvale Cemetery, Bear Road, Brighton, family vault Grave 47/48/49.
Location of VC: Royal Engineers Museum.

Citation: *Cool and gallant conduct in establishing a lodgement in Tryon's Rifle Pit, and assisting to repel the assaults of the enemy. This brilliant operation drew forth a special order from General Canrobert.*
(*London Gazette*: 24 February 1857)

Major Edward MANNOCK

(Eventually Major E. Mannock, VC, DSO**, MC*)
Born 24 May 1887, died 26 July 1918.

Won VC in France and Flanders on 17 June 1918. Unit: 85 Squadron, Royal Air Force.

VC presented by King George V to Major Mannock's father at Buckingham Palace on 16 November 1919.

Grave or cremation details: not known. Commemorated on Arras Memorial, France.

Location of VC: not publicly held.

Citation: *On 17 June 1918, he attacked a Halberstadt machine near Armentières and destroyed it from a height of 8,000 feet. On the 7 July 1918, near Doulieu, he attacked and destroyed one Fokker (red-bodied) machine, which went vertically into the ground from a height of 1,500 feet. Shortly afterwards he ascended 1,000 feet and attacked another Fokker biplane, firing 60 rounds into it, which produced an immediate spin, resulting, it is believed, in a crash. On 14 July 1918, near Merville, he attacked and crashed a Fokker from 7,000 feet, and brought a two-seater down damaged. On 19 July 1918, near Merville, he fired 80 rounds into an Albatros two-seater, which went to the ground in flames. On 20 July 1918, near La Bassée, he attacked and crashed an enemy two-seater from a height of 10,000 feet. About an hour afterwards he attacked at 8,000 feet a Fokker biplane near Steenwercke and drove it down out of control, emitting smoke. On 22 July 1918, near Armentières, he destroyed an enemy triplane from a height of 10,000 feet. This highly distinguished officer, during the whole of his career in the Royal Air Force, was an outstanding example of fearless courage, remarkable skill, devotion to duty and self-sacrifice, which has never been surpassed. The total number of machines definitely accounted for by Major Mannock up to the date of his death in France (26 July 1918) is fifty.*
(*London Gazette*: 18 July 1919)

Second Lieutenant Cyril Gordon MARTIN

(Eventually Brigadier C.G. Martin, VC, CBE, DSO)

Born 19 December 1891, died 14 August 1980.

Won VC at Spanbroekmolen, Belgium, on 12 March 1915. Unit: 56 Field Company.

VC presented by King George V at Buckingham Palace on 12 July 1915.

Grave or cremation details: cremated at Blackheath; ashes scattered on Pew Tor, Devon.

Location of VC: Royal Engineers Museum.

Citation: *For most conspicuous bravery at Spanbroek Molen on 12 March 1915, when in command of a grenade throwing party of six rank and file. Although wounded early in the action, he led his party into the enemy trenches and held back their reinforcements for nearly two and a half hours, until the evacuation of the trench was ordered.*
(*London Gazette*: 19 April 1915)

Captain James Thomas Byford McCUDDEN

(Eventually Major J.T.B. McCudden, VC, DSO*, MC*, MM)

Born 28 March 1895, died 9 July 1918.

Won VC in northern France on 2 April 1918. Unit: 56 Squadron, Royal Flying Corps.

VC presented by King George V at Buckingham Palace on 6 April 1918.
Grave or cremation details: Wavans British Cemetery, France.
Location of VC: Royal Engineers Museum.

Citation: *For most conspicuous bravery, exceptional perseverance, keenness, and very high devotion to duty. Captain McCudden has at the present time accounted for 54 enemy aeroplanes. Of these 42 have been definitely destroyed, 19 of them on our side of the lines. Only 12 out of the 54 have been driven out of control. On two occasions he has totally destroyed four two-seater enemy aeroplanes on the same day, and on the last occasion all four machines were destroyed in the space of 1 hour and 30 minutes. While in his present squadron he has participated in 78 offensive patrols, and in nearly every case has been the leader. On at least 30 other occasions, whilst with the same squadron, he has crossed the lines alone, either in pursuit or in quest of enemy aeroplanes.*
The following incidents are examples of the work he has done recently:
On 23 December 1917, when leading his patrol, eight enemy aeroplanes were attacked between 2.30 p.m. and 3.50 p.m. Of these two were shot down by Captain McCudden in our lines. On the morning of the same day he left the ground at 10.50 and encountered four enemy aeroplanes; of these he shot two down.
On 30 January 1918, he singlehanded attacked five enemy scouts, as a result of which two were destroyed. On this last occasion he only returned home when the enemy scouts had been driven far east; his Lewis gun ammunition was all finished and the belt of his Vickers gun had broken.

As a patrol leader he has at all times shown the utmost gallantry and skill, not only in the manner in which he has attacked and destroyed the enemy, but in the way he has during several aerial fights protected the newer members of his flight, thus keeping down their casualties to a minimum.

This officer is considered, by the record he has made, by his fearlessness, and by the very great service he has rendered his country, deserving of the very highest honour.
(*London Gazette*: 2 April 1918)

Colour Sergeant Henry McDONALD
(Eventually Captain H. McDonald, VC, DCM)
Born 28 May 1823, died 15 February 1893.
Won VC at Sebastopol on 19 April 1855. Unit: 10th Company, Royal Sappers and Miners.
VC presented by Queen Victoria at Southsea Common, Hampshire, on 2 August 1858.
Grave or cremation details: Western Necropolis, Glasgow.
Location of VC: Glasgow Art Gallery and Museum.

Citation: *For gallant conduct when engaged in effecting a lodgement in the enemy's Rifle-Pits, in front of the Left advance of the Right Attack on Sebastopol; and for subsequent valour, when, by the Engineer Officer being disabled from wounds, the command devolved upon him, and he determinately persisted in carrying on the sap, notwithstanding the repeated attacks of the enemy.*
(*London Gazette*: 2 June 1858).

Corporal James McPHIE

Born 18 December 1894, died 14 October 1918.
Won VC on the Canal de la Sensée, near Aubencheul-au-Bac, on 14 October
1918. Unit: 416 (Edinburgh) Field Company.
VC presented by King George V to Corporal McPhie's mother at Buckingham
Palace on 3 April 1919.
Grave or cremation details: Naves Communal Cemetery Extension, France, Plot
II, Row E, Grave 4.
Location of VC: Imperial War Museum.

Citation: *For most conspicuous bravery on 14 October 1918, when with a party of sappers maintaining a cork-float bridge across the Canal de la Sensée, near Aubencheul-au-Bac. The farther end of the bridge was under close machine-gun fire and within reach of hand grenades. When infantry, just before dawn, were crossing it, closing up resulted and the bridge began to sink and break. Accompanied by a sapper, he jumped into the water and endeavoured to hold the cork and timbers together, but this they failed to do. Corporal McPhie then swam back, and having reported the broken bridge, immediately started to collect material for repair. It was now daylight. Fully aware that the bridge was under close fire and that the far bank was almost entirely in the hands of the enemy, with the inspiring words, 'It is death or glory work which must be done for the sake of our patrol on the other side,' he led the way, axe in hand, on to the bridge, and was at once severely wounded, falling partly into the water, and died after receiving several further wounds. It was due to the magnificent example set by Corporal McPhie that touch was maintained with the patrol on the enemy bank at a most critical period.*
(*London Gazette*: 31 January 1919)

Captain Coulson Norman MITCHELL

(Eventually Lieutenant-Colonel C.N. Mitchell, VC, MC)
Born 11 December 1889, died 17 November 1978.
Won VC on the Canal de l'Escaut, north-east of Cambrai, on 8–9 October 1918.
Unit: 1 Tunnelling Company, 4th Canadian Engineers.
VC presented by King George V at Buckingham Palace on 3 April 1919.
Grave or cremation details: Field of Honour, Pointe Claire, Montreal, Quebec.
Location of VC: Military Engineers Museum, Chilliwack, British Columbia.

Citation: *For most conspicuous bravery and devotion to duty on the night of 8–9 October 1918, at the Canal de l'Escaut, north-east of Cambrai. He led a small party ahead of the first wave of infantry in order to examine the various bridges on the line of approach, and, if possible, to prevent their demolition. On reaching the canal he found the bridge already blown up. Under a heavy barrage he crossed to the next bridge, where he cut a number of 'lead' wires. Then, in total darkness, and unaware of the position or strength of the enemy at the bridgehead, he dashed across the main bridge over the canal. This bridge was found to be heavily charged for demolition, and whilst Captain Mitchell, assisted by his NCO, was cutting the wires, the enemy attempted to rush the bridge, in order to blow the charges, whereupon he at once dashed to the assistance of the sentry, who had been wounded, killed three of the enemy, captured 12, and maintained the bridgehead until reinforced. Then, under heavy fire, he continued his task of cut-*

ting wires and removing charges, which he knew well might at any moment have been fired by the enemy. It was entirely due to his valour and decisive action that this important bridge across the canal was saved from destruction.
(*London Gazette*: 31 January 1919)

Lieutenant Philip NEAME

(Eventually Lieutenant-General Sir Philip Neame, VC, KBE, CB, DSO)
Born 12 December 1888, died 28 April 1978.
Won VC at Neuve-Chapelle, France, on 19 December 1914. Unit: 15 Field Company.
VC presented by King George V at Windsor Castle on 19 July 1915.
Grave or cremation details: St Mary the Virgin Church, Selling, Kent.
Location of VC: Imperial War Museum.

Citation: *For conspicuous bravery on 19 December 1914, near Neuve-Chapelle, when, notwithstanding the very heavy rifle fire and bomb-throwing by the enemy, he succeeded in holding them back and rescuing all the wounded men whom it was possible to move.*
(*London Gazette*: 18 February 1915)

Lieutenant-Colonel Augustus Charles NEWMAN

(Eventually Lieutenant-Colonel A.C. Newman, VC, OBE, TD)
Born 19 August 1904, died 26 April 1972.
Won VC at St Nazaire, France, on 27–28 March 1942. Unit: The Essex Regiment, att No. 2 Commando.
VC presented by King George VI at Buckingham Palace on 11 December 1945.
Grave or cremation details: Barham, Kent.
Location of VC: not publicly held.

Citation: *On the night of 27/28 March 1942, Lieutenant-Colonel Newman was in command of the military force detailed to land on enemy occupied territory and destroy the dock installations of the German controlled naval base at St Nazaire.*

This important base was known to be heavily defended and bomber support had to be abandoned owing to bad weather. The operation was therefore bound to be exceedingly hazardous, but Lieutenant-Colonel Newman, although empowered to call off the assault at any stage, was determined to carry to a successful conclusion the important task which had been assigned to him.

Coolly and calmly he stood on the bridge of the leading craft, as the small force steamed up the estuary of the River Loire, although the ships had been caught in the enemy searchlights and a murderous crossfire opened from both banks, causing heavy casualties.

Although Lieutenant-Colonel Newman need not have landed himself, he was one of the first ashore and, during the next five hours of bitter fighting, he personally entered several houses and shot up the occupants and supervised the operations in the town, utterly regardless of his own safety, and he never wavered in his resolution to carry through the operation upon which so much depended.

An enemy gun position on the roof of a U-boat pen had been causing heavy casualties to the landing craft and Lieutenant-Colonel Newman directed the fire of a mortar against this position to such effect that the gun was silenced. Still fully exposed, he then brought machine gun fire to bear on an armed trawler in the harbour, compelling it to withdraw and thus preventing many casualties in the main demolition area.

Under the brilliant leadership of this officer the troops fought magnificently and held vastly superior forces at bay, until the demolition parties had successfully completed their work of destruction.

By this time, however, most of the landing craft had been sunk or set on fire and evacuation by sea was no longer possible. Although the main objective had been achieved, Lieutenant-Colonel Newman nevertheless was now determined to try and fight his way out into open country and so give all survivors a chance to escape.

The only way out of the harbour lay across a narrow iron bridge covered by enemy machine guns and although severely shaken by a German hand grenade, which had burst at his feet, Lieutenant-Colonel Newman personally led the charge which stormed the position and under his inspiring leadership the small force fought its way through the streets to a point near the open country, when, all ammunition expended, he and his men were finally overpowered by the enemy.

The outstanding gallantry and devotion to duty of this fearless officer, his brilliant leadership and initiative, were largely responsible for the success of this perilous operation which resulted in heavy damage to the important naval base at St Nazaire.

(*London Gazette*: 19 June 1945)

Private John PERIE

(Eventually Mr John Perie, VC)
Born August 1829, died 17 September 1874.
Won VC at Sebastopol on 18 June 1855. Unit: 8th Company Royal Sappers and Miners.
VC presented by Queen Victoria at Hyde Park, London, on 26 June 1857.
Grave or cremation details: Plot I or J/43, St Peter's Cemetery, Aberdeen.
Location of VC: Royal Engineers Museum.

Citation: *Conspicuous valour in leading the sailors with the ladders to the storming of the Redan on 18 June 1855. He was invaluable on that day. Devoted conduct in rescuing a wounded man from the open, although he himself had just previously been wounded by a bullet in his side.*
(*London Gazette*: 24 February 1857)

Lieutenant Harry North Dalrymple PRENDERGAST

(Eventually General Sir Harry Prendergast, VC, GCB)
Born 15 October 1834, died 24 July 1913.
Won VC at Mundisore, India, on 21 November 1857. Unit: Madras Engineers (B Company Madras Sappers and Miners).
VC presented by Queen Victoria at Windsor Castle on 4 January 1860.
Grave or cremation details: Richmond Cemetery, Surrey.
Location of VC: Royal Engineers Museum.

Citation: *For conspicuous bravery on 21 November 1857 at Mundisore, in saving the life of Lieutenant G. Dew, 14th Light Dragoons, at the risk of his own, by attempting to cut down a*

Velaitee who covered him (Lieutenant Dew) with his piece, from only a few yards to the rear. Lieutenant Prendergast was wounded in this affair by the discharge of the piece, and would probably have been cut down had not the rebel been killed by Major Orr. He also distinguished himself by his gallantry in the actions at Ratgurh and Betwa, when he was severely wounded. Major General Sir Hugh Rose, in forwarding his recommendations of this officer states: 'Lieutenant Prendergast, Madras Engineers, was specially mentioned by Brigadier (now Sir Charles) Stuart, for the gallant act at Mundisore, when he was severely wounded; secondly, he was "specially mentioned" by me when acting voluntarily as my aide-de-camp in the action before Nesilging Ratgurh, on the Beena River, for gallant conduct. His horse was killed on that occasion. Thirdly, at the action of the Betwa, he again acted voluntarily as my aide-de-camp, and distinguished himself by his bravery in the charge which I made with Captain Need's troop, Her Majesty's 14th Light Dragoons, against the left of the so-called Peishwa's Army under Tantia Topee. He was severely wounded on that occasion.'
(*London Gazette*: 21 October 1859)

Lieutenant Claud RAYMOND

Born 2 October 1923, died 22 March 1945.
Won VC at Talaku, Burma, on 22 March 1945. Unit: 58 Observation Squadron, 303 Indian Brigade.
VC presented by King George VI to Lieutenant Raymond's parents at Buckingham Palace on 12 February 1946.
Grave or cremation details: Taukkyan Cemetery, Burma, Plot 12, Row G, Grave 9.
Location of VC: Royal Engineers Museum.

Citation: *In Burma on the afternoon of 21 March 1945, Lieutenant Raymond was second-in-charge of a small patrol, which was acting in conjunction with a larger detachment of a special force, whose objective was to obtain information and create a diversion in the area of Taungup, by attacking and destroying isolated enemy posts some 40 miles in advance of an Indian Infantry Brigade, pushing down the road from Letpan to Taungup.*

The patrol was landed on the south bank of the Thinganet Chaung, an area known to be held by numerous enemy strong-posts and gun positions, and marched about five miles inland. As they were nearing the village of Talaku and moving across an open stretch of ground, they were heavily fired on from the slopes of a jungle covered hill by a strongly entrenched enemy detachment.

Lieutenant Raymond immediately charged in the direction of the fire. As he began to climb the hill he was wounded in the right shoulder, but he ignored this wound and continued up the slope firing his rifle from the hip. He had advanced only a few yards further, when a Japanese threw a grenade which burst in his face and most severely wounded him. He fell, but almost immediately picked himself up again, and, in spite of loss of blood from his wounds, which later were to prove fatal, he still continued on, leading his section under intense fire. He was hit yet a third time, his wrist being shattered by what appeared to have been an explosive bullet. In spite of this third wound he never wavered, but carried on into the enemy position itself, and, in the sharp action that followed, was largely responsible for the killing of two Japanese and the wounding of a third.

The remaining Japanese then fled in panic into the jungle, thus leaving the position in our hands, together with much equipment.

The position itself was strongly fortified by foxholes and small bunkers and would have proved extremely formidable had not the attack been pressed home with great determination under the courageous leadership of Lieutenant Raymond.

Several other men were wounded during the action and Lieutenant Raymond refused all treatment until they had been attended to, insisting despite the gravity of his injuries, on walking back towards the landing craft in case the delay in treating his wounds should endanger the withdrawal of the patrol.

It was not until he had walked nearly a mile that he collapsed and had to allow himself to be carried on an improvised stretcher. Even then he was continually encouraging the other wounded by giving the thumbs up sign and thus undoubtedly helping them to keep cheerful and minimise the extent of their injuries until the landing craft was reached. Soon after he died of his wounds.

The outstanding gallantry, remarkable endurance and fortitude of Lieutenant Raymond, which refused to allow him to collapse, although mortally wounded, was an inspiration to everyone and a major factor in the capture of the strong point. His self-sacrifice in refusing attention to his wounds undoubtedly saved the patrol, by allowing it to withdraw in time before the Japanese could bring up fresh forces from neighbouring positions for a counter attack.
(*London Gazette*: 28 June 1945)

Corporal John ROSS

(Eventually Sergeant J. Ross, VC)
Born 1822, died 23 October 1879.
Won VC at Sebastopol on 21 July 1855. Unit: 2nd Company, Royal Sappers and Miners.
VC presented by Queen Victoria at Hyde Park, London, on 26 June 1857.
Grave or cremation details: Finchley Cemetery, London, Block 2, Section I, No. 9765.
Location of VC: Royal Engineers Museum.

Citation: *Distinguished conduct 21 July 1855, in connecting the 4th Parallel Right Attack with an old Russian Rifle-Pit in front. Extremely creditable conduct on 23 August 1855, in charge of the advance from the 5th Parallel Right Attack on the Redan, in placing and filling 25 gabions under a very heavy fire whilst annoyed by the presence of light balls.*

Intrepid and devoted conduct in creeping to the Redan in the night of 8 September 1855, and reporting its evacuation, on which its occupation by the English took place.
(*London Gazette*: 24 February 1857)

Lieutenant Philip SALKELD

Born 13 October 1830, died 10 October 1857.
Won VC at Delhi on 14 September 1857. Unit: Bengal Engineers.
VC sent by post to father, Reverend Robert Salkeld, on 7 July 1858.
Grave or cremation details: Delhi.
Location of VC: not publicly held.

Citation: (*MEMORANDUM. Lieutenants Duncan Charles Home and Philip Salkeld, upon whom the Victoria Cross was provisionally conferred by Major-General Sir Archdale Wilson,*

Bart., KCB) For their conspicuous bravery in the performance of the desperate duty of blowing in the Cashmere Gate of the Fortress of Delhi in broad daylight, under a heavy fire of musketry, on the morning of 14 September 1857, preparatory to the assault, would have been recommended to Her Majesty for confirmation in that distinction had they survived.
(*London Gazette*: 18 June 1858)

Corporal Michael SLEAVON

(Eventually Mr M. Sleavin, VC)
Born 1827, died 14 August 1902.
Won VC at Jhansi, India, on 3 April 1858. Unit: 21 Field Company.
VC presented in India in 1860.
Grave or cremation details: Bannagh Churchyard, Tubrid, near Ederney, Co. Fermanagh, N. Ireland.
Location of VC: not publicly held.

Citation: *For determined bravery at the attack of the Fort of Jhansi on 3 April 1858, in maintaining a position at the head of a sap, and continuing the work under a heavy fire, with a cool determination worthy of the highest praise.*
(*London Gazette*: 11 November 1859)

Sergeant John SMITH

(Eventually Ensign J. Smith, VC)
Born February 1814, died 26 June 1864.
Won VC at Delhi on 14 September 1857. Unit: Bengal Sappers and Miners.
VC presented in India in 1858.
Grave or cremation details: Artillery Cemetery, Jullundur.
Location of VC: not publicly held.

Citation: *For conspicuous gallantry, in conjunction with Lieutenants Home and Salkeld, in the performance of the desperate duty of blowing in the Cashmere Gate of the Fortress of Delhi in broad daylight, under a heavy and destructive fire of musketry, on the morning of 14 September 1857, preparatory to the assault.*
(*London Gazette*: 27 April 1858)

Second Lieutenant Edward Talbot THACKERAY

(Eventually Colonel Sir Edward Thackeray, VC, KCB)
Born 19 October 1836, died 3 September 1927.
Won VC at Delhi on 16 September 1857. Unit: Bengal Engineers.
VC presented by Major-General the Hon. Arthur Dalzell at Dover in July 1862.
Grave or cremation details: The Cemetery, Bordighera, Italy.
Location of VC: South African Military History Museum.

Citation: *For cool intrepidity and characteristic daring in extinguishing a fire in the Delhi magazine enclosure, on 16 September 1857, under a close and heavy musketry fire from the enemy, at the imminent risk of his life from the explosion of combustible stores in the shed in which the fire occurred.*
(*London Gazette*: 29 April 1862)

Captain Alfred Maurice TOYE

(Eventually Brigadier A.M. Toye, VC, MC)
Born 15 April 1897, died 6 September 1955.
Won VC at Eterpigny Ridge, France, on 25 March 1918. Unit: 2nd Battalion
The Middlesex Regiment (Duke of Cambridge's Own).
VC presented by King George V at Aldershot on 8 June 1918.
Grave or cremation details: Tiverton Cemetery, F/36 (or XF/36).
Location of VC: not publicly held.

Citation: *For most conspicuous bravery and fine leadership displayed in extremely critical circumstances. When the enemy captured the trench at a bridgehead, he three times re-established the post, which was eventually recaptured by fresh enemy attacks. After ascertaining that his three other posts were cut off, he fought his way through the enemy with one officer and six men of his company. Finding 70 men of the battalion on his left retiring, he collected them, counterattacked, and took up a line which he maintained until reinforcements arrived. Without this action the defence of the bridge must have been turned. In two subsequent operations, when in command of a composite company, he covered the retirement of his battalion with skill and courage. Later, with a party of battalion headquarters, he pressed through the enemy in the village, firing at them in the streets, thus covering the left flank of the battalion retirement. Finally, on a still later occasion, when in command of a mixed force of the brigade, he re-established, after hard fighting, a line that had been abandoned before his arrival. He was twice wounded within ten days, but remained at duty. His valour and skilful leading throughout this prolonged period of intense operations were most conspicuous.*
(*London Gazette*: 8 May 1918)

Captain William Spottiswoode TREVOR

(Eventually Major-General W.S. Trevor, VC)
Born 9 October 1831, died 2 November 1907.
Won VC at Dewangiri, Bhutan, on 30 April 1865.
VC presented by Major-General Fordyce, commanding the Presidency Division,
at The Maidan, Calcutta, on 23 March 1868.
Grave or cremation details: Kensal Green Cemetery, Plot 179/PS/31775.
Location of VC: Royal Engineers Museum.

Citation (to be read in conjunction with Lieutenant James Dundas): *For their gallant conduct at the attack on the blockhouse at Dewan-Giri, in Bhootan on 30 April 1865.*

Major General Tombs, VC, CB, the officer in command at the time, reports that a party of the enemy, from 180 to 200 in number, had barricaded themselves in the blockhouse in question, which they continued to defend after the rest of the position had been carried, and the main body was in retreat. The blockhouse, which was loopholed, was the key of the enemy's position. Seeing no officer of the storming party near him, and being anxious that the place should be taken immediately, as any protracted resistance might have caused the main body of the Bhooteas to rally, the British force having been fighting in a broiling sun on a very steep and difficult ground for upwards of three hours, the General in command ordered these two officers to show the way into the blockhouse. They had to climb a wall which was fourteen feet high, and then to enter a

house occupied by some 200 desperate men, head foremost through an opening not more than two feet wide between the top of the wall and the roof of the blockhouse. Major General Tombs states that on speaking to the Sikh soldiers around him, and telling them in Hindoostani to swarm up the wall, none of them responded to the call until these two officers had shown them the way, when they followed with the greatest alacrity. Both of them were wounded.
(*London Gazette*: 31 December 1867)

Major Arnold Horace Santo WATERS

(Eventually Colonel Sir Arnold Waters, VC, CBE, DSO, MC)
Born 23 September 1886, died 22 January 1981.
Won VC on the Sambre-Oise canal near Ors, France, on 4 November 1918. Unit: 218 Field Company.
VC presented by King George V at Buckingham Palace on 15 March 1919.
Grave or cremation details: cremated at Sutton Coldfield; ashes laid to rest at All Saints, Foley Road East, Streetly.
Location of VC: Royal Engineers Museum.

Citation: *For most conspicuous bravery and devotion to duty on 4 November 1918, near Ors, when bridging with his Field Company the Oise-Sambre canal. From the outset the task was under artillery and machine-gun fire at close range, the bridge being damaged and the building party suffering severe casualties. Major Waters, hearing that all his officers had been killed or wounded, at once went forward and personally supervised the completion of the bridge, working on cork floats while under fire at point-blank range. So intense was the fire that it seemed impossible that he could escape being killed. The success of the operation was due entirely to his valour and example.*
(*London Gazette*: 13 February 1919)

Lieutenant Thomas Colclough WATSON

(Eventually Lieutenant-Colonel T.C. Watson, VC)
Born 11 April 1867, died 15 June 1917.
Won VC at Bilot, Mamund Valley, India, on 16 September 1897. Unit: Bengal Engineers.
VC presented by Queen Victoria at Windsor Castle on 23 June 1898.
Grave or cremation details: cremated at Golders Green; buried at Finchampstead Churchyard.
Location of VC: not publicly held.

Citation: *This officer, on 16 September 1897, at the village of Bilot, in the Mamund Valley, collected a few men of the Buffs (East Kent Regiment) and of No. 4 Company Bengal Sappers and Miners and led them into the dark and burning village to dislodge some of the enemy who were inflicting loss on our troops. After being wounded and driven back, he made a second attempt to clear the village, and only desisted after a second repulse and being again hit and severely wounded.*
(*London Gazette*: 20 May 1898)

Captain Theodore WRIGHT

Born 15 May 1883, died 14 September 1914.

Won VC at Mons on 23 August 1914 and Vailly on 14 September 1914. Unit: 57 Field Company.

VC presented by King George V to Captain Wright's mother at Buckingham Palace on 16 November 1916.

Grave or cremation details: Vailly British Cemetery, France, Grave II-2-21.

Location of VC: not publicly held.

Citation: *Gallantry on 23 August 1914 at Mons in attempting to connect up the lead to demolish a bridge, under heavy fire; although wounded in the head, he made a second attempt. At Vailly, on 14 September, he assisted the passage of the 5th Cavalry Brigade over the pontoon bridge and was mortally wounded whilst assisting wounded men into shelter.*

(*London Gazette*: 16 November 1914)

Some Notes on Visiting the Sites

These notes are designed for the guidance of anyone wanting to visit the sites where the VCs were won and to study them in a general way. There are many specialist tour operators who can offer tours with expert guides to give a more in-depth account of the battles concerned. However, except in such famous cases as Rorke's Drift, the sapper aspects will necessarily be only a small part of the presentation. With the help of these notes, the accounts in this book and the maps and bibliography, the 'DIY' sapper-minded tour planner should be able to have an enjoyable visit to the recommended sites. I have personal knowledge only of the European sites – Author

The Crimea (Ukraine)

The Crimea sites can now be visited. The principal battle sites remain reasonably preserved but little can be seen of the Redan. Several companies run tours to the area. Advice may be obtained through the Crimean War Research Society (Secretary: David Cliff, 4 Castle Estate, Ripponden, West Yorkshire HX6 4JY).

The Indian Sub-continent

The *Kashmir Gate* is intact and still carries the scars of the battles of September 1857. Little remains of the walls of the old city, however. Tracing the other sapper VC sites of the 1857 Uprising with any accuracy would be unrewarding.

Afghanistan, *Bhutan* and the *North-West Frontier* are currently not practical propositions.

Nilt can be reached by the Karakoram Highway which passes through the Nilt valley. The configuration of the land gives a good idea of the problems that faced Colonel Durand's force, though nothing remains of the village.

Africa

Ashanti (Ghana) While access to Kumasi is perfectly straightforward, it would be difficult to pinpoint the exact location of Bell's action. A short journey into the rainforest would, however, give a good idea of the difficulties encountered by Wolseley's army.

Zululand The Zulu War sites are well catered for by tour operators. While nothing significant remains of the old mission station, the building which replaced it on the same site is now a museum. A line of stones marks the outline of the mealie-bag wall and the progress of the battle can easily be followed from a study of the lie of the land.

Boer War sites While it would be impractical to try and locate the site of Kirby's great feat near the Delagoa Bay Railway, Wagon Hill at Ladysmith is eminently worth a visit and carries a memorial to Digby Jones.

The Western Front

(The 1:100,000 scale map IGN (Institut Géographique National) Série Verte is an invaluable asset on these visits. The 1:25,000 is even better.)

Mons The Mons canal has been realigned and rebuilt since 1914 and nothing can be seen of the sapper VC sites. There is, however, a well-stocked museum and much of the general action of the first day of the First World War can be followed. The Commonwealth War Graves Commission (CWGC) St Symphorien Cemetery, with British and German graves, is well worth a visit.

The Aisne The sites at Vailly, where Theodore Wright was killed, and at Moulin des Roches at Missy, can be located quite simply using the map. On the latter site a sugar factory makes the approach from the south difficult, but from the north, where the bank is now wooded, the approach is straightforward.

The Salient There are many tours specialising in the Salient, some locally based starting in Ypres. The area is so full of incident, and the way in which the ground was fought over during the whole war so complex, that some such orientation tour is to be strongly recommended. The museum in the Cloth Hall in Ypres is a must if only for the marvellous model of the city in its state of devastation towards the end of the war. Also a must is the 8.00 pm ceremony at the Menin Gate at which the Last Post has been sounded every night since 1 May 1929, apart from during the years of the Second World War. With the help of a local tour and a map, Westhoek ridge, where Clifford Coffin won his VC leading his brigade, and the Hill 60 area, where John Carmichael won his, can be found.

Another essential visit in the Salient for sappers is the Pool of Peace at Spanbroekmolen. This crater, one of the 19 fired to launch the Battle of Messines, was purchased by Lord Wakefield in 1930 and it has been left ever since as a permanent memorial. The tunnel in which the mine was laid started some 500 yards to the west and this is also the general area in which Cyril Martin won his VC.

Neuve-Chapelle and Givenchy Although it is hard to find the actual location of the trench where Philip Neame won his VC, the area of the battle is worth a visit and particularly to see the Indian memorial on the cross-roads on the D947 just to the south of the town. A few miles south of Neuve-Chapelle lies Givenchy-lés-la Bassée beneath whose soil lies William Hackett and whose name is recorded on the Ploegsteert Memorial in the south of the Salient. There are no remains of Shaftesbury Shaft. Some idea of the conditions in the tunnels can be gained from a visit to Vimy ridge where guided tours of a preserved section are given by the Canadians.

Loos The Loos battlefield is one of the most satisfactory visits as the countryside remains surprisingly clear and the events are reasonably easy to follow from the high ground around Vermelles, which lies between the N43 Lens–Béthune and the D947 Lens–La Bassée roads. The farm tracks from Vermelles to Auchy-les-Mines are negotiable by car. From Auchy-les-Mines the CWGC Quarry Cemetery can be reached on foot, and the area of the Hohenzollern Redoubt is on the high ground to its east. Hill 70, the scene of Frederick Johnson's VC, lies in the angle between the D947 and the D165 which runs through Loos south-west from the D147.

The Somme The actual battle of the Somme in July 1916 brought no sapper VCs. There are, however, many tour operators and guide books which can be used to explore this fascinating battlefield. Within the general area lie the two sapper VC sites resulting from the Kaiserschlacht battles in March 1918. Cecil Knox's bridge, or rather its replacement, can easily be found at Tugny-et-Pont, a few miles to the east of Ham on the D67. Eterpigny, where Maurice Toye made his great stand with the 2nd Middlesex, is located to the north of Brie on the N29 St Quentin–Amiens road at the point where it crosses the Somme canal.

Bapaume, Cambrai and the Canal de la Sensée Grévillers, the scene of Samuel Forsyth's VC, can easily be found to the west of Bapaume. From there the N30 leads to Cambrai, passing just to the south of Bourlon Wood where Frederick Johnson was killed during the 1917 Battle of Cambrai. Pont d'Aire, Coulson Mitchell's bridge, is best found by skirting the city of Cambrai to the north-east and going out on the very minor D6 to Morenchies. The site looks very much as it must have done in 1918. From there it is possible to continue on to Ramillies-Eswars-Abancourt-Fressies and so to Aubencheul-au-Bac, the site of James McPhie's VC. Unfortunately, the canal here has been developed into a much wider waterway than the one which McPhie so gallantly crossed in 1918 and it is difficult to picture his situation.

Sambre-Oise The Sambre-Oise canal is probably the best of all the Western Front sapper VC sites to visit. Little seems to have changed since 1918 and it is easy to envisage the probable approach routes, assembly and harbour areas for the field companies and their bridging materials and the daunting obstacles which they faced. A good route to follow is the D959 leading north-east from the N43 Le Cateau-Cambresis–Catillon sur Sambre road. This passes through the Forêt Dom de Bois L'Evêque which is partly a French military training area, and Ors is signed to the right. The road crosses a level-crossing as it emerges from the wood and the crossing made by Arnold Waters and Adam Archibald, just south of the bend in the canal, can be reached by a muddy track which runs north-east alongside the railway after the level-crossing. There are several cemeteries in Ors. A small one in a field quite close to the crossing contains the graves of several sappers. In the village itself is the Communal Cemetery in which the CWGC section is located in the local cemetery. It contains the graves of the two posthumous VCs from the Ors crossing, James Neville and James Kirk, as well as that of the poet Wilfred Owen.

Even more accessible is George Findlay's crossing at Lock No. 1 south of Catillon. The best approach is from the west by means of the D86 running south out of Bazuel to Mazinghien and Rejet de Beaulieu. The track from Rejet de Beaulieu, more or less Findlay's route, can be found quite easily and leads to the lock.

Brett Cloutman's bridge site is about 20 miles further north at Pont-sur-Sambre. It is not where the main D961 crosses the canal but can be found by taking the minor road leading eastward out of the town. The lock has been resited and rebuilt since 1918 but the new bridge is still in the same place and the original stone abutments can be seen under the new bridge.

The Second World War
St Nazaire The Forme Ecluse attacked so dramatically by Charles Newman and Robert Ryder has been restored and can be seen from a good outlook point on the top of a nearby museum devoted to submarine exploration. From there a good view can be obtained over the Loire estuary to the point where Tom Durrant made his last stand. The course of the battle can easily be followed from the general layout of the surrounding area. The memorial to those who died in the raid and the submarine pens are also worth visiting. Many of those killed in the raid are buried in the CWGC cemetery at Escoublac-la-Baule, ten miles to the west of the port.

In the following index, page numbers in **bold** refer to maps and illustrations.